ENCYCLOPAEDIA OF ENVIRONMENTAL EDUCATION

Edited & Compiled by

DR. PREM SUNDER
Principal,
Darsh College of Education
Gohana (Sonepat)
Haryana

KSK

K.S.K. PUBLISHERS & DISTRIBUTORS
7/26, Ansari Road, Darya Ganj,
New Delhi – 110 002.

Published by:

K.S.K. PUBLISHERS & DISTRIBUTORS

7/26, Ansari Road, Darya Ganj,
New Delhi – 110 002.
Phones 011-42564726, 47090343, 43551324, (M) 9811088729
E-mail: khelsahitya@rediffmail.com, vivekthani@gmail.com
Website: www.khelsahitya.com, www.kskpublisher.com

ISBN: 978-81-89983-23-9

PRINTED IN INDIA 2022

Typeset by:
K.S.K. DTP UNIT,

7/29, Basement, Ansari road,
Daryaganj, New Delhi-110002

Printed at:
S.K. OFFSET, DELHI

Price : Rs. **2000/-**

PART-I

ENVIRONMENTAL EDUCATION

CONTENTS

PART-II

ENVIRONMENT STUDY

CONTENTS

PART-I
ENVIRONMENTAL EDUCATION

1

HUMAN POPULATION AND ENVIRONMENT

Population Growth

Population is the number of individual organisms of same species in a given area. Population dynamics refers to the trends of growth of population with time. The study of human population is called demography. Some of the topics studied under demography area the rate and trends of growth of population with time, ratio of females to males, percentages of population in each age group etc.

Exponential Growth and Doubling Time

Exponential growth means growth in the population of organism at a constant rate per unit of time. It is called exponential growth because existing population is multiplied is geometrical ratio.

The geometric pattern of increase is 2, 4, 8, 16 and so on. By contrast, a pattern of growth that increases at a constant amount per unit of time is called arithmetic growth. The sequence is this case might be 1, 2, 3, 4, or 1, 3, 5, 7.

In India we usually talk about population growth of human beings. Population also increases of animals and other organisms too. In overseas countries attention is also paid to changes in the population on organisms.

The moose population as well as other organisms have the ability to grow exponentially. The reflect growth of moose and wolf population on Isle Royal National Park from 1900-1985. Moose first appeared on the island shortly after 1900. By 1929, the moose population had grown to about 5000 and had exhausted the easily available food supply. A catastrophic die-back occurred during the 1930, when 97 percent moose died. The appearance of wolves after 2940 at first reduced the moose population but then established a dynamic equilibrium around what appears to be the carrying capacity.

Reasons for exponential growth - the main reasons with regard to the growth of population with given appropriate environmental are as follow:

(i) Biotic Potential - Biotic potential means maximum reproductive rate of an organism. There are many other organisms which have fastest reproducing capacity compared to moose and humans. Housefly has fastest reproducing rate. Each female fly lays an average of 120 eggs in each generation. The eggs hatch and mature into sexually active results and lay their own eggs in fifty six days. In one year if all its offspring survived long enough to reproduce, a single female could be the ancestor of 5-6 trillion flies. The result is astounding.

(ii) Biological Reproduction - Experience of biologists reveal that each cow moose reaches sexual maturity at the age of three or four. If she remains healthy and has enough to eat and survive it can produce one to three calves each year for the next eight to ten year. This means that each female moose can produce as many as 30 calfs during her life time. If half of those calves are female then the population will increase at a 14 to 35 percent annual growth rate. But within a very short time, the numbers began to increase. The growth curve produced by this constant rate of unfettered growth is called a J curve because of its shape. Moose population growing at 35 percent doubles every two year. You can also apply this rate to calculate doubling time of human population. Countries growing at 4 percent per year will double their population in 17-5 years.

Growth of Population

Growth of population is a function of birth rate and death rates. Number of persons born per thousand people during a certain period of time in a country is called birth rates. Growth rates is the rate at which the population grow in a country during a certain period. It is the difference of the birth rate and death rate during the period. If birth rates exceed death rates population will grow and it is called growth of population.

During the early period of Human history, population growth was extremely slow because death rates were higher than birth rates. Reasons for high death rates are as follow:

a. Absence of medical aid.

b. Hostile environment and prevalence of fatal diseases.

c. Scarcity of food and the cave man had to struggle hard for survival.

This happened during 1821. It was called period of great divide. Discovery of agriculture lead to more settled life. Famines and deaths due to scarcity of food registered a decline. All this lead to higher survival rate. Population did increase but slowly. People migrated to new areas and more land was brought under-cultivation. These developments made world population 300 million. It happened at the beginning of the Christian era.

Industrial revolution marked the next important stage in the growth of human population followed by advancement in medical science. Advances in the field of medicine resulted in the control of plague, smallpox, malaria and other deadly diseases.

Protected water supply, sanitation of other preventive measures further reduced death rates. Not only that, settlements encouraged population growth. This happened with the opening up of lands in North-America. South America and Australia. So population increased by immigration as well.

Factors Affecting variation in a Population

The main factors that affect distribution of population are natural resources, climate conditions, soils, cultural factors, age of human settlement, industrial development and means of transport and communication. The factors affecting distribution of population are described below one by one in a nutshell manner:

(i) Cultural factors - Cultural factors like the modes of life of the people also affect the density of population. The density of population is low in equatorial forests and deserts because nomadic tribes live in regions are often found engaged in food gathering to support their families. The regions inhabited by pastoral nomads also have low density because they migrate with their animals is search of pastures.

(ii) Age of human settlement - Australia and USA have low density of population. Human habitation in these countries is of recent origin compared to river valley of the ancient period. Besides this, these countries also practise strict immigration procedures. This system keep population density far below the total potential.

(iii) Means of Transport and Communication - Highly development means of air, surface and water add to the density of population in a particular region because there the people can manage and carry on agricultural, commercial as well as industrial activities very safely and swiftly.

(iv) Soils - Rich and fertile soil always help in the growth and development of agricultural activities with substantially high yield per hectare. This is so because fertile lands produce a variety of crops to support dense population. Son on that East and South Asian Region and northern plains of India are densely populated.

(v) Climatic Conditions - Climate also influence growth of population. Moderate climate leads to the growth of population because it is pleasant and refreshing. In these regions density of population is high. On the other hand people to not like to live in too hot and too cold climates. This is the reason that Canada is sparsely populated. Average density of population in Canada is 2.5 per sq. km. metre. Similarly in India, Rajasthan, Deccan hills, plateaus and the Himalayan regions are sparsely populated.

(vi) Natural Resources - The region having rich wealth of natural resources like coal, water, minerals and forest wealth favour the growth of population. These resources help in the development of trade, commerce and industry. This promote cluster of population and thereby increase density of population. This is the reason that North-West Europe, Bihar and West Bengal in India have high density of population.

Distribution of Population

The total of the world have crossed about 5.8 billion in July 1996 and in the year 2000 it was estimated to be 6055 million. Annual addition to the world population in the next decade will average 97 million. All this population growth will be in Africa, Asia and Latin America. Over half of it will be in Africa and South Asia alone. The details of this uneven distribution is given below:

(i) the countries such as China, India, Russia, Indonesia, Brazil, Japan, Nigeria, Bangladesh and Pakistan are the top ten nations in order of having more than 100 million persons.

(ii) The continent of Asia including Russia has nearly two-thirds of the world's population.

(iii) More than 90% of the population live in the Northern Hemisphere.

Density and Regions of High density of Population

Density of Population which means population per sq. km is necessary to be studied because absolute number of people living in a country do not provide any indication of the impact of population on the land and its resources.

The average density of population for the world as a whole is about 38 person per sq- km according to 1992 estimates, assuming that the entire population is spread uniformly over the land area. The actual density of population varies from region to region. This variation depends upon environmental conditions.

Variation in density of population is classified broadly in three parts as described below:

a. Low density Regions - The density of population in these regions is less than 50 persons per sq. km. Over three-fourth of world's area has density below 50. Low population density regions are:

(i) Tropical deserts like Sahara and Western Australia.

(ii) Equatorial rain forest regions such as Amazon and Zaire.

(iii) High mountains and dissected plateaus with rugged relief.

(iv) Polar regions such as Antarctica and Greenland.

b. Moderate Density Region - These are those areas where 50-100 persons live per Sq. Km. These are regions of extensive agriculture and pastoral activities. Industrial development in these regions is quite more. These regions are:

(i) Coastal low-lands in middle latitudes regions of South America and South Africa.

(ii) European Russia.

(iii) Central and Southern Europe.

(iv) River valleys of South-East Asia.

c. Regions of high density - Areas where over 100 persons are found living per sq. km. are called region of high density. Broadly there are four major regions of high density of population. These regions are:

(i) North-Eastern United States comprising, the region between the Great Lakes and Atlantic coast.

(ii) North-West Europe includes Great Britain, France, Belgium. the Netherlands, Denmark and Germany.

(iii) Southern Asia comprise India, Pakistan and Bangladesh.

(iv) Eastern Asia which include China, Japan and Korea.

Population explosion

Baby boom is called population explosion. There is sudden and fast increase in the birth rate of babies. India is caught in the grip of population explosion. Here birth rates are higher than death rates inspite of family planning measures. The population in the organism tends to increase as long as its environment allows. Thus, most populations are in a state of dynamic equilibrium which is influenced by the local environment and by the interaction of the organisms with other populations in the community. Malthus concluded that human populations tend to grow until they exhaust their resources and become subject to famine, disease or war. Mathusian theory of population appeared to be correct in case of India because he said population has tendency to be doubled after 25 years. Malthus painted a bleak picture of the countries if the population continue to rise at such as learning speed. He opined that there will be imbalance between population growth and the food supply. Under these circumstances, T.R. Malthus predicted cannibalism in the future. In order to control the population growth, he suggested preventive and positive checks. These are as follows:

a. Positive checks - These exercise their influence on the growth of population by increasing the death rate. These checks are natural catastrophics, famines, droughts, floods, and spread of epidemics etc.

Malthus further stressed that the nation should immediately adopt preventive checks to control the population otherwise nature shall interfere through its untold miseries, which has been discussed in the preceding paragraph.

Malthus's theory of population to some extent is found applicable in under-developed, developing countries amongst which India is one. A critical study of Indian economy reveals that population of this country has almost doubled after a period of 25 years. The population of India in 1950-57 was 34.7 crores and now it stands more than 1`00 crores. India is having food problem due to faster growth in population. Increasing rate of population has reduced the ratio between man and land. As described by Malthus, we are using family planning methods to control our population,

Today India is the second populous country in the world; the first is China. Amongst States, Population-wise U.P. is the biggest state, Kolkata is the most population city but now Mumbai has been declared most .populous city,. Being the second populous country in the world according to 1991 census. India constitute about 16 percent of the total population of the world. In other words, every seventh person on the earth is an Indian. India on the other hand, has got only 2.4 percent of the total land area in the world. China with about 20 percent of the world's population has nearly 7 percent of the land area, the U.S.A. maintains only 6 percent of the total world population and about 7 percent of the total area.

India is overpopulated country. Thomas Robert Malthus in his book Essay on the Principles of Population mentioned that human population in every country increase faster than the means of subsistence. Though the population has increased in every country of the world but in India the growth rate of population is quite high., In 1951 the population of India was 34.7 crore which increased to 54.7 crore in 1971. Today India's population is approximately more than 100 crores and 20 lacks.

Causes of Population Growth - Population growth is a function of birth rates and death rates. If BRs increases. In India BRs increase faster than Drs population increases. In India BRs are more than Drs for which following are the main reasons.

(i) Children in rural areas are considered asset rather than liability and 75% of India s population live in villages.

(ii) Wide spread poverty and no source of entertainment.

(iii) The joint family system further provide spurt to population growth.

(iv) the population of women in the age of child bearing age in 15.49 years and 84.53 percent of the total female population falls in the reproducing age.

(v) The average age of women in India for bearing conception is low.

(vi) Marriage is universal in India which means every girl get married sooner or later.

2. Preventive checks - These checks exercise influence on the growth of population by bringing down the birth rates. These checks are used as family planning methods such as contraceptives, late marriage and self-restraint.

Demographic transition theory of population

In the theories of population it is mentioned that population increases fast but its rate of growth falls with the industrial development. Improved medical facilities also ensure low death rates. The historical sequence led to demographers to ask whether this process will continue with industrialization. The theory to demographic transition explains that a stage is arrived at where population tends to stabilize once a certain level of economic development is achieved. There are three stages of demographic transition. These are as follow:

Stage one - In this stage both death rates and birth rates are high. Due to this reason population growth remain fairly stable. This stage is found in traditional societies.

Stage two - In this stage birth rates remains high but

death rates fall due to availability of medical facilities and better living standards. This stage is found in all development societies. Population increases quite fast in this stage.

Stage three - In this stage both death rates and birth rates starts declining and settle at a low level.

Stage four - Population growth rage gradually declines toward zero and remains fairly stable. This stage is found in advanced industrial societies.

The transition has been completed in Europe, Japan and North America. India is at the second stage of demographic transition. The problem of recognizing demographic theory of transition is that it is only a bypothesis and every society do not behave as explained in this theory . Japanese method of controlling population after world war second has been abortion. Secondly decline in birth rates is closely connected to socio-economic development per capita income and educational level.

Optimum Theory of Population

The exponents of this theory comment that population growth as described by Malthus is not always bad. Increase in population helped the economic growth of Western European countries rather than hindering it. This theory of population tries to explain that the size of population which is the best for a country of a particular time. The theory conceives the right number of population relative to the amount of actually developed natural resources, availability of capital and technology. Optimum population is that level of population at which output per capita for real income per head is the highest. If the population happens to be less than optimum level, it is underpopulated and if this is more than optimum level, it is over populated.

Let us assume that the stock of natural resources, capital and technology is given and remains fixed at a given time. Now also assume that the population at initial stages is found less but begins to increased. With the increase in population, the labour supply also increase. With small population and large resources, the production appears to be less because resources are not fully and optimally utilized. So there will be three advantages if population increase:

1. Food problem shall be caused due to over population.

2. Open and disguised unemployment.

3. Low standard of living. So when resources are not fully utilized due to less man power because manpower resources are short then it is the resources then it is a symptom of economic development than retardation.

Dalton has given a formula through which it can be judged to what extent actual population of a country deviates from the optimum population. The degree of deviation is called maladjustment.

Maslthusian theory of population

Robert Malthus, an English clergyman put forward the theory of population in his boom An Essay on The Principle of Population in 1798. He was impressed by the unlimited urge of sex to produce children and limited power of earth to produce food. His explanation has been reduced to the following points:

(i) Law of diminishing returns apply to agriculture. Population get food from agriculture.

(ii) Population has a tendency to be doubled after a period of 25 years.

(iii) There are two ways viz., positive and preventive checks which can keep the level of population checked.

(iv) Population always increases when the means of subsistence increase.

(v) Human population increases faster than food production. Population increases in geometric progression and food production in arithmetic ratio. Geometric progression is 2, 4, 6, 16, 32, 64, 128, and arithmetic progression is 1, 2, 4, 6, 8, 10.\

Malthus painted a bleak picture of the countries if the population continue to rise at such an alarming speed. He opined that there will be an imbalance between population growth and the food supply. Under these circumstances, T.R. Malthus predicted cannibalism in the future. In order to control the population growth, he suggested preventive and positive checks. These are as follows:

(i) Positive checks - These exercise their influence on the growth of population by increasing the death rate. These checks are natural catastrophes, famines, droughts, floods, and spread of epidemics etc.

b. Preventive checks - These checks exercise influence on the growth of population by bringing down the birth rates. These checks are use of family planning methods such as contraceptives, late marriage and self-restraint.

Malthus further stressed that the nation should immediately adopt preventive checks to control the population otherwise nature shall interfere through its untold miseries, which has been discussed in the preceding paragraph.

A storm of controversy was raised over Malthusan theory of population with the following pints of criticism.

(i) Malthus gave no exact proof about his assertion that population increases in geometric progression and food supply in arithmetic progression.

(ii) Malthus held the view that with the increase in subsistence, food supply will increase population. But in western countries, there has been control over birth rates in-spite of increase in subsistence resources.

(iii) Malthusian concept of population is believed to be governed by the law of diminishing returns as applied to agriculture. Advancement in technical know-how and application of technology is agriculture has failed this law.

(iv) In western countries population has failed to grow as rapidly as predicted by Malthus. As a result the living standards of people have increased.

Family Welfare Programme

Most population experts believe that less developed nations must initiate family planning or welfare program in order to check population growth. This programme allows couples to determine the number and spacing of offsprings. For less developed countries family planning programme can accelerate the decline in birth that occurs slowly through economic growth and the demographic transition. Some researchers believe that family planning program are responsible for a 40% to 50% decline in fertility in these countries.

It means smaller size of family that is one to two children may be both male or females. The family should by health accept car and not baby. Family planning programme has been initiated by health department of the Government. Huge amount of money is been spent by the Government of India because India is second populous country in the world only second to China. We have already crossed one hundred crores people by now. More than 30-40 crores are married couple in our country. If we observe the principal of the family planning than by the end of a few years the population of this country shall be more than China. Family welfare programme which is a need of the day stress the following recommendations.

1. Providing incentive to those who can have small size of family.

2. Opening more and more family welfare centre in rural planning measures.

3. Spreading and advertising about the use of family planning measures.

4. Children may not be considered gift of nature but result of mating either sexes.

5. Disseminating education in rural areas in such a style that they prefer small size of family.

6. Spreading family planning programmes in rural areas of Indian society.

7. Educating woman for having smaller size of family.

8. Banning universal marriage.

9. Fixing marriage age of both male and female. It is 18 years for female and 21 years for male. In urban areas this age is on the hire side.

10. Late marriage.

11. Sterilization both bisectomy and vasectomy.

12. Using contraceptives at the time of male-female mating.

13. Having healthy children and not bringing them up in a proper standard is violence.

14. Child by choice and not by accident.

15. One or two children to a family.

If above measures are adopted effectively than

sufficient economic welfare can be exercised to India society.

Future of Human Population

World population is estimated to have grown at the annual rate of 1.4% during the year 1990-2000. There is net increase of three humans per second in the world population because in every second, on average, five children are born somewhere on earth and in that same second, two other people die. In other words BRs are five per second and Draw are two on earth.

The difference between BRs and DRs it three humans. If you multiply this out, you will find we are growing at a rate of about 11,000 per hour, 2,65,000 per day, or almost 100 million more people per month. By 1995, the world population had reached about 5.7 billion. Many people worry that overpopulation will cause resources depletion and environmental degradation that threatened the ecological life. Others believe that human population is useful because it provides technology and enterprise that extend the world's carrying capacity which allows us to overcome any problem we encounter.

A larger population means a larger workforce, more genius, more ideas about what to do. Along with every new mouth comes a pair of hands.

Environment and Human Health

Health means disease free body. The state of the people does not depend on the number of doctors and hospitals, but also on clean environment. An unclean environment can cause a number of health problems because ecological changes have a direct impact on human health. There are certain changes in the human environment that increase the incidence of many diseases. Such changes include socio-economic and cultural changes leading to stress of many kinds of human health.

For instance, urbanization and industrial stress, population stress and others ultimately bring about changes in the human environment, making it a paradise for infectious agents. Nearly 80% of the world's diseases, particularly in developing world can be linked with water. In our country there are 14 river systems. About 90% of pollution load in river system is due to human waste. For instance during Kumbh coliform increases from 300/100 ml to about 165,000/00 ml. In our country Kerala has much lower mortality rates that even the nation average. The reason are high literacy in women and better environmental sanitation. In Rajasthan the situation is very bad. Nearly 8000 villages in Rajasthan and Central India are affected with Guinea worm disease. Return of malaria and filaria and kalabaazar in Japan is also due do to adverse environment conditions.

Keeping the dangerous effects of bed environment following points must be kept in view:

1. Health care should not be biased towards cities. There should be proper care in villages also.

2. Disease control should not be taken in isolation. There should be cooperation of doctors, health educators, social anthropologists, media men, engineers, socio-economics and others.

3. Habitat management is very vital.

5. Future impact assessment of all development projects must include health aspect as well.

Contaminated water is the main cause of bad human health. The potable water contaminated with faeces is the chief cause of some important diseases of man. The enteric diseases are transmitted mainly by swallowing food or drinking contaminated with faeces. Typhoid fever, dysentery, cholera and other enteric diseases are caused by consumption of contaminated water. Some common human bacterial disease transmitted by factually contaminates are water:

Sanitation Bulletin: An emergency sanitation bulletin should include the following:

1. Milk and Food - Use only pasteurized milk. When the safety of milk is in doubt, or when only raw milk is available, bring the milk to a boil and cool in a clean container. If boiling is not possible, canned or powdered milk mixed with safe water can be used.

Cook all foods thoroughly. Frozen foods that have been thawed should be discarded if not consumed immediately or kept refrigerated at 450 F for lower. Avoid creamed dishes, hash, puddings, meat, poultry, and pre-prepared salads unless refrigeration can be assured.

Utensils can be used if clean and not exposed to flood waters. Raw foods exposed to flood waters should be avoided unless cooked because of possible contamination. If raw foods necessary to be used, clean thoroughly and soak in chlorinated water at least for 5 minutes.

Destroy the contents foods in tins where selling, leaking, rusting, or serious denting is visible. Wash off and immerse all hermetically sealed cans in good condition in a bleach disinfecting solution for at least 5 min prior to use in the same manner as above.

Clean and then disinfect all utensils and equipment prior to use in the same manner as above. Silfer should be immersed in boiling water for at least 2 min. Use single-service paper or plastic dishes, cups, and utensils where possible.

2. Safety Precautions - Entering into Damaged Buildings- Proceed with caution. If you have any doubts about the structural safety of a building, seek professional advice or assistance before going in. Check for visible signs of buckled walls, loose bricks, cracks, or shifting of foundation.

3. Household Cleanup Procedure - Cellars- If possible, wait for the groundwater level top drop below floor level. Otherwise, drain or pump water from flooded cellars, being careful to avoid the collapse of walls caused by the pressure of the water-saturated ground around the basement. Postpone pumping if groundwater level is high. Wash down the walls, floors, and other areas exposed to floodwater; keep windows and doors open for ventilation.

Disinfect the washed area by applying a solution of bleach with a broom or stiff brush. Allow the solution to remain in contact for approximately 10 min. The solution is prepared by adding 2 oz of bleach to 5 gal of water. Rinse with cold water as soon as possible to minimize staining. Any commercially available disinfectant can be used.

(i) Furniture - Clean and then wash metals, plastic, and leather surfaces with mild soap and water and wipe dry immediately. Some upholstery may be washed on the surface with soap and water and wiped dry. Expose to open air and sunshine.

(ii) Floor Coverings - Flush rungs and carpets with house and squeegee, the wash with lukewarm water containing a detergent. Rinse and dry in sun.

4. Refuse Collection, Storage, and Disposal - Drain and warp garbage in several layers of newspaper to absorb moisture. Store garbage in watertight, rodent-and insect-proof containers having a tight-fitting cover. Use

plastic linear if available. Bury garbage when necessary in a hole deep enough to provide for at least 18 in. of dirt cover and located at least 100 ft from any well of surface water.

Store all other refuse in a convenient place until normal collection services are provided, or take to the nearest designated place established by local authorities. Bury all dead animals as quickly as possible at a distance of a least 100 ft from any well or surface water and cover to a depth of at least 2 ft.

5. Insect and Rodent Control - To prevent breeding, store and dispose of garbage, sewage, and dead animals according to instructions. Drain standing water where ever possible, including containers of stagnant water. Treat standing water with kerosene, fuel oil, or commercially available larvicide during mosquito breeding season; apply 3 oz per 100 ft of water surface or in accordance with the manufacturer's instructions.

To kill rats, when trapping proves unsatisfactory, use commercially available quick kill poisons- such as zinc phosphide or red squill. Follow directions on the label. USE WITH CARE! Keep these poisons out of the reach of children and away from animals. Store in a locked cabinet.

6. Sewage and Excreta Disposal - When flush toilets cannot be used, use a small covered watertight bucket with a removable plastic liner to receive body wastes. Use a small amount of chlorine bleach, chlorinated lime, or any commercially available preparation which disinfects and deodorizes; follow manufacture's instructions. Remove the plastic liner as necessary; tie and place into a large watertight, rodent- and insect-proof garbage can with a tight cover for temporary storage. The wastes may be disposed with the garbage when

normal collection is restored, or by burial in a deep hole with at least 18 in. of dirt cover located at a distance of not less than 100 ft from any well or surface waters, or when and where feasible, by emptying the contents into the flush and carefully disposing of the plastic bag with the garbage.

Use the temporary public toilets established in the disaster area; they may be located over sewer manholes.

7. To Disinfect Your Well - First, pump well until water is clear; then:

(i) Pump heavily chlorinated water to waste, away from grass and shrubbery.

(ii) Repeat steps 1 through 3 to ensure that the chlorinated water has circulated through the entire toilet flushing.

(iii) If possible, reopen one tap and recirculate water back into well by means of a garden hose for a least 1 hour, then close tap.

(iv) Pump until chlorine odour appears at all taps, then close taps.

(v) Pur solution into well though top of casing or use vent pipe where available.

(vi) Mix one of liquid bleach in 5 gal water.

8. Drinking Water - Use Only Safe Water - Assume all sources are unsafe for use until approved by your local health department. Meanwhile, use health department-approved bottled water, or water distributed by health department-approved tank truck.

Or, disinfect water using a household liquid bleach disinfectant containing at least 5 percent available chlorine by weight. To one gallon. Of clear water, mix 6 to 8 drops of bleach; let the solution stand for 30 min before drinking. If the water is cloudy and contains particles, allow the particles to settle. Pour off the clear water into a separate container and add to it double the amount of bleach mentioned above; or heat water and a rapid boil for 2 min; or disinfect water using purified water using purification tablets. Carbonated beverages are satisfactory.

Value of Education

The environmental scenario of India is wide and diversified. Climatically, geographically, geologically, socially, economically and ethicality this country is highly diverse. It is, therefore suggested that while imparting environmental education special attention must be paid to school going children and women because they alone constitute about 50% of the population. They should be made aware of health, nutrition, sanitation, hygiene, water and food contamination. The main objectives of environmental education should be improving the quality of environmental, creating an awareness among people on environmental problems and conservation, creating such an atmosphere so that people find themselves fit enough to participate in decision making so that development programmes are presented after evaluation.

Role of I.T. in Environment and Human Health

Information technology is the need of the day. Computers, satellites and other technological developments have enabled environmentalists to gather informations and forecast the disasters much quickly with I.T. The engineer or environmentalists can gather world wide information on his table and make use of the same as per his requirements. Through GIS and GPS, a large amount of information along with photographs are easily accessible.

ENVIS, set up by the Ministry in 1982 as a decentral information system network continued its activities in collection, storage, retrieval and dissemination of environmental information to decision makers, policy planners, scientists, engineers, environmentalists, research workers and the general public all over the country. The ENVIS network besides the focal point in the ministry presently consists of 13 subject oriented centres, known as ENVIS Centres, set up in the various institutions/organizations of the country in the priority areas of environment like pollution control, toxic chemicals, energy and environment environmentally sound and appropriate technology, bio-degradation of wastes, deserification, estuary, mangroves, corals and lagoons, media and environment etc.

ENVIS has been designated as National Focal Point and Regional Service Centre for South Asia sub-regional countries by INFOTERA of United Nations Environment Programme. It caters to the environmental information needs more than 500 Indian Protectial Sources in the international directory of UNEP of providing information in the field of environment and its related areas.

Women and Child Welfare

Two-thirds of the world is done by women, whereas they own less than 7% of world's wealth. Women play a great role in unbringing family. Child welfare is situations which comes after bodyhood. She has the responsibility of child welfare. Fastest growth takes place during the first 2 years of life and again between 10 and 15 years for girls and 12 to 17 years for boys. They need the best food but many do not have. During this time they develop a lot of physically, mentally and lots of skills and ideas. The vocabulary develops from 0 and 1 year ago to about 2500 words at 6 years. Ideas about right and wrong develop through the example and teaching of adults. Through games one learns the importance of rules to that the game of life runs smoothly. Simultaneously, friends become very important and influential too.

In 1971 member countries of United Nations agreed on the declaration of rights of the child. A treaty was brought out by united nations of the Convention on the Rights of the Child", which was published in 1919. Out of 159 countries 100 countries accepted the rights of the children and the role of women towards child welfare. Following are the highlights of this convention.

1. Education which play facilities must be provided so that they grow well on all fronts.

2. Every effort should be made for medical care.

3. Clean and ventilated housing should be arranged for them.

4. Children should be provided nutritious food.

5. All children have the right to love understating.

Remote Sensing

Remote sensing is an art by which information can be acquired about an object or a surface feature from measurement at a distance without coming in physical contact with object or feature of interest. This information by noncontact methods is acquired usually from airplanes or satellites. It is one of the areas of rapidly advancing technology, very useful in ecosystem and environmental management. Photography from the ground or aerial platforms is a conventual form of remote sensing being used by foresters, geologists and geographers. Information on photographs or other images can be evaluated qualitatively and quantitatively. The method of concluding relationships by visual examination is called photointerpretation whereas the procedure of making photographic measurement is called photogrammetry.

Role of remote sensing in ecological research is enormous. It contributes to inventory and mapping of resources, quantifying the environment, describing the flow the matter and energy in the ecosystem, and evaluating change and alternative solutions for management of ecosystem. All these together help in environment management.

Remote sensing is proved very useful in soil and agriculture, town and country planning, detecting depiction of forest cover mapping etc. Remote sensing provides information about various agricultural resources that may have effect of the crop production. Many countries including USA and USSR have got remote satellite programme for land resources survey, environment impact assessment, weather forecasting and ocean studies. The proper know-how and technology is also developing in India by National Remote Sensing Agency assisted by Indian Institute of Remote Sensing, Dehradun. This Institute impart training to scientists and engineers in the field of remote sensing and photointerpretation since 1086. India launched many remote sensing satellites such as Bhaskra II and India satellite for earth imageries with coverage of sufficient radius. The use of this information can be made to exercise environment management and planning.

Global Positioning System

The Global Positioning System is an excellent example of information system based on modern radio and satellite systems. GPS demonstrates the technology and capabilities that were inconceivable a short time ago. GPS incorporate diverse types of information technology and it serves a broad range of utility guiding smart bombs or missiles to locating fish in water.

The basic function of GPS is to determine the position of GRS receiver anywhere on or above the earth in terms of latitude, longitude and elevation above sea level, with a clear view sky so that signals can be received from at least three GPS satellite at different locations in the sky. Once the position in the unit are determined by the receiver, the processor may then convert that location something useful to the user.

If the signals are from three satellites the GPS can determine the location anywhere in the surface. With signals from four or more satellites, the altitude can also be determined so that position in 3 dimensions may be determined. GPS is an excellent example of generating new products and capabilities. For a environmentalists GPS can be of great use. It can be used for many purposes, which could not be covered by remote sensing.

Geographic Information System

The management of resources need detailed inventory of all natural resources- abiotic and biotic. GIS study is very beneficial in this direction. The information so collected and compiled is quite useful to future generation. Help of computer is necessary to avoid negative consequences while compiling information because information collected manually shall become outdated because the resources would disappear as they get spoiled in the process of environmental degradation with passage of time. With the introduction of commercial geographic system, it has been possible to creatively analyse and interpret the data, eliminating the slow, laborious methods of data handing. Both CAC and CAD on the one hand and GIS on the other are equally beneficial. The GIS is an important tool for converting the spatial data into information which can be utilized to support the decisions for the intelligent use of earth resources and to manage the man made environment. Contents of GIS are given below:

(i) One can develop a small database of his own against which he can compare the test results.

(ii) It is possible to preserve the majority of the attributes data.

(iii) The conversion between rester and vector is quite common.

(iv) GIS use raster or a vector format to represent location.

(v) It provides specific location data with location, attribute and time.

Need for Planning Future

A review of the above description suffice to bring out the necessity of a direct attack on the problem that should aim at a rapid reduction in the birth rate. Based on the experience of western countries economic development and industrializations are quite often stressed as the best contraceptive. Besides this there are a number of remedies stated below if exercised effectively can check population in planning future.

Family planning is limiting the number of children to the born to a couple to one or two, More intensive research in family methods and practices, Creating grater awareness of the opportunities for legal fermentation of pregnancies, Setting up of family planning centres to make available the various related family planning, Using various means of communication to persuade people to through different outlets in urban, semi-urban and rural areas, Determining the spacing of children.

Density of Population

The density of population is calculated as ratio of the number of persons per sq. km. of land area. According to the 19912 census, the density of population in the country is 267. In Burma it is 50, Japan 316. One can know 3 interstate variation i.e., 6,319 but Arunachal Pradesh has only 10. The factors governing density of population are:

1. Rainfall irrigation facilities and agricultural development.

2. Better climate.

3. Trade and Business.

4. Industrial advancement.

Ecosystem Case Study/Environmental Case Study

Kolleru lake, a wetland located in Andhra Pradesh, is one of India's largest freshwater lakes and a bird sanctuary. Between 1985 and 1087 a study identified more than 185 bird species in the area, and new species continue to be found. The lake harbours four rare bird species and 12 endangered ones. It was declared a protected area of pelicans- about 8,000 pelicans came in 1961- but since 1972, none have visited. But today, economic and industrial development, expanding fisheries and pollution threatens Kolleru.

1. Ecological degradation - Pressure on the lake has led to proliferating weeds and fewer visiting birds. The catchment area has shrunk. This has led to eutrophication, loss of drinking water and declining fish catechus. Obstructions on the lake's periphery lead to flooded agricultural land even during normal rainfall.

The shape and area of the lake is difficult to assess because floods submerge large areas. The water spread varies from 135 sq km at + most level to 901 sq km at +10 mst. The average depth of the lake varies from 0.5 metres to two metres: the lake is silting gradually, raising the bed level.

Sewage inflow from the towns of Eluru, Fudivada and even Vijayawada and industrial effluents, pesticides and fertilizers from the Krishna-Godavari delta region contaminate the lake. Eleven major industries release about 7.2 million liters of effluents into the lake every day. An Andhra Pradesh Pollution Control Board report states that more than 17,000 tones of fertilizer wash enters the lake annually. Studies have shown the presence of organic pollutants in lake sediment and the weeds to growing fast. The sewage and discharge from factories have also affected the growth of water-bone organisms that the fish consume.

An ecological survey conducted in 1978 with financial assistance from CSIR, found no evidence of algal blooms and no significant contrast between the concentration of dissolved oxygen at the surface of the lake and at the bottom. However, in 1980 by the Administrative Staff College of India stated that the weed problem in the lake was caused by high levels of pollution. In 1972, state pollution board member warned that and dead zone would be created if pollutants were not checked.

2. Fishing - The roads and bridges that had come up with agricultural development in the area, along with an increased demand for fish, especially from Kolkata, created a new and vast market for fish by 1978. Pisciculture suddenly became profitable. By 1984, 5,000 acres of government lake bed land were converted to fish tanks under corporative societies. The government did well. Financial help was provided by pledging the

petty lands to cooperative banks in order to construct fish tanks. Our department provided technical help and training. Unfortunately, due to poor maintenance and low productivity of these tanks, fishefolk could not repay the loans. The government auctioned the tanks to private investors.

3. The led of Kolleru Lake has been used for ages to cultivate yerra vari, a native paddy variety. Since 1940 the cultivated area increased as the British government granted pattas on payment of market value for the land. 1954 on, the government initiated cooperative farming and organised 93 farming societies on 2.1 million acres of the lake bed. By 1969, almost the entire lake came under cultivation with huge bunds constructed to keep water out. The native paddy was replaced with shorter, high-yielding varieties requiring more fertilizers and pesticides.

Effects of Population

Reduction in death rates per 1000 and not controlling of birth rates to desirable limits has led to what has been described as population explosion. Rapid increase in population is threat to the nation's development. Population growth has nullified the efforts and improvement in the quality of life. Unlike developed countries, in developing countries like India where labour is abudant and capital scarce population growth is liability rather than an asset. Discussion to this reflect effect of population on nation's growth rate has been shown as follows:

(i) Illiteracy and ignorance shall prevail everywhere in India in the near future due to rapid growth of population according to available estimates. Newly born children will need one or two more fully equipped schools in each district every week.

(ii) At present food production in the country is about 180 million tonnes which is just sufficient to maintain the present level of population at the existing standard of nutrition. Any further increase in population, unless met with an equal proportional increase in food supply, will certainly lead to the shortage of food which will lead to famine, resilience, malnutrition, epidemics etc.

(iii) The pressure of population on land which is already high, is rising further as a consequence of growing population.

(iv) Growing population adds to the problem of under-utilization of labour.

(v) The growth in numbers has itself contribute to environmental damage, especially through reduction of soil cover and consequent flooding.

(vi) Population has adversely affected the growth of per-capita product.

(vii) High fertility rate and declining mortality in younger and old age group, the population is acquiring an increasing proportion of people in the non-working age groups relative to those of working age.

Declining Death Rates

India is fast in closing the gap with the rest of the world with regard to death rates. Death rate in the world in 1991 11 per 1000. This means 1.1% Following are the reasons leading to fall in death rates:

1. Food shortage which used to cause famine deaths have been overpowered.

2. Provision of better maternity and post-natal care has helped to bring down the death of infants.

3. There is growth of sanitation and cleanliness which help to reduce the incidence of morality.

4. Plague, Smallpox, Typhoid which used to finish villages in past have now been controlled with the use of antibiotics and other life-saving medicines.

5. Technology with regard to diseases control.

2

COMMUNITY AND ENVIRONMENTAL EDUCATION

All over the world, drinking water and sanitation projects are being viewed as a base for promoting public health. In India, the coverage of sanitation services are poor, to achieve the Million Development Goals (MDG) there appears to be insufficient resource allocation to the sector. Hence, under sector reforms the government replaces heavy subsidized programme with demand driven and community led approach, where community share/recovery of partial capital cost, to reduce burden on state exchequer. This study investigated how and to what extent this shift help in achieving the set objective by choosing a similar project implemented in Karnataka state with the following objectives:

- To examine community contribution for environmental sanitation.
- To examine impact of community participation in expected outcomes.
- To examine the contribution by different stakeholders during implementation of project

Approach and Methodology

To test the objectives, a multiple sampling method was used to select the villages and households. The result in analysis shows that the communities were unable to contribute for the capital cost. As a result, there was inequity in sharing the benefits of the project among the community. Hence, it necessitates redesigning the project with specific role for each actor in the project.

Introduction

In recent years, there has been increasing recognition of the limitations of the capacity of government agencies to effectively manage the rapidly increasing multiplicity of development programmes. As a substitute the governments have been assigning greater roles to the Non-Government Organisations (NGO), private sector and communities for greater participation. This shift in approach was observed in various sector including drinking water and sanitation services, to increase efficiency, for cost recovery and sustainability of the schemes/assets, this has been experienced in many countries. In fact, the drinking water and sanitation sector received attention to promote public health in turn the productivity of human resources can be enhanced, thus poverty can be reduced.

In India, just 22 per cent of the households have access to sanitation in rural area (NSS 1998; Census 2001). This level needs to rise to 53 per cent by 2015 to meet the MDG target, a huge challenge. There appears to be a shortfall of some Rs 287 billion in the financing needed from 2002-15 (Water Aid 2005). Toward this goal the Government of India is making all the efforts, traditionally relied on high level of subsidies to construct latrines. The high subsidy approach has been now replaced with the principle of demand driven and community led, with the introduction of the Total Sanitation Campaign (TSC) in 1999. The concept of sanitation has now been expanded to include liquid and solid waste disposal, personal, domestic as well as environmental hygiene.

Location of Project

The Karnataka (Federal State) state implemented three major projects supported by multilateral and bilateral agencies, the new approach introduced in TSC was in-built in these projects. This study investigated how and to what extent the paradigm shift took place in demand driven and community led. For investigation, the Karnataka Integrated Rural Water Supply and Sanitation Services (KIRWSS) project was selected, which was implemented during 1994-2002, in 1104 villages (rural settlements), supported by World Bank.. Two sets of villages were selected for investigation, first set of villages were randomly selected ten per cent of the 1104, project villages. Purposively all the nine pilot phase villages spread across the state were selected for investigating impact of project at household level, the households were selected proportionately to total households. Thus, 121 villages (112+9) and 755 households were finally selected and examined. According to methodology (see Appendix), the required secondary and primary data was collected from different agencies and households.

Situation Analysis and Description of Problem

According to the latest statistics in state only 18 per cent of the households have access to latrines and 35 percent for drainage systems (Census 2001). Of the total access to latrines only 9 percent were have pit latrine. The reasons for the low coverage vary; however, the common factors are religious beliefs and culture, the advent of Hinduism and its caste system (Cooper 1997). The community often unable to perceive a direct relationship between the current health profile of household and sanitation services. (Veerashekharappa,

2001; 2004) As the project was based on need and demand driven concept, the primary objective was to create awareness on impact of water and sanitation related diseases, in turn to create demand for project. For this, the Information, Education and Communication (IEC) strategy was adopted. Under the project, the entire investment on water was met by the project funds, while for environmental sanitation 30 per cent of the cost has to be met by the community in the ratio of 70:30. The NGOs, beneficiaries and private sector have participated; the beneficiary was involved in all stages of implementation through Village Water Supply and Sanitation Committees (VWSC). The concept followed in the project was with better resources and community participation; the expected outcomes can be derived. The process and expected outcomes were well defined under the project, which was reproduced here briefly.

Resource

1. Finance
2. Human resources
3. Institution

Process

1. Participation
2. Accountability
3. Transparency

Expected Outcomes

1. Equity
2. Efficiency
3. Sustainability

As mentioned earlier, the community has to share 30 per cent of capital cost of sanitation. To tender water work construction, the VWSC has to mobilize 25 per cent of the 30 per cent, thus the community was made accountable for initiation of the project. Of the total 12 district (provinces) where project implemented, except in two districts, in all other districts the agreed amount was mobilized, but in none of the district the amount was entirely mobilized from the household source. The balance amount has come from non-household sources, such as Gramapanchayat, cooperative societies, contractors, etc. Of these, the role of local leaders, contractors and Gramapanchayats was important in that order, because together they met the biggest chunk of the gap left by the households, which amounted to 41.6 per cent. Of the total selected (112) villages, including four villages, where no contribution has taken place, in total 21 villages the contribution was less than 25 per cent. The major concern in this context was, of the 29 contractors, 45 per cent of them contributed an amount varying from 40 per cent and upwards of the total contribution in the village (in one village 80 per cent). Finally, the total amount mobilized at state level from all sources under community contribution was Rs 130 million as against the expected Rs 300 million (GOK 2003), thus, 43 per cent of the agreed amount was mobilized. Within that, what was actually mobilized from the household was just around 60 million.

As mentioned earlier, 25 per cent of the agreed amount had to be mobilized for tendering villages for water works, but in practice the norms were flouted. The reasons attributed were that the tendering was done on global competition, to achieve the economy of scale and a couple of villages were combined as a slice on cluster basis. In the process, the villages that had not mobilized the agreed amount also tendered on the pretext that community would mobilize the agreed amount later. But, that could not take place at all, thus the accountability on the part of community was relaxed. In pilot villages, the pattern of contribution was more or less same what was observed in large sample. The most identified reason for less number of household contributions was the inefficiency of NGO in convincing the household about the benefits of the project.

Most of the households were under impression that 'none pays' or 'nothing happens even if we did not pay'. Thus, the NGO could not make much effort in changing of mindset of the household, which was very crucial for successful implementation of the project. The inefficiency of NGO was turned out be an advantage to contractors in each village. If the households had been convinced on the relation between contaminated water and health profile of the households the situation would have been different. The role of NGO, along with creation of awareness, it has to facilitate VWSC in its various functions, such as facilitated to conduct meetings, provide technical training in operation and maintenance of assets, etc. As per the norms, VWSC meetings were scheduled every fortnight, but, the minutes of meeting book show that in all the villages, in aggregate 43 per cent of meetings held as per schedule. The reasons for not holding meetings as per scheduled was attributed to the factions in village and reconstituting of VWSC in couple of villages, due to change of party in power. It is observed that women and vulnerable section of the community attended the meetings, because of appropriate reservations were made to them while constituting the committee. But, their presence was not felt in meetings.

The VWSC had been authorized to award contract for the construction of sanitation services. In practice, the persons, who played a key role in mobilizing the large amount, took the decision. In each village, the contractor was awarded to the person recommended by them. If any person questions the award of contract was cornered and suppressed with questions like 'Why should you interfere? Are you going to pay for it? Why bother who gets contract. If you want to interfere, why don't you mobilize more? Moreover, when the contractor was willing to contribute on our behalf, we have saved of paying towards our share of capital cost. Thus, there was no community participation and transparency in awarding contract, as there was nexus between elite group of village and contractor.

Thus, though finance (enough funds), human resources (NGO) and organisation (VWSC) was provided in the project as input in. But, it is noticed that there is not equity provision of services, which were biased towards wealthy localities in terms of accessibility and adequacy of water supply. Of the total households, 82 per cent of the wealthy households found the source located within short distance, 32 per cent drew water 40 lpcd and above, whereas on an average, 17 per cent of the poor drew water less than 40 lpcd. The quantity of water obtained was positively associated with the landholding and wealth status. Similarly, there was inequity in provision of sanitation services. As mentioned earlier, sanitation services made available largely on demand based by sharing proportion of total investment cost. As a result there were large variations in the components provided and proposed, considering the mobilization of agreed amount. For instance, the drainage construction was not taken place in one village, in three villages it was partially constructed that too in wealthy locality. The box type drainage was constructed in wealthy locality, while in other localities the L shape drainage was constructed. Of the total selected households, on an average, 17 per cent of them had Individual Household Sanitary Latrine (IHSL), against the targeted 30 per cent by the project. The 17 per cent were a cumulative figure of various other similar programmes, such as Nirmal grama yojana (NGY) implemented in respective villages.

The reasons for low coverage were attributed, for linking sanction of subsidy to the household toilets with community contribution and private household connection (PHC) of water. The beneficiary had to meet at least one of these two conditions to get the benefit. This undue practice had kept away many deserving households from opting for latrines. At the same time, our investigation found a couple of households misusing the facility, with the nexus of officials and key persons within the village, by showing latrines constructed under NGY or self initiated against the KIRWSS and claimed the subsidy.

Lessons Learnt and Alternatives

The above analysis brings out that; the concept of community participation through cost sharing and recovery in development projects had been theoretically established and empirically tested in many parts of the world. The international agencies have been promoting this idea by funding directly and indirectly, countries are accepting these policies to reduce the financial burden on public exchequer of their county.

The lessons learn from this project was, the programme not deep rooted in minds of people, to achieve this, the approach has to be revised. Both the institutions (NGO and VWSC) were ineffective in various aspects, in fact the VWSC was functioning as an extended arm of the gramapanchayat. Thus most of the demerits of that institution have been inherited by this organization. As a result, neither the beneficiary shared the capital cost nor user charges were paid in many villages. In fact, the project helped the key persons in the village to capture benefits, without accountability. Subsequently, most of the villages (except 10 to 12 villages) were transferred to gramapanchayat, the operation and maintenance cost is met largely from state budgetary allocation.

Hence, there is a need to re-examine at the design of similar projects, particularly designing the process, which is most important. Particularly the job of regulator and service provision has to be separated, to achieve equity and efficiency in service provision, if necessary partially privatization can be acceptable by involving Self Help Groups (SHGs) through linking up micro-finance activities. Indeed this approach might be an alternative in future.

HOME HYGIENE AND ENVIRONMENTAL SANITATION: A COUNTRY SITUATION ANALYSIS FOR INDIA

Problems of the environment and of domestic hygiene are always related to poverty of population and the sanitation of settlements. Most cities and towns in developing countries, like India, are characterised by over-crowding, congestion, inadequate water supply and inadequate facilities of disposal of human excreta, waste water and solid wastes. Inadequacy of housing for most urban poor invariably leads to poor home hygiene. Personal and domestic hygiene practices cannot be improved without improving basic amenities, such as water supply, waste water disposal, solid waste management and the problems of human settlements. But even under the prevailing conditions, there is significant scope of improving hygiene practices at home to prevent infection and cross-infection. Unfortunately, in developing countries, public health concerns are usually raised on the institutional setting, such as municipal services, hospitals, environmental sanitation, etc.

There is a reluctance to acknowledge the home as a setting of equal importance along with the public institutions in the chain of disease transmission in the community. Managers of home hygiene and community hygiene must act in unison to optimise return from efforts to promote public health. Current practices and perceptions of domestic and personal hygiene in Indian communities, the existing levels of environmental and peri-domestic sanitation and the 'health risk' these pose will be outlined, as well as the need for an integrated action for improving hygiene behaviour and access to safe water and sanitation.

UNICEF Partners with Community to Initiate a Cleanliness Drive in Relief Camps

UNICEF partnered with the government and NGOs to mobilise communities in relief camps to clean up the open defecation and build toilets for men and women within the camp area. The exercise kicked off from the Nilayathachiamman Kovil, in Nagapattinam the men and older children enthusiastically shovelled the earth to clean up excreta lying scattered in the open. Government workers and 50 volunteers recruited by the NGO SCOPE supported community.

TRAINING THE COMMUNITY AND THE VOLUNTEERS

Community members and volunteers recruited in

Trichy by SCOPE were first trained in the Centre on the need for maintaining environmental sanitation that focused on the prevention of open defecation, provision of appropriate toilets, refuse disposal, and the importance of washing hands with soap after defecation. Soap provided to UNICEF by Rotary and P&G was distributed by the trained volunteers to complete the process.

The Joint Secretary Health, Supriya Sahu requested the UNICEF team to deploy trained volunteers to three camps where sanitation and water is a critical problem. The Water, Environment and Sanitation (WES) officer at Nagapattinam will deploy 15 of these volunteers at each of the Centres.

The roll out plan of the Community Centre sanitation programme will be need-based covering all Centres in the district that do not yet have any toilets. The Joint Secretary will maintain contact with the UNICEF WES officers to co-ordinate the efforts.

Temporary Toilets

Trenches 3 ft. deep, 2 ft. wide and 7 ft. long were dug in the open compound of the temple, enough for 45 people to use the toilets at one time. For privacy, the trenches were covered with coconut thatch "walls". Special women's toilets were created to protect their privacy - a major issue at the camps.

The UNICEF initiative will ensure that all relief camps have sanitation facilities and the community will be in charge of maintaining cleanliness in these temporary structures.

Community takes responsibility to clean up toilets

The 15 members of the Fishermen's committee along with women groups agree to take responsibility to maintain the cleanliness of the toilets and ensure that no body in the camps defecates anywhere in the open but in the toilets.

Women and children began using the toilets minutes after they were constructed. "This is a great relief. We were defecating and eating food in the same grounds. Many of us felt giddy while eating due to the stench from the excreta," says Meenakshi who comes with her child six year old child the newly built toilet.

Community Water and Sanitation Facility: A Cities Alliance Initiative

In February 2003 the United States launched the Community Water and Sanitation Facility as a Global Development Alliance (GDA), public-private partnership, with the multi-donor supported Cities Alliance to expand water and sanitation services in urban slums. The Facility works towards achieving the objectives of Target 11 of the Millennium Development Goal Number 7 to improve water and sanitation and significantly improve the lives of at least 100 million slum dwellers by 2020. The U.S. launched the Facility with seed funding of $2 million and technical assistance from other agency programs.

The Community Water and Sanitation Facility supports local authorities and their partners in working through public-private partnerships to expand water and sanitation services to slum communities, fund community endorsed construction, promote risk-sharing and innovative financing to mobilize funding resources.

Cities Alliance is a donor coalition committed to the vision, "Cities Without Slums" and has 14 contributing members, including Brazil, Canada, France, Italy, Japan, Germany, the Netherlands, Nigeria, Norway, South

Africa, Sweden, the United States, the United Kingdom, the Asian Development Bank, the United Nations Environment Program, UN-Habitat and the World Bank, plus the four major global municipal organizations under United Cities and Local Government (UCGL).

Public-Private Partnerships Are Essential to Bringing Water and Sanitation Services to Slum Communities

USAID-sponsored Community Water and Sanitation Facility (CWSF) activities underscore and promote the importance of public-private partnerships to achieve sustainable provision of water and sanitation services in slum communities. Several USAID country missions are working with partners to broker activities for Facility support.

USAID-Sponsored Projects

USAID/South Africa has worked with the British Department for International Development (DFID) and the Municipal Infrastructure Investment Unit (MIIU), a non-profit corporation funded by the Government of South Africa, to increase access to water and sanitation services for over 1 million disadvantaged persons in five municipalities. The partners are using the CWSF to support water system upgrades, promote local capital investment, and better managed services for the urban poor. USAID has provided use of its innovative Development Credit Authority (DCA) credit instrument to facilitate local lenders making funds available to these municipalities. With an expected leverage of over 36:1, the Facility contribution of $300,000 should generate $16,675,000 in partner contributions. In a related municipal finance partnership, USAID and private sector partner, Evensen Dodge, are assisting the Cities of Tshwane and Durban to obtain access to up to $1 billion over the next three years to finance infrastructure investments such as in water services.

USAID/Mozambique is now supporting local governance programs which may results in CWSF projects in six cities and a proposed UN-HABITAT initiative to address interlinked problems of poor access to safe drinking water and efficient waste management in Quelimane City. The goal being to promote participatory development strategies and implementation of innovative tools resulting in improved water and sanitation solutions.

In India, USAID and Shelter Associates, a community based organization representing slum dwellers in Sangli, constructed community toilet facilities for the use of 25,000 persons. The project objectives were to:

a. Develop community-level toilet construction and management plans in consultation with local government authorities,

b. To assist the municipality in implementing the community-level plans and

c. To begin the preparatory work for a citywide slum upgrading strategy.

The Facility was asked to fund technical assistance and construction materials for public toilets. Added resources were provided by private sector and community partners. Upcoming CWSF efforts are in development, where USAID/India will partner with local stakeholders and the Government of India in Bangalore and Agra to address long-term city wide infrastructure planning, delivery of basic services and test a pilot "willingness-to-pay" demonstration program. The pilot will showcase how low income communities can acquire reliable services when community residents pay for individual connection charges and monthly water and sewerage tariffs. This win-win mechanism has enhanced revenues for the utilities thereby enabling it to improve service quality to slum residents.

USAID/Panama has been working with local stakeholders in Panama City to plan a CWSF program to address public health concerns and bring sewerage lines and treatment facilities to a marginalized community of 12,500 people in the Panama Canal watershed. Through a series of community meetings, participants identified how toddlers and women were disproportionately affected by skin and gastro-intestinal problems due to the lack of sanitation services. In response to the community's needs, USAID through the CWSF is helping to broker a public-private alliance with the Ministry of Health, Panama Canal Authority, the National Institute for Water and Sanitation, the Municipality of Panama, local business and community residents to construct a affordable sewerage system. This partnership will help protect the Panama Canal watershed and tap into local and international capital financing for scaling up the intervention into other communities in the watershed.

Future Water Partnerships to Deliver Services to Urban Poor

USAID's Urban Programs Team is now actively work with other USAID/Washington programs and various Field Missions throughout the world to initiate new CWSF and slum upgrading projects in cooperation with this Facility. For example, USAID is now working with local stakeholders to plan and consider the development of future CWSF projects in Nepal, Ecuador, Jamaica, Mozambique, Angola and Iraq.

3

ENVIRONMENT—SCIENCE AND ENGINEERING

Environment engineering is the technical method used to minimise pollution and other industrial hazards. The permissible limit as approved by Central Pollution Control Board, and State Pollution Control Board of a country is considered by an environmental engineer. It is felt that as we move into twenty-first century, the use of technology problems will increase. Role of engineering and technology in environment matters therefore is now changing in to importance areas.

There areas are (i) sustainable development and (ii) preventive technology. Sustainable development primarily deal with global problems whereas preventive technology is designed to reduce the environmental effects of processes, operations and products. Global sustainable development require a stabilized world population living in secure social and physical environment. These requirements are being badly hit by engineering, technological and scientific practices such as overfertilizing the land, harvesting old grown forests, avoiding pollution control etc.

Preventive technology decisions are guided by market and profit concerns, with little or no consideration for environmental and social at the cost of their health and safety. Environmental science try to explain how diversified pollutions can be checked without causing health hazards to organisms living in this world. So its study in the field of engineering becomes quite important.

Environmental Science and Sociology

Sociology is body of learning about society interacting with social groups. It is a social science which includes the study of social institutions, religions, family, values, customs, caste and habits etc. While living in society, man changes environment very quickly in order to meet his biological and social needs. So on the social front man tries to possess materials for life and for this purpose he removes raw materials from his environment by way of deforestation, extraction of minerals, erection of thermal power stations and construction of concrete jungles for habitat. Indiscriminate construction and expansion of settlement activities collectively pose threat to the environment leading to serious problem of environmental degradation.

Environmental science evolve the study that seeks to describe problems caused by our use of natural world. In addition, it seeks some of remedies for these problems. It tries to protect environment from hit and attach by social- economic activities. Protection of environment from hit and attack by socio- economic activities. Protection of environment with the application of environmental science is as important and focal point before society. It teaches development without polluting the environment with the application of environmental science is an important and focal poind before society. Teach development without polluting the environment. It is agreed that there should be environment development. To this the straight reply is that there should be development within the environment. One should not find these two things separate development and clean. If one cannot breathe pure air, cannot drink clean water and if one has come from west and live on mineral water then there is something fishy somewhere. Birds in this direction assist in communicating environmental pollution because their metabolic rate is much higher than those of humans beings. They predict environmental se up of a region.

Environmental Science and Eco- system

The natural world is organized into interrelated units called ecosystems. Ecosystem is a collection of living and non-living organism connected by a complex web of interactions. Eco-system is a region in which the organism and the physical environment form an interacting unit. This is true in case of lake or island; transition from grassland to desert. Of course it depends on the historical pattern of rain fall in an area. Eco-system look at the ways and means by which natural world is organized. It answers to questions like- where do the rivers flow? What are the typical plants and animals in the area? How does human activity affect the nature?

Environmental scientists recognizes and understand the natural interactions that take place. He integrates these in such a hammer that men make use of this natural world. A few studies made from time to time illustrate this explanation.

North American continent is dominated by intensive agriculturc. This mcans that thc original, natural eco-systems have been replaced by managed agricultural enterprise. It is important to mention that this area was at one time wilderness. Today it is difficult to find large regions of true wilderness. The economic value generated by the use of rich soil is tremendous, and consequently most of the land is privately owned. Government cannot control easily what happens on these privately held lands, but do indirectly encourage certain activities. It provides special subsidies to farmers and develop markets for products. Inspite of these facilities, economic risks involved in farming are great. Drought, disease and lack of markets result in failures and on account of this reason, the numbers of farmers constantly decline. Not only this, many communities due to the use of pesticide and fertilizers because they potentially enter the ground water. In addition many farmers use ground water for origination which result in lowering of the water table and less availability of groundwater for other purposes. To stay in this region, to do business and preserve way of life, farmers must make careful use of tools and technology in a responsible manner. Irresponsible use causes increased erosion, water pollution and risks to humans. Environmental sciences teach perfect control and maintenance of eco-system for living.

Environmental Science and Agriculture

There is growing realization that natural farming methods in and answer to the environmental and agricultural problems. The National Academy of Science, Washington has found that farmers who apply few or no chemicals to crops are usually as productive as those who use pesticides and synthetic fertilizers. The group has therefore recommended changing federal subsidy programs that encourage use of chemicals. In the federate corn programme, for instance, farmers are paid a subsidy or roughly $1 for every bushel they produce. The incentive is to produce more bushels, without disturbing environmental condition.

Environmental Science and Economics

Poverty, hunger, malnutrition, unemployment and poor medical facilities are very serious and acute problems in the developing countries. Environmental pollution is another equally serious problem being faced throughout the world due to struggle for economic development. Economic development which require fast industrial development is being made everywhere in the world, in order to needs of teeming millions. To need the needs of increasing population, more and more resources are being tapped from nature. Reckless use of natural resources cause disharmony between human being and the natural environment. This is not economic growth but enactment, hazardous to economic growth. Use of clean technology and pollution free environment ensure higher rates of economic growth because this practice leads to enhanced longevity of life.

A statement issued by the Royals Society of London pointed out that the world population is growing at the unprecedented rate of almost 100 million people every year and human activities are bringing major changes in the global environment. Sustainable development implies a future in which life is improved world- wide through economic development where local environments and biosphere are protected with the application of environmental science assist creates new opportunities for human progress.

Growth and development are fundamentally different goals. Growth results in an increase in material production and consumption that may be unsustainable in the long run : development is a strategy that calls for improvements is culture that do not necessarily require further increase in resources consumption, and environmental degradation.

Environmental Science and Biotechnology

In today's world, biotechnology occupies and Important position in applied sciences in its effort to improve the quality of human life and the living conditions through the development of bio-diversed products, because biotechnologist search nearly all types of herbs through assistance of environmental studies.

It is a observed that the environment come through increased population pressure leading to over exploitation of land, and available water resources, destruction of biowealth, biodiversity a d also injection of various hazardous xenobioti substances into the environment affecting its self-purification potential and carrying capacity. The enormity of the problem has drawn attention of scientist, technologists, administrators and citizens to find ways to sustain and to preserve eco-health along with conservation of invaluable natural resources.

The emerging science of biotechnology is found to be an essential tool in this endeavour it can provide new approach for understanding, managing, perceiving and restoring the quality of environment.

The methodologies of biotechnology not doubt can be suitably utilized to asses the health and well being of ecosystems, transformation of pollutants into harmless substances, to generate biodegradable materials from renewable resources and for developing eco friendly products and manufacturing processes and also disposal methods. Ass these products and process are studied under environmental biotechnology.

Environment Science and Biology

The term biology is mode of two words. One is called bios in Greek which means life and the other logos means study. So biology is the science of living things.

Biology makes to understand ourselves better and the nature in the best possible way. It explain intricate relationship among the organisms in the ecosystem. Studies reveal that about 50,000 children die everyday of various prevented if we commit ourselves to environmental science.

Environmental sanity which means the state of being sane/wise and hygienic. The practising of cleanliness away of maintaining good health which control all the factors in the physical environment. There are a large number of disease which are communicable and non-communicable The various non-communicable disease are hypertension, stroke, cancer, diabetes act. There are many intestirory infectious diseases such as Viral hepatitis, Cholera, Typhoid, Food Poisoning etc. One can protect himself from such disease because health in man's natural condition. It is the result of living in accordance with natural laws pertaining to the body, mind and environment. These laws relate to fresh air, sunlight, diet, exercise. Rest and relaxation of mind. The pure treatments and gifts of environment. The use of these gifts treat mental health and ensure the balanced development of man's personality and emotional attitudes. Worry, low temper, insomnia, fluctuation in mood, cuneus dislike and constant bitterness in feelings. You are always right and others always wrong are a few aches and pains which no doctor can cure to these diseases. So there is interrelationship and interdisciplinary relationship between biology and environment science.

Environmental Decision Making Process

Environmental science teachers that all organisms have an impact on their surroundings. It regnancies development of compromise between different geographic regions. Environmental decisions are therefore often compromising. As already discussed, environment means surroundings. It is a system in which various living beings like animals including man birds, insects, rodents, micro organisms like algae, fungi, protozoa and non-living beings like the soil, the water and the air and interrelated in life sustaining system.

It is a complex web and man occupies a very tiny space in it. Man lives in two environments - one is natural environment of water, air, soils, hills, trees and other living beings etc. The other environment is his social environment. It is an artificial environment, a man-made ecosystem. This environment is created himself alone by using science, technology, religion and politics. Both the environments are lively and lovely, beautiful and bountiful. But some times man meddles too much with Mother Earth to extract much more than what he deserves. Then she becomes crues, hostile and devastating. Environment governs everything that earth provides to people. So environmental problems are people's problems. These problems occur due to unrestricted use of natural resources, which some people feel are justified, result in a diminished environment for other in the region.

For instance insecticides have been applied to crops since they were introduced in the mid 40s to increase yield; prevent pests from devouring food for people more damage to the public health and the environment than the benefits gained from them. There is now a growing body of scientific evidence indicating that pesticides provide only a short term solution to pests and increased agricultural productivity. The two major areas of concern in pesticide use are the crop residues that contain the poison and the phenomenon of resistance that makes insects immune to pesticides. The residues carry not only the portion the kills insects but also the substances that cause cancer, birth defects and many other ailments after contaminating the air, land and water. The tragedy here is that insecticides do not know when to stop killing.

Hot Spot Biodiversity

Studies reveal that wetlands and water bodies in Assam have been identified as a hot spot of biodiversity. It is regretful to notice that wetland in Assam continue to be assaulted by developments. There are many as 3,513 fresh water wetlands. They develop various characteristics on the basis of their location, nutrient dynamic of the soil and vegetation. One of the serious problems associated with wetlands is the construction of embarkments to check floods. The result is the feeder channel which is the umbilical cord of the wetlands is cut off. This action affects the nutrient input and the output ratio between the lake and the main feeder channels.

Consequently, there is an acceleration in the lane use pattern, particularly increased agricultural activities. One of the implications is the change in the fish community composition of the wetlands. A few species have become extinct, leaving this aside, the discharge of effluents for paper mills, woolen factories, refineries and insecticides from agricultural fields have affected the quality of wetland resulting in low productivity and increased incidence of disease both in man and cattle. Scientific management is the only option left for the preservation of Assam's wetlands.

Environmental decision making process occur due to the uses of natural resources. Economic consideration is the backbone of environmental decisions. This is so because a group of people receive value from the natural resources when used whereas another group perceives an economic loss because a use from natural resources been withdrawn. So a conflict is created between two groups. In other words cold war between environmentalist, chemical scientists and economics is generated.

Environmentalists object the use of insecticides and pesticides as well as felling of trees for the construction of river valley projects but economists and chemists do not agree to this proposal. Environmentalists want to protect environment because all these activities affect ecology. The call it mismanagement of resources done in the form of large-scale deforestation, unplanned discharge of residual waste, handling of toxic chemicals, indiscriminate construction and expansion of settlement activities because they collectively pose threat to the environment.

Now the question arises how this dispute should be settled. Environmental decision makers give their views in the following manner.

(i) Some are against these changes; others identify that change must occur.

(ii) Some argue that Government and authorities should take all necessary measures for protection quality of environment, by laying down standards for discharge of environmental degration.

(iii) Some comment that economic considerations should not be given any importance whereas other argue that economic considerations can resolves it.

Now what to do? What potions should be selected what should be. With all these issues in view, compromise is the only way to resolve the conflicts. The social institutions and economic evaluators play an important role in this direction. The field of environmental science seeks to find the middle path and ground. The environmental science teachers the impact on environment when natural resources are converted into goods. It is therefore, argued and suggested that before natural resources are converted into artifacts that is when deforestation is exercised for making diversified use of wood and elephants are killed to get ivory, what impacts they have upon environment should not be forgotten. Environmental impacts while underrating River Valley Projects in no way less important because this action lead to degradation of catchment areas, rehabilitation of those who are affected by environmental changes, increase in water borne disease, reservoir inducing seismicity and causing loss of flora and fauna. To minimize these changes some standards are framed. International standard organization has framed some standards for better environmental management. India has also adopted IO 14000 which incorporate series of management standards. The components of ISO 14000 are as follow:

a. Environmental Management System :- It is a system for maintaining development in the environment. It's aims are recognizing impacts and risks of environmental degradation and developing all environmental control policies so that environmental performance is improved.

b. Environmental Performance Evaluation :- ISO 14000 is applicable to all types and sizes of organization. Its applicability is traceable at irrigation Department, Forest, Extraction of Oil and Natural Gas and various industrial units. Any organization where nature of activity and service have direct and indirect effect on environment can adopt these standards. The success of this system depends on commitment from all level. EPE unit try to achieve standards as per ISO standards after examination an d evaluation.

c. Environmental Auditing :- It aim is maintaining programmes and procedures for periodic EMS audit. Auditing is done to know whether or not the environmental management system conform to the Environmental management standards.

d. Environmental Aspects of Products Standards :- It includes element of an organization' activities, product or services which can interact with environment.

e. Life- cycle Assessment :- Under this the organization establishes and maintains documented procedures to monitor key characteristics of its operations and activities that can have significant impact on the environment.

e- Environmental Labelling :- It ensures conformance with stated environmental policy and make a self determining declaration of conformance with the standard.

Environmental Impact Assessment

Environmental impact means effect on environment due to human activities directed in pursuit of fulfilling ever increasing needs of life. Assessment refer to evaluation and estimation of exploitation and processing of natural resources. The EIA is therefore a method of evaluating environmental consequences i.e. environmental changes which are likely to be caused by the proposed human activity related to land use construction of dams, reservoirs, industrial location, urban expansion etc. and the possible adverse effects of these environmental changes which may cause ecological imbalance and ecosystem dis-equilibrium etc.

Methods of Checking Environmental Impacts

(i) Polluters should pay for their environmental impacts through internationalization of costs, the use of appropriate taxes, changes and incentives for environmental protection.

(ii) Unsustainable patterns of production and consumption must be reduced and appropriate demographic policies must be promoted.

(iii) Environmental protection must be an integral part of development.

(iv) Creation of an agency to prepare an environmental impact statements for analysing the major effects of projects to be undertaken. EIS will reconsider a harmful project.

(v) Society need urgently many more teacher at every level who should be trained in environmental education. Outdoor activities and natural sciences are important components of this mission.

(vi) Outdoor activities are an essential part of environmental education, which strives to introduce environmental literacy to the general population and to encourage students to prepare for environmental careers.

(vii) Providing environmental literacy - a sense of duty to care for and managing wisely our natural endowment and productive resources for the long haul.

(viii) Encouraging pose secondary students to pursue careers related to the environment, appreciation of our natural environment, knowledge of basic ecological concepts, acquaintance with broad range of current environmental problems.

(ix) Improving understanding among the general public of the natural and built environment.

(x) Promoting efforts to prevent damage to the environment and the biosphere.

(xii) Environmental careers are required to be expanded because environmental studies is a very vast subject. So far perfect assessment and evaluation environmental professionals such as engineers are needed to develop technologies and products to clean up pollution, economists , geographers, and social scientists are needed to evaluate and other specialists to develop government and industrial policy, laws, and regulations to protect the environment. The EPA estimates, for example, the 100,000 new professionals will be required in the United State in the next five years alone to deal with hazardous waste problem.

Dharma Ecology

On the occasion of the World Environment Day, one aminate environmentalist presented he concept of Dharma on Ecology. According to him there is a need to have global ethic to meet threat to our environment. Planners must make use to this concept and educate the people over this ground, because the major challenge facing the human race is to move towards susceptibility.

Following six principle of Dharma Ecology as recognize by environmentalist are mentioned below:

(i) Halting and revising the arms built-up.

(ii) Meeting genuine social needs.

(iii) Willingly adopting sustainable way of life.

(iv) Crating awareness about concealed social, economic and environmental costs.

(v) Protections and nurturing renewable resources, conserving non- renewable resources and avoiding conserving non-renewable resources and avoiding waste by exercising economy.

Need for Public Awareness

The enhanced pace of developmental activities and rapid urbanization have resulted in stress on natural resources and quality of life. The trend of increasing pollution in various environmental media is evident from the deteriorating air and water quality, higher noise levels, increasing vehicular emission etc. Realising the urgent need for arresting the trend, Ministry adopted Policy for Abatement of Environmental Degradation. But this is only a approach and not a movement. Till movement is not effect, approach shall stand null and void. To make movement effective public support is very necessary. So a clarion call of public awareness becomes essential. There is no urgent need for public awareness about cleaner environment.

It is, therefore suggested that while imparting environmental education special attention must be paid to school going children and women because they alone constitute about 50% of the population. The should be made aware of heath, nutrition, sanitation, hygiene water and food contamination. The main objectives of environmental education should be (i) improving the quality of environment (ii) creating an awareness among people on environmental problems and conservation of (iii) creating such as atmosphere so that people find themselves fit enough to participate in decision making so that developmental programmes are presented after evaluation.

However, a number of environmental management

approaches have bee developed with the lapse of time and the same are discussed below in a lucid manner.

Scope and Importance of Environmental Studies

Scope means coverage, end aimed at, purpose, intention, outlook, purview and sphere of observation. The scope of environmental subdues is vast and wide. Sky is its limit and ocean is its depth. What is not covered in environmental studies shall take years and years yet to think as how to cover. Studies reveal that during the past, few decades there has been fundamental change in the attitude of man towards environment. There was time when environment meant only sanitation and health.

Today, the environment is conceived in its totality and a holistic approach is designed while planning a better quality of life stressing upon sustainable development. Who with not agree with this fact that human activities have been changing with greater speed and velocity. Our number population- wise is changing fast.

Environmental studies Teachers us deforestation and forest conservation

Increasing population, along with widespread poverty, has generated pressure on our natural resources. Of the 329 m ha. of the total land area in the country, it is estimated that about 174 m. ha. is degraded; this consists of agricultural as well a non- agricultural lands and forest resource. The forest resources are threatened due to overgrazing and other forms of exploitation, both for household and commercial needs, encroachments, unsustainable practices like unscientific cultivation and degradation of forests and tree lands. Environmental science teaches how forest can be covered. National afforestation and Eco-development programmes provide methods of forest wealth conservation, because trees and plants are the life and blood of human civilization. They have served and are serving man-king in various ways from days of yore Media Parkar Sunder Bahuguna, the leader of the Chipko Movement, rightly pointed out that preservation of trees and plants alone can save the human species from environmental pollution. The fist and foremost advantage of forests is that they absorb carbon dioxide, provide water and control soil erosion. To save trees in to save civilization.

(ii) Environmental Studies Teaches us Diversified Ecologies

Conservation ecology deal with the application of ecological principles to the proper management of resources leading to sustained yields of useful resources to human welfare. Resource ecology deals with the renewable and non-renewable resources and their judicious management. Pollution ecology deals with problems associated with the movements of pollutants in the environment, environmental deterioration and the maintenance of its cleanliness. System ecology deals with the analysis and modeling of ecological systems. Radiation environment. Paleoecology deals with organisms and their environment in the geological past.

(iii) Environmental Studies deal with air pollution check-up - Chemical and allied industries are the major source of air pollution because these industries discharge tons of noxious gases. With the increasing standard of living and a growing end for a faster moving life, the numbers of automobiles on the Indian roads have been increasing and simultaneously so is the pollution from them. The exhaust of automobiles and diesel driven heavy vehicles contain many harmful gases and the problem of air pollution is more significant at found level. Since the major activities of human beings are at this level, the pollution from automobiles has been gaining notoriety day by day. It has been determined that they contribute 39 percent of the total air pollutants in terms of tonned is the USA. Air pollution caused by motor vehicles contaminate surroundings. Smoke, odour and irritating compounds are causes of nuisance, especially to a person standing next an idling vehicle. The cumulative effect of many vehicles, plying especially on busy roads during peak hours has highly deteriorate effects. Those residing in the vicinity of such roads are worst affected and they often suffer from chronic heart and oxides of nitrogen, and under certain favourable conditions of temperature and sunlight, certain photochemical reactions are highly toxic, irritate the eyes and the respiratory system, damage vegetation and impair visibility. Today the number of planes, rails and vehicles which emit carbon mono-oxide along with smoke is much larger than earlier. According to one estimate the oxygen consumed by one automobile after covering a distance of 960 km. is enough for a man for one year. Tokyo is the most polluted town in the world.

Every policeman there is provided with an oxygen cylinder so that he may use it when the need arises. In Los Angeles people are advice not to undertake any exercise and inhale air in foggy environment. The toxic vehicular exhaust are sources of considerable air pollution. The ever increasing vehicular traffic density pose continuous threat to the ambient air quality. It is estimated that in all the major cities of a country about 800-100 tonnes of pollutants are being emitted into the air daily; of which 50% comes from automobile exhausts alone. The sources of emission in atomiles are: (i) Crankcase , (ii) Fuels tank and carburetor.

Broadly two types of air pollutants- primary and secondary air pollutants are emitted. Primary air pollutants are carbon monoxide, hydrocarbons, particulates, sulphur dioxide and nitrogen compounds. These five pollutants are released into the atmosphere in an unmodified as well as in sufficient quantities which pose hazards and risks to human health.

Environmental science teaches how to maintain AAQ and keep air pollutants within the permissible limits. Replacements of diesel driven heavy vehicles with CNG is one important attempt in this direction. Hats up to environmentalists.

(iii) Environmental studies is useful in controlling water pollution - In India, there are several river systems which accounted for 83% of the land mass, 80% of the population and 85% of the water discharge. A survey report reveals that 90% of pollution load in the river systems in on account of human wastes. The different types off diarrhoea, which in themselves may not be killers, but could prove very dangerous when accompanied by malnutrition and about 3 mullion children die per minute. Water borne disease occur primarily due to the lack of proper environmental sanitation.

We are told that almost 13,000 litres of blood enter everyday in Yamuna because of slaughters. More than 100 different virus types are known to be found in human refuse. Viruses are quite common in sewage. They can survive for months in water and soil. Recently a number of diseases have been linked to contaminated water are increasing. The contaminated water use for irrigation purposes has adverse effects on the fruits, vegetables that we consume in our day to day life. The extension of irrigation is creating excellent breeding grounds for disease by leaps and bounds. Intensive agriculture based on chemical agents for fertilizers and crop protection has also become a major cause of water contamination by ammonia.

The major causes of water pollution are sewage and other waters, industrial effluents and agriculture discharges. Broadly biodegradable and non-biodegradable pollutants are responsible for water pollution. Environmental engineers suggest the various ways of controlling water pollution as follow:

a. Sodium Salts : These could be removed by reverse osmosis method. Sodium sulphate from a rayon mill effluent cab be easily removed. The water for reuse cab be recovered by this method. From Cheese whey, we may recover 70% of protein a d 80% of lactose by this method.

b. Decolorization of water : The waste water from printing and sari dying industries could be decolorized by an electrolyte decomposition technique.

c. Phenolics : This can be removed from waste water of pulp and paper mills, carbonization plants, petroleum refineries, tanneries and resin plants by the use of polymeric absorbents.

d. Mercury : This could be removed from Chloro-alkali effluent plants by using mercury selective ion-exchange resin.

e. Ammonia : This cab be removed from waste water of industry by ion- exchange technique.

f. Re-utilization and recycling of waste : Different types of wastes such as industrial effluents, sewage and sullage of municipal and other systems and thermal pollutants can be recycled for beneficial use. Urban waste may be recycled to generate cheaper fuel gas and electricity.

Technology has been developed for magnesium not of radio-active wastes and chemical wastes. In Okhla, New Delhi is large treatment plant for sewage recycle is already in operation. Waste water reclamation through aqua culture, utilization of domestic and industrial waste water in agriculture and detoxification of phenol is a suitable technique developed. On distillery in Gujarat is able to treat 4,50.000 litres of waste daily and generate energy equal to that produced in 10 tonnes of coal.

g. Stabilization of the ecosystem : It is the most scientific way of controlling pollution and is done by reducing waste input, harvesting, removal of biomass, trapping of nutrients, fish management not and aeration. This can be done by biological and physical methods to maintain ecological balance.

Environmental studies is very useful for ecological health

Environmentalists teach disposal of the dead and burning. Provision of gas or electric crematoria have been made in all major town and cities. Planting of trees in an integral part of school and college education. No student should be given his degree or diploma unless he or she produces a certificate of having planted and nurtured at least ten or twenty trees during his or her students life.

We must understand the nature of human cells and the nature of plants cells which provide nourishment and around which animals and man have evolved. It is the quality of plant life on which the quality of human life depends. Ecological health depends upon keeping the surface of earth rich in humus and minerals so that it can provide nourishment and around which animals and man have evolved. It is the quality of plant life on which the equality of human life depends. Ecological health depends upon keeping the surface of earth rich in humus and minerals so that it can provide a foundation of health property and cultural stability. When the trees are in plenty there is a natural cycle involving the trees and the soil. In autumn the trees drop their leaves returning them to the earth where they decompose. A complex mixture of bacteria and fungi inhabit the soil. These microbes plan an extremely important role in the biochemistry of the soil.

It is a well known fact that after the ruthless deforestation, it is impossible for us to have plant food grown without the help of artificial fertilizers for the millions of people in our country and suffering from the consequences thereof. The most important measures of population control is the grow more and more trees in the hills and foothills, plains and in clusters in the fields everywhere and every nook and corner of the country on a war-footing. The symbolic rituals of getting a few trees planted by visiting dignitaries here and there, is of no use.

4

BIO-DIVERSITY AND ITS CONSERVATION

Introduction : Definition of Bio-diversity

The term biodiversity is made of two words- bio and diversity. Bio means living things whereas diversity means state of being varied or variety. So in nutshell biodiversity means varied type and king of species. Different organisms and species are examples of bio-diversity. Earth's bio-diversity is organized into three levels :

(i) At the top are the ecosystems such as rain forests, coral reefs and lakers.

(ii) At the bottom are the variety of genes, making up the heredity of each species.

(iii) Third down are the species that compose the ecosystems such as swallow tail butterflies, moray eels people.

Now one question arise in the minds of readers as how much biodiversity is there. Biologists have described a total of between 1-5 million and 1-8 million species. Yet this impressive achievement is only a small beginning. Estimates of the true number of living species range, according the method employed, from 3-6 million to more than 100 million. Least known are the smallest organisms. By repeated sampling, biologists estimate that as few as 10% of the different kinds of insects, worms and fungi have been discovered for bacteria and other micro-organisms, the number could be well below 1%. Even the largest and most intensively organisms are incompletely catalogued. Four species of mammals, for example have recently been discovered in the remote Aminate Mountains along the Vietnam- Loas border. One of them, the saola or spindlehorn is a large cowlike animal distinct to be classified. Earth, as far as life is concerned, is little known planet.

Genetics

Genetics is the study of the laws of inheritance. The first scientific study on genetics was carried out by Gregor Mendel an Austrian Monk, biologists and a famous geneticist. Being son of a successful horticulturist, Mendel developed a love for gardening. His father initiated him into the art of grafting of fruit and trees. Later he entered a monastery in Bruin, Where he carried on his scientific investigations on hybridization of plants. Mendel died before he could see his work accepted and appreciated. Genetics is the modern experimental study based on the discovery of Mendel's experiments.

Genetic is the study of heredity and variation in animals and plants. Every organisms carries genes. This is true of bacteria, fungi, plants, animals and human beings. These genes are called codes. These codes are nothing but massages. They carry information about organisms as what chemicals are needed to grow, survive and reproduce. Genetics try to solve puzzle of what genes are, how they are duplicated and transferred. Genetic engineering studies about moving of genes form one organism to another. It is the manipulation of heredity material. It seeks to change not only the species that provide us with food and drink but also those involved in sewage disposal, pollution control and drug production. It also seeks to create micro-organisms, plants and animals that can make human products such as insuling and even possibly to change the genetic make-up of humans.

Contribution/Applications :

The genetic engineering hopes to provide society with a vast range of innovations such as-

(i) Biologists use genetics to identify the genenes that function in the life of the cell and those control the development of complex organism from a fertilized egg.

(ii) Rapidly growing biotechnology industry is using genetics to produce a range of products from pharmaceuticals to micro-chips.

(iii) In agriculture, genetics is the basis of breeding new crop plants and livestock.

(iv) Scientific investigations seeking to understand the molecular basis of genetic diseases and to effect its cure.

(v) Providing counselling to families who are at risk of producing children with genetic defects.

(vi) Understanding the inheritance of genetic diseases.

(vii) Diagnosis and correction of genetic disorders.

(viii) New approaches to the generation of energy.

(ix) Recovery of resources and pollution control.

(x) More abundant food products.

(xi) More effective and cheaper pharmaceutical products.

Species

Species literally means kind. Species are all the organisms of the same kind able to breed in nature and produce live fertile offspring. Species also include plants- the definition of which provide exception but for our purposes this is a useful working definition. Species living in a given area at the same time consists of a population. Problems are faced with species definitions based on reproductive isolation. Investigators mostly cannot know whether two groups that live in different places are capable of interbreeding. Species identification therefore becomes a serious problem. Morphological characteristic such as size, shape, colour and skeletal structure is the only way opened for species identification.

How many species are there on Earth is an important question. Though it is difficult to answer yet some scientists confidently declared that every important king of living thing on Earth would soon be found and named. Most of these findings concentrate on species such as birds and mammals. Recent studies of organisms such as insects and fungi suggest that millions of such species and varieties to be studied scientifically. Based on new discoveries and research taxonomists estimate that there may be somewhere between 3 million and 50 million different species alive today.

In fact, there may be 30 million species of tropical insects alone. About 70 percent of all known species are invertebrates. This group perhaps makes up the vast majority of organism yet to be discovered. They may constitute 95 percent of all species. We now believe that the 2-1 million species presently known represent only a small fraction of the total number that exist.

Plant Diversity

Animals and human beings are deeply indebted to plants on account of their following diversified uses :

(i) Green plants, some of them when appear in the shape of forests covering 22.7% of the total land area of

India provide natural habitat and food to wild life, raw material for use in industries; supplying oxygen gas during photosynthesis; checking soil erosion by way of binding re-roots; cool atmosphere and influence the local rain-fall.

(ii) One has rightly asserted that the existence of man would have been unthinkable and impossible without plants as they provide oxygen for respiration and food for nutrition.

(iii) Plant exercise monopoly by way of preparing food such as starch a chief constituent of rice, wheat and potato etc., by obtaining carbon dioxide from the air, water and inorganic salts from the soil.

(iv) Green plants purify the atmosphere by absorbing carbon-dioxide from it and releasing an almost equal amount of pure oxygen into it.

Bicdiversity in India

India's biological diversity is quite immense. She has over 45,000 plant species which represent about 7% of world's flora and 6.5% of world's fauna. India is one of the 12 countries identified as mega-centres of biological diversity.

Embracing 10 biogeographic Zones and 25 biotic provinces, India incorporates an exceptional range of bio-diversity, including all the world's major ecosystem. As one of the eldest and largest agricultural societies, India also has an impressive diversity of at least 166 species of crop plants and 320 species of wild relatives of cultivate of cultivated crops.

(i) Wild Life - Regarding wild life presently, the protected area network comprises 84 National Parks and 447 wildlife sanctuaries. The Protected area covered is 4.5% of the total geographical area of the country. There are over 200 Zoos and 23 Tiger reserves in the country.

Financial, technical and scientific assistance are provided to states. The national Wildlife Action Plan adopted in 1983 provides the frame work of strategy as well as programme for conservation of wildlife.

10 to 15 percent of all the world's species live in North America and Europe. New species of higher plant and animal are rarely found in developed countries of the world. Tropical areas are the centres of greatest biodiversity. They have never been studied by scientists thoroughly. The Malaysian Peninsula, for example has at the least 8000 species of flowering plants, Britain double the area has 1400 species. South America has fewer botanists available to study perhaps 200,000 species of plants. Twelve countries, mainly in the tropics, account for at least 60-70 percent of the world's bio-diversity.

(ii) Coral reefs - Coral reefs are shallow water tropical marine ecosystems characterized by high biomass production and rich flora and fauna diversity. The Four Indian coral reefs are : Gulf of Manner, Andaman and Nicobar Islands, Lakshadweep Islands and Gulf of Kutch. The survival of resources is threatened by factors like oil spillage etc., and often because they fail in the shipping route.

(iii) Fauna - Mammal fauna comprises 372 species, with 63% found in Assam, India's 1,228 bird species represent about 13% of the world's total. Reptilian and amphibian fauna include 446 and 204 Species respectively, with concentration in Western Ghats. Faunal endem's varies substantially from 3.5% in mammals and 14% in birds to 32% in reptiles and 62% in amphibians. Among the larger animals, 101 of birds. 15 of reptiles, 3 of amphibians and 2 of fish are considered endangered.

(iv) Flora - Indian flora comprise about 15,000 flowering plants, an estimated 33% of which are endemic and roughly 1500 plant species are threatened. Areas rich in endemism are the North-East, the Western Ghats and the North-Western and Eastern Himalayas, however, the Andaman and Nicobar island contribute at least 200 endemic Species.

Universal Ethical Principles

There are four schools of thought which respond to moral laws such as Universalists, Relativists, Nihilists and Utilitarians. The thinkings of these schools towards environment are explained below turn in a nutshell manner.

(i) Utilitarians - Bentham is called utilitarian. He was English philosopher. Bentham was an eccentric genius. He equated goodness with happiness, and happiness with pleasure. Studies reveal that the views of Bentham. He regarded pleasure as the only thing worth having in its own right.

(ii) Nihilists - Thinker Schopenhauer is recognized Nihilist. In spite of living in a civilized and comfortable society. Schopenhauer painted dark picture of the world. He commented that everything is arbitrary and there is no purpose in life other than the dark and unceasing struggle for existence. So according to the views of Nihilists there is no reason to behave morally. We live in the world of uncertainty, pain and despair and there is no such thing as good life, Might is right eat or be eaten.

(iii) Relativists - Sophists are called relativists. The oppose views of Plato. The opine that moral principles are relative to circumstances and are always contextual. They relate to a particular person, society, or situation.

(iv) Universalists - Plato and Kant talk about the universality of ethical principles. According to these moral philosophers fundamental principles of ethics are universal and eternal. These rules of right and wrong are valid regardless of out interests and preferences. Some believe these rules are revealed by God while others maintain that they are discovered through reason and knowledge.

Social, Ethical, Aesthetic values

Ethics is one branch of philosophy. It seeks to explain the difference between right and wrong, regardless to cultural attitudes. Now one feeling must be creeping in out minds as what ethics has to do with environment. To this is replied that there is definite interrelationship between ethics and environment. All environmental issues involve consideration of ethics. Sufficient food and fabric is available in the world to feed people. It is unethical to allow some people to starve and others consume more than what they need.

Developed nations do not realize it. They have enough and still they need more. Their greed for more is ever increasing. They do not surrender before morals and ethics of life and share with others what they have. The must think less about conquering nature and more about learning to work with nature. Each person must realize his interdependence with the rest of he nature including his fellow human beings. To safeguard life on earth, people must learn to control and adjust the balances in nature that are altered by their activities. One more reason is placed in this context. Members of the society very well realize this view. They view the world's energy situation as serious and have reduced their own consumption. But may do not believe and realize this problem. They continue to consume energy as long as it is available and do not accept any cut on the use of it. Other similar issues are the population problem and pollution. It is ethical to have more than two children when the world is facing problem of over-population. Similarly an industrialist may not probably look on the negative aspects of pollution compared to one who is outdoor. Some sixty American cities have been declared having unsatisfactory water supply due to toxicity of pollutants released by industries.

Every year in the United States, 20 million tones of paper and 200 million tons of domestic garbage in junked. Keeping this in view the Massachusetts Institute of Technology, USA reveals that there shall be disastrous collapse in the coming hundred years if both population growth and industrial growth are not brought to an immediate halt. So the first task is to educate economic harpers about the value of environmental ethics. Clean and unpolluted air away from the chimneys of industries, free from fumes and smoke has a great cleaning and purifying effect for sustainable growth. For this purpose, taking ethical stand is important regardless to those who disagree with it.

Emerson, a pioneer philosopher environmentalist in his first essay Nature published in 1836 objected fast economic development by way of invading nature. Another naturalist who held the beliefs similar to Emerson was Henry David Thoreau. According to Thoreau, Truth in nature and wilderness over the deceits of urban civilization. He summarized his feelings about nature as But most men, it seems to me, do not care for nature and would sell their share in all her beauty, as long as they may live, for a stated sum-many for a glass of rum. He further concluded Thank God, men cannot as yet fly, and lay waste in the sky.

Rachel Carson rank above all naturalists of her time who generated widespread discussion about pesticides and its potential dangers to food, wild life, and humans in her work Silent Spring published in 1962. Carson's early death from cancer came before her book was recognized, establishing pesticides can contaminate and cause widespread damage to the ecosystem. In style and content, Rachel Carson designed Silent Spring to shock the public into action against the misuse of chemical pesticides. She described the poisons, pointed out the failure to grasp biological principles that allowed us to direct broadsides of these poisons against the environment and detailed the resulting disasters. According to one report DDT tends to accumulate in the fatty tissues of wildlife. In 1957, the waters of California's Clear Lake were found to contain only .02 parts per million of DDD, a close relative of DDT. Microscopic plants and animals in the water stored residues at five parts per million. Yet fish eating large quantities of microscopic organisms, concentrated these residues to over 2,000 parts per million. Grebes which fed on these fish died in great numbers.

Ethics being a part of philosophy relates to morals and values. Morals tell difference between right and wrong whereas values are concerned with the ultimate worth of actions or things. Western countries consider the roots of morals and values as posed by Socrates and the Greek philosophers 2500 years ago. According to these philosophers what is the good life and how should we as moral beings behave. Environmental ethics asks about the moral relationships between humans and the world around us. We know that besides human beings, we are surrounded by species and nature. Do we have ethical principles, duties and responsibilities towards these. Are these ethical principles that constrain to use resources or modify our environment. Are we not going against the nature? Do we listen what nature speak to us? Nature will not speak, nature goes its way, headlines and heartless. No matter whether man responds to it or not. How are our obligations and responsibilities to nature weighed against human values and interest? Do some interests or values supercede others? These are very important questions posed to us.

Values, Rights and Obligations

Human beings are moral agents, because they are capable of acting morally or immorally. Capabilities that enable humans to form moral judgements include moral deliberation. Moral deliberation are capacity to carry out decisions and the responsibility to answer all those right things which he fails to carry out. All humans do not have all these capacities, children, mentally retarded and mentally ill are not regarded moral agents. If a child murder someone, we do not hold him responsible, because children are considered moral subjects.

Weaker members of society dissever equal treatment with those who are stronger was not universally accepted. Powerful people always considered women, children, outsiders and serfs as their property. Even Greek philosophers accepted slavery as natural and necessary. But on ethical grounds it is incorrect. No one can ethically treat another human as a mere object for their own pleasure or profit.

Like human beings, do other species have some rights is an important question covered in environmental ethics. Though non-humans are encompassed in moral extensionism yet some philosophers do not agree and claim animals automa. Pet owners claim of course while animals may not have clear feelings. This is all about organisms but what about bugs, rocks and landscape. Should we extend moral considerations to these non-sentiment beings is an equally important with regard to ethics. Value measure the worth of something. All human beings have inherent value because they are human. Tools on the other hand have instrumental value. Tools have value because those who use them have value.

Now the question arises as do non-sentiment things have inherent value. Non-sentiment things are non-humans. Some people believe that even non-living things also have inherent value. Rocks, rivers, mountains, landscapes and earth certainly have value. These things exist since time immemorial even before our arrival and we cannot recreate them if destroyed . In a landmark, 1969 court case, the Sierra Club sued the Disney Corporation on behalf of the trees, rocks and wildlife of Mineral King Valley in the Sierra Nevada Mountains where Disney wanted to build a Ski resort and the Ski was never built. Expansionists and ecological world view give the following statement in support of non-sentiment thins :

(i) Development means essentially the same thing as growth.

(ii) Technological innovations can sustain an ever-increasing human populations.

(iii) Progress means the satisfaction of increasing levels of human wants.

(iv) Nature is a storehouse of raw materials to be used to satisfy ever increasing human needs.

(v) Earth's resources can support unlimited economic growth.

In view of above statements many tribals both hunters

and gathers have a strong sense of responsibility to act as custodians of resources. They feel to have proper role as working together with human and non-human forces to sustain life. Human are seen as partners in natural process rather than masters - not outside of nature but part of it. Egocentric claims moral values and rights for ecological processes and systems. According to them if you kill an individual organism, you deny it a few months or years of life, but if you eliminate and entire species or a whole landscape, you have destroyed something that took millions of years to create.

Value of Bio-diversity

We benefit from biodiversity in many ways. Some of them are discussed below :

(i) Drugs and Medicines : Living organisms provide useful drugs and medicines. More than half of all prescriptions contain some natural products. The value of pharmaceutical products from the plants and animals of third world countries are accounted to be worth $30 billion according to the UNDP. Indigenous communities that have protected and nurtured these organisms on which these products happens to be based are much less compensated. Realize the success story of vinblastine and vincristine. They are anticancer alkaloids. They are derived from the rosy periwinkle from Madagascar. This organism provide anticancer drugs. It use inhibit the growth of cancer cells and is found very effective in controlling cancer. This drug also make childhood leukemias and Hodgkin's disease highly remissible.

Pharmaceutical companies are actively engaged in search of herbs in tropical countries. Merck-world's largest biomedical company is paying $1 million to INBIO of Costa Rica for supply of plants. INBIO also impart training to natives to locate and catalogue all the native flora and fauna between 500,000 and 1 million species in Costa Rica. This is good scientific information besides sharing profits from native resources.

(ii) Human Food Supply - Human Food of everyday use comes from other organisms. So many wild plant species therefore make important contributions to human food supplies. According to noted ecologist Norman Meyears nearly eighty thousand edible wild plant species for food and medicine beings. Some four thousand native plant, animal species for food and medicine are used by villagers in Indonesia. Indonesia has 250 edible fruits and only forty-three of which are cultivated widely Academy of Science. Studies reveal that unfortunately human disturbance are destroying valuable food supplies and domestic crops before identification and prevention of their genes on account of the following :

1. Conversion of natural landscapes to agriculture.
2. Forest clearing.
3. Overgrazing

(iii) Aesthetic and Cultural Benefits - The diversity of life on this planet open many doors of aesthetic and cultural benefits to man in innumerable manner. Millions of people enjoy hunting, fishing, hiking, wildlife watching and other outdoor activities based on nature. These activities provide invigorating physical exercise. Observing and protecting nature has religious or moral significance for many people. Nature's appreciation is economically important also. Note the important information communicated by U.S. Fish and Wildlife Service :

a. To enjoy nature and experience other cultures inexpensive intercontinental air-fights are arranged to visit remote and exotic planes in USA.

b. 8 million on cinema tickets and $ 5.9 billion per year compared to $ 5.8 billion on cinema ticket and $ 5.9 on sports events.

c. Americans spend $ 18 billion every year watching wildlife.

(iv) Ecological Benefits - Biodiversity provide ecosystem stability. Soil formation, air and water purification, nutrient cycling, solar energy absorption and management of hydrological cycles all depend on the biodiversity of life. Nature as a matter of fact maintain ecological processes automatically with no cost to us. Besides this it provides a genetic library of information about ecology which man could never reproduce.

There have been a great deal of controversy about the role of biodiversity in ecosystem. Ecologist like David Tillman opine that plant communities withstand environmental stress better and recover more quickly than those with fewer species. But this is not agreed in toto. Since we do not understand fully the complex interrelationships between organisms so we are often amazed at the effects of removing insignificant members of biological communities. Wild species provide significant services in suppressing pests and disease carrying organisms. It is estimated that 95% of potential pests and disease-carrying organisms in the world are controlled by species.

The PRAYING MANTIS is an effective predator against garden pests and is harmless to human. Ladybird beetles prey on a variety of pests both as larvae and adults. For a few dollars you can buy several thousand of these hardy and colourful little garden protectors from gardening supply stores. So by preserving natural areas and conserving wild species, we utilize the stabilizing diversity of nature that keep pests organisms in balance. Hence Bio-diversity is beneficial in preserving ecological balance.

Biodiversity Threatens

Extinction of species is of great concern because despite our increased ability to alter and restructure our surroundings, people depend on other species is many ways. Extinction eliminates species from the planet and this elimination is a natural process. They eliminate in many ways such as species die out and are replaced by others, i.e. by their descendants. Thousands of species disappear due to human interference because man disturb ecosystem. Not only species but sub-species also extinct every now and then. Though it is difficult to provide accurate data on species distinction yet one feeling is very clear that if present trend continue, we may destroy millions of kinds of plants, animals, and microbes in the next few decades.

(i) There are two distinct forces which express concern about the conservation of Bio-diversity. One is recognized as ecological conservation and the other commercialized conservation. Ecological conservation of biological diversity arises due to severe genetic erosion. Genetic erosion takes place as a result of commercialization of agriculture and forestry. Genetic erosion is an ecological hazard because it leads to the extinction of life forms which have value in themselves.

(ii) Endangered creatures called Olive Redley Turtles are being slashed by the propeller blades of fishing trawlers or caught in fishing nets. The death toil of the turtles from 1991 was 50,000.

(iii) 70 percent of all recorded wolf mortalities in Kutch are due to spraying of position around their dens.

If this trend continues, we will soon lose the entire carnivores guild of Kutch. Wolves, even although they are known to be hardy race, are on the endangered list of wildlife. Earth is one intricate ecosystem of links by which all life is shaped. Lose one species, and a thousand others will be on the brink eventually threatening our survival.

Human caused reduction in bio-diversity

The rate of species's extinction is dramatic for the last 150 years. Between A.D. 1600 and 1850, disparaging of species from this planet has been due to alarming increase in human activities. According to Harvard university entomologist E.O. Wilson, we are pushing 20,000 or even more species per year into extinction. This is only a tentative data about the extinction of biodiversity because many parts of the world are not thoroughly explored and many species might have disappeared before they were studied and classified by biologists. The greatest loss of extinction is to tropical zones of the world because 90 percent species belong to this group. Human caused reduction in biodiversity is exercised by way of habitat destruction, hunting, fishing, commercial products and live specimens. The details of these reasons are given below to facilitate understanding of readers :

a. Genetic Assimilation - Endangered species like mammals and birds crossbreed with closely related species and opportunistic plants introduced into a habitat or displaced from their normal ranges by human actions genetically overwhelm local populations. This process is called genetic assimilation. Many endangered species are threatened by genetic assimilation because they crossbreed with more vigorous related species. Hatchery raised trout are introduced to streams where they genetically dilute indigenous stocks. On account of this reason black-ducks have declined severely in USA and Canada.

(ii) Pollution - Toxic pollutants have disastrous effects on local populations of organisms. Declining marine mammals, alligators and fish populations show complex interrelations between pollution and health. Widespread deaths of seals on both sides of the Atlantic are due to persistent accumulated chlorinated hydrocarbons such as DDT, PCBs and toxins in their body which weekend their immunity system. Similarly deaths of pacific seal loins and striped dolphins in the Mediterranean are thought to be caused by accumulation of toxic wildlife. The U.S. Fish and Wildlife Service estimates that 3000 metric tons of lead-shot are deposited annually in wetlands and that between 2 and 3 million waterfowl die each year from lead poisoning. Scavengers such as bald eagles eat birds and mammals that have lead shot or bullet fragments in their bodies. Though lead-shot is banned yet spent shot remain in bottom sediments of lakes, ocean and water-reservoirs where bottom feeders consume it.

(iii) Diseases - Pathogens and disease organisms are also recognized as predators. To be successful over a long period of time, a pathogen must established a balance in which it is vigorous enough to reproduce, but not so lethal that it absolutely and completely destroys its host. When a disease is introduced in the new environment, this balance may be lacking and an epidemic may seep through the area.

The American chestnut was one very popular amongst hardwood forests. One among four trees was chestnut. This tree was over 45 m tall and 3 m in diameter. Its nutritious nuts were important for birds particular for passenger pigeon, forest mammals and humans. The wood of this tree was quite useful for making fence posts to fine furniture. In 1904s, a shipment of nursery stock from China brought a fungal blight and within forty years, the American chestnut disappeared. A similar disaster has devastated American elms.

(iv) Induction of Exotic Species - Exotic species are non-native organisms. They are aliens. They are both animals and birds. They have been introduced intentionally and accidentally. Zebra mussels and spiny water flues are introduced accidentally. English sparrows and common pigeons are aliens and introduced by acclimatizers who spent considerable sums of money to import these species from Europe. Exotic species in the United States. Alien species from around the world now threaten native species throughout the Great Lakes. Probably the most endangered group in the United States are fresh water mussels, of which more than half of the 297 known species are threatened, endangered, seriously declining or already extinct. Pollution, siltation, and competition from exotics like zebra mussels are largely responsible. Some of the exotic organisms that have, with human help invaded the Great Lakes. These aliens are driving out native species and irreparably damaging the ecosystems.

Plants when introduced into a new environment also multiply explosively. Kidzu-a legume that grow in Asia when brought in United States grow and run with so much of wild expansion that it covers trees, houses and whole hillside. Not only that, this plant also reduced the growth of native plants, this is a non-native plant which cause hinderance to the growth of native-plants besides damaging houses and hillsides. Similarity water hyacinths are floating plants with waxy green leaves were brought from Argentina to United States in 1880 for exhibition. People took plants home and intentionally put them into lakes. Results reveal that within a period of ten years, this prolific weed had spread across the South from Florida to Texas, completely covering the surface of many waterways, blocking boat traffic and smothering fish and native plants. So extinction is also caused not only by introducing non-native animals but due to non-native plants too. Kudzu-a-States and were brought from Asia and Argentina. These plants extended the growth of native plants.

(v) Predator and Pest Control - Some animal populations have been internationally exterminated because they are dangerous to humans and livestock. Animal control agents in USA trap or even shoot thousands coyotes bobcats, prairie digs because they are considered threat to people, livestock or crops. To lill 86,500 coyotes the cost involved is worked out by Office of Animals Damage Control amounted to $ 38 million. Animal rights activities oppose the killing of predators and comment that they have equal right to inhabit the landscape as humans. They suggest guard dogs predators thought to be dangerous. One may comment anyway he likes but one issue cannot be ignored that some animal population is exterminated.

(vi) Commercial Products - A variety of commercial products like furs, hides, horns and live specimens are being obtained from nature in addition to harvesting wild species for food. People consider it better and sustainable harvest compared to agriculture and industry. Despite international bans on trade in products from endangered species, man is involved in the smuggling of these products worth millions of dollars each year. Developing countries in Asia. Africa and Latin America with the richest biodiversity in the world are the main source of wild animals and animal products. North America and some wealthy Asian countries are the chief important.

Places below is information with regard to trade and commerce of animal and animal products :

a. The trade in wild species for pets is an enormous business. Worldwide some 5 million live birds are sold each year for pets.

b. Plants also are threatened by overharvesting. Wild ginseng has been nearly in many areas because of the Asian demand for roots that are used as an aphrodisiac and folk medicines.

c. In 1980, there were 1.3 million elephants in Africa. A decade later only 625, 000 remained. 1000,000 elephants were killed by poachers for ivory trade.

d. The population of African black rhinos dropped from 100,000 in the 1960s to about 3000 today due to demand of their horn. In Asia powered rhino fetches \$28,000 per kg because it has medicinal properties. In Yemen, a rhino horn dagger handle is sold up to \$1000.

e. Profits on wildlife smuggling is very high. Tiger of leopard fur coats can bring \$100,000 in Japan.

f. The united States imports 90% of all live cacti and 75% of all orchids each year.

g. European countries buy 3/4 of live birds.

h. Japan, Taiwan and Hong Kong by 3/4 of all cat and snake skin.

(vii) Hunting and Fishing - Overhunting and overharvesting is responsible for depletion of many species. Ectopistes migratorius in classic example which exterminated due to overhunting and habitat destruction. 200 years ago this was the world's most abundant bird with a population between 3 and 5 billion. It once accounted for about one quarter of all birds in North America. In 1830, John James saw perhaps a flock of billion Ectopistes migratorius. Between 1870 and 1890 hunting and habitat destruction caused the entire population to crash. The last known passenger pigeon was shot in 1900 and the last female bird died in 1914 in the Cincinnati Zoo. Overhunting cases also include extermination of great whales and American bisons. Bisons are killed for hides, tongues, food, clothing and shelter.

Studies reveal that 2.5 million great whales once inhabited the world's ocean. The blubber of whales was highly prized as a source of oil. Initially the slowest whales were caught by hand-thrown harpoons but in the 19th century with the introduction of steam ships and explosive harpoons it became possible to catch and kill even fastest whales. The International Waling Commission has prohibited catching of great whales. But countries like Iceland, Japan and Norway continue to catch whales under the guide of scientific research. They restore meat and blubber of these animals in their programme of scientific research and sell the same at a handsome profit.

It is a difficult task to count whales accurately. Should man catch whales is an ethical question. Do you think and find acceptable to hunt and kill large, rare, intelligent wild creatures like whales? Fish stocks have been seriously depleted by overharvesting. With the result, a huge increase in fishing fleet size and efficiency in recent years has led to a crash of many oceanic populations. Worldwide, 13 to 17 principal fishing zones are now reported to be commercially exhausted. Canada cut nets or seized foreign boats violating their territorial waters.

(viii) Habitat Destruction - Habitat is called living place of species. Many species are endangered by multiple threats to habitats by humans. Exotic species receive a greater threat to their habitants. For plants, trampling, grazing, collecting, flooding and other human actions constitute serious dangers. The current increase in extinction is habitat loss. Habitat fragmentation which means dividing and sub-dividing of dwelling places of species divides population of species into isolated groups that expose to catastrophic events. In a state of habitat fragmentation, very small populations may not have enough forests to breed adults under normal circumstances. This happened due to decrease in wooded area of Cadiz township in Southern Wisconism during Eurcpean settlement. Saded area reduced miserably and drastically from 1831 to 1950. By destroying habitat, man eliminate not only prominent species but also many rare once of destruction of forests, wetland, and other biologically rich ecosystems around the world. Endangered species are kept in Zoological Parks. Zone are just jails additional solicitor general Altaf Ahmad told to Supreme Court days after 12 tigers died in Bhubaneswar's Nandan Kanan Zoo.

(ix) Tiger and Peacock Deaths - The death of 12 tigers at the Nandankanan Zoo musical Park in Orissa in July 2000 has raised serious questions about inbreeding over crowding professional management stocking of drugs, and availability of funds for the zoos in the country.

During the last six years, 44 tigers in Orissa, 18 Lions in Guwahati, 10 tigers in Hyderabad and six hunters in Patna - totalling 78 in all have died captivity. The death of the big cats are a lesson not only the zoo custodians but also for the scientific community and veterinarians. Doctors at the Orissa Veterinary College, Bhubaneswar, as well as senior forest officials in-charge of the zoological park, said the deaths could have been due to trypanosomiasis, a parasitic infection, which is endemic in nature and is spread by a particular type of fly.

All the victims belonged to group of 17 tigers which were administered the Beneril injection, a preventive medicine. Dr. A.T. Rao, Professor of Pathology in the OVC, who conducted the post-mortem on four tigers said that a possibility was that the preventive medicine was administered when the infection had reached its final stage. In July 2000, about 80 peacocks died in Morena district of Madhya Pradesh. Fifty peacocks were found dead at Maharajapur village and nearby areas and twenty-nine at Sitapur village in the district. The deaths were caused by the birds consuming bajra containing pesticides. The post-mortem report revealed that the death of 19 peacocks was due to the birds consuming foodgrains containing chemicals of he Organo-Phosphate category. The post-mortem indicated they had died due to hemorrhage of the stomach caused by chemicals belonging to the mercuric and carborate group.

Natural causes of extinction

99 percent of all species that ever existed are now extinct. Studies of fossils records provide this information. Most of those species were gone long before humans came on the scene. Species appear and disappear through process of mutation. Evolution can proceed slowly and gradually over millions of years. New forms of species replace completely lost. The do exist. Tiny Hypohippus has been replaced by a large modern horse but the genes of tiny Hypohippus perhaps still

survive on its distant offspring.

Mass extinctions have wiped out vast numbers of species even whole families. This happened when dinosaurs disappeared. An even greater disaster occured around 250 years ago when 2//3 of all marine species and nearly half of mass extinctions of species were :-

(i) Release of greenhouse gases in the atmosphere.

(ii) Large asteroids structuring to earth.

(iii) Catastrophies caused by climate changes.

Biodivesity in India

India's biological diversity is quite immense. She has over 45,000 plant Species which represented about 7% of world's flora and 6.5% of world's fauna. India is one of the 12 countries identified as mega-centres of biological diversity.

Embracing 19 biogeographic Zones and 25 biotic provinces, India incorporates an exceptional range of biodivesity, including all the world's major ecosystem. As one of the eldest and largest agricultural societies, India also has an impressive diversity of at least 166 Species of crop plants and 320 species of wild relatives of cultivated crops. Among the most neglected and threatened parts of India are its extensive coastal and marine areas. These areas are home to a high percentage of biodivesity, and the lifeline of at least 10 million fisherman and many million other residents

Biological Diversity Bill- 2000

The Biological Diversity Bill 2000, awaiting Parliamentary sanction and presidential approval, is a landmark legislation aimed at protecting India's bio assets and ensuring equitable benefit-sharing by the users and the owners.

Bill No. 93 for the year 2000 was tabled in the Parliament on May 15, 2000. Christened the Biological Diversity Bill 2000, it is intended provide for conservation of biological diversity, sustainable use of its components and equitable sharing of the benefits arising out of the use of biological resources and for matters connected therewith or in dental thereto. This preamble is same as the objectives spelt out the Convention on Biological Diversity Signed in 1992 at the UN Conference on Environment and Development at Rio de Janeiro. While 150 countries signed the treaty, the US was an exception, arguing that it will set back research efforts in biotechnology and protection of intellectual property. Subsequently, the US Congrees agreed to implement the terms of the treaty.

The various provisions of the Biological Diversity Bill, 2000, are as follows:

(i) Ecomarks - It is a labelling for environment-friendly household and other consume goods which satisfies the requirements of Indian standards for that product. The Bureau of Indian Standards is the implementing agency for this scheme.

(ii) Funds - Biodivesity Funds to be set up Central, state and local levels.

(iii) Authorities - National Biodivesity Authority to deal with request for access from foreigners; to grant approval for seeking IPRs in or outside India for any invention pertaining to be biological resource obtained from India. State Biodivesity Boards to deal with matters relating to access by Indians for commercial purposes and restrict activities violating objectives of conservation, sustainable use, and equitable sharing of benefits.

(iv) Safeguards and exemptions - Free access to Indians to use biological resources within the country for research. Use of bio-resources by vaids and hakims. Traditional knowledge to be protected.

(v) Objects and reasons - Regulate access to biological resources. Respect and protect knowledge of local communities. Protection and rehabilitation of threatened species. Involve self-government institutions in implementation.

Biodivesity Protection

Biological diversity is important and irreplaceable assets. Slowly and gradually we have become aware of the harm we have done and continue to do to wildlife and biological resources. Now we are adopting national legislation and international treaties to protect endangered species and biodivesity.

Hunting and fishing bill was introduced in the United States congress to protect American bison in 1874. This initiative remained ineffective because many legislators believed that all wildlife was so abudant that it will never deplete by human activity. But this feeling proved quite wrong. By the end of 19th century bisons had plunged from some 60 millions to only a few hundred animals.

By the 1980s most states had enacted hunting and fishing laws to restrict liberal shooting and poaching. The general idea being is to protect and conserve biodivesity and natural resources for future generation. The wildlife regulations and refuges established since that time have been remarkably successful for many species. At the turn of century, there were an estimated half a million white-tailed deer in the United States; now there are 14 million or more in some places that the environment can support. Wild turkeys and wood ducks were completely extincted some fifty years ago but now situation is different. They are now restored to several millions due to restoring habitat, planting food crops, building shelter or houses, protecting them during breeding season and other conservation measures.

The Endangered Species Act and CITES represent a new attitude towards wildlife in which we protect organisms just because they are rared and endangered. A few acts passed from time to time to preserve and protect species of diversity are stated below to save nature because saving nature means serving human population.

Endangered Species Act : U.S. Endangered Species Act of 1973 and COSEWIC 1976 provide powerful approaches to wildlife protection. The regulations under these acts identify endangered species and save biodivesity regardless of its usefulness to humans. The species under the Acts are classified into three sections.

a. Vulnerable Species - These species are naturally rare, or we can say that activities have put them to such a low level of numbers that their risk of being depleted is being felt. They are Bald eagles, gray volvas, brown bears and sea otters.

b. Threatened Species - These are those species that have declined significantly in total number and are on their verge of extinction. Spotted owl and gizzly bear are recognized in threatened species.

c. Endangered Species - These are those species which are considered in imminent danger of extinction. These worldwide endangered species are mammals, birds, reptiles and plants. The Untied States has some 1359 species in its endangered species $39 million per year is being spent to protect these species annually by USA.

In-situ Ex- situ Biodiversity Conservation

Many strategies have been used over the years to try to conserve biodiversity. They can broadly be divided into in-situ and ex-situ approaches. Both approaches are useful in biodiversity conservation. Ex- situ approaches involve collecting storing and conserving things away from the environment in which they were found. Thus seed collections, gardens, orchards and zoos all seek to preserve biodiversity in a safe and controlled environment away from where they were found naturally. While such an approach removes biodivesity from its threatened environment to safe area, it also removes it from the dynamic environment in which it was growing and evolving. Recreating the ideal conditions is an exaction task, and reproduction to propagate the species can be difficult or impossible. This form of conservation preserves species, but not necessarily habitats or ecosystems.

In-situ approaches concentrate on preserving and conserving bio-diversity within the environment in which it is found. In-situ conservation is the conservation of ecosystems and natural habitats and the maintenance and recovery of viable population of species in their natural surroundings and in the case of domesticated or cultivated species, in the surroundings where they have developed their distinctive properties.

In-situ conservation allows the ecosystem and species to continue to evolve within their environment, adapting and changing in response to changing environmental conditions. Thus the focus is on the habitat and ecosystem, as well as the species.

Although viable populations of some organisms can be maintained ex-situ either under cultivation or in captivity, these methods are far less effective than in-situ methods, and, generally, they are extremely costly. Likewise, although ex-situ methods are important under a number of conditions, in-situ methods are generally recognized as being more secure and financially efficient. The challenge in using in-situ methods is to expand our vision of protected areas to includes multiple use and extractive reserves and to develop new models for conservation including; Such innovative proposals as using damaged ecosystems to preserve rare, endangered, and threatened species; conserving Biodiversity in seed Banks and gene Banks ; Restoration on Bio-diversity : vegetation panting to control erosion : removal of contaminated soil : Fencing to prevent cattle : Reintroduction of exculpated species : imparting environmental education, Enforcing Environmental Legislation.

Advantages, Risks, and Opportunities

In-situ maintenance of biodivesity through the establishment of conservation and multiple-use areas offers distinct advantages over off-site methods in terms of coverage, viability of the resources, and the economic sustainability of the methods :

1- Economic sustainability - A country that maintains specific examples of biodivesity stores up future economic benefits. When the need develops and this diversity in thoroughly examined, commercially valuable genetic and biochemical material may be found. Establishing a conservation are in just not sufficient to assume its bio-diversity till protected automatically without risk. Many other risk both natural and man-made, remain. They are mentioned below :

a. Genetic uncertainty or random changes in genetic make-up due to genetic drift or inbreeding in-situ programs such as national parks, biological reserves, and other conservation areas appear to be somewhat favourable.

b. Natural catastrophes such as floods, fires, or droughts, which may occur at random intervals.

c. Demographic uncertainty resulting from random events in the survival and reproduction of individuals.

d. Environmental uncertainty due to random, or at least unpredictable, changes in whether, food, supply, and the populations of competitors, predators, parasites, etc.

2- Viability - Natural selection and community evolution continue and new communities, systems, and genetic material are produced.

3- Coverage - A worldwide system of protected and multiple-use areas would allow a significant number of indigenous species and system to be protected, thus taking care of the unknown until such time as methods are found for their investigation and utilization.

5

MARKET LINKAGES

The distance factor plays a significant role between the two main factors of the market, i.e., the producer and the consumer. Whatever goods the producer produces has to reach to the consumers who are located at distant places. For this he adopts various means and ways. These means and ways that the producer adopts to approach or establish links with the consumer are called as Market Linkages. The various means or modes of transportations like head load, roadways, railways, ropeways, pipelines, waterways, airways etc. serve as the main forms of market linkages.

Nature of Linkages

The market linkages are instrumental in the movement of goods from the producers to the consumers from the production of raw materials to their movements to the factories and markets or from the factories to the markets or from the markets to the consumers. In every stage, some of the other means of transportation is necessary.

Functions of transport in support of commerce

The development of the various modes of transportation or linkages affect expansion of trade and widening of the market. The entire economic and commercial life of a country depends upon services of transport. In fact, at every stage in the activity of production and marketing of goods some or the other mode of transport is needed. It is an element of cost, both in the production as well as in the distribution or marketing of goods, as the cost of transportation is included in the sale price of the product. Sale price of the goods affect both the producers and the consumers. Therefore knowledge of transportation is must for the selection of best and suitable transport services.

A planned approach towards development of transportation is essential for the industrial and commercial development of a country. As large markets, mass production and specialisation in industry and commerce can be made possible with its help. It also enables numerous goods, irrespective of size, weight, etc. to enter in the market to satisfy ever-increasing and varied consumer demand both on national and global level. Further, it also reduces the cost, increases the speed and safety in the physical distribution of goods.

1. Transport and Consumption - Efficient and cheap transport reduces cost of production as well as cost of marketing. Hence, it can reduce the prices charged to the consumers. Lower prices help quick distribution of goods and encourage mass consumption.

Supply of goods can be equalized from place to place and through proper adjustment of supply with the changing market demand, we can have stable prices. A single price can be established for a commodity all over the country. Transport creates place utility, e.g., sand at the seashore has no value but in the city it has a price. Complete system of physical distribution involves two complementary functions, viz, transport involving the creation of place utility and storage or warehousing involving the creation of time utility. Both these functions of transport and storage must be closely coordinated in modern marketing and both together shall determine the cost and efficiency of physical distribution for consumption or use.

2. Transport and Exchange - Transport is a major factor in marketing, it helps exchange, i.e., buying and selling of goods. It promotes competition in commerce. It widens the market and allows each area or region to produce only those goods in which it enjoys superior advantages, e.g., Bengal has specialised in the production of jute and jute textiles for the world market, U.P. in sugar, Assam in tea, M.P. in wheat and cotton, Maharashtra in cotton textiles, etc. Such areawise specialization of production is possible due to easy transport facilities. International exchange of goods depends upon the best means of transport. Eighty years ago, Mumbai could get coal more cheaply from South Africa than that from Raniganj.

3. Transport and Production - At every stage in the production of goods we require some kind of transport. Production for the market whether agricultural or industrial, depends upon the means of transport. Adequate and cheap transport facilities can reduce the cost of production of goods, and can enable production of goods for distant markets also. Transport helps considerably agricultural, mining and manufacturing operations.

Services of Transport

Services of transport are summarized below:

1. It provides employment to a very large population.

2. Its equalizes supplies place-wise and provides stable prices in all markets.

3. It creates place utility.

4. Transport widens the market.

5. Defence demands adequate and efficient transport.

6. It spreads culture and civilization promoting higher standard of life. We can have close social and cultural contacts.

7. It increases localisation of industries.

8. It helps agricultural and industrial marketing.

9. It makes persons and goods mobile freely moving.

10. It helps quick industrialization of a country.

In short, we can satisfy our innumerable and varied wants through monetary exchanges very easily due to modern means of transport. If there be a strike in our transport services, our entire daily life will be simply paralysed. Transport is an essential public utility service and it is now a specialized and independent branch of industry. It is no longer merely and auxiliary agency or aid to trade. It has assumed national importance. All-round -planned industrial and commercial development of every nation primarily depends upon efficient and cheap transport- land, water and air transport.

Influence of Geographical and Economic Factors

Geographical factors, e.g., topographical features and climate, restrict the development of different means of transport and limit their use and efficiency. Mountainous regions like the Himalayas and the Rockies; ice-bound regions like Greenland, North Canada; marshy forested regions of the Amazon and the Congo basins; sandy dry desert areas of North Africa and west Australia- all these have continued to be poor in the means of transportation. Apart from unsuitable topography, climatic conditions, excessive cold climate and frozen lands do not facilitate transport. Stormy and cyclonic weather conditions and flood-prone areas restrict the use of all means of transport.

The development of railways depend upon physical terrain and the climate of a region. The construction of railways in the plains is easy and economic. But it is very difficult to build them in forest, deserts, ice-bound and hilly regions. In the mountainous areas, the cost of providing railway transport is always high because valleys are to be bridged and hills are to be cut into tunnels.

As per the schedule is concerned, among all the means of transports, railway transport is least affected by weather conditions and therefore sticks to a regular schedule. But it is different for road transports which are profoundly affected. Also affected are air and water transports.

Economically advanced and prosperous nations have the greatest facilities of transportation, while economically backward countries have poor transport facilities. The economic factors affecting water transport are the volume of traffic, port facilities and charges, location of refuelling stations, perishability of products, cargo handling charges. The size of ship and canal charges.

Co-existence of Different Modes of Transport

There are several modes of transport employed in the world of commerce. At present, the businessman has a choice of many different forms of transport for his goods-by road, by railway, by inland waterway, or by sea or by air. The reasons for the existence of variety in the forms of transport is that each mode of transport has its own peculiar advantages and disadvantages. In some cases road transport is to be preferred to rail transport; in others railway transport is superior to road transport. In some circumstances, goods may be sent by coastal steamer rather than by railway; for other goods sea transport may be the only suitable form of transport; in certain circumstances, a trader may prefer even air transport. Thus, the businessman makes his choice. In judging competitive efficiency of different means of transport and their coexistence we have to consider carefully the following points:

1. Availability - In the mountainous regions, e.g., in Kashmir valley or Simla, businessmen and have only animal or human beings as a mode of transport and, in foreign trade in the absence of common land frontiers, businessmen may have to rely only on sea transport. For reaching the interior and village population, we may have at our disposal only bullock carts or trucks. In India, air transport is not available for all markets.

2. Regularity and Punctuality - Railway transport usually provides a higher degree of regularity and punctuality and it is more dependable in this respect. Air transport may not provide expected regularity and punctuality, particularly in bad weather. In winter transport may not be available as water may be frozen in cold regions.

3. Flexibility - Road vehicles are extremely flexible. At present in the U.S.A., computerised routes and charts are prepared and these charts give the most direct, or most economical route to be followed. Railway transport is not so flexible.

4. Safety - During transportation, goods are subjected to many uncertainties and risks of loss. If a certain mode of transport provides necessary safety and security to goods, there will be minimum chances of damages or losses during transit. The businessmen prefer truck transport. Goods enjoy a damages or losses are leisurely in truck transport. Goods enjoy a higher degree of safety and security. Sea transport is not reliable.

5. Cost - Every person wants cheaper transport. Air

transport is very costly and it cannot be used for heavy goods. Cheaper and economical transport can reduce production and marketing costs and the consumer can buy goods at reduced prices. This means cheaper transport can expand our markets, increase our sales and profits. Transport cost plays a important role in commerce.

6. Speed - Quick delivery is essential, e.g., in perishable goods. Roses are exported by India by air transport as they are perishable and they must reach the market overnight.

7. Suitability - It must suit to our needs, e.g., buoyancy of the water makes the effective weight zero. Hence, sea transport is very suitable for heavy and bulky goods.

Water Transport

Since the earliest times, water transport has been availed of to carry men and materials. The earliest boats were made of different materials. Simple boats are still in use in different parts of the world. The range and importance of water transport increased when wind power was harnessed with the use of sails. Overtime increase in the size and complexity of sailing has facilitated the growth of trade. Traders from Egypt and the Mediterranean coast have moved towards south-east Asia for trade by boat.

The invention of the steam engine has brought a revolution in water transport. Steam gave greater power so that ships could travel at greater speed and carry larger loads. Ships were built of iron and steel instead of wood; and they were safe and efficient. Ships now use nuclear power. Bigger and bigger ships are built to serve different purposes.

Water transport is available for oceans, coastlines, rivers, lakes, and canals. The bulk of international trade is carried on by means of ocean transport. Coastal and inter-coastal traffic contribute to a great extent to international trade. Inland water transport has promoted inland trade, stimulated the paces of industrialization and assisted in the distribution of commodities on a larger scale. It is now the cheapest mode of transport because it does not incur the capital and maintenance costs of transport by land-by roads and railways.

Water transport is divided into three groups:

(i) Coastal shipping.

(ii) Inland waterways.

(iii) Ocean or sea transport.

Ocean Trade Carriers

The trade carries or merchant ships that are employed to carry passengers and cargo are:

1. Bulk-cargo carriers - Carriers or ships carrying dry and liquid bulk cargos have been continuously increasing in size to earn better and higher revenues and returns. This is necessary to ensure their operational viability. Bulk carriers which carry dry bulk cargo are available in various sizes. The most common among them are 40000 DMT size of carrier.

2. Tankers - Tankers are special ships, designed to carry mineral oils and petroleum products. Petroleum has become an important source of energy after the Second World War. Ocean-going tankers, therefore, were brought into use for mass-scale movement of oil from the areas of production to the areas of demand. Bigger and bigger tankers, known as super tankers, are now built.

3. Cargo boats - It is a steamer that performs the

functions of a liner as well as a tramp. This ship carries a large quantity of bulky goods and a limited number of passengers. Most of the ships are special purpose ships and have cold storage facilities. Cargo liners have specialized their functions; therefore, they are designed and fabricated to suit a particular purpose. The carriage of passengers give them additional income in the form of fares. Cargo liners are generally equipped to load and unload the goods. Sometimes they use crane facilities available at ports.

4. Tramp - The tramps are small cargo vessels which carry bulky goods. They are generally chartered to carry full cargo. But often take the cargo wherever can, and do not follow any definite route.

5. Liners - Liners are steamers which follow a definite route on their schedules, irrespective of whether they operate at full capacity or not. They carry passengers, mail and a small quantity of cargo. Modern liners offer many good facilities to passengers.

The Suez Canal

The Suez canal is one of the largest shipping canals of the world. It has been constructed by cutting across the isthmus of Suez to provide water transport facilities between Mediterranean sea and Indian ocean. It is the oldest oceanic canal and carries a lion's share of international waterborne commerce between the west and east.

The canal was opened for navigation in 1869. It is 160 kms long with a minimum width of 60 metres and a depth of 13 metres. The canal is at sea level throughout its length. The canal connects two important lakes the Great Bitter lake and Timsah. The canal can handle 49 ships per day with a tonnage upto 50,000. It takes nearly 13 hours to complete the journey through the canal.

The canal is not only link between the two seas but also a vital artery of world commerce. It has resulted in enormous saving in time, distance and money. It has resulted in enormous saving in time, distance and money. It has opened up a new route to Africa, Asia, Australia and New Zealand.

Advantages

1. Many ports of call and ports are developed along the Suez Canal route as a result of the construction of the canal, e.g., Aden, Karachi etc.

2. It helped Britain to maintain political control over her colonies and seas by dispatching her army and navy through the canal.

3. Revenue amounting to millions of dollars annually from toll is collected by Egypt. Egypt's economy is based on this canal.

4. The canal served as lifeline to Britain as the trade between Britain and Common Wealth countries of the East was carried by this canal route.

5. The canal reduced the distance as well as saved time for ships moving between the eastern and the western countries. Thus distance between London and Mumbai via this route was reduced by 6760 km and time saved was by 23 days. Distance between London and Singapore was reduced by 3535 kms and time saved was of 17 days. This route even brought the eastern coast of North America closer to the Far East Countries of Asia. The distance from New York to Hong Kong was reduced by 2290 kms. Similarly distance between New York and Mumbai was reduced by 4409 kms.

6. One more shipping route made available to western countries to trade with the countries of Asia, Africa and Oceania.

Future Potentials of other important canals

In these days of oil crisis, construction of canals has gained more importance. In order to conserve exhaustible fuel resources and to make distribution of goods more economical, construction of shipping canals, wherever possible, has become a need of the day. Such canals reduce distance of hundreds of kilometres to few kilometers. Construction of new canals such as Isthmus of Kra in Thailand will shorten the distance between Rangoon of Burma and Bangkok of Thailand by nearly eleven hundred kilometers. Similarly, there is a greater possibility of construction of one more canal which will connect Gulf of Aquba with Mediterranean sea. This will pass through Israel, benefitting her in the time of political crisis.

Kiel Canal

Kiel Canal is an artificial waterway and is located in western part of United Germany. It connects Baltic Sea with North Sea, reducing the distance of nine hundred kilometers to ninety kilometers. It has mainly benefitted United Germany. Though constructed for strategic purpose it has been now internationalized, i.e., open for all the countries since 1962. The ships passing through this canal mostly carry bulky goods like iron-ore and coal as well as forest products.

The Pnama Canal

The Panama Canal connects the Atlantic and Pacific oceans. It has brought the East and West of North America close to each other. The canal has provided the shortest route between ports on the Atlantic and those on the Pacific. It is 80 km long and 12-26 metres deep. The water level of the canal is higher than the sea level. Hence, six lock gates have been provided to maintain the proper level.

Advantages

The Canal has eliminated the long and difficult trip around Cape Horn and brought the West coast of the USA nearer to Europe by more than 8000km. The canal has brought the Western part of countries of 9. America closer to the Eastern parts of the USA and the countries of Europe. Nearly 50% of the total traffic through the canal is American. It has opened up a new route for Europe for going to Australia and New Zealand. The distance between Liverpool and Great Britain and Willington of New Zealand is reduced by about 640 km.

Disadvantages

1. There is lack of major ports and islands on the route.

2. The canal route passes through thinly populated hilly areas.

3. The system of locks, for maintaining the water level, is very inconvenient.

4. It is a narrow shipping canal of a width ranging between 92 meters and 309 meters.

Shipping Canals

Shipping canals are the artificial construction of waterways through a narrow strip of land lying in between two water bodies. Construction of such shipping canals shorten the distances among number of areas of the world, saving time and fuel, both. In the world, there are three important shipping canals today.

1. KIEL CANAL.

2. PANAMA CANAL.

3. SUEZ CANAL.

Panama Canal Route

This ocean route came into being in 1914 when

Panama canal was opened for the traffic. This route is of vital commercial importance to U.S.A. This route gets divided into many branches, one going up to the western coast of South America and the other to the western coast of North America. While crossing Panama from the pacific to the Atlantic, the route gets divided into further three branches; one branch runs to the northern and eastern coasts of South America, the second branch runs to the eastern coast of North America; and the third joints the South Atlantic ocean route to Western Europe, via the Caribbean countries.

The chief ports on this ocean route are Boston, New York Orleans, Seattle, Los Angeles, San Francisco of U.S.A., Valparaiso of South America, London, Liverpool, Glasgow, Manchester, etc. The Panama Canal route serves Europe, the eastern and western coasts of Canada and the U.S.A., the Caribbean islands, Central American countries and countries on the coasts of South America, Australia and New Zealand. The export of important minerals, such as bauxite, iron ore, copper, lead, magnesium, tin, zinc, and nitrates are facilitated from South America to U.S.A. and Europe. The Panama Canal route has helped to improve the economic conditions of Central and South American countries.

Suez Canal Route

The Suez canal route came into existence after the construction of Suez Canal through Isthmas of Suez, connecting Mediterranean Sea with Red Sea. It is a great international trade route, connecting the East and the West. The Suez Canal route has been of immense commercial and strategic value to European countries and the U.S.A. in maintaining trade relations with East African countries, south and south-east Asian countries, the Far East and the Middle East. The canal route was a vital link between European colonists and their poor Asian and African colonies- a link between the modern Western civilization and the old Eastern civilizations. Trade in agricultural products and minerals to feed industries in Europe and the quick supply of finished products in the markets of the colonies continued through this route till the middle of the 20th century. New systems for defence, administration, education, cultural ideas, transport, business, banking, recreation, etc., were promoted and transferred by this route from the West of the East. It assisted the Europeans to become industrially, economically and politically strong.

Due to this canal route the distance between India and England was reduced by about 9,6000 kms. This route also eliminated the trip around to Cape of Good Hope. However, it was closed from 1967 to 1975 because of Arab-Israel war. Fuel supply on this route has never been a problem. The important coal refuelling stations on this route are Gibralter, Port Said, Aden, Colombo, and Hong Kong. As regards oil refuelling stations, Indonesia, Sarwak, the Middle East, the Black Sea, and the North African countries are the important countries on this route.

Most of the ports on this route are well-equipped with modern equipments for loading and unloading operations. These ports are: London, Southampton, Liverpool, Glasgow, Le Harve, Mumbai, Colombo, Hong Kong etc. The first division of traffic is related to the trade of Mediterranean countries with each other. Food and raw materials are important by France, Italy; oil from the Middle East by the West; cotton, tobacco, chromite from Turkey; and grains, oil, manganese from the C.I.S. The East-bound traffic is generally of manufactured goods.

The second division of traffic is relates to the trade between West European countries and Mediterranean countries. The commodities like fruits, wines, cotton, corks, silica, sulphur, etc. move towards Western Europe; while coal, forest products, machineries, tools, textiles and manufactured goods move towards the Mediterranean lands.

The third division of traffic relates to the trade among North America and East Africa and Asian countries from the eastern coast of Canada and the U.S.A. There has been a considerable flow of traffic through the Suez between these two ends. Rubber, tin, manganese, tea, tobacco, spices, coffee and jute products- are the major commodities which are carried towards North America Automobiles, machineries, petroleum-products and other manufactured goods move of East African and Asian countries.

The fourth division of traffic relates to the trade between West European countries and East African and south and south-east Asian countries. West-bound export consists of a variety of food products, agricultural products, minerals, oil and other industrial raw materials. Eastbound export consists of iron and steel products, locomotives, machineries, tools, chemicals and a variety of manufactured goods.

The fifth division of traffic relates to the trade between North America and Western Europe in the west and between North America and the Far east, Australia and New Zealand in the east. Japan and the Philippines have trade links with West European countries and North America. Rubber, tobacco, spices, tea, jute, sugar, wool, animal products, manganese, etc. move towards the European countries and the eastern coast of North America. Automobiles, petro-products, machineries and other manufactured products move from eastern North America and European countries to the Far East and Oceania. The trade of Australia and Now Zealand with European countries and North America is more on this route across the Pacific.

Pacific Ocean Route

The Pacific Ocean is the biggest water route in the world, and was developed mostly between western coasts of Canada and the U.S.A. and the Far East and Oceania. It was the last route to be developed because, of economic and physical conditions. The submerged islands, shoals in the ocean, cyclonic weather conditions and long vast stretches of water without land were the major problems. There water moreover, no refuelling centres for ship. Traffic on this route is poor.

The route links the eastern coasts of Asian countries-Japan and the Philippines- with the western coast of North America via Hawaii. A branch of this route form the western coast of North America goes south to Fiji, Australia and New Zealand. The far eastern countries though densely populated, do not have much purchasing power. Agricultural products are not grown in exportable surplus quantities. Japan in the east is leading in trade with U.S.A. and Canada on this route.

The important ports on the Asiatic side are Tokyo, Manila, Seoul, Yokohama, Kobe, Osaka. Shanghai, Hong kong and Canton. Those on the American side are Vancouver, Portland, Prince Rupert, San Francisco and Los Angeles. The U.S.A. and Canada export lumber, wood pulp, cereals, petroleum-products, minerals and various manufactured goods. Japan exports silk, tea, electronic goods, and automobiles. The other countries export sugar, rubber, tea, corpa, tobacco. Australia and New Zealand export minerals wool and other animal products.

South Atlantic Ocean Route

The South Atlantic ocean route does not lie exactly in the Southern part of the Atlantic Ocean. The route was established between European colonists and their colonies in Central and South America. European countries, Canada and U.S.A. were connected with Central and South American countries. The route did not develop in the southern part of the Atlantic Ocean because African and South American countries have little to exchange. Their geographical environments are similar; their products are the same; and both the continents are thickly populated.

The South Atlantic route has been developed by the Europeans and the Americans to import raw materials and seek markets for their finished goods. Therefore, the pattern of trade has been, till recently, more or less the same. Now the process of industrialization has begun in Mexico, Brazil, and Argentina. Agricultural products, pastoral products and minerals move from Central and South America countries including wheat, corn, coffee, sugar, cotton, tobacco, wool, vegetable oils, fats, waxes hides and skins, iron ore, bauxite, manganese, tin, oils, copper, etc. , to European countries, Textiles, iron and steel, medicine, paper, wines, electrical and electron goods- these are exported by Canada, U.S.A. and West European countries to Central and South American countries.

European, American and Canadian ports have contributed to the development of trade on this route. But there are only few ports in South American countries. Kingston, Havanal Pernambuco, Santos, Sao Paulo, Rio de Janeiro, Montevideo and Buenos Aires are the major ports through which trade is handled by the South and central American countries. The volume of trade on this route is comparatively small.

North Atlantic Ocean Route

The North Atlantic ocean route has been the busiest among all for more than a century. It lies in the northern part of the Atlantic Ocean and links Western Europe with the eastern coast Of Canada and U.S.A. Nearly 25 percent of the world's vessel tonnage is handled on this route. The countries on this route are the leading producers of the wide variety of goods. They exchanges good in large quantities. The volume of trade between them is always large. Passenger traffic on this route has also been regular because of old cultural ties. The world's fastest and largest ships operate on this route. People from either side enjoy a high per capita income and a fairly high standard of living.

The North Atlantic route is a great trunk route with a number of branch lines. The terminal branches extend from the Mediterranean to the North Sea in Europe and from New Found land in Canada to the Caribbean Islands and Central America. The North Atlantic route is the shortest route between Western Europe and North America.

There is no shortage of fuel on this route. Cheap and abundant supply of coal is available on both ends of the route. Oil-burning ships from North America carry enough oil for their return journey because of the high oil cost in Western Europe.

As large number of natural ports have deep waters, well protected sites and highly developed integrated hinterland. Most of the ports are free from ice during the major part of the year and they are well equipped with modern facilities for bulk cargo handling. The important ports on the American coast are Halifax, St. John, Montreal, Quebec, Boston, Baltimore, New York,

Charleston, Philadelphia and Noe Orleans; the important ports on the European coast are Liverpool, Glasgow, Cardiff, Southampton, London, Le Harve, Amsterdam, Bremen, Rotterdam, Hamburg, Antwerp, Oslo, Stockhol, Bordeaux and Lisbon.

Forty percent of the world's trade is handled on this route. The passenger and mail traffic has decreased recently because of the development of air transport. The shipments from Europe to North America mainly consist of manufactured goods, cars, wines, paper pulp, dairy products and luxury goods, while those from North America to Europe consist of iron ore, forest products, dairy products, grains, cotton, meat, petroleum and petro-products, machinery, vehicles, fruits, etc.

Geographical conditions are generally very favourable for navigation on the North Atlantic route. But the icebergs and dense for near New Foundland has prevented this route to follow great circle route. Cyclonic weather in winter also pose some problems for the ships on this route.

Cape Route

The Cape of Good Hope route is the world's oldest route which links West European countries, the Southern and South-East Asian countries, the Western and South African countries, as well as Australia and New Zealand. European colonists established their colones in Asia and Africa travelling by this route. They traded in industrial raw materials and agricultural products via the Cape route. They sought good markets for their finished goods; and spread modern ideal culture, etc. Political dominance over Asian and African countries was established by Europeans by travelling through this route.

Refuelling along this route is done at Madeira and

the Canary Islands. Colonists tried to develop new ports in their colonies. The important ports on this route are London, Liverpool, Cardiff, Swansea, Le Havre, Libson, Cape Town, Port Elizabeth. Durban, Dar-es-Salaan, Mombasa, Colombo, Mumbai, Adelaide, Melbourne, Sydney and Brisbane.

This route declined in importance when the Suez Canal was opened in 1869. But is promoted a vital trade link between the East and West till then. The importance of this route increased again following the closure of the Suez Canal in 1967.

Copper, gold, iron ore, uranium, cobalt, tin, lead, zinc, bauxite, diamonds, chromite, etc., and agricultural products, such as tea, sugar, cotton, jute, jute goods, hides and skins, coffee, wool, tobacco, cocoa, rubber, limber, vegetable oils, etc.- all these goods moved through this route towards the European countries and U.S.A. The east-bound movement was of manufactured goods, such as textiles, chemicals, medicines, drugs, electrical goods, machines and tools, transport equipment and a variety of manufactured goods. The traffic on this route declined following the opening of the Suez Canal.

Charter Party

It is an agreement whereby the shipowner agrees to let the entire ship or a part thereof to any person, called the Charterer, for the carriage of goods on the specified voyage of during a specified period of time for a sum of money which the Charterer undertakes to pay as freight for the carriage of the cargo.

The form of Charter Party contains the following information:

1. The lay-days. The Charter Party also contains

terms and conditions on which the ship-owner agrees to charter the ship.

2. The time required for the voyage.

3. The freight agreed upon.

4. The list of cargo specifying the goods by number, weight and marks.

5. Ports of loading and discharge.

6. Registered tonnage.

7. Name of the Charter of the shipper.

8. Name of the ship.

Contract of Affrerightment

A consignor who wants to ship the goods by sea has to enter into a contract with the ship-owner unless he owns the ship himself. When the ship-owner agrees to carry the goods by sea or furnish a ship for the purpose of carrying the goods in return for a sum of money, such a contract is called the Contract of Affreightment, and the sum of be paid is called the Freight. The cargo of a ship is also called Freight.

A contrast of Affreightment may be embodied in a document called the Bill of Lading, or in another document called the Charter Partly. The Bill of Lading is issued by the ship-owner to the shipper when he agrees to carry goods which forms a small part of the entire cargo. When the agreement is to carry a complete cargo or to furnish a substantial part of it, the Contract of Affreightment is embodied in a document called the Charter Party.

World Shipping Routes or Ocean Routes

The ocean routes, generally known as international trade routes, are influenced by geographical and economic conditions. These are:

1. The Pacific ocean route.
2. The South Atlantic ocean route.
3. The North Atlantic ocean route.
4. The Cape route.
5. Canal routes and canal charges.
6. Refuelling facilities.
7. Availability of ports and harbours.
8. Weather conditions.

The Suez Canal route and the Panama Canal route are also considered as international trade routes.

Containerization

The term containerization refers to the shipment of goods in uniform, sealed and reusable containers. This is a recent development in the handling of shipments in large quantities. It is damage free, economic and fast across land and sea. Recently, shipment in containers was introduced in air transport. The container facilitates the combined and coordinate-carrier cars are especially designed and fabricated to carry very large and bulky goods. Containers are made of waterproof and fireproof materials. The container are made of waterproof and fireproof materials. The container service is mainly for such commodities as perishable, chemicals, and drugs.

The consignor enjoys the benefits of container service, which are: reduction in the packaging cost; less likelihood of damage to goods; fast delivery; door-to-door service, and unit-load movement from factory to warehouse; no chance for rough handling of goods; loading and unloading by mechanized means; and safer and economic.

Container transport service is not useful for all kinds of goods. Coal, ores, steels, fertilisers, grains, jute, jute goods, hides and skins, etc. These are some of the commodities which cannot be transported by containers. Engineering goods, cotton textiles, manufactured goods, frozen foods and well-packed commodities are generally considered suitable for container transport.

Container transport service is widely used in industrially advanced countries. U.S.A., CIS, Japan, and the European countries often use this method of transportation, It would be worthwhile if all forms of transport adopt uniform, standard-size containers. Each mode of transport can then offer the best possible service, even if there is a break-of-bulk in transit. Container transport service is now becoming popular in developing countries. India introduced a railroad coordinated system in the sixties. Some marketing and sales organisations and Government undertakings have started using the container service very progressively. Oils, chemicals, liquefied gases and milk are transported in containers by road and rail.

The use of containers by Indian merchants, business houses and shipping companies is increasing day-by-day. At present, the facility of container cargo is provided at the ports of Mumbai, Chennai, Kolkata, Haldia and Cochin. The cargo-handling charges at Indian ports are generally high. Secondly, congestion at the lort in another problem. Mountains of cargo eat up the precious dock space in India. The Container Corporation of India is planning to introduce some measures to relieve the congestion such as:

1. The Inland Container Depots and Container Freight Stations are to be set up at major ports. The Wadi Bunder Container Terminal is the best example of the port side container terminal at Wadibunder in Mumbai.

2. Modern loading system to be employed to double the speed of operations.

3. Many of the port functions are to be taken out of the port areas.

Chief Trade Carriers

The trade carriers or merchant ships that are employed to carry passengers and cargo are:

1. Bulk Cargo Carriers - Carriers or ships carrying dry and liquid bulk cargos have been continuously increasing in size to earn better and higher revenues and returns. This is necessary to ensure their operational viability. Bulk carriers which carry dry bulk cargo are available in various sizes. The most common among them are 40000 DMT size of carrier.

2. Tankers - Tankers are special ships, designed to carry mineral oils and petroleum products. Petroleum has become an important source of energy after the Second World War. Ocean-going tankers, therefore, were brought into use for mass-scale movement of oil from the areas of production to the areas of demand. Bigger and bigger tankers, known as super tankers, are now built.

3. Cargo Liners - It is a steamer that performs the functions of a liner as well as a tramp. This ship carries a large quantity of bulky goods and a limited number of passengers. Most of the ships are special purpose ships and have cold storage facilities. Cargo liners have specialized their functions; therefore, they are designed and fabricated to suit a particular purpose. The carriage of passengers give them additional income in the form of fares. Cargo liners are generally equipped to load and unload the goods. Sometimes they use crane facilities available at ports.

4. Tramps- The tramps are small cargo vessels which carry bulky goods. They are generally chartered to carry full cargo. But often take the cargo whereever they can, and do not follow any definite route.

5. Liners - Liners are steamers which follow a definite route on their schedules, irrespective of whether they operate at full capacity or not. They carry passengers, mail and a small quantity of cargo. Modern liners offer many good facilities to passengers.

Communication

The word communication is derived from the Latin communis which means common. We attempt to communicate, that is, to establish a commonness with another person. There are three essential parts of communication. They are the source, the massage and the receiver. True communication takes place only when the massage means the same thing to both the parties.

The effective communication occurs when a sender sends a massage and a receiver responds to the message in a manner which satisfies the sender. Both must have identical meaning of the message.

In any exchange activity, communication is absolutely necessary. You may have the best product, package and so on. It may have fair price. But people will not buy your product, if they have never heard of it, or if they are simply unaware of its existence. The marketeer must communicate to his prospective buyers and provide them adequate information. People must know that the right product is available at the right place and at the right price. Here, comes, the need of proper communication system which can move forward a product, service or an idea in a channel of distribution. Through this, the marketer, informs and persuades buyers to accept, recommend or use the product, service or idea which is being promoted. Both the transportation and the communication are complementary to each other and serve the world of commerce as prime aids to the trade. They combat the world of distance by shortening them.

Modern Communication facilities

The present state of commerce can be mainly attributed to the role played by various communication modes. There have been rapid advancement in the development of communication systems and their services. The development has come as a boon to the modern commercial world.

The modern communication systems have been playing very significant roles in present human societies. Besides all modes of transport services that man has been using for last so many centuries, it is science and technology that have enabled man to transmit his messages in words and pictures to any corner of the world within a moment and at any time. Post and telegraph service has been the oldest among all. Telephones, radio, television, teleprinter, fax and telecommunication through satellite have become very popular during twentieth century.

The postal services have been in use from centuries ago. But an organized and government controlled postal service was introduced by Europeans. It was by British colonists in India. Telegraph service was introduced in second half of the last century in Europe, mostly attached to the postal services. Today it serves the largest number of people and covers the longest area. It depends upon other means of transportation, however it is the cheapest Post and telegraph services have played a great role in establishment of trade links in the world.

Telephone service cause in existence in fourth

quarter of last century. A direct conversation through wire could establish a very quick and assured link between two persons. This service became very useful during war times and other emergencies. Telephone service could not reach to rural areas except in developed countries. Teleprinter service in newspaper agencies while telex in industries and business are the improved facilities to get machine typed matters within few moments. Fax is a further improved facility to get photocopy of the printed massage at other destination.

Radio service and then television made a real revolution in communication systems in the world. Not only geographical but all other barriers are crossed by this new means of communication systems. The world has shrunk into a small place. People of different culture and taste have come closer and closer. These services have enabled man to established links with people of remote areas. They propagate and circulate news, educational programme entertainment and advertisement to establish trade links. Also the informations about any warning of naturally calamities like earthquake, volcanic eruptions or floods can be spread rapidly and thus the relief work. Radio service has been of an eminence use to military and in border areas.

The satellite communication of enormous significance since last few decades. At least 200 satellites have been launched in the space by various counties in the world for communications to receive different informations and relay the massages, news, programmes, sports, and business news, etc. Weather forecast, resource exploration and spying are some other jobs performed by satellite for other countries. Telecommunication service is very common in developed countries like the U.S.A., European countries,

Canada, Australia and Japan.

The communication services are poorly developed in developing and backward countries of the world because of-\

1. Less demand of such services because of poor development.

2. Lack of scientific and technological know-how.

3. Economic and cultural backwardness.

Air Transport

In recent years, air transport has been assuming increasing international important although it has not yet been able to render all types of commercial services. The two world wars gave a great impetus to the development of aerial transport.

The supreme advantage of air travel is its speed. Aeroplanes have been travelling with a speed greater than the sound and for this reason air transport is eminently suitable for passenger and postal services. During 1940-80, the number of passengers carried by airlines increased over forty times and the amount of mail by twenty times in many advanced countries like U.S.A. and the U.K. The advent of Jumbo Jets since 1970, has further revolutionized the air transport all over the world.

Market research on air freight costs conducted by Air Canada was published recently and has proved the fact that air transport is practicable and economical method of transport for many transport is advantageous only for passengers, mail, perishable goods and light goods having high value. Fruits, tea, drugs, vegetables and many other perishable goods have entered international market due to air transport. Even valuable components of machineries are being carried by air transport.

Advantages - It is most suitable for carrying goods of goods high value such as diamonds, bullion, perishable commodities which necessitate rapid transport, Customs formalities can be very quickly complied with and thus delay in obtaining clearance is reduced, It is quite suitable for carrying goods with normal bulk and in small quantities. It is most comfortable for passengers and safe for goods, It provides regular, efficient and quick service.

There are two types of air vessels- airships and aeroplanes. The airship is higher than air, while the aeroplane is heavier than air. Now we have jumbo jets. It can carry 362 passengers and can travel at about 2000 kilometres per hour. Supersonic Anglo-French Concorde is recently introduced which can travel at a speed of about 3,000 k.m. per hr. During the last fifteen years, commercial and civil air transport has gained considerable importance all over the world. Today, we are living in the space age and the Jumbo Jet Age. Businessmen, tourists and politicians have become reminded.

Disadvantage - It is costly for goods transport. Too many international restrictions and regulations over its services arrest the growth of air network in the world, Air transport is controlled to a great extent flying operations temporarily and cause uncertainty in its timetable, Chances of breakdown and accidents are frequent owing to the fact that all the technical aspects of air transport have yet to be exploited, It cannot carry bulky commodities on a large-scale and hence, it is not of much use to the mercantile community, Costs of operation and maintenance of aerodromes and ground organization are heavy. Its carrying capacity is not very large.

(i) India - Among the developing countries, India has acquired an important place in civil aviation. Her midpoint location on the routes between the East and the West gives her a key position in international aviation. The Indian Government, therefore, has been taking a keep interest in developing air transportation in the country. The air transport industry was nationalised in 1953 by the Indian government. And it has established two corporations: The Indian Airlines Corporation and Air India. The Indian Airlines Corporation is for traffic within the country and with the neighbouring countries. Air India operates flights at the international levels. Since the corporations were formed, there has been a rapid progress. Both airlines operate their scheduled services on various routes, linking major Indian cities and towns with those in the world. The process of modernization has been continuous and modern aircrafts are purchased replacing the old. Boeing 747 are operated by Air Indian and A-310 AIRBUS by both Air India and the Indian Airlines Corporation. There are about four more domestic airlines.

The Indian Airlines Corporation operates regular flights between important cities - Mumbai-Delhi, Mumbai Chennai, Mumbai-Kolkata etc. Air India has air transport agreements with a large number of countries, and is among the ten leading airlines in the world. It runs regular flights on the principal routes- Mumbai-Nairobi, Mumbai-Delhi-London-New York, Kolkata-Singapore-Tokyo, Kolkata-Jakarta, etc. A well-organised network of airports and air routes is very essential for the expansion of air traffic. About 85 airports are maintained by the Civil Aviation Department of the Government of India.

(ii) Asia - Most of the Asian countries are linked by

air from the east to the west from the north to the south. Almost every Asian country has tis own airline, providing international air services. Three-fourth of the Asian air traffic is by south-east Asian countries. Japan and India together, have more than three-fifth of the traffic in south-east Asia. China, another Asian country has comparatively less air traffic at the international level.

(iii) Africa - Many African countries are linked with North America vis Europe or South America. The route via Europe is preferred because there are more halts and, therefore, greater traffic. Many routes link African countries with Europe because of colonialism in the past. A route from North-West Europe links Tunis and Algier via Madrid and Rome. Other route links European cities with south cities on the Atlantic coast and the eastern coast of Africa. Cairo in Egypt is a nodal point for all international airlines. Most of the African countries have their domestic airlines. A few have international airlines too.

(iv) South America - International air traffic is (v) Europe - The second large volume of air traffic in the world is in Europe. Every major industrial city and capital is linked by airlines. Passenger traffic and mail service by air are quite regular. European airways account for about 25 percent of the world's air traffic. Most of the European countries operates one or two international airlines. The U.K. has three airlines, British Airways is the most important airline. Germany's Lufthansa, Switzerland's Swiss Air, France's Air France, the Netherlands's KLM, Belgium's Sabena, Italy's Alitalia are the world's leading airlines operating in the European countries. Scandinavian Airlines services is jointly operated by Norway, Sweden and Denmark. The

European Airlines have links with the entire world towards the east and west, North and South. International air-traffic in all European countries is of greater importance than the domestic traffic, because every European country is small in size and has an adequate network of roadways, railways and inland waterways.

Fifteen independent countries after the former Soviet Union split up all could not establish their airlines independently. The former Soviet airline, now the Russian Airline Aeroflot is operated all over the world. The other countries such as Ukraine, Urbekistan, Georgia etc. will soon come in the international scene. The capital leading commercial centre of Russia, Moscow, is linked with all the major international centres and capital cities.

(vi) North America - The greatest volume of air traffic is in North America. The busy mode of life, level of development and high standard of life may be the reasons. Regional and feeder, inter-continental and trans-continental air services are easily available in North America. There has been a dense network of air routes over the entire territory and the U.S.A. International routes operate from the Pacific coast to the Far East and Oceania and from the Atlantic coast to Europe, Asia and Africa. The busiest air traffic is between north-east U.S.A. and Western Europe across the North Atlantic.

The U.S.A. alone has 9,000 airports and more than 60,000 registered civil aircraft. The country is served by four large corporations:

1. The United Airlines.
2. Eastern Airlines.
3. The Pan-American Airlines.

4. Transworld Airlines.

Besides there are about 45 domestic air services. The chief commodities moved by air are light machinery, electrical and electronic goods, meals, liquor, fish, fruits, vegetables, fish etc. Canada has a dense network of air route in the southern part of the country. The domestic airlines operate east-west in the agricultural, industrial and mining areas. The leading airline is Trans-Canada Airlines.

CIS

The CIS made remarkable progress in making high power TU-104 jets and TU-114, the turbo-prop aircraft. Greater attention is concentrated on the development of big sized speedy aircraft with a huge carrying capacity. A large number of air routes link Moscow with major international centres and capital cities - London, Warsaw, Buddhapast, Berlin, Parague, Sofia, Bucharest, Beijing, Havana, New Delhi, etc.

6

ENVIRONMENTAL POLLUTION

Introduction

The Planet Earth along with its living organisms and atmosphere which sustains life is known as the Biosphere. The different components of the biosphere interact in a delicately controlled and orderly manner and it is this factor that ensures the survival and growth of the biotic elements or living beings. Any adverse effect of disturbance of the delicate balance of the biosphere caused by man's careless or excessive exploitation of natural resources, can lead to the by man's careless or excessive exploitation of natural resources, can lead to the creation of unfavourable conditions for the well-being or even survival of mankind.

1. Environmental Degradation - Environmental degradation means deterioration of the environmental quality at global, regional and local levels by both-natural processes and human activities.

2. Environmental Pollution - Environmental pollution can be explained as lowering of the quality of environment of local level caused by human activities for exploitation of resources.

Pollution

Pollution indicates the adverse changes brought by human activities in the environmental quality at local level. Sometimes, the effects of human activities are so wide that the environment is degraded not only at local level but at global and regional level too.

As such we define Pollution as an undesirable change brought in the physical, chemical and biological characteristics of air, water and soil that may harmfully affect the or create a potential health to any living organism. In this way, Pollution is direct or indirect change that has come in any component of the biosphere that is harmful to living organisms and man that has come. It has an adverse effect on cultural and natural resources or general environment.

Meaning of Pollutants

Pollutants can be defined as any substance which causes lowering the quality of environment or pollution. A pollutant is any solid, liquid or gaseous substance found in such a concentration that it may have adverse or harmful effect or may be injurious to the environment, Pollutants are the residues of things, which we make or use or throw away. We know that the rivers are polluted by wastes emanated from factories, air is polluted by the gas, smoke emanated from chimneys of the factories, industries and thermal power plants etc.

According to Smith Every human society, be it rural, urban, industrial and most technologically advance society dispose of certain kinds of by-products and waste. Products which are injected into the biosphere in great quantities and they affect the normal functioning of ecosystems and have an adverse effect on plants, animals and man are called pollutants.

Thus a pollutant can be as under:-

1. Indirect being mediated via his resource organisms or climatic change. We may illustrate it with the help of an example. A water pollution can mean anything put into water which was not there in its natural state. In this way, any substance can be a pollutant if too much of it is present having an adverse

effect.

2. Direct.

3. Any physical property e.g., noise, heat. It is released intentionally or inadvertently by man into the environment with actual or potential adverse, harmful or unpleasant and inconvenient effects.

4. Any Geochemical e.g., dust, sediment, substance, biological organism or product.

5. Any chemical e.g. organic or inorganic compounds, radionuclide, organophosphorus compound, or trace gas.

Classification of Pollutions

Pollution have been classified on various bases. Chief bases are as under:

1. Classification on the Basis of Cast Pollution - It is discovered by the research studies that billions of tons of municipal waste are generated each year. About 60-70% of it including paper, yard and food wastes are easily biodegradable. As such, it is especially amenable to biological treatment. Again, about 12-16 percent rubber, leather and plastic waste are potentially biodegradable. At present, merely a small faction of the potential waste is treated by utilizing biotechnology.

2. Classification on the Basis of Nature of Pollutants - Pollution is classified on the basis of the nature of pollutants. Pollutants are broadly classified into two categories as under- Biodegradable Pollutants, these pollutants are the domestic wastes that can be rapidly decomposed under natural conditions and create problems when they accumulate. Non Degradable Pollutants, these pollutants include the materials and poisonous substances which either do not degrade or degrade very slowly in nature such as aluminium,

mercuric salts, long-chain phenolics, etc. evidently they are not naturally cycled in ecosystem.

3. Classification of the Basis of Human Activities - Pollution is generally caused by human activities. On this basis pollution can be divided into two broad categories- Social Pollution is caused in different aspects of the society. It is on account of cumulative effects of extreme events/hazards and pollution. Physical Pollution is caused by human activities by human activities due to lowering of the quality of physical components of the environments.

4. Classification of Pollutions on the Basis of Environmental Types.

Types of Pollutants

A proper balance between these two factors (Resources production, Waste disposal) is necessary for a healthy biosphere. The resources are created with a useful purpose of some economic advantage for the human being. However on actual use it is observed that some such resources like synthetic detergents, persistent pesticides, medicinal drugs, non-biodegradable substance, etc., have highly serious side-effects. Some of these wastes are of such a nature as cannot be degraded or processed by nature within a reasonable period of time Consequently, such wastes begin to accumulate and pollute the environment. Some device is indispensable to convert such wastes into usable form. Such a device would not only relieve of pollution but also improve, or at least, maintain environmental quality and the production of future resources. Reversal of environmental deterioration is one of the major goals of our society.

Various types of pollutants are as under:-

1. Agrochemicals such as fungicides and fertilizers.

2. Photo chemical oxidants.

3. Radioactive waste.

4. Solid waste.

5. Gases such as nitrogen, carbon monoxide, sulphur oxides.

6. Deposited matter such as dust, smoke, tar, grit, etc.

7. Complex organic substances such as ether, acetic acid, benzene, etc.

Natural Degradation

Micro-organisms cause much of the natural degradation that slowly remediates contaminants released into the environment. The specific mechanisms involved include:-

1. The bioregeneration of granular activated carbon.
2. Formation of biological barriers.
3. Bioenhanced filtration.
4. Accumulation.
5. Biodegradation.

Genetic modification of the micro-organisms involved can sometime further improve the above methods. At present, attempts are being made to improve micro-organisms through selective breeding.

Water Pollution: Meaning and Causes

Water, is one of the most important and most precious of natural resources. A regular and plentiful supply of clean water is essential for the survival and health of most living organism. On account of rapidly expanding industrialization and excessive population growths, most of our rivers, lakes, streams and other water bodies are being increasingly polluted.

Water is regarded as Polluted when it is changed in its quality or composition, directly or indirectly as a result of mankind's activities so that it becomes less suitable for drinking, domestic, agricultural, recreational, fisheries or other purposes for which it would otherwise be quite suitable in its natural state.

According to P. Viver, "Water pollution is defined as a natural or induced change in the quality of water which renders it unsuitable or dangerous as regards food, human and animal health, agriculture, fishing or leisure pursuits."

According to World Health Organization, "Foreign materials either from natural and other sources are contaminated with water supplies and may be harmful to life, because of their toxicity, reduction of normal oxygen level of water, aesthetically unsuitable effects and spread of epidemics."

Causes of Water Pollution

Main Causes of water pollution may be classified under two heads and under:-

1. Heat - It comes from power and manufacturing plants using water for cooling purposes.

2. Radioactive substances- They result from mining and processing of radioactive ores and the use of radionuclides in industry, medicine, research and nuclear weapon testing etc.

3. Sediments or silt - i.e., particles of soil, sand and minerals.

4. Persistent substances - e.g., non-biodegradable organic and inorganic substances.

5. Groundwater Pollution - Groundwater is the water that naturally flows through and is stored in soil and rock bodies beneath the land. Groundwater

contamination occurs when liquids, usually rainwater move through waste disposal sites and into the groundwater, carrying pollutants with them. The resulting mixture of liquid and pollutant is called leachate. The groundwaters are threatened with pollution from seepage pits, refuse dumps, septic tanks, barnyard manures, transport accidents, etc., and with diverse agricultural, chemical of biological pollutants. One major that arises from the effluents that are discharged on the ground so as to prevent pollution in rivers and streams. Other important sources of pollution of groundwater are inclusive of sewage and soluble salts.

6. Mercury Pollution - Rapidly increasing amounts of metals have been discharged into the environmentally industrial establishments. Out of these, mercury has been one of the worst offenders as a dangerous pollutant. It is responsible for several deaths in Sudan and Japan. It has caused the Minamata disease in Japan. Various Swedish rivers and lakes have already become heavily polluted by the widespread use of mercury compounds as fungicides and algicides in paper making and pulp lumber industries. The problem of mercury pollution in Sweden has been studied by Ackfors with particular reference to conditions in the aquatic habitat. Fishes have been found to absorb and concentrate mercury, in the form of methylmercury, to dangerous levels.

7. Thermal Pollution- In the category come mainly Heat and radioactive substance. These are the wastes chiefly from thermal and nuclear power plants- which use large quantities of water. There are some other industries also that give out waste water after use. Nuclear power plants emit ratio nuclides. In our country the quantity of waste water in highest in the thermal power plants. After use at very high temperatures this

waste water in highest in the thermal power plants. After use at very high temperatures this waste water is drained out to the streams, rivers and lakes. It adversely affects the aquatic life in these water bodies. It is given the name thermal pollution because heat acts as pollutant. The nuclear power plants cause fall out problems as well as release waste heat. It contributes to thermal pollution. A great number of plants and animals are killed outright by the very hot water. The waste water from nuclear power plants has following adverse effects on quintic life:-

(i) It is studied that thermophilic algae, cyanobacteria and fungi have been isolated from many hot habitats in the past few years.

(ii) Many workers have enumerated the effects of thermal pollution on microbes, Plankton, plants and animals. It is shown by Vannote and Sweeney that adult body size and fecundity of several aquatic insects depend mainly on thermal conditions during larval growth. It was found when growing in non optimal temperature range, the larvae developed into smaller-sized and less found adults.

(iii) Effluents from thermal power plants sometimes exerts adverse affect on the fish population by inhibiting the spawning run which blocks the access of fish to spawning grounds. It is found in an study of the effects of thermal effluents on marine organisms in the USA, Warinner and Brehmer that carbon assimilation by natural phytoplanktons was affected by an artificially induced increase in water temperature.

(iv) Discharge of waste heat in rivers affect the indigenous fish population as well as their migration or spewing.

(v) It is studied that the rapidly spreading weed Elodea

condenses has become the dominant species at thermal outfalls and heated areas in Alberta and that in such areas this weed has tended to replace species of Myriopyllum.

(vi) Discharge of heated effluents affects species composition and production of submerged macrophytes, in a water body.

(vii) Heated water produces more serious effects in those cases where an important biological resources is diminished. Although fish and other swimming animals can move freely in an out of a thermal plume yet sessile, benthic invertebrates cannot do so. Therefore in their case a plume can exert a much more profound effect.

(viii) Warm water holds less oxygen and hence its BOD rises. Water ooC. has approximately 14 ppm of dissolved oxygen whereas that at 200C has only 9 ppm.

(ix) Significant shift is caused in algal forms and other organisms towards more heat-to learnt forms. It results in decrease in species diversity.

(x) It leads to early hatching of fish eggs.

8. Industrial Effluents - In this category come the effluents from breweries, tanneries, dying textiles, steel industries, paper and pulp mills, mining operations etc. These effluents are both, inorganic and organic pollutants. Among them are included oils, greases, plastics, metallic wastes, plasticizers, suspended solids, phenols, toxins, cynides, DDT; acids, dyes, etc. Many of those create serious pollution problems. Sulphuric acid waste from coal mines increase the hardness of water. It has naturally disastrous effects on living organism. The heavy metal effluents, discharged from industries, include Nitrates, Cadmium, Mercury, Copper, Chromium and lead etc.

9. Domestic Wastes and sewage - Discharge of untreated or partially treated sewage into rivers is main cause of pollution, especially near big cities. Waste disposal in many countries is still archaic. Discharge of treated or untreated sewage into water bodies can produce some or all of the following symptoms:

1. Stimulation of algae growth and also a shift in the algal flora to the blue-green algae, leading to production of obnoxious blooms, floating scums or blankets of algae, etc. Decomposition of such algal masses in turn leads to oxygen depletion. Sewage discharge into waterways can lead to the spread of waterborne diseases.

2. Depletion of oxygen content due to biological oxidation of organic matter.

Sewage is the waterborne waste derived from home and animal or food processing plants. Domestic waste includes human excreta, paper, cloth, soap, detergents etc. These are a major part of the pollutants that enter water. Uncontrolled dumping of wastes of rural areas, towns and cities into ponds, lakes, stream of rivers, is being observed. Due to accumulation of sewage and other wastes in these water sources, it does not remain possible to recycle it. As a result, their self regulatory capability is lost. Due to accumulation of sewage and other wastes in these regulator capability is lost. Due to higher levels of pollution the decomposition of these waste by aerobic microbes decreases. The water loses its self-purifying ability. Water is rendered unfit for drinking and other domestic uses. The decomposition of sewage and other wastes being largely an aerobic process, their accumulation in water increases its oxygen requirements.

Phosphates, the major ingredient of most detergents, leads to luxuriant growth of algae. It forms water blooms.

This extensive algae growth consumers most of the available oxygen from water. It becomes detrimental to growth of other organisms. It produces a foul smell upon decay. Some decomposing plants also grow. These plants are known to produce toxins as strychnine. The latter kills animals.

Effects of Water Pollution

1. Metals - Metalliferous mining, smelting, and refining release metals to the soil atmosphere, water and sediments, e.g. electricity generating plants, incinerators, sewage sludge, and residues from leaded gasoline. Studies are made to know the long-term effects of metal accumulation in the soil resulting from applications of sewage sludge.

2. Fertilizers and Detergents - Some of fertilizes and detergents are fairly persistent pollutants. A major ingredient of most detergents is phosphates. When discharged into water, these phosphates support luxuriant growths or blooms of algae. After dying the algae release their component inorganic and organic substances back into the water. Thus, they become pollutants themselves. Excessive growths of algae rob the water of its oxygen.

3. Silt - The dirt and dust particles which are carried from land to water. It constitutes a very serous pollutant. These particulates originate from the weathering and erosion of rocks. Silt particles are mainly composed of silicates and carbonates with some phosphates and heavy metals absorbed on them. Silting can choke irrigation channels and rives. Edible fishes, e.g., salmon, are unable to spawn on silted gravel beds.

4. Weedicides - Residues of various weedicides and insecticides often accumulate in agricultural; soils rapidly. Insecticides are designed to kill insects. Some

herbicides differ from insecticides in killing both desirable species as well as the intended targeted. Their impact may not be confined to the plant community or agricultural crop but they many also act indirectly through effects on such soil microbes as nitrogen fixing blue-green algae and bacteria. This in turn may cause harm to the growth and production of higher plants. The impact of such chemical wastes as phenols, acids, metals, etc. applied to soil can also be fairly high and may tend to complete destruction of vegetation and also soil sterilization.

5. Man's Activities - Almost all of man's activities produce wastes. Many wastes can be recycled or reduced at source. Yet there are but some wastes and their residues which are inevitable and have to be placed in landfall sites. Up to 80-90 percent of our refuse has generally been disposed off on the land. Hazardous wastes come from industries, agriculture, and other sources. In fact, much of a nation's prosperity and economic well-being originate from activities that have produced hazardous wastes. Their proper disposal often presents tricky problems and needs careful consideration. However, some big chemical companies are now installing huge incinerators with a view to handle the wastes produced by them.

6. Acid Mine Drainage - Acid main drainage is chief source of pollutant. The reason is acid generation and discharges continue even after mining has ceased. Coal mining operation releases some acid arising from the exposure of iron sulphide minerals found in the coal for the purpose of keeping control, certain steps may be followed during the mining operation to prevent the acid from being formed.

7. Mining Activities - Mining activities constitute one

of the largest producers of solid waste. Extraction of fuel being a destructive process, environmental degradation is an inevitable result of such mining. The various environmental pollution problems arise from mining. The chief is of solid wastes. The handling and disposal of the solid waste is the principal cause for disturbed lands. During mining and benefaction, environmental problems can arise from the runoff from the disturbed area, and dust form blasting, extraction, haulage, storage, and grinding, etc.

8. Municipal Solid Waste - It is reported that most manipulates face the problem of managing the ever-increasing volume of municipal solid waste in an environmentally acceptable manner. An integrated strategy using the Four Rs is regarded as the most efficient and cost effective way of reducing the MSW requiring landfill, yet it is not being done. So there is continued reliance on landfilling. Given the current landfill capacity crisis, incineration may gain support as an integral part of an effective waste management strategy.

Measure to Check Water Pollution

Some measure to check water pollution are as under:-

1. Detention and National Treatment - In recent year storm-generated pollution has become one of the greatest offenders in the area of water pollution. It can contribute heavily to BOD, COD total suspended solids, total N and orthophosphate loads of water. An effective means of managing storm-generated pollution involves source control of storm water runoff by detection and natural treatment in a lake. By using this procedure it is possible to bring about an immediate improvement of runoff quality and make it possible to remove pollutants

on a long term basis.

2. Reverse Osmosis - For a number of industrial effluents, reverse osmosis has proved to be very effective for reclaiming or concentrating specific chemical or materials. However, less attention has been paid to the use of reverse osmopsis as a municipal wastewater treatment technique where the concentrations of toxicants and heavy metals are relatively low. Reverse osmesis is found capable of removing essentially all viral and bacterial particles of cells as well as most suspended and dissolved inorganic and organic chemicals from water. This technique can be used for separation of heavy metals from water and secondary municipal effluents. The pesticides and organic phosphates can, some time, be completely removed from water by using this method. The removal efficiencies of various toxicants vary with their chemical nature.

3. Ozonization - It is found that ozonization is useful to disinfect drinking water in Switzerland and some other countries. Treatment of such polluted waters with ozone and do as under-

a. Improve its taste and odour.

b. Disinfect the water.

c. Oxidize of pollutants.

Thus, water is made suitable for drinking. Some of the pollutants are directly oxidized by ozone while others react slowly with ozone decomposition.

4. Various Techniques - Various techniques are currently being devised to control water pollution. The techniques aim at removing various chemical, biological and radiobiological pollutants through various methods as under:-\ a. Ion exchange and reverse osmosis.

b. Electrodialysis.

c. Physio-chemical methods as absorption.

In most such methods, the high costs constitute the main obstructions and are the limiting factors for general and wider application to control water pollution. The reverse osmosis can be used to separate any substance in liquid or gaseous solution. It involves the use of a porous membrane the chemical nature can be made such that it has a preferential attraction for the solvent and a similar repulsion for the solute. This technique was, in the beginning, developed to purify seawater but is now playing a significant role in the Waste reclamation, Water purification, Water rnovation and Water pollution control. The technique is found valuable in the treatment of hard waters rich in calcium and magnesium. Reverse osmosis can be used as an economical and effective method for upgrading sewage other countries. Treatment such polluted waters.

5. Efforts by WHO - The World Health Organization, has proposed International Standards for Drinking Waters on the basis of which five classes of quality as distinguished, viz., as under :-

1. Characteristics affecting the acceptability of water. WHO has prescribed the maximum permissible concentrations of various kinds of pollutants. The characteristics for water acceptability include such properties as colour, smell, taste, tepidity, pH, hardness, etc.

2. Specific chemicals affecting health.

3. Toxic substances.

4. Radioactive pollutants.

5. Biological pollutants, e.g., microbes and pathogens.

6. Suggestions Given By EFWP - At its 16th

Symposium held in Zurich in 1972, the European Federation for Water Protection has given its valuable suggestions as under:-

a. First, a greater importance should be given to water bodies, both flowing and stationary, used for recreation, nautical sports, bathing, fishing etc. This should be more particularly for their value as sources of industrial and drinking water supplies.

b. Secondly, the groundwater should be suitably conserved and protected.

c. Thirdly, it should be kept in mind that it is not only biodegradable pollutants that cause the major pollution load. Instead there are several kinds of ingredients such as heavy metals, refractory chemical compounds, mineral oil, exist which cannot be decomposed by mechanical or biological means; inorganic fertilizers and various biocides.

d. Fourthly, preventive measures against possible future detrimental effects of pollution are even mor important than the repair of damage already inflicted. Hence, further efforts should be made to reduce the amounts of solids and liquid wastes by reutilizing or recycling some of their components.

e. Fifthly, efforts for control of water bodies and of plants serving the purpose of water protection should be reinforced and carried out by all available means, including legal enforcement.

5. To Stabilize the Eco-system - The most reliable way to control pollution and improver water quality is undoubtedly to stabilize the ecosystem by balancing the input and output of energy and nutrients. Some reasonable ways to increase stability of aquatic eco-system are as under:-

a. Fish management and aeration.

b. Trapping of nutrients.

c. Harvesting and removal of biomass.

d. Reduction in waste inputs.

Air Pollution

It need nor iterate that no life is possible without air. A living being can survive for a few days without water and for a few weeks without food but can nor survive even for a few moments without breathing i.e., inhaling air. Our atmosphere is gaseous envelope which surrounds the earth from all sides. The air is composition of several gases mainly nitrogen, oxygen, argon and carbon dioxide.

Air pollution takes place through enrichment of our atmosphere or air with noxious gases and other undesirable substances, caused largely on account of burning of fuels and through the release of gases by various industries and automobiles, the burning of fossil fuels releases huge amounts of CO_2 and other gases.

Thus Air pollution can be defined as the contamination of air with dust, smoke and harmful gases. The air pollution is generally made though the pollutants of gases and solid and liquid particles of organic and inorganic chemical. The various kinds of gases such as carbon monoxide, sulphur dioxide, hydrogen sulphide emissions from volcanoes, swamps, dusts, salt spray, pollens from plants, etc. are continuously added to the air by natural processes. Air pollution can be defined as the state when the natural composition of air is distributed either by natural of man-made sources of activities or by both.

Position of Air Pollution

It is revealed that in industrially SO2 advanced

countries, sulphur oxides constitute a very harmful air pollutant. Excessive enrichment of air with these oxides can have grave, and even lethal, effects on human beings as well as animals and plants. SO2 is the most common pollutant in human beings as well as animals and plants. About 60 percent of the SO2 emissions come from power stations wherein coal is used. In North America, photochemical oxidants, sulphur oxides and nitrogen oxides are common air pollutants. It is also revealed that, now the major cause of air pollution has shifted from SOx to photochemical air pollutants. Researchers have revealed cases of serious vegetation damage, caused by smog, ozone, peroxyacetyl nitrate, fluorides or ethylene, and polluted air has been established as being responsible for adverse effects on forest yields.

Increasing quantities of air pollutants are now causing changes in the atmosphere. Through our emissions of CFCs and other compounds, making has disrupted the ozone balance in the stratosphere. Hence, several countries have signed an agreement-the Montreal Protocol- to reduce and eventually eliminate emissions of substances that destroy the ozone layer. The latest research findings indicate that the depletion of the earth's ozone layer is proceeding at a faster rate than expected.

Causes or Sources of air pollution

The causes of air pollution are as under:-

1. Man-made causes or sources - These causes include human activities, such as industries, factories, urban centres, aircraft, nuclear experiments, automobiles, agriculture, power plants etc.

2. Natural Sources or sources - These sources include volcanic eruptions, deflation of sand and dust, forest, or wild fires of natural vegetation, etc.

Main Sources of Air Pollutions

Main sources of air pollution are as under:

1. Textile Mills - Textile mills emit great amounts of cotton dust. Pandit et al., have highlighted the concentration of airborne cotton dust particles from coarse and fine cloth mills located in Maharashtra, Vidarbha and Gujarat, and recorded average dust contents of 176,274 and 763 mg/100 m3 for fine mills, coarse mills and ginning presses respectively. Cotton dust implicate in the disabling occupational disease known as Byssinosis which is widespread in textile workers in India.

2. Furnaces - Future projections indicate that coal will be utilized to produce synthetic fuels by gasification and liquefaction. These processes, in turn, may pose new toxicological problems. The aqueous condensates derived from coal gasification and diliquefaction processes constitute primary effluents. The major organic components in the condensates are phenols, cresols and some low molecular weight carboxylic acids.

3. Thermal Pollution - In our country, there are a number or thermal power stations and super thermal Power stations. The National Thermal Power Corporation is setting up four mammoth coal-powered power stations to add to the energy generation situated as under-

a. Farakka in West Bengal.

b. Ramagundam in Andhra Pradesh.

c. Korba in M.P.

D. Singrauli in U.P.

The coal consumption of thermal plants is several million tonnes. The main pollutants are fly ash, sulphur oxide and other gases and hydrocarbons. The are tree thermal power stations at the Indraprashta Estate,

Rajghat and Badarpur in Delhi. They add to the air pollution. The Indraprastha plant consumers about four thousands tonnes of coal and in the fire units. Badarpur, the largest, consumes daily about 10 thousands tonnes of coal.

4. Industrial Air Pollution - In our country, there is rapid development in the agricultural technology and engineering. There is also rapid industrial development.

Nitrogen oxides probably pose the most serious air pollution control challenge. These oxides come both from automobiles and from certain stationary combustion sources. About 95 percent of the NOx act photochemically with hydrocarbons and SO2 to form undesirable compounds, with a shift of residual No to NO2.

5. Automobiles of Air Pollution - At present there is a rapid increase in number of Automobiles e.g. cars, trucks, buses and two wheelers. It is has raised the traffic density in towns and cities. They pour tonnes of gaseous pollutants into the air daily.

It is reflected from the studies that ever increasing vehicular traffic density poses continuous threat to the ambient air quality. About a decade and a half there were over 300 million cars, trucks and buses the world over and their number is increasing rapidly., India 2.8 million vehicles of which more than 65% were two wheelers operating in petrol. There has been an addition of not less than thirty percent vehicles now.

In the major cities of the country about 1100 to 1500 tonnes of pollutants are being emitted into the air daily, of which 50% come from automobile exhausts. It is revealed by the cities that in the major metropolitan cities, vehicular exhaust accounts for 70% of all Co2, 50% of all hydrocarbons, 30-40% of all oxides and 30%

of all SPM. In Delhi, there are more than three million vehicles which are registered there as well as registered in other status but being plied there. During peak traffic hour automobiles of all classes emit as much as 900 kg of CO, 350 kg of hydrocarbons and 90 kg of nitrogen oxides.

Causes of Air Pollution

Main causes of air pollution are as under:-

1. Metals - These include nickel, vanadium, titanium, beryllium, arsenic, tin, lead, cadmium, etc. They have been detected in the atmosphere in the form of solid particles or liquid droplets or gases. Mostly they come from fumes and dust from metallurgical processes.

2. Naturally produced air pollutions - In this category come pollen, volcanic gases, marsh gas, etc.

3. Particulate matter - The come mostly from industries, power plants and refuse disposal. Most of this particulate matter has not yet been adequately identified.

4. Hydrocarbons - They are mostly discharged by motor vehicles and industries.

5. Ozone - On account of human activities, its level may rise in atmosphere.

6. Nitrogen oxides - Nitrogen oxides include mainly nitrogen monoxide, nitrogen oxide, nitric acid mostly released by automobiles, power plants and industries.

7. Sulphur compounds - These Compounds include SO2 H2S and sulphuric acid. They are mostly released by fossil fuel i.e. coal, etc. based power generating plants and industrial units as refineries.

8. Carbon compounds - Carbon compounds include carbon dioxide and carbon monoxide. Carbon dioxide is released by complete combustion of fossils fuels. The

carbon monoxide is released by automobile exhausts.

Effect of Air Pollution- Man and Environment

Air pollutants can seriously harm materials, crops and livestock. They can spoil fabrics, surface coatings, metals and other commercial materials:-

1. Fluorides and arsenic found in air have caused serious injuries to livestock and cattle. When eaten, this fodder possess the cattle.

2. Ozone produces damaging effects on fabrics, dyes and rubber.

3. It is detected that Sulphur compounds can corrode or damage many metals, stones, electrical equipment, painted surface, textiles, paper and leather.

In fact, most of the air pollutants can cause human sickness or even death. Cases of air pollution disasters have been recorded from many countries. In the town of Donora, Pennsylvania, in October 1948; a temperature inversion trapped the emissions of certain industrial establishments and factories. Nearly 5,000 inhabitants fell ill, and at least 20 of them died following this calamity. A 50 day episode of severe air pollution in London in 1952 took a toll of some 4,000 deaths.

The researches done by Hickeyt and associates in 38 large American cities have highlighted that increasing concentrations of nitrogen dioxide and SO2 in the air are statically correlated with increasing death rates from chronic diseases associated with ageing and senescence, e.g. cancer, heart diseases, diabetes mellitus, etc. The air pollutants can and do cause long-term, slow and chronic effects on health in addition to their immediate and acute effects.

Some studies have indicated that the atmospheric SO2, NO2 and lead can cause mutations in human beings. These noxious gases are ocular and respiratory irritants. Concentrations of SO2 and No2 in the atmosphere constitute statistically significant predictors for maritally rates for various diseases of aging, including cancer and arteriosclerosis. In the same way, the lead concentrations were significant predictors for infant mortality rates and congenital malformations. Atmospheric NO2 can cause the potent mutagen nitrous acid and possibly bisulfites atmospheric chemical mutagens alter resting DNA in such a way that mutations appear after subsequent replications. Replication errors could sometime lead to a gradual accumulation of nutational errors.

Polluted air of big cities also contains carcinogens, e.g., benzopyrene, and other polycyclic compounds. Main sources are tobacco smoke, automobile exhaust and effluents from industry and electric power stations. The various kinds of particulates in the atmosphere cause soiling of various objects and are responsible for various nuisance effects. High dust levels in some occupational environments are also definitely harmful regardless of chemical composition.

Evil Effect of Air Pollution On Environment

1. Historical Monuments - A expert Committee appointed by the Government of India on Environmental Impact of Mathura Refinery has expressed the view that there may be a serious threat to the Taj, and that appropriate precautions should be taken to preserve the Taj from the adverse effects. They have warned that the Taj and various other ancient monuments may be irreparably affected by the corrosive fumes and pollutants discharged from the refinery, so much so that more money have to be spent on protecting Taj Mahal from the adverse impact of the Refinery than it took Shah

Jhan to build it. The work done at the National Environmental Engineering Research Institute at Nagpur has revealed that SO2 and other emissions from refinery and foundries can certainly affect marble as well as the red sanstone buildings of the tomb of Ehmad-ud-dulah, the Fatehpur Sikri complex, and the Red Fort. Some of the ancient temples in Mathura and even the famous bird sanctuary in Ghana forest near Bharatpur may be affected sooner or later.

This is the reason why the Department of Environment, Government of India, has ordered the closure of two coal-fired power stations in Agra and has also persuaded the railway authorities in Agra to switch over from coal to diesel. With a view to protect the Taj Mahal from pollution effects. A green belt is also being created around the Taj for the same purpose.

The crude oil to be processed in the refinery contains up to about 2 percent sulphur. This is oxidized to SO2 and will be emitted from the chimney of the refinery. Thereafter, in the moist atmosphere it is converted to dilute acid which causes decay of stone and marble.

2. Effects on Plants and Animals - Air pollution affects crop yields. Studies carried out in England have revealed great reductions in they yields of such plants as radish, lettuce, various flowering annuals and other crops when grown in the more highly polluted parts of big industrial cities. The smelting of ores causes serious damage to vegetation. Pollutant particles some time settle down on levels or nearby trees and may block the stomatal pores. In this way they affect gas exchanges, water relations and other physiological processes. Ozone can cause damage to palisade cells which lose water and disintegrate. At levels of 0.02 ppm, it damages tobacco, tomato, bean, pine and other plants.

Plants possess a gaseous environment. When the composition of this environment exceeds the capacity of plants to tolerate or adapt to the change, some stress is imposed. Thus the sensitive components of the ecosystem start malfunctioning. When the gas reaches inside the leaf, the cell membranes are affected. Alterations take place in SH/SS ratio. There can be permeability dysfunction as well. Free radicals are formed and ion transport can be inhibited and normal functions disrupted.

Plants growing in polluted environment often show symptoms of injury, and general debility. In temperate counties some findings are as under:

a. Reduction in fruit size.

b. Necrosis of fruit tips.

c. Necrosis of stigmatic surface.

d. Hardening of floral buds.

e. Tobacco to ozone and ptunia to photochemical smog. In this topics, mango is especially sensitive to polluted air. The aerial parts of the trees growing near thermal power stations, brickkilns, steel factories and smelters exhibited.

3. Cloud Structure - The particles called ice nuclei found in our atmosphere in low concentrations modify the cloud structure at subzero temperatures and the effects of ice nuclei are some time so severe that the precipitation potential of such cold could may also become altered. Two main sources emanating ice nuclei are steel miils and automobile emissions.

Forest fires and pulp and paper mills are the sources of certain other particles called could condensation nuclei. The CCN particles can modify precipitation from clouds that have temperatures above 00C. Other air pollutants like acid fumes, aerosols, ammonia, and SO2 affect the pH of rainwater. Certain chemicals in the discharge can interact in the atmosphere resulting in an amplification of their effects e.g., although SO2 and NH3 by themselves react slowly, their reaction rate is greatly increased in the presence of could droplets.

Surface active pollutant molecules are able to coat cloud particles and influence could and aerosol coagulation and evaporation. Some air pollutants are able to affect aerosols involved in could processes. The structure and distribution of clouds can be effected by such pollutants. It causes alterations in precipitation and optimal scattering properties. Besides, affecting some aspects of weather, these pollutants are also now believed scattering properties.

4. Acid Rain - The acid rain causes both air and water pollution. Some scholars have tried to identify the problem of acid precipitation which causes both air and water pollution. Some have even gone to the extent of describing acid precipitation as one of the gravest threats man.

To understand the concept of acidity is a basic requirement in any attempts to design ecosystem studies for answering questions about. The classical definition describes acids as proton donors and bases as proton acceptors. This means that acidity is a relative property and a substance may simultaneously act both as an acid and a base.

Acid rain is the principal cause of the acidification of soils and fresh-waters in several countries. It may b e deemed as rain with pH of less than 5.6 It follows from the definition of acidity in natural waters. The pure water in equilibrium with atmospheric CO2 has pH of 5.6 at 1000 C and zero alkalinity by definition. Thus rain with pH less than 5.6 is acid rain. The input of acid from the atmosphere imposes and acid load on ecosystems which receive it.

It is discovered that the HCI in acid rain comes mostly from the combustion and decomposition of organochlorine compounds and polyvinyl chloride plastics. The sulphuric acid comes from oxidation of sulphur in fossil fuels, and nitric acid comes from nitrogen fixation.

Acid precipitation affects water bodies. Lakes can lose as much as 70 percent of their bicarbonate alkalinity and in decade, due to the input of acid precipitations. Such a loss a alkalinity makes it difficult for crustaceans to moult their exoskeletons; in some cases, many crustaceans may die. Another indirect effect of the fall in water pH is the release of heavy metals such as mercury and aluminium in water, these metals in turn produce adverse effects on the indigenous biota.

5. Ozone Formation - Ozone, like several other photochemical oxidants is formed primarily from nitrogen dioxzide. Ozone like other oxidants such as PAN, harms plants. Ozone can also react with nitrogen monoxide, whereby the ozone is used up and nitrogen dioxide forms anew. If only these compounds are present, the ozone levels will not be very high. But when hydrocarbons enter into the picture, really high levels of ozone are reached. The reason is the hydrocarbons can transforms nitrogen monoxide to nitrogen dioxide without using up the ozone.

6. Photochemical smog - Photochemical smog is caused, in the presence of sunlight, by hydrocarbons and other organic substances and nitrogen oxides, most of which arise from the fumes and exhaust of motor vehicles. Smog formation atmosphere, the chief reaction

being the formation of certain free radicals of oxygen, hydrocarbon and nitrogen dioxide.

In Photochemical smog are found mixtures of ozone, nitrogen dioxide, nitrates, and other gases or dry particles. Intermittent fog in the same geographical area can be acidic with high concentrations of nitric acid. The various components of photochemical smog are toxic to agricultural crops and forest tress. Photochemical smog is known to cause serious health hazards. A particularly serious episode of heavy smog formation occured in July 1970 in Tokyo, New York, Rome and Sydney. Epidemics of such diseases as asthma and bronchitis occurred immediately after the smog.

Measure To Control The Air Pollution

Today it has become possible to control several types of air pollutions by employing modern technology and scientific researchers. It involves the benefits to improve the quality of the environment and human health, agriculture and vegetations. It also improves the ecological balance and stability of ecosystem. Some suggestions are as under:-

1. Control Through Law - Acts of Industries should be enforced to prevent gaseous pollution. Both the air pollution and noise pollution are included under Air and Noise Pollution Prevention Act. Legal steps already been taken by state and central government, to control the air pollution. Education can also play a vital role in preventing and controlling air pollution. It is essential to arouse wide awareness and to develop consciousness among students about air pollution and its resources and ways. Formal, non-formal and adult education programmes should aim at arousing and developing feelings and attitudes or consciousness about the problem which has serious adverse effects on human

health. Dr. Vibasi has suggested for preparation of Charts and mottoes on air pollutions, resources and remedial measures. Media and newspaper slogans should be used Save the Oil protect the air pollution.

2 Control on Industrial Air Pollution - The following methods are suggested to be used to control air pollution from gaseous pollutants -

a. Wet Dry Systems - This method is found successful in dry cleaning plants, printing shops, paint factories, food processing plants, etc.

b. Dry System - When water comes in contact with sulphur dioxide, it produces sulphuric acid.

c. Wet system - The alkali liquid reacts with sulphur dioxide to produce a precipitate.

3. Control on Automobiles Air Pollution - Some measures to reduce air pollutants from the transport sector in the advanced countries are as under:

a. To control through law such as Motor Vehicles Act, 1988 and other Acts of engine.

b. To use the filters.

c. Control evaporation from fuel tank and carburettor.

d. To check pollutants emission from vehicular lexhaust.

e. To adopt speed limits for road traffic at a maximum of 100 kph.

f. To adopt properly regulated emission standards for all new motor vehicles, including aeroplanes and ships.

g. To adopt plans and timetables with a view to reduce significantly the total European volume of road and air traffic.

h. To implement volume control, no investment in

public transport and railway freight systems should be increased.

4. Various Measures - A range of measures should be adopted including as under :

a. Applying best available techniques in the energy, transport, industry, and agriculture sectors.

b. Switching to less polluting fuels.

c. Increasing the efficiency of energy production, transmission, and use.

d. Increasing to conservation of energy.

e. Using renewable energy sources.

5. Ascertainment of Critical loads - With a view to check the continuing deterioration of the environment, concentrations and depositions of air pollutants must be reduced to below the critical loads. We can define critical loads as a quantitative estimate of an exposure to one or more pollutants above which adverse effects on receptors, such as plants, ecosystems or materials, may take place.

Soil Pollution

We can define soil pollution as the contamination of soil with excess of chemicals, fertilizers, insecticides and herbicides. Soil is very important environmental component for human beings, animals and plants. It is the basic medium for food, vegetation and natural resources as well as the base for the development of human culture and civilization. Various aspects and components of soils and texture, structure, moisture, profiles and horizons.

The decrease in the quality of soil either due to human activities or natural sources or by both is give the name soil pollution or soil degradation. It is caused by various reasons as under:

1. Lack of Human content.
2. High fluctuations of temperature.
3. Excess of deficit of moisture content.
4. Decrease in soil micro organisms.
5. Decrease in plant nutrients.
6. Soil reason.

Main Causes of Soil Pollution

There are various causes of soil pollution. Accelerated rate of soil erosion, silk eruption, deforestation, excessive use of pesticides, insecticide, chemical fertilizers and herbicides, polluted waste water from industries, forest fires, urban areas a few micro-organisms, dummying of urban and industrial wastes, water-logging and related capillary process, drought, leashing processes etc. Main causes of soil pollution are as under:-

1. Resistant Object and Recalcitrant Wastes - Various large, resistant objects such as cans, tyres, other metallic or plastic junk or even parts of old cars, etc., act as pollutants. The polychlorinated biphenyls is a serious pollutant. At present PCBs are used primarily as dielectric fluids and coolants for electrical equipment. They are also used in paints, paper coating, carbon-less paper and chlorinated rubber. Mineral oils can become contaminated with low concentrations of PCBs. It should be noticed that PCBs are highly stable under most conditions and this resistance to degradation increases their polugenic nature.

2. Metals - Metalliferous mining, smelting, and refining release metals to the soil atmosphere, water and dediments, e.g. electricity generating plants, incinerators, sewage sludge, and residues from leaded gasoline. Studies are made to know the long-term effects

of metal accumulation in the soil rustling from applications of sewage sludge.

McGrath reports the results of a long-term experiment which received metal-contaminated sewage sludge from 1942 to 1961 and inorganic fertilizers thereafter. Additions of sewage sludge and a sludge-straw compost increased considerably the concentration of Zn, Cu, Ni, Cd, Cr and Pb in the plough-layer soil, these have persisted for over 4 decades now. Metal concentrations in the soil started failing since 1941 when the sludge applications were stopped. Most workers agree that the soil and organic litter layer components of woodland ecosystems are the ultimate sinks for heavy metals in aerially contaminated areas. It is found that once soils have become contaminated, they are unlikely to be depleted of lead and other metals by leaching.

3. Fertilizers and Detergents - Some of fertilizers and detergents are fairly a very serious pollutant. These particulates originate from the weathering and erosion of rocks. Silt particles are mainly composed of silicates and carbonates with some phosphates and heavy metals absorbed on them. Silting can choke irrigation channels and rivers. Edible fishes, e.g., salmon, are unable to spawn on silted gravel beds.

4. Silt - The dirt and dust particles which are carried from land to water. It constitutes a very serious pollutant. These particulates originate from the weathering and erosion of rocks. Silt particles are mainly composed of silicates and carbonates with some phosphates and heavy metals absorb on them. Silting can choke irrigation channels and rivers. Edible fishes, e.g., salmon, are unable to spawn on silted gravel beds.

5. Weedicides - Residues or various weedicides and insecticides often accumulate in agricultural soils

rapidly. Insecticides are designed to kill insects. Some herbicides differ from insecticides in killing both desirable species as well as the intended target. Their impact may not be confined to the plant community or agricultural crop but they may also act indirectly through effects on such soil microbes as nitrogen fixing blue-green algae and bacteria. This is turn may cause harm to the growth and production of higher plants. The impact of such chemical wastes as phenols, acids, metals, etc. applied to soil can also be fairly high and may tend to complete destruction of vegetation and also soil sterilization.

6. Man's Activities - Almost of man's activities produce wastes. Many wastes can be recycled or reduced at source. Yet there are but some wastes and their residues which are inevitable and have to be placed in landfill sites. U to 80-90 percent of our refuse has generally been disposed off on the land. Hazardous wastes come from industries, agriculture, and other sources. In fact, much of a nation's prosperity and economic well-being originate from activities that have produced hazardous wastes. Their proper disposal often presents tricky problems and needs careful consideration. However, some big chemical companies are now installing huge incinerators with a view to handle the wastes produced by them.

7. Acid Mine Drainage - Acid main drainage is chief source of pollutant. The reason is acid generation and discharges continue even after mining has ceased. Coal mining operation releases some acid arising from the exposure of iron sulphide minerals found in the coal for the purpose of keeping control, certain steps may be followed during the mining operations to prevent the acid from being formed.

8. Mining Activities - Mining activities constitute one of the largest producers of solid waste. Extraction of fuel being a destructive process, environmental degradation is an inevitable result of such mining. The various environmental pollution problems arise from mining. The chief is of solid wastes. The handling and disposal of the solid waste is the principal cause for disturbed lands. During mining and benefaction, environmental problems can arise from the runoff from the disturbed area, and dust from blasting, extraction, haulage, storage, and grinding, etc.

9. Municipal Solid Waste - It is reported that most municipalities face the problem of managing the ever-increasing volume of municipal solid waste in air environmentally acceptable manner. An integrated strategy using the Four Rs. is regarded as the most efficient and cost effective way reducing the MSW requiring landfull, yet it is not being done. So there is continued reliance on landifilling. Given the current landfill capacity crisis, incineration may gain support as an integral part of an effective waste management strategy.

Effect of Soil Pollution

Main effects are as under:-

1. Evil Effects of Fertilizers on Soil - Some adverse effects of fertilizer on soil use are:-

(i) Disturbance in the ionic balance and equilibrium in soils. High acidity, nutritional imbalance, shortages of certain trace elements and molydbenum or selenium toxity.

(ii) Stimulating of weed growth in crop fields.

(iii) Deterioration of water resources caused by eutrophication.

(iv) Changes in mobility status of various nutrients in soils.

2. Evil Effect of Nitrates - The excessive and indiscriminate application of inorganic fertilizers is found leading to accumulation of nitrates in water. When such waters are drunk by cattle or human beings, these nitrates are reduced to the toxic nitrites by intestinal bacteria. Nitrates can cause a serious diseases known as methemoglobinemia damaging respiratory and vascular systems and may even cause suffocation.

3. Evil Effect of Asbestos - Asbestos is widely used as in insulating material. Its recognition as a pollutant was realized in 1973, when the American Environmental Protection Agency reported that the water of Lake Superior contained hazardous amounts of asbestos as the iron ore wastes were being dumped in the north western portions of the lake. The recent medical opinion attributes such hazards as cancer of lungs, stomach and intestines to asbestos pollution. Asbestos is now also recognized as a dangerous air pollutant since its particles can be carried into the atmosphere.

4. Effect of Pesticides - The pesticides of their residues pollute the soil as under:-

(i) They may cause the adverse effects as resistance, fungal displacement and other population changes.

(ii) Many of them persist and thus cannot be disposed off.

(iii) Their concentration and magnification in biological systems may lead to certain unexpected or untoward results.

(iv) They strike the intended pests as well as several non target organisms.

3. Health Hazards - Pesticides pollute the

environment causing health hazards. A decade ago, a mysterious disease involving pain in joints afflicted poor farmers in several villages in Karnataka State. It was detected that the crustaceans had become contaminated with parathion and endrin which were used in the paddy fields. The pesticides ultimately were ingested by the farmers. As such, they developed the disease.

4. Poverty and Malnutrition - In developing countries, poverty, malnutrition and weak health of the agricultural workers can be linked with improper storage of the chemicals and the use of pesticide containers for storing food and drinks in villages. These factors contribute to accidents of pesticide poisoning. It is observed that most poor peasants live in a single-room hutment where the probability of pesticides getting into the food which is often cooked in the same room is high. Besides, the access of the chemicals to children is easy. These hutments are frequently very close to the crop fields. When the crops are sprayed, the spray frequently drifts into the house, exposing the children to grave risks.

5. Effect on Insects - The effects of pesticides on various kinds of insects , earthworms, invertebrates, protozoa, and microbes found in soils, especially the reduction in natural enemies due to pesticide usage, increased resistance to pesticides in insects and mites, and honey bee poisonings account for about 70 percent of the calculated socio-environmental costs for pesticides in the USA.

6. Effect of Honey Bees - Bees aid the pollination of several plants. Pesticides have significantly affected some honey bees and other useful insects so their populations have declined. According to Pimental et al. annual agricultural loses due to poor pollination from pesticides can be as high as $ 4000 million in the USA.

Some effects are as under:-

(i) Drifting or leaching pesticides drain into nearby water in rotation. Drifting or leaching pesticides drain into nearby water bodies, and cause fishery and wildlife losses. It is observed that wild birds and mammals exposed to pesticides suffer by death from direct exposure to high doses.

(ii) Persistent herbicides also can injure crops planted in rotation.

(iii) Herbicides that drift from a treated crop to a nearby crop also cause serious environmental problems.

(iv) Crops are damaged instead of being protected by improper pesticide applications e.g., application of improper dosage under unfavourable conditions.

7. Effect on Ladybird Beetle - The consequences of pesticides are almost invariably adverse and harmful. Here one case study can be cited. In the nineteenth century, the ladybird beetle was brought from Australia to California to control a scale insect pest of oranges. The beetle kept the pest under check for more than five decades. However, in 1946 when DDT began to be used in the citrus orchards, its existence was endangered. The beetle was susceptible to DDT and hence its population declined. This led to a marked increase in the population densities of the pest. A subsequent withdrawal of DDT again restored the natural balance of biological control within a few years. It is established that DDT is one of the most effective pesticides known. It was banned in the USA in 1972.

It is believed that the most serious threat to public health is from the uncontrolled use of pesticides for agronomic practice. Chapping and Wessertrom found so in 1981. In India, widespread resistance to pesticides has developed in Anopheles spa particularly in areas which have recently shifted to high-yielding farmers of agricultural production Resistance may be clearly seen in the areas where Green Revolution technology, has been introduced.

8. Effect of DDT - Extensive researches in the USA have established widespread distribution of DDT residues through food chains in several lakes. Residues were detected in shallow and deep water mud samples, the whitefish, duck, crustaceans ring-billed and herring gulls and other fauna adversely affected. Residues of Dieldrin, Endrin, DDT and DDE have been detected in all major river basins in the United States. It is also believed that the declining percentage of immature birds in the American bald eagle population is due to DDT and other hard biocides.

Control Measures

1. Processing Sludge Ash - It is proved that processing sludge ash into lightweight aggregates for the concrete industry is the most promising utilization option. Lightweight aggregate may be produce by firing pelletized or slabbed sludge ash at 1100 to 12000C produce a hard, ceramic-like material. It can later be crushed, sized and graded to conform to required aggregate specifications. The low thermal conductivity and high fire resistance of the aggregates make them suitable for thermal conductivity and high fire resistance of the aggregates make them suitable for use in thermal insulation and fire protection applications such as fireproof wallboard.

2. Ban of Pesticides - As the surviving biocide residues are found uncontrollable, insidious and unpredictable in their actions, Rudd has advocated a complete ban on such pesticides whose toxic effects

cannot be confined to the site of application. In fact, substantial harm has already been done by these biocides. In such a position even if their future use were banned now, sufficient amounts of residues will still persist in the various ecosystems to cause serious ecological effects for decades.

3. Technologies - Attempts are under way in Canada and other countries to evolve suitable technologies for destroying PC Bs contained in both liquid and solid wastes.

4. Limitations on Concentrations of Harmful Substances - Some limits are imposed on the concentrations of harmful substances in the effluent, however not on the production rate of the mine. The maximum authorized monthly average concentration prescribed in Canada is 0.5 mg/litre for arsenic, nickel and zinc; 0.3 mg/1 for copper, 0.2mg 1 for lead, and 10 pCi/ litre for randium 226.

5. Limitation By Enactments - In several countries, regulations are enacted to limit the concentrations of the following metals in the mining effluents: copper, lead, arsenic, nickel, zinc and radium 226.

Here mines are taken as all metal mining and milling facilities and associated smelters, refineries, acid plants, pelletizing plants, sinter plants and any similar operations where the effluent from several such operations is combined with effluents form mining and milling.

Noise Pollution

The word noise is an unwanted or unpleasant sound that causes discomfort. Noise is Wrong sound, in the wrong place at the wrong time. Noise pollution is the unwanted sound dumped into the atmosphere leading and health hazards. Noise Pollution may be defined as the state of discomfort and restlessness that is cause to man by unwanted high intensity sound known as noise. Unbearable high pitched sound is called noise pollution.

Effects of Noise Pollution

Some effects of noise pollution are as under -

1. Psychological Effects - The noise pollution exercises psychological effects. It causes a great number of behavioural change among human beings as well as animals. Disco music some times, causes temporary deafness in the listens.

2. Non-auditory Effects - These include the interference with speech communication, physiological disorders irritation/annoyance and loss of working efficiency etc.

3. Auditory Effects - As clear from the name, these include auditory fatigue and deafness. Deafness is caused by continuous noise exposure in the biggest cities like Delhi, Mumbai, Kolkata and Chennai, etc.

Auditory fatigue appears in the 90 dB and may be associated with side effects as whistling and buzzing in ears. Deafness can be cause due to continuous noise exposure. Temporary deafness occurs at 4000-6000 hz. Permanent loss of hearing occurs at 100 dB. Mumbai and Kolkata are the nosiest cities in the world.

Methods of Control Noise Pollution

Main methods to control noise pollution are as under-

1. Education - The students and public should be educated about the harms caused by noise nuisance though news media.

2. Preventive Acts or Law - Air pollution Control Act is enacted to check the noise pollution. In should be enforced strictly.

3. Plantation or Vegetation - Big trees should be planted along high ways, streets and other noisy places. They absorb noise.

4. Ear Protection - Various devices such as ear plugs and ear muffs may be provided the workers of industries.

5. Transmission Control - Another suggestion is to cover the room at source.

6. At Source Control - Another suggestion is to cover the room walls with should absorbers.

Marine Pollution

Our age long concept that oceans are limitless or bottomless is erroneous for the oceans are quite limited in respect of their capacity to act as huge sink and receptacles for wastes.

Ocean pollution can be cause by ship-generated discharges of oil and petroleum products, noxious liquids, packaged dangerous goods, sewage and garbage, etc.

Process

The fate of pollutant discharged into the sea is determined by many route and processes. It is studied that the pollutant may become dispersed in any of the following ways:

1. Such biological processes as may include uptake by seaweeds, fish, birds and phytolankton. From the latter it may pass on through a food web involving zooplankton, fish and mammals.

2. Transported by cocoon currents and migratory birds.

3. Turbulence and ocean currents.

Sources

Terrestrially produces or eroded substances and

pollutants are mostly carried into an ocean through:

1. Deliberate disposal of substances by man through pipelines.

2. Rivers.

3. The atmosphere.

In fact, oceans can cope up with reasonable amount of particulate minerals, common soluble chemicals, mud and salt, but they are unable to rot or decompose organic matter. Organic materials however, are generally:

(i) In sedimates containing high concentrations of fine particles of Ca Co3 precipitation of disclosed phosphate occurs on the surfaces of CaCo3 grains. As such, phosphate concentrations in the interstitial water of such sediments much lower than those in anoxic siliceous sediments.

(ii) Heavily polluted sediments are subject to faster decomposition of their organic matter than less polluted ones.

(iii) Dissolved ammoniac and phosphate originate from the same general organic decomposition process which in some marine sediments is believed to be brought about by microbes in addition to those concerned with sulphate reduction.

(iv) Eaten, digested and execrated by marine animals.

Effect of Sea Pollution

1. It is revealed by the studies of fishes in polluted and non-polluted areas near Helsinki that the production and biomass of fish in polluted areas was great yet the species diversity was less.

2. The greatest diversity of bottom fauna was found in clear or only slightly polluted water and it was found to decrease progressively with increasing load of

pollution.

3. Most crustaceans avoid polluted areas.

4. The most common pollution-tolerant benthic animal of Macoma ballica.

5. In highly polluted areas, no macroscopic bentic animals are found however chironomid larvae occur at the sea bottom.

6. The bottom fauna of polluted coast shows a zonation in keeping with the extent of pollution.

7. Any serious pollution of seawater can result in a loss of diversity in the marine organisms and unstabilize and simplify the otherwise complex and stable ecosystem. The pollution is the Baltic Sea as reported by Bagge, along the coast of Finland mainly comes from sewage and effluents from wood-processing industries.

Oil Pollution

In recent years oil pollution has become formidable. Recent increases in shipping and drilling operations have caused increased contamination of our oceans with chemical pollutants, including petroleum hydrocarbons. These adverse effects are as under:-

1. Aquatic species may be more sensitive than mammals to the acute lethal effects of a variety of chemicals.

2. Marine fish, crustaceans, molluscans, and zooplankton accumulate hydrocarbons from polluted water.

Spills

Much of the oil and petroleum products are shipped by sea and any spill of this oil can cause serious pollution problems. Spills are occasional discharges or dumping that happen due to:

1. Convenience dumping into sewers, streams,

estuaries, coastal waters.

2. Deliberate dischages of ballast water.
3. Malfunctioning of vehicles and equipment.
4. Human error.
5. Accidents.

Some of these spills cause obvious, damage to marine fish, birds, invertebrates, algae, and mammals. Sometimes the spills themselves may not be very harmful to marine life, but the detergents used to clean up the spill prove extremely harmful. It is studied that those areas of British coasts around which large amounts of toxic detergents were used to clean up the oil slick caused by the notorious Torrey Canyon accident a few years ago, witnessed a high morality of marine life.

Thermal Pollution

Thermal pollution is the pollution caused by the discharge of heat in the form of hot water, air of effluent into the environment. Many industries use a log of water for cooling purposes and return this water to the stream at a higher temperature. High temperature can exert a lethal effect on the biotic communities in an equated habitat. Some animals are killed our-right by the hottest water, with less hot water some harmful effects can result e.g. a bacterial disease of salmon in some rivers is though to become aggravated by a slight rise in water temperature.

Effect of Thermal Pollution

The thermal pollution can affect the entire ecological balance of stream. For Instance:

1. In USA Warinner and Brehmer found that carbon assimilation by natural phytoplanktons was affected by an artificially induced increase in water temperature.

It is found that the greater the temperature rose caused by thermal pollution, the greater was the depression in primary production.

2. Many research workers have narrated their findings regarding the effects of thermal pollution on microbes, plankton, plants and animals.

3. Discharge of waste heat in rivers can not only affect the indigenous fish population but may also affect their migration or spawning.

4. The rapidly spreading weed Elodea condenses has become the dominant species at thermal outfalls and heated areas in Alberta and that is such areas this weed has tended to replace species of Myriophyllum, Chara and Potamgeton.

5. It affects species composition and production of submerged macrophytes.

6. Heated water produces more serious effects in those cases where an important biological resources in diminished. The sessile, benthic invertebrates cannot move freely so. Hence in their case a plume can exert a much more profound effect.

7. High water temperature adversely affects the daily and seasonal behaviour and metabolic responses.

8. Salmon often fails to spawn in such conditions. Warm water holds less oxygen and hence its BOD rises. Water 0oC has approximately 14 ppm of dissolved oxygen whereas that at 200 has only 9 ppm.

9. The trout eggs commonly fail to batch in water that is too warm.

10. The discharge of warm water may cause fish eggs to hatch so early in the spring that the natural food organism needed by the young fingerlings would not be available.

7

HEREDITY AND ENVIRONMENT

Far from satisfying our psychological curiosity, the fact of individual differences in intelligence and personality spurs us on to trace out the causes of these differences. The question thus raised is a large scientific problem with important practical bearings. For if it is true, as some believe, that one person's superiority over another due mostly to heredity, then the best hope for the future of mankind lies in improving the breed. If the contrary view is nearer the truth, and the main causes of individual differences lie in the environment, then it is the environment rather than the breed which needs to be improved. Shall the gardener pin his hope on careful cultivation of the soil, or on selection of the best seed? The practical gardener knows perfectly well that both are necessary.

He could never grow a superior crop from inferior seed, no matter how rich the soil, nor from even the best of seed down in poor soil. The development of a plant is clearly a response of the heredity present in the seed to the environmental stimuli of soil, moisture and sunlight. It is equally true of the animal that development depends on both heredity and environment, and that one individual differs from another sometimes because of different heredity, sometimes because of different environment, and usually no doubt from both causes combined. This rather dogmatic statement needs to be scrutinized in the light of the main facts in individual development, and it is not enough if we push our study back to the very birth of the individual, for both heredity and environment have exerted decisive influences during the prenatal period. We need to see the young individual's mental development against the background of early physical development against the background of early physical development as studied by the biological sciences of genetics and embryology.

EXPERIMENTS ON HEREDITY AND ENVIRONMENT

The logic of investigation is clear from what has just been said. To bring out the importance of heredity, take two individuals of different heredity and let them develop in identical environments; if they develop differently the cause must certainly be the difference in heredity. Similarly, in investigating the influence of environment, the experimenter takes individuals of identical heredity and lets them develop under different environmental conditions, so that any difference which results must be attributed to environment. These two types of experiments have been tried many times and in many ways on plants and animals.

Monsters prove the importance of environment in causing individual differences

Is development what its name would seem to imply, a mere "unfolding" of characteristics which are predetermined by heredity? The negative is proved by a second type of experiment, in which an individual of normal heredity is subjected during early development to abnormal environmental conditions. There are obvious difficulties in the way of performing this type of experiment on unborn mammals, but the eggs of birds can be tampered with during incubation, and those of fishes and amphibians as they develop in the water can be heated or chilled or treated with chemicals or electric currents or rays of any kind. The result is frequently the production of a "monster," an individual differing in some striking way from the norm of the species. For example, a collection of young fish embryos, just as the stage when the eyes begin to form, is placed in the icebox for a number of hours, with the result that some of the fish become Cyclopen monsters, having a single centrally located eye.

The difference between these monsters and normal two-eyed fish is due to a difference in environment. Instead of saying that heredity unfolds itself, it would be nearer the truth to say that development consists in the unfolding of heredity by environment. Heredity is like a rocket lying on the shelf, a potential firework, containing within itself some of the conditions for a display, but dependent also upon external conditions. One display may differ from another be cause of a difference in the way the rockets are made or because of a difference in the way they are set off.

Hybrids prove the importance of heredity in individual differences

If a male of one species is mated with a female of a different species, the offspring is known as a hybrid. With the male parent a donkey and the female a horse the hybrid offspring has the same prenatal environment as a normal horse and should therefore be born a horse, if only environment counts. But the new born hybrid turns out to be a mule, differing considerably from a horse. Moreover, though the postnatal environment may be the same for both, the young mule becomes more and more a mule, and the young horse more and more a horse.

The difference between a mule and a horse must therefore be laid to heredity. Half of the mule's chromosomes, in fact, are donkey chromosomes and are responsible for his unhorselike peculiarities. Cross-breeding experiments in great variety have been made by students of genetics, and the wonderful body of knowledge thus achieved from the day of Gregor Mendel, 1866, down and especially during the present century should certainly be examined by anyone who is skeptically inclined towards heredity.

ORIGIN AND EARLY DEVELOPMENT OF THE INDIVIDUAL

About nine months before birth the human individual begins his career, in the from of a one-called organism, the fertilized ovum, which is an ovum from the mother's gonads combined with a spermatozoon from the father. In the favourable environment supplied by the mother, this microscopic individual grows and divides into two cells, into four, into eight, into many, many millions. Along with growth occurs 'differentiation,' which means that the cells derived from the fertilized ovum, the 'daughter cells,' differ among themselves, with the result that the individual develops a great variety of tissues and organs. Amid all this multiplication and differentiation, the parts of the organism remain in union and interaction with each other, and the individual remains an integral whole, a perfect example of unity in multiplicity.

Environmental factors in development

A hen's egg, though fertilized and containing all the

heredity necessary for the development of a chick, remains quiescent necessary for the development of a chick, remains quiescent while in cold storage and develops only when incubated. Environmental conditions must be favourable or the fertilized ovum will not develop at all, and if they are unusual development is apt to take an unusual course. The prime conditions to be met by the environment are protection, warmth, food, oxygen and the elimination of waster products.

It might seem, and indeed has sometimes been asserted, that heredity, however potent in the first stage of development, must become less and less important as the effects of environment accumulate. If all of heredity is present in that microscopic cell, the fertilized ovum, how can it be more than an infinitesimal factor in the individual at a later stage, as at birth, when eight pounds of material from the environment have been incorporated? The answer is that this absorbed material has not simply been added: it has been built into the organism in accordance with the organism's own hereditary characteristics. All the milk absorbed by the infant in his first year does not make him more and more milky, for he changes it chemically into human muscle, bone and brain.

The chromosomes keep pace with the growth of the individual and are just as potent a factor in the later stages of development as at the very beginning.

No native traits, and yet native differences

What we have just said forces us to desist from speaking of native and acquired traits, "native" meaning due to heredity and "acquired" meaning due to environment. Every trait of an individual depends on both heredity and environment. This conclusion certainly seems at first thought to run counter to common sense. If one individual has blue eyes and another brown, is not the difference due to heredity and to heredity alone? If one speaks Swedish and the other Italian, is not this difference due entirely to the differing social environments in which they have grown up? Yes—but nothing we have said forbids us to speak of native differences and acquired differences. Consider the rectangle once more.

While the area of any single rectangle certainly depends on both base and altitude, the difference between two rectangles may lie wholly in one dimension. In the same way, two individuals of the same heredity may differ because of differing environments: and two individuals exposed to identical environments may differ because of differing heredity.

Chromosomes and genes

This bare sketch of embryonic development needs a little more details in order to reveal the effects of heredity and environment. Within the general fluid mass or cytoplasm of any living cell is contained a small nucleus of somewhat denser material; and while the cytoplasm performs the distinctive activity of the cell—the secretion of the gland cell, the contraction of the muscle cell, or the rapid conduction of the nerve cell—it is the nucleus that takes the lead in the processes of growth. In cell division the first thing that happens is a division of the nucleus.

The chromosomes rod-like bodies which make up the nucleus, deploy in regular order and split, each forming two daughter chromosomes one for each of the daughter cell. This splitting of the chromosomes occurs in every successive cell division, and thus the chromosomes of the fertilized ovum are reproduced in every cell of the developed organism. Every cell of the same individual possesses identical chromosomes. Now the chromosomes are-the carriers of heredity. Half of them were brought into the fertilized ovum by the spermatozoon and the other half were present in the ovum itself prior to fertilization. From these facts we can draw two highly important inferences: (1) the individual's heredity is derived in equal measure from the maternal and paternal sides: and (b) the individual's complete heredity is present in every cell of his body. The chromosomes are not ultimate units: each one is conceived to be an aggregation of numerous parts called "genes."

The genes are too small to be seen with the microscope, but the location of single genes within the chromosomes has been discovered by indirect means. Each gene carries a unit factor of heredity. The whole heredity of the individual consists of many unit factors corresponding to as many genes. That is to say, unit factors of heredity have been located in definite parts of certain chromosomes. The gene is of course a theoretical concept, like the molecule or atom or electron, with the same sort of scientific justification.

Development is the product, not the sum, of heredity and environment

The relation of heredity and environment is not like addition but more like multiplication. The individual does not = heredity + environment, but = heredity × environment. Let heredity be represented by the base of a rectangle, and environment by its altitude. Then development, or the developed individual, is represented by the area of the rectangle, the product of base and altitude. We cannot say that the area depends more on the base or more on the altitude; for if either should drop out there would be no area left. In the same way it is absurd to think of either heredity or environment as being more important than the other in the process of development. The conclusion that all development depends on both heredity and environment is of importance in psychology, since what holds good of development holds good of the developed structures and of the activities of those structures.

HOW UNIFORMITY OF BEHAVIOUR IS PRODUCED

In spite of all the differences which we have been discussing, is it not true that people are, after all, very much alike both in structure and in behaviour? They breathe alike, they pass through the same stages of growth, and within the same social group they talk and conduct themselves in much the same manner. Now if differences are due to either heredity or environment, to what are uniformities due? We easily fall into the error of attributing certain uniformities to heredity and others to environment. Uniformity in breathing is said to be handed down by heredity, and uniformity in language by tradition.

Biological uniformities are said to be transmitted by the chromosomes, and cultural uniformities by the social environment. But this way of thinking runs counter to our previous decision that all behaviour depends on both heredity and environment. Let us go back once more to our rectangle. Two or more rectangles cannot have the same area just because they are alike in one dimension; they must be alike in both, or else differences in one dimension must be compensated by reverse differences in the other. By the same logic, if two identical twins develop alike, they must have been exposed to practically equal environments.

Uniformity in development or behaviour means, not that either heredity or environment has been uniform for all the like individuals, but that both heredity and environment have been uniform, or else that the difference in heredity has been balanced by a reverse difference in environment. This is sound logic, but the conclusion does not appear entirely convincing. It would seem that individuals of differing heredity become more and more alike when kept together in the same environment. They speak the same language, no matter what language was spoken by their parents.

The reason is obvious: it is well within the native capacity of the average child to pick up the rudiments of any human language. The heredity of all normal individuals can be regarded as the same, so far as simple speech is concerned. Therefore, having sufficiently uniform heredity, they develop alike with respect to the rudiments of a language when exposed to the same environment. Our logic is not overthrown. A similar example is afforded by the use of the bow and arrow in nearly all tribes and peoples, the world over, prior to the introduction of firearms. This is called an instance of social transmission, but it depends also on uniform heredity to the extent of capacity for using the bow and arrow. None but human beings have the hereditary capacity for this mode of behaviour, and even the chimpanzees have not picked it up from their human neighbours.

SEX DIFFERENCES

Sex itself is determined by heredity. Of the 48 chromosomes of the human fertilized ovum, there is one which determines the sex of the individual. It occurs in two alternative forms, one giving male gonads, the other female gonads. Whatever differences between the sexes are dependent on the gonadal hormones are thus to be called hereditary sex differences. In addition, the sex chromosome contains other genes besides those which determine sex itself and these genes are sex-linked factors in the development of the individual, i.e., they are hereditary factors which differ from one sex to the other. We know little about them in the human species, but would expect them to amount to not over 1/48 of all hereditary factors.

These sex-linked genes, plus the gonadal hormones, are responsible for the familiar sex differences in the plumage of birds and in the size and build of men and women. Probably due to heredity is the well-known difference between men and women in muscular strength. Man surpasses not so much in endurance as in intensity of muscular action. He can squeeze harder and punch harder and run faster. This sex difference is not due simply to occupation, since it appears even in those tribes where the women do much of the hard labour. Men's muscles are somehow capable of using fuel and oxygen more rapidly, and their red blood corpuscles, which carry the oxygen from the lungs to the muscles, are ten percent more abundant those of women. Another sex difference comes to light in the earlier and more rapid maturing of girls.

They reach sex maturity and adult stature a couple of years younger than boys, and it is probable, though not proved as yet, that they reach mental maturity earlier. You have then a difference in size and in muscular strength favouring men and a difference in early maturity favouring women. Add to these the obvious difference in reproductive functions and you have perhaps listed all the important sex differences which are strictly hereditary. These few biological differences are responsible indirectly for considerable divergence between the occupations and achievements of men and women.

When we find among primitive tribes that man is the hunter and woman the gardener, we are inclined at first to say that it is just a matter of tradition; but we soon see that this division of labour is much more economical biologically than the reverse. If this case is typical, the behaviour differences which exist between men and women are neither forced by heredity nor due simply to tradition; for while the individual id following tradition, tradition is following lines of least biological resistance.

It is important to remember that sex differences in behaviour or achievement are differences between the male and the female averages, and that the distributions overlap. Even in stature, though men average two or three inches taller, many individual women are taller than the male average. The same overlap is found in muscular strength and is still greater in the more intellectual performances. Usually the sex difference in any performance in small in comparison with the range of variation within either sex.

Sex differences in test results

In intelligence tests of the Binet type, girls, show a slight superiority over boys of the same age, while in performance tests the slight advantage in with the boys. On the whole the sexes are practically equal in tested intelligence. Memory tests give the advantage to the girls. Their learning of either connected or disconnected material is more rapid than that of boys. Girls surpass in various language tests, such as naming all the words possible in three minutes, or saying the opposites of a given list of words. Girls seem indeed to have a definite advantage in all sorts of language activity. As babies they begin to talk a month earlier than boys, they pick up a vocabulary more rapidly, and they use longer sentences in the early years. In school they surpass the boys in language work. Boys surpass in the tests that have been prepared to measure general information; and in school they carry away more information from geography, history and the sciences. Boys surpass in most of the motor tests, though decided not in handwriting.

Their superiority in managing mechanical contrivances is as marked as that of the girls in language. Can we accept these as native sex differences? There is really no good evidence on the question. We can argue that boys simply have more experience with tools and mechanical toys, but the answer is that they certainly seem to have more spontaneous interest in such things. But possibly this difference in interest in merely the result of adult steering—possibly, not probably. We might expect to find greater differences between the sexes in personality than in intelligence, but so far as tests have gone there is not much that is definite to say. Would you expect men to be more inclined to introversion than women, or the reverse?

The best indications are that the sexes do not differ in this respect. On the whole the sexes are much more on a par mentally than our ancestors would have believed. Biology gives us no reason to expect large differences, tests do not reveal any. But we have to leave unanswered one specially intriguing question: why are the great geniuses and producers, and the great criminals and scoundrels, still predominantly men in spite of the increased freedom of women during the past hundred years? One theory is that the male sex is inherently more variable and so presents the more extreme deviations from the average, both upwards and downwards. Another possibility is that men have more energy because of their more abundant red blood corpuscles. Both theories are speculative at the present time.

HOW DIFFERENCES IN INTELLIGENCE ARE CAUSED

The human species presents a difficult field for the student of heredity and environment. The interval from one generation to the next is so long that investigation has to advance very slowly. Breeding cannot be controlled by the investigator who is therefore forced to deal with individuals of undefined heredity, and environment can be controlled only to a slight extent for scientific purposes. The logic of investigation remains the same as in the hybrid and monster experiments, but the difficulty is to find individuals of identical heredity or individual exposed to identical environments.

Identical twins are the only exception

It sometimes happens that two individuals come from a single fertilized ovum, by a splitting of the embryo at a very early stage of development. Theses two individuals therefore have identical chromosomes, identical heredity. At birth such individuals usually resemble each other so closely as to be scarcely distinguishable and this resemblance persists. It extends to such details as the finger prints. These are identical, or unioval twins. "Fraternal twins" occur when two separate ova are fertilized at practically the same time. Coming from different fertilized ova, with different chromosomes, fraternal twins are simply siblings, with no more in common, so far as heredity is concerned, than can be expected from two children of the same parents. Fraternal twins are as often of different sexes as of the same, while identicals are always of the same sex. Even when of the same sex, fraternal twins often differ considerably in appearance and constitution. Now the question is whether identical twins are more alike mentally than fraternals or than siblings. One convenient way of handling test data to obtain an answer to such a question is by use of the correlation coefficient.

The higher the correlation the closer the resemblance. Much work on anatomical measurements of siblings has indicated a normal correlation of approximately .50. In intelligence tests it is probably a little closer, though not above 60. Such moderate values of the correlation coefficient mean that siblings differ considerably. Between fraternals a little higher correlations are found than between siblings. Since fraternal twins are presumably no more alike in heredity than siblings, the higher correlations found suggest that the sum total of effective environmental influences, prenatal and postnatal combined, differs less between fraternal twins than it does between siblings born at different times.

When we come to the identicals, we find correlations

that are much closer than between fraternals or siblings. To explain this result in terms of environment we should assume that the environment is much more alike for two identicals than it is for two fraternals. This assumption appears rather strained, and the explanation in terms of heredity is simpler, since we already know the hereditary difference between fraternals or siblings to be much greater than between identicals. Another method of handling the data is simply to find the difference in IQ between the members of each pair of twins and so to obtain the average IQ difference between identicals, between fraternals, and so on.

The difference between identical twins is no greater than between repeated tests of the same individual. If the reader is predisposed to stress heredity, he will notice that the results obtained conform very well with the known differences in heredity. An environmentalist finds comfort in the very same table of results, for he points out that fraternals are certainly more alike in environment than other siblings, and possible less alike in environment than identicals. We could never reach a unanimous verdict on the strength of the evidence so far presented.

The differing environment of siblings

Environment covers a multitude of factors capable of affecting the individual's development. Food supply, poisons, infectious diseases may act either before or after birth. School and community are important, and the home deserves special emphasis. That the home is not the same for two brothers is clear from the fact that one has an older, the other a younger brother, a difference which may be quite important. One child may be mother's pet and the other father's; and this difference in companionship may amount to something in intellectual stimulation. Besides, it can fairly be said that each individual creates his own environment, in large measure, and that if two siblings differ by heredity they are sure to differ correspondingly in environment. They pick out different toys, companions, reading matter, even radio programs, and thus to be treated differently, for it is practically impossible to treat two individuals alike if they are unlike in intelligence or personality.

Evidence from foster children

Foster children deserve attention here because they are usually adopted by superior foster parents, while their own parents are not above average in intelligence or in social status. Foster children seem to be treated in general as well as own children in superior homes, and they turn out encouragingly well. But the scientific question is whether they turn out equally well with own children from superior homes. The best foster children to study are those adopted soon after birth, whose whole childhood is passed in the superior environment of their foster homes. Children who come into the hands of child-placing agencies soon after birth are commonly the children of unmarried mothers, who feel compelled to leg their babies go at the earliest possible moment. Unfortunately for our purpose, little can be learned regarding the intelligence of the own fathers of most of these children. Form their parentage we should expect these foster children to show an average IQ of not far from 100; while own children of their foster parents, or of parents of the same class, have an average IQ of 115. Two large samples of such children, taken into superior foster homes within the first year after birth, have been tested, one sample in Chicago and the other in California.

The IQ of the Chicago sample in later childhood averaged 104, and that of the California sample averaged 107. The difference between 100 and 104—107 would accordingly be ascribed to difference in environment, and the difference between 115 and 104—107 to difference in heredity. The weak point in the argument in our uncertainty regarding the heredity of these children: if it was lower than estimated, environment had a greater effect than appears from the figures; but if it was little higher, there remains no difference to attribute to environment. The only sure difference is that between foster children and own children from equally superior homes, and this difference must apparently be due to heredity.

There are several other ways of utilizing the data from foster children, and some of these ways strongly indicate a real difference due to environment. But none of the indications are entirely conclusive as yet. More definite results can be expected from the continued study of foster children as well as of twins. From all the evidence it is fairly certain that both heredity and environment are real factors in causing individual differences in intelligence. Brain disease or injury—an environmental factor—can certainly lower the individual's intelligence to near zero. Social environmental factors in the home, school and community can raise the individual's level by a moderate amount at least. There is no evidence to indicate that any environmental influences, whether physical or social, can bring the person of low heredity up to average intelligence or personality, or the person of average heredity up to a really superior level.

The differing heredity of siblings

Brothers and sisters—"siblings," as they are called

without distinction of sex—are indeed more alike in heredity and in home environment than children taken at random from the community; but they do not have the same heredity nor the same environment. To justify this statement with respect to heredity, we need one additional biological fact. Every human cell possesses 24 pairs of chromosomes, each pair including one from the individual's father and one from the mother. But the ovum in ripening prior to fertilization extrudes one chromosome from each pair—either one, just at random—and the ripe sperma-tozoon, similarly, contains only one of each pair. In the fertilized ovum the pairs are restored, but the whole combination is new and is practically certain to be different in any two fertilized ova even from the same mother. Therefore siblings do not have identical heredity.

Identical twins reared apart

If we could arrange to have one of a pair of identical twins reared in Russia and the other in France, we could safely predict a difference in language and probably in social and economic ideas. If one were brought up in the city and the other in the country they would certainly differ in their manners and in the kind of knowledge and skill acquired. But could we produce a difference in intelligence in any such way? Of late years attempts have been made to discover pairs of identical twins who have been separated soon after birth and reared indifferent families and communities. Several pairs have been found; more are needed. Here is the history of one pair. Identical twins girls were adopted by different relatives at the age of five months and brought up one in the city and the other on a farm.

The city girl had the more schooling and became a

clerical worker and also a piano teacher. The farm girl became competent in running the farm. Neither married up to the age of 28 when they were tested. The farm girl was found to be an inch taller than the city girl, 28 pounds heavier, more muscular and in better physical condition. She appeared to be more of a leader, more conversational, and fully as competent in general. In the intelligence tests, however, the city girl made the better scores. In educational tests the difference was about the same, while in a non-verbal performance test it was smaller, with the city girl still leading. The rather large difference of about 19 points in IQ must be due to environment, and the question is whether this is a real difference in intelligence.

Were the tests equally fair to city and country?—a question raised before. If we accept the usually obtained differences between city and country children as proof of genuine intellectual differences, then we can say that the country girl in this pair of identical twins was less intellectual than her city twins because of environmental factors. But if we doubt that the tests are fair to city and country, or to different races, social classes, etc., then we must discount the difference found in this pair of identical twins. This particular pair showed a greater difference than has usually been found in identical twins reader apart. Of ten cases so far reported, six show only a trifling difference between the twins, four show rather substantial differences of 12—19 points, and the average for all is 8 points. In several cases it is difficult to judge which twin had better environmental advantages.

If we should expect to find still larger differences in test results, but the question would remain whether we were making a fair comparison. This subject will continue questionable until the old slogans are laid aside and new problems formulated, such as these: What kinds of difference in intellectual performances are produced by differences in environment? What environmental factors are effective in producing intellectual differences? If identical twins reared apart can afford a measure of the environmental factor in intellectual differences, where shall we look for comparable evidence on the hereditary factor? We need to locate individuals of unequal heredity growing up in the same or equivalent environments.

8

POPULATION POLICY

Population policies are deliberately constructed or modified institutional arrangements and/or specific programs through which governments influence, directly or indirectly, demographic change. For any given country, the aim of population policy may be narrowly construed as bringing about quantitative changes in the membership of the territorially circumscribed population under the government's jurisdiction. Governments' concern with population matters can also extend beyond the borders of their own jurisdictions. Thus, international aspects of population policy have become increasingly salient in the contemporary world. Additions to the population are primarily the result of individual decisions concerning childbearing. Within the constraints of their social milieu, these decisions reflect an implicit calculus by parents about the private costs and benefits of children. But neither costs nor benefits of fertility are likely to be fully internal to the family: they can also impose burdens and advantages on others in the society. Such externalities, negative and positive, represent a legitimate concern for all those affected. The present study briefly discusses how individual and collective interests were reconciled in traditional societies, summarizes the population policy approaches adopted by the classic liberal state, and sketches government responses to the low-fertility demographic regime that emerged in the West between the two World Wars. In greater detail it considers international population policies after World War II and contemporary population policy responses to below-replacement fertility.

Population policy may be defined as deliberately constructed or modified institutional arrangements and/or specific programs through which governments influence, directly or indirectly, demographic change. The generality of the definition lends itself to varying interpretations. For any given country, the aim of population policy may be narrowly construed as bringing about quantitative changes in the membership of the territorially circumscribed population under the government's jurisdiction. Additions to membership are effected only through births and immigration, losses are caused by emigration and by deaths. Concern with this last component is usually seen as a matter for health policy, leaving fertility and migration as the key objects of governmental interest in population policy.

More broadly, policy intent may also aim at modification of qualitative aspects of these phenomena—fertility and international migration—including the composition of the population by various demographic characteristics and the population's spatial distribution. Furthermore, governments' concern with population matters can also extend beyond the borders of their own jurisdictions. International aspects of population policy have become increasingly salient in the contemporary world.

POPULATION CONTROL IN TRADITIONAL SOCIETIES

Rulers of any political unit have a stake in the size and composition of the population over which they have authority, hence an incentive to try to influence demographic change in a desired direction. Thus "population policy" may be said to have a long history, starting at least with the empires of the ancient world. Greater numbers tended to connote greater wealth and power, at least for those at the apex of the social pyramid. Measures encouraging marriage and sometimes immigration testify to the prevailing populationist sentiment among rulers throughout history. But the leverage of the weak pre-modern state over fertility in traditional societies was necessarily limited. The dominant influence setting the patterns of reproduction was located, instead, in a deeper layer of social interaction. Births, the key element affecting population change, are produced by individual couples—seemingly an intensely private affair yet one in which the immediate kin group and the surrounding local society in which that group is embedded have a material stake. All societies, if at varying degrees, grant a measure of self-sovereignty to their members. An individual has certain rights over his or her direction in life. But this is always subject to some constraints, not only biological but also social. Well before rights and obligations are formally codified in legal terms, they are established through spontaneous social interaction—a self-organizing process. Restrictions on freedom to act take the form of social expectations and pressures that individuals can ignore only at considerable personal costs to themselves.

Typically, there is a strong expectation that men and women should marry and have children. Parental and kin obligations in the matter of bringing up children are well understood by all adults and informally enforced by the community. In most societies there is the expectation that children are to be born to married couples only; that a man can have one wife at a time;

that a husband is obligated to support his wife and a father his children; and that he can expect reciprocal services from them. And informal rules shaped by community interest tend effectively to regulate the entry of foreigners. The fabric of such demographically relevant behavioural stances, supported by internalized personal norms and buttressed by religious injunctions, is a product of social evolution; how effective such institutions are becomes an important determinant of societal success. As a classic statement of the British demographer Alexander Carr-Saunders (1922: 223) put it, persons and groups of persons are naturally selected on account of the customs they practise, just as they are selected on account of their mental and physical characters. Those groups practising the most advantageous customs will have an advantage in the constant struggle between adjacent groups over those that practise less advantageous customs.

Few customs can be more advantageous than those which limit the number of a group to the desirable number....[In the traditional society] there would grow up an idea that it was the right thing to bring up a certain limited number of children, and the limitation of the family would be enforced by convention. Given the harsh biological and economic constraints pre-modern societies invariably experienced, that "desirable number" presupposed fairly high fertility: high enough to provide a sufficient margin of safety over mortality. Successful societies—societies that survived to the dawn of the modern era—thus obeyed the biblical injunction to be fruitful and multiply, even though such multiplication as a matter of historical record was necessarily very slow. But traditional demographic regimes resulting from spontaneous social interaction achieved modest growth rates at varying levels of fertility and mortality. Early modern Western Europe succeeded in maintaining a relatively low average level of mortality by means of keeping birth rates low, primarily by means of a fairly high average age of marriage and substantial proportions that remained permanently single. A contrasting pattern, such as in India, combined early and universal marriage and a consequent high level of fertility with slow population growth by virtue of death rates that were also high, approximating the level of the birth rate. With respect to the rate of population growth, these different combinations of birth and death rates in traditional societies were very similar. The potential for rapid population growth that might be triggered by a fall of mortality was, however, much higher when the pre-modern equilibrium was the result of a combination of high mortality and high fertility.

RATIONALE FOR POPULATION POLICY

Modernity—the rise of democratic state formations reflecting the public interest and the emergence of rapid economic development—brought about the realistic promise of realizing age-old human aspirations for a better life. The state increasingly came to be seen as an institution created by the voluntary association of free individuals to further their interests. The central function of the state was to produce public goods—goods that individuals cannot secure for themselves. The US Constitution, promulgated in 1789, articulated key items in the collective interest concisely and with universal validity. The aim of the Union formed by the People was, in the words of the Constitution's Preamble, to "establish Justice, insure domestic Tranquillity, provide for the common defence, promote the general Welfare, and secure the Blessings of Liberty to ourselves and our Posterity." In pursuing such goals, regulation of immigration into a state's territory is clearly defined as a public good, thus delineating a particular role for population policy. And aggregate fertility may also be construed as a public good, if its level as determined by spontaneous social interaction is too high or too low in terms of the collective interest.

The potential role of the state in regulating immigration is straightforward: individuals wishing to restrict or promote it cannot set up their own border patrols or issue entry visas. Individual preferences in the matter, however, are likely to differ. It is the task of the government to weigh and reconcile conflicting individual desires and come up with a policy deemed the best under the accepted rules of the political process. To claim a role for the state in the matter of fertility is more problematic. Additions to the population are the result of a multitude of individual decisions concerning childbearing. Within the constraints of their social milieu, these decisions reflect an implicit calculus by parents about the private costs and benefits of children to them. But neither costs nor benefits of fertility are likely to be fully internal to the family: they can also impose burdens and advantages on others in the society. Such externalities, negative and positive, represent a legitimate concern for all those affected. An individual's influence on the fertility of other families, however, is very limited: there are no private markets offering preferred patterns of aggregate demographic processes to individual buyers. Remedying such market failure may then be attempted through intervention by the state so as to affect individual behaviour in order to best serve the common good—the good of all individuals.

The earliest clear formulation of the population

problem as a problem of coordination among individual preferences, hence establishment of the rationale for potential state intervention in the matter of fertility, was given by William Foster Lloyd, an Oxford mathematician and economist, in an essay published in 1833. In the spirit of the Malthusian concerns of his time, Lloyd (1833/1968: 22–23) envisaged the possibility of overpopulation even under conditions when all families have only the children they actually want and suggested the direction in which remedy ought to be sought:

The simple fact of a country being overly populous...is not, of itself, sufficient evidence that the fault lies in the people themselves, or a proof of the absence of a prudential disposition. The fault may rest, not with them as individuals, but with the constitution of society, of which they form part. Population policy should therefore strive toward institutions and incentive systems—a constitution of society—that provide signals to individuals guiding them to behave in harmony with the collective interest.

POPULATION POLICY IN THE LIBERAL STATE

Technological progress and consequent improvements in the standard of living in modernizing societies result in a far more effective control of mortality than was possible in the traditional society. But the fall of the death rate accelerates the rate of population growth, which, in turn, could strain the capacity of the economic system to accommodate the increased population numbers. Falling living standards then would once again increase death rates, reestablishing an approximate balance between births and deaths at a low standard of living. This was the pessimistic central vision of T. R. Malthus's 1798 Essay. But this outcome, although held to be highly probable, was, according to Malthus, avoidable. Given sound public policies, there was an alternative to subsistence- level equilibrium, both agreeable and achievable.

A salient element in the 1798 Essay, and in subsequent writings influenced by it, was disapproval of the schemes for poor relief prevailing in Britain and elsewhere in Europe—on the grounds that they were likely to encourage irresponsible reproduction. Efforts of the paternalistic state to reduce poverty were held to be misguided; by stimulating fertility, hence population growth, such efforts would generate only more misery. Malthusians argued that the state's correct stance in demographic matters, as in the economy at large, was laissez faire. This would foster the prudential habits among the general population similar to those that already existed among the propertied classes. It would do so by assuring that the costs of childbearing were not shared by society at large but were primarily borne by the individual couples having children.

Heeding such a prescription did not imply that the state was to play a passive role in demographic matters. Malthus's own writings, most clearly his 1820 tract Principles of Political Economy (1989: 250–251), spell out a broad agenda which expresses the philosophy that came to be dominant in the liberal states of the West in the nineteenth century. Material improvements, such as higher wages for labour, could indeed be defeated if they would be "chiefly spent in the maintenance of large and frequent families." But Malthus also envisaged a different, happier possible outcome: "a decided improvement in the modes of subsistence, and the conveniences and comforts enjoyed, without a proportionate acceleration of the rate of [population] increase." The possibility of such diametrically different responses to the stimulus of higher wages suggests a large element of indeterminacy in fertility behaviour. To Malthus, the causes of these divergent responses were to be found in the circumstances, social and political, in which people lived—in particular, whether those circumstances hindered or rewarded planning for the future. From his analysis he derived a prescription for a population policy that would yield the hoped-for demographic outcome:

Of all the causes which tend to generate prudential habits among the lower classes of society, the most essential is unquestionably civil liberty. No people can be much accustomed to form plans for the future, who do not feel assured that their industrious exertions, while fair and honourable, will be allowed to have free scope; and that the property which they either posses, or may acquire, will be secured to them by a known code of just laws impartially administered. But it has been found by experience, that civil liberty cannot be secured without political liberty. Consequently, political liberty becomes almost equally essential. During the long nineteenth century—which may be thought of as stretching to the outbreak of the First World War—the politics in Europe and in its overseas offshoots favoured, even if imperfectly, the development of institutional and legal frameworks in harmony with such principles. This, in interaction with economic and cultural changes shaped by the industrial revolution, created a milieu that fostered the prudential habits of parents, rendering the micro-level calculus of the costs and benefits of children increasingly salient. Rising demand for labour, including greater use of child labour, and rising income levels tended to sustain high fertility or even to stimulate it.

But rising material expectations, broadening opportunities for social mobility, and the patterns and circumstances of urban living pulled in the opposite direction. This was powerfully reinforced by some programmatic activities that were consistent with the limited role the liberal state claimed in managing the economy. These included public health programs and projects aimed at improving basic infrastructure for transport and communication. And most importantly, the state, or local government, assumed a key role in fostering, organizing, and financing public education. At basic levels school attendance was made mandatory and enforced and, in parallel, labour laws curtailed the employment of children.

Reflecting long-standing cultural values and religious injunctions, and contrary to laissez-faire principles, the liberal state generally banned the spreading of contraceptive information and the sale of contraceptive devices and made abortion illegal. Such restrictions typically remained in effect well into the twentieth century. But by all evidence, any upward pressure on fertility from these restrictions was swamped by the downward pressure on parental demand for children resulting from the state policies and programs just mentioned. By the last quarter of the nineteenth century birth rates were falling rapidly in the countries of the West. In many cases, rates of population growth fell also, despite continuing improvements in mortality. In Europe this trend was facilitated by emigration, which both sending and receiving countries—notably the United States, Canada, and Australia—either positively encouraged or at least permitted. The stance of the liberal state on population policy thus brought about the prospect of a new demographic equilibrium in the West that could be consistent with continuing material progress: achievement of a stationary population at low levels of fertility and mortality and allowing freedom of movement internationally.

POPULATION POLICY BETWEEN THE WORLD WARS

The massive losses of life resulting from World War I and from the influenza pandemic in its immediate aftermath, and the sharp drop in the number of births during the war years, were temporary disruptions in the steadily declining trends of fertility and mortality characterizing the prewar decades in the West. Those trends soon made it evident that there is no built-in guarantee that the sum total of individual fertility decisions will eventually settle at a point at which, in the aggregate, the rate of population growth will be exactly zero or fluctuate tightly around a zero rate. Although, owing to relatively youthful age distributions, the rate of natural increase remained positive, by the late 1920s demographers realized that fertility rates in several Western countries had fallen to such a low level that, in the longer term, natural increase would become negative. This trend became more accentuated and more general under the impact of the Great Depression. Some observers foresaw a "twilight of parenthood." Just as excessive reproduction called for corrective public policies, there were calls for corrective action achieving the opposite result: enhancing fertility so as to assure at least the simple maintenance of the population. In some countries the ban on contraceptives was tightened and the penalties on abortion were increased. These measures had little effect. Neither did, predictably, governmental exhortation appealing to families to have more children. The most promising avenue for population policy seemed to be to use the instruments available to the state for redistributing income so as to reward demographic behaviour considered socially desirable (and to discourage contrary behaviour). By the 1930s such pronatalist policies came to be fairly widely if rather tight-fistedly applied in a number of countries. Among Europe's emerging democratic welfare states, Sweden and France were pioneers in providing financial rewards and services in kind to families with children, especially to larger families. (Sweden, however, also allowed liberal access to contraception.) Similar policies were applied with equal or greater vigour in fascist Italy and Nazi Germany.

Invariably, the proponents of such policies claimed some results in terms of birth rates somewhat higher than would have been expected in their absence. But the latter quantity is a hypothetical one, which introduces a necessary caution to such claims. More pertinently, when average fertility is low, the birth rate in any given year is an unreliable measure of long-run fertility. Couples have considerable latitude to time the birth of their children earlier or later, without affecting the number of children they ultimately wish to have. Logically, pronatalist policies seek to affect that lifetime total rather than aiming at temporary increases in the birth rate.

INTERNATIONAL POPULATION POLICY AFTER WORLD WAR II

In the countries that the United Nations categorizes as less developed, population policy issues attracted little attention until the middle of the twentieth century. Fertility remained high, more or less at its pre-modern level. Population growth was slowly increasing, however, as a result of improvements in mortality. Following the end of World War II, mortality decline accelerated greatly and as a result so did population growth. In 1950, the world population was 2.5 billion. Some 1.7 billion of that total was in countries classified as less developed, with an average annual birth rate of 44 per 1000 population —twice as high as in the more developed group. Unless a decline of the birth rate got underway fairly rapidly, an unprecedentedly large expansion of human numbers was inevitable.

Although the trigger of such population growth was a welcome development—falling death rates—growth rates that would double or even treble a population within a generation seemed a major obstacle to development. And the large and widening differential between the more developed and the less developed countries in terms of population size and average income levels was seen as holding out the prospect of major dislocations and long-term instabilities within the international system. As a result, in the 1950s an intense debate started on what policies could reduce fertility in the less developed world. This policy debate was primarily Western, much of it American, just as the diagnosis of the problem itself had been. The proposals that emerged were to be applied in countries representing a large and growing share of the global population. Population policy became international.

The West of course already had relatively low fertility, and with it much historical experience on why birth rates fell. Social science analysis was virtually unanimous in interpreting this experience. The explanation centred on the role of changing structural conditions of the economy, conditions to which micro-level units of the population tended to respond, in demographic as well as in other matters. Demand for smaller families was seen as the primary force determining birth rates; the means by which couples regulated their fertility was not unimportant, but seen as a distinctly secondary factor. If the demand was strong enough, fertility would be low, even if birth control technology was primitive. A transition to low fertility presupposed changing preferences, and such preferences were responses to market signals. If policy was to have an explicit role, it would be through reinforcing those signals. In the experience of past fertility transitions, four components of the incentive structure seemed especially pertinent: (1) the direct costs parents must incur in bringing up children; (2) the opportunity costs of children to parents, that is, the earnings a couple must forgo because of children; (3) the contribution of children to family income through labour services; and (4) the contributions of children to parents' economic security in old age, in comparison to alternative sources of security.

Fertility declines when shifts in these components make family limitation advantageous to couples, overcoming cultural resistance supporting traditional behaviour. Patterns of development generate that effect when at least some, but especially when all of the following conditions are fulfilled: (1) social expectations and formal institutional arrangements place on parents the major financial responsibility for raising their own children, including much of the cost of education and health care; (2) women have access to income-earning opportunities in the labour market, including jobs not easily compatible with childbearing and child-rearing; (3) social institutions make formal education (primary and early secondary) compulsory and effectively enforce school attendance; (4) child labour is made illegal; (5) effective legal guarantees of property rights, legal enforcement of private contracts, and the development of public and private insurance and pension schemes provide attractive and comparatively secure alternatives to children as a source of old-age security.

Social and institutional conditions that make such changes potent generators of fertility decline include the following: (1) emphasis on personal economic contribution (rather than, for example, class status or political loyalty) as the primary factor determining a person's earnings, thus providing an incentive for increased investment in human capital; (2) systems of promotion that provide opportunities for upward social mobility according to merit and tolerate downward social mobility; (3) openness to outside influences that create rising expectations with respect to material standards of living; and (4) emphasis not only on the rights but also on the social and economic responsibilities of the individual. Some of the factors that prompted the fall of fertility in the West also became potent in the less developed countries as concomitants of successful economic and social progress. International conferences, for example the 1974 Bucharest conference on population, spelled out many of the essential socioeconomic changes necessary for fertility to shift from high to low levels. But assembling the instruments so identified into a coherent development strategy of institutional-structural reforms, reforms justified also by demographic objectives, remained an elusive task. In promoting development governments came to see their roles not in supporting institutions harnessing the market, but replacing the market in key developmental tasks through specific goal-oriented categorical programs. In the matter of population policy, the rapid postwar progress in the technology of birth control provided an appealing apparent short-cut for achieving fertility decline through programmatic means. Markets, it was held, could not be relied on to bring that technology to those wishing to practice birth control. Governments could, instead, organize free delivery of birth control information, and provide effective means for preventing births to all those, primarily (it was assumed) women, who wished to plan their families. Surveys indicated that there existed a substantial latent demand for such services. Satisfied customers, in turn, would serve as role models, bringing new clients to the program.

By the mid-1960s, in programmatic terms the international population policy debate on the relative importance of demand versus supply was essentially decided in favour of the latter. For the next quarter-century, population policy in the developing world became essentially synonymous with family planning programs.

Financial and administrative limitations within developing countries necessitated the heavy involvement of foreign assistance in launching and sustaining family planning programs. Although donor countries' own domestic experience in this area was practically nonexistent, such aid, justified by the seriousness of the "population problem" (a problem whose cause was defined in terms of aggregate indexes of population growth), was readily forthcoming, partly in the form of bilateral assistance and partly through international aid institutions.

The cost of birth control technology was, in itself, relatively modest. But sustaining an effective delivery service did represent significant claims on scarce human and material resources. Declared demand for birth control does not necessarily translate into effective willingness to practice it: conflicting desires may interfere. Weakness of measures of latent demand, or "unmet need," is reflected in the requirements that programs are supposed to satisfy if they are to be successful. These typically included such items as "doorstep accessibility of quality services," "broad choice of contraceptive methods," "forceful IEC [information, education, and communication] programs," "sound financing strategies," "sound management with proper logistics," "evaluation systems," "a continuous process of strategic thinking, planning and management, " and "staff leadership for program parameters".

The effectiveness of family planning programs in reducing fertility remains a matter of controversy. According to international guidelines, programs recruit their clients on a strictly voluntary basis. By accepting the service voluntarily, the individual acceptor demonstrates that she values that service. But some of the more successful programs, notably in Asia, tended to increase acceptance by often heavy-handed methods of persuasion, and , in the especially important case of China, by coercion backed by legal sanctions. Where fertility fell in less developed countries with active family planning programs, it is typically found that program-provided free services account for a large percentage of those practising contraception. This non-surprising result is then often taken as an indicator of success in reducing aggregate fertility. But what would have happened in the absence of the program is conjectural, hence routinely ignored.

Some less developed countries that lacked government programs also experienced major falls of fertility: Brazil is a conspicuous example. Similarly, if programs have seemingly only minor success in reducing fertility, this can be taken as evidence that the program is inadequately financed, organized, and managed: greater efforts would have led to better results.

Family planning programs as they were commonly conceived had a strong resemblance to health programs. But given the special priority accorded to family planning services in foreign assistance, typically they were organized as a separate "vertical" program, or kept administratively distinct within the broad health program. The justification for such treatment was that while acceptors of family planning services are recruited because the program satisfies their individual need, the program also serves a national developmental need by helping to reduce aggregate population growth, hence deserves priority. Once a family planning program is organized, its managerial and professional cadres form a natural advocacy group strongly interested in the program's sustenance. Invoking the public interest in lowered fertility, as distinct from simply serving the needs of the clients of the program, has long served as a key supporting argument in that endeavour.

Over time, this developmental prop has eroded. This was in part a result of criticisms of the intrinsic scientific merit of the argument but most of all a reflection of the extensive decline of fertility that has occurred, a decline often attributed to the success of the family planning programs themselves. On the eve of the 1994 International Conference on Population and

Development, a review, considered highly respectful of the importance of fertility decline for successful development, reached the guarded conclusion that the data on the subject "mostly support the view that rapid population growth in poor countries under conditions of high fertility is inimical to many development goals"—with stress on the qualifying words "mostly," "high fertility," "many development goals," and "rapid," and with the last-mentioned term defined as "in excess of 2 percent annually" (Çassen 1994: 13). By that time, among world regions, only Africa and West Asia had a population growth rate meeting that criterion. Accordingly, the development rationale of family planning programs was gradually dropped and was replaced by the argument that the programs satisfy important health needs and help people exercise a fundamental human right. The Cairo conference formalized this shift: even though the name of the conference for the first time included a reference to development, scant attention was paid to that concept. Family planning programs were redefined, instead, as reproductive health programs, responding to a broader range of women's health needs, such as prevention of unsafe abortions and sexually transmitted diseases, including HIV/AIDS. But beyond this, new emphasis was put on some requirements that would contribute to women's empowerment: reduction of infant and maternal mortality and improvement in girls' education and women's opportunities for employment and political participation. Although the connection was not highlighted, these are conditions that are likely to help reduce the birth rate through stimulating the demand for smaller family size. The Cairo conference, in effect, reverted to some key elements of a demand strategy for reducing birth rates. The future of family planning service programs is thus left in a somewhat tenuous status. Without invoking a collective interest in a wider practice of birth control, it is not clear what level of priority should be accorded to such programs as just one part of publicly financed health programs, or indeed relative to many other social welfare programs that also serve demonstrable human needs. Not surprisingly, there are increasing efforts in national programs to rely on the market in enhancing access to contraceptives and to provide program services on a fee-for-service basis.

POPULATION POLICY IN RESPONSE TO BELOW-REPLACEMENT FERTILITY

During the second half of the twentieth century debates about population policy, and consequent programmatic action, were centred on the issue of rapid population growth in the less developed world. Toward the end of this period, however, a quite different demographic phenomenon has begun to attract increasing attention: aggregate fertility levels that are inadequate for the long-run maintenance of the population. Analytically, the potential population policy issue raised by low fertility is identical to the problem inherent in rapid population growth: it is caused by the disjunction between the sum total of individual reproductive decisions and the collective interest in a long-run demographic equilibrium. But this time individual aspirations generate a deficit rather than an excess in population growth. The syndrome, as was noted above, is not entirely novel: it was detectable in fertility trends in the West, especially in Europe, in the 1920s and 1930s, and in some instances, notably in France, even earlier. But in the decades immediately following World War II, the baby boom seemed to make the issue of low fertility moot. Indeed, by any historical standard, population growth was rapid during the second half of the twentieth century even in the developed world. Europe's population, for example, grew during that period from 550 million to about 730 million.

The baby boom was, however, a temporary interruption of the secular downward trend in fertility. By the 1970s, the net reproduction rate was at or below unity in most countries in Europe and also in the United States. In the US fertility stabilized at or very close to that rate, but in Europe fertility continued to decline. By the beginning of the twenty-first century, the average total fertility rate in Europe was 1.4. Such a level, if maintained indefinitely, would result in a population loss of one-third from generation to generation, that is, roughly, over each period of some 30 years. In some countries, notably in Southern, Central, and Eastern Europe, period fertility rates were at low levels without historical precedent for large populations. If continued, in the absence of large compensatory immigration this would not only lead to rapid population decline but also result in very high proportions of the population at old ages. It might be expected that in the affected countries such prospects would generate not only concern, but also vigorous remedial policy action.

By and large, however, this response has not been evident. Most governments as well as the general public tend to view below-replacement fertility with an equanimity quite unlike the alarmed reaction that the same phenomenon elicited when it first emerged between the two World Wars. And explicit pronatalist policies, common in the 1930s, are conspicuous by their absence. There are a variety of reasons explaining this indifference. First, the preeminent population issue confronting policy-makers in the post-World War II period was rapid global population growth. Programs aimed at moderating fertility in the developing world received assistance or at least encouragement from the rich, low-fertility countries. Although the rationale was modified over time, such assistance and encouragement have continued, as indeed substantial further population increase in the less developed countries is still anticipated in the early decades of the twenty-first century. Even though population issues tend to be sui generis, reflecting differences in demographic behaviour country-by-country, there was, and remains, a perceived dissonance between fertility-lowering assistance to other countries and engaging in action at home serving the opposite aims. Faulty logic notwithstanding, the international terrain has not been favourable for domestic pronatalism. Second, the natural rate of increase—the difference between the number of births and the number of deaths—is still positive in many of the countries with fertility well below replacement. This is the result of age distributions—reflecting past fertility and mortality and notably the effects of the postwar baby boom—that still favour population growth. While this momentum effect is temporary, the longer-term implications for population decline and population aging are only dimly perceived by the general public and provide an excuse for inaction on the part of policy-makers.

Third, when those longer-term demographic effects are understood, a calmer attitude still prevails. There is an inclination, reinforced by increasing concern with the quality of the natural environment, to regard a degree of demographic "decompression" as a not necessarily unwelcome prospect, especially in countries with an already dense population. And it is assumed that the economic and social disadvantages that might be imposed by a declining population can be effectively dealt with through institutional adjustments and social policy measures other than measures aiming for a higher birth rate. A demographic policy often regarded as potentially helpful in this regard is encouragement of immigration. That willing immigrants are available to compensate for low birth rates is taken for granted—a realistic assumption in high-income countries.

Fourth, there is a vague expectation that the population decline, impending or already begun, will in due course trigger corrective homeostatic mechanisms, leading to a spontaneous rebound in the level of fertility. Another baby boom may not be in the offing, but fertility may rise sufficiently to once again reach or at least approximate replacement level. Governments, it is assumed, would be ill-advised to interfere with this natural process by trying to increase birth rates and then seeking to fine-tune them at the desirable steady-state level. According to this view, a laisser-faire fertility policy is justified since, apart from broad upper and lower limits, governments are not competent to determine what constitutes an optimal fertility rate, or growth rate, or population size in any given year, decade, or even longer time interval.

Finally, even if the will were there, there is a paucity of effective pronatalist policy instruments. Exhortation from governments is not promising, and in any case unlikely to be tried in a democratic polity. Restrictions imposed on access to modern contraceptive technology are not politically acceptable; they would be also certain to prove a failure. This leaves the traditional levers of social policy: dispensing material incentives and disincentives so as to increase the willingness of couples to have children. Such incentives can be engineered by the government through fiscal measures, such as differential taxation, and/or through provision of services in kind. This approach was tried in the interwar years, but, as noted above, with at best limited success. After World War II many similar measures continued to be applied; in fact, with the steadily expanding welfare state, they were often upgraded and their scope, too, was extended.

However, they were no longer considered "pronatalist" but were absorbed within the more encompassing frames of family and general welfare policy. The new label partly reflected a political-ideological preference, but in part also the fact that some distinctive features of pronatalism—such as differential rewards that favoured large families, and non-means-tested or even regressive allocation of family and child benefits—were generally no longer acceptable.

Although the redistributive policies of the contemporary welfare state are biased in favour of the elderly and the poor, government-organized transfers to parents of children, or to children directly (such as through publicly financed day-care services and free or subsidized education often beyond the secondary school level, which lessen the cost of children to parents), are substantial in all low-fertility countries. Indeed, it is typically assumed that existing family and welfare policies sustain fertility above a level that would ensue in their absence. Accordingly, making these policies more generous—socializing an even larger share of child costs—is often seen as a means toward increasing fertility, whether as an outright policy objective or, more in the prevailing spirit of the time, as an unintended but welcome by-product. Such extension, however, is difficult, given the fiscal constraints of already over-committed welfare states. And more to the point, the net effect of family friendly redistribution of incomes and provision of services is uncertain. It is notable that in the US, where such schemes are distinctly less well funded than, for example, in Western Europe, fertility is, nevertheless, relatively high.

In recent decades, in modern industrial economies, participation of women in the formal labour force expanded rapidly. This tendency, reflecting market forces but also encouraged by government policy (partly as an antidote for deteriorating dependency ratios as the population becomes older), is likely to continue. Among the factors explaining the low level of fertility despite general material affluence, many observers point to the double burden on women of both raising children and working outside the home. To the extent that higher birth rates are seen to be socially desirable, the derived policy prescription is to adopt measures that make motherhood and women's labour force participation more compatible. The higher fertility in countries (notably in Scandinavia) where such measures are strongly applied, compared to countries (especially those in Southern Europe) where they are largely absent, suggests that enhanced compatibility (through day-care services, flexible work-hours, liberal sick-leave allowances, and the like) is an effective pronatalist policy even if motivated by other considerations. But it is far from clear whether the fertility differential so generated is high enough to bring the total fertility rate back to replacement level. Steady labour force participation of women during the childbearing years can certainly be made compatible with having one child or even two. It is likely to be far less compatible with sustaining, or even increasing, the proportion of women who have more than two children. Many career-oriented women voluntarily remain childless; many others prefer a single child. It follows that, to achieve average replacement-level fertility, the proportions of such women need to be counterbalanced by high enough proportions of women who have chosen third-, fourth-, or even higher-order births. There is little indication at present that policies directed at enhanced compatibility achieve that result.

When fertility is high, as it still is in most developing countries, it is a safe prediction that with economic development it will eventually decline, at least to replacement level. Since population growth cannot be sustained indefinitely, in the longer term, apart from out-migration, the only alternative is higher mortality. The record of the high-income countries indicates, however, that replacement-level fertility is not a necessary resting point. Once fertility is lower than that, predictions become highly hazardous.

European and also East Asian experience suggests that fertility has a tendency to settle below an average of two children per woman, hence a tendency toward sustained population decline. The question, to which no good answers exist at the dawn of the twenty-first century, is "how far below?" "Scandinavian"-style family policies may stabilize fertility only modestly below replacement—such as around a total fertility rate of 1.8. That would imply a fairly moderate relative shortfall of births compared to deaths, and population stability in rich countries with such vital rates could be fully or nearly compensated with a modest level of controlled immigration. Population aging would be then kept within relatively narrow limits, which post-industrial economies could readily adjust to. The demographic weight of such countries within the global total in the foreseeable future would continue to shrink, raising possible problems of a shifting geopolitical balance. Still, such demographic configurations would be likely to push the day of demographic reckoning beyond the policy horizons that governments feel an obligation to be actively concerned with. Pronatalist interventions would find at best a marginal place on governments' policy agendas.

On the other hand, fertility levels in the lowest-fertility countries—countries with a total fertility rate of 1.3 or below around the turn of the century—might stabilize at that level, or even shrink further, reflecting the decentralized and uncoordinated decisions of individuals and individual couples. Such an outcome might also foreshadow future reproductive behaviour in countries in which fertility is still fairly close to replacement level. This would create a qualitatively different demographic situation for which there are few precedents in modern history. It would represent a clear threat to the continuing viability of the countries affected. Compensatory immigration flows would have to be so large as to be inconsistent with any reasonable degree of cultural and ethnic continuity. Alternatively, population aging in the absence of immigration would create virtually unsolvable challenges, and there would be a likely drastic loss of relative geopolitical status. Spontaneous homeostatic mechanisms may not come into play to save the day, or may do so too sluggishly to matter. A radical rethinking of fertility policy would then become a necessity for social—and national—survival.

HEALTH AND POPULATION

POLICY INITIATIVES

Over the last fifteen years India has witnessed a sharp decline in the state's commitment to public health. Thus today our country has the fifth lowest public health expenditure in the world. As the National Health Policy admitted, this is, at 0.9 per cent of the GDP, lower than the average in even Sub Saharan Africa. Along with decreasing state spending on health, increasingly policy measures have encouraged the growth of the private sector in health care so that today we have the largest and least regulated private health care industry in the world. Evidence from across the country indicates that access to health care has declined sharply over this period. The policy of levying of user fees has impacted negatively upon access to public health facilities, especially for poor and marginalised communities and to women. As health care costs have increased sharply, it is not surprising that medical expenditure is emerging as one of the leading causes of indebtedness. At the same time, this has been accompanied by policies that have reduced access of the poor to public distribution systems of food so that per capita availability of food has shown an alarming decrease.

It is thus not surprising that in addition to starvation deaths, the huge load of preventable and communicable diseases remains substantially unchanged. Infant and child mortality take an unconscionable toll of the lives of 22 lakh children every year. We are yet to achieve the National Health Policy 1983 target to reduce the Infant Mortality Rate to less than 60 per 1000 live births. More serious is the fact that the rate of decline in the Infant Mortality Rate, which was significant in the 1970s and 80s, has remarkably decelerated in the 1990s. 130,000 mothers die during childbirth every year. The NHP 1983 target for 2000 was to reduce Maternal Mortality Rate to less than 200 per 100,000 live births. However, 407 mothers die due to pregnancy related causes, for every 100,000 live births even today. As per the National Family Health Surveys in the last decade, the MMR has increased from 424 to 540 maternal deaths per 100,000 live births. Partially as a result of population policies, the disincentives and the two-child norm contained in them – at variance with the National Population Policy (2000) and the commitments made at the ICPD in Cairo – there is a massive shortfall of girls in the 0-6 years age group due to Sex Selective Abortions (SSA). Violence against women has grown, and taken many new forms, including a huge increase in so-called "honour killings". Indeed it would be no exaggeration to state that population policies have added to this violence.

HOPE FROM UPA GOVT

It is thus with hope that we looked forward to the United Progressive Alliance government to initiate policy measures to arrest these trends. Although the Common Minimum Programme was committed to a substantial increase in health spending, this is not evident in the financial allocations made: the budget outlay for 2004-05, adjusted for inflation, shows no increase in the outlay for health and an 11.9 per cent increase for family planning, clearly indicating skewed priorities.

However, more alarmingly, the single line, "A sharply targeted population control programme will be launched in the 150-odd high-fertility districts", from the CMP has been acted upon to unveil policy measures for 209 districts in the country. This is a truly unfortunate move, with grave consequences for thousands of women and children from the poor, marginalised communities, especially dalits and adivasis, who along with deprivation, suffer higher levels of morbidity and mortality, and a high unmet need for health and family planning services.

REGRESSIVE PROGRAMME

These 209 districts in which the "sharply targeted population control programme" are to be launched are precisely the same districts with poor indicators for social development, especially female literacy, infant and child survival, maternal morbidity and mortality and other indicators of human and gender development. Instead of a package of health and development measures, what is being proposed is concentrating on a sharply targeted population control programme in these districts in five states. This profoundly regressive policy relies on targets for sterilisation, coercive incentives and disincentives, and massive subsidies to the private sector, recalling the worst days of India's family planning history. Not only do such measures violate basic human rights, they have also been shown to be demographically unnecessary in bringing down population growth rates.

The declining Child Sex Ratio (CSR) is one deeply worrying indicator of the outcomes of such short-sighted population policies. Between 1991 and 2001, in urban areas, the CSR has declined from 935 to 903 and in rural areas from 948 to 934. More ominously, between January and June this year, in Delhi the Sex Ratio at Birth indicates 819 females being born for every 1000 males; in the prosperous and educated South Delhi zone, where demographic transition has by and large been completed, only 762 females were born for every 1000 males. A recent study by the Ministry of Health also indicated the dolorous outcome of the imposition of the two-child norm for contesting elections. A large majority of those disqualified on this ground were dalits, the adivasis and women from poor families, defeating the very purpose of democratic decentralisation. Further, the study indicated that this norm had acted as an incentive for SSA. Clearly then population stabilisation in this form cannot be the goal since it leads to profoundly unbalanced populations.

We therefore demand that the programme measures for these 209 districts be unreservedly scrapped. We cannot have a population policy that does not hinge on equity and gender justice. There should thus be no National Population Mission. Issues concerning women's health and reproductive rights can only be part of a larger package of a health and social development policy.

We welcome the UPA's commitment to increasing state spending on health, but this should be entirely devoted to strengthening the universal and comprehensive primary health care (PHC) system. Increasing state spending cannot become the vehicle to increasing public subsidy to the private or NGO sectors, which in fact require regulation. It is evident from the CSRs that the private sector has played a deeply regressive role in health care provision.

The Tenth Plan proposals for health and nutrition need to be reviewed keeping epidemiological priorities in mind. A basket of technologically determined vertical programmes cannot substitute for a systematic strengthening of a comprehensive, universal, integrated PHC system.

Ten years after Cairo, if the commitments made there

have to have meaning, it is clear that we cannot have RCH without PHC; nor indeed can we have gender-just population policies without the enabling conditions of health and development. What we have demanded is the minimum and non-negotiable.

9

CONCEPTS OF GROWTH AND DEVELOPMENT

Life of human being never remains same. With the time, various kinds of changes take place in various aspects of the life. Various kinds of changes can be seen in the body of human beings. Not only external, various kinds of internal changes take place in a human being's body. With these changes, a lot of physical as well as psychological changes take place in the human beings. These kind of changes are described by the terms of Growth and Development.

Concepts of Growth and Development

Growth

The process through which body increases in size and weight is known as growth. It is with the help of this process that an individual's body becomes larger and heavier. Actually, when we speak of growth of human body, it results from the growth of muscles, brain and of the skeleton. Various kinds of physical changes that take place in human being as a result of conception to maturity are parts of the concept of growth. An increase in mass of the body is termed as growth. Thus, a quantitative increase in the size and shape of the body is termed as growth. When these organs changes in size and shape, it is known as physical growth. With this process, all the organs of the body got enlarged in size, they become longer, thicker and heavier in weight.

Meredith has defined the concept of growth as the entire series of anatomical and physiological changes that take place between the beginning of the parental life and ends after death of the individual.

Development

Concept of development is different from that of growth. Under this process, various kinds of changes take place in the human being which help him to become mature. These changes take place as a result of maturation and experience. Generally, various kinds of internal changes that place in an individual are included in the process of development. These changes can be qualitative as well as quantitative in nature. Development consists of various kinds of structural and functional changes which can be of positive as well as negative nature. These kind of change take place in any phase of the life. Development take place in an individual in the early phase of life, the stability which is generally found in young age and the deterioration in the capacity of individuals during old age are important constituents of the concept of development. Development is a phenomena with a wider scope, which consists of different kinds of changes taking place in an individual.

Different Stages of Growth and Development

Science has developed to very large extent and it is because of the studies done by scientists that the manner or process in which human beings take birth is being presented by the scientists. According to their studies, when two germs from the body of partners indulging in relationship gets united, a single cell is being produced, which is being called the zygote. In a very rapid pace, this cell gets multiplied. It took around 7 to 8 months to develop properly, and it is after this long period of time that the weight of this cell can be measured.

A child grow in a very set or sequential pattern. One can easily divide this sequential pattern into some parts, which are as follows :—

Pre-Natal Stage,

Post-Natal Stage,

Infancy,

Childhood,

Adolescence,

Adulthood, and

Old Age.

Various kinds of changes take place in an individual during these stages, which have been discussed in the following manner :—

Pre-Natal Stage : It is during this period or stage that two cells get united from the bodies of people of two sexes and give birth to a new cell, which is called Zygote. In the beginning, this cell has a very small size and it begins to accelerate in a very slow speed. It takes around a period of two weeks to get attached to the uterine wall and this process is being called the embryo. It is in that stage that mass cell gets divided into three layers, which are called the Ectoderm, Mesoderm, and Endoderm. All these layers grow in different organs of the body. For instance, ectoderm grows into the skin, nervous system, eyes, tooth and oral passages. This layer is the outer layer of the cell. After this situates the Mesoderm, which is the middle layer of the cell. Skeletal, kidneys, muscular tissues and blood are the main organs into which this layer grows. The innermost layer is called the Endoderm, which generally grows in digestive system and some special cells of thyroid and parathyroid glands. At this stage, cell grows at a very rapid speed and after a period of six weeks, fetus stage comes into being. During this stage, rate of growth of the cell increases to a considerable extent, and it is during this period that cell gains weight. After a period of three months, child becomes able to move in some manner. By seventh month, various organs of the body of the child gets developed. It is only in the ninth month that blood passage of blood cells gets directed into fetal blood streams. Placenta begins to break down in the ninth month and mother's blood flow in the child's blood stream at this period. Various kinds of genetic as well as environmental factors affect the pre-natal stage.

Post-Natal Stage : Parturate stage begins after the birth of the child till the severance of umbilial cord. It is after passing from this stage that child gets detached from the body of the mother. Upto this period, muscle fibres of the child do not get developed properly. At the time of birth, brain has a weight which is being equitable to the one-eighth of the entire weight of the body. After birth, period of around two to four weeks is called Neonate stage. It is during this period that various organs of the child's body adapt themselves according to the outer environment.

Infancy : The period until child attains the age of two years is known as infancy. It is during this period that a child acquires various kinds of capacities at a rapid speed. Various organs of the body gets developed at a constant speed during this period. All the children do not grow at the same speed, but pattern in which they grow is quite the same. Various kinds of hereditary and environmental factors affect the growth of the body of the children. During this period, bones of the child develop at the considerable pace.

At this stage, fatty acids present in the body grow up as a result of which child's body weight gets increased. With the time, bones and muscles of the body gets developed because of which the process of increase in body weight also gets increased. Height of child's body at this stage varies from 9 to 20 inches. In sixth or eight month, first temporary tooth starts appearing out of the gums of the baby. In comparison to upper teeth, lower teeth appear first.

During this period, nervous system of the body gets developed which result from the development of immature nervous cells. These nervous cells are being present in the human body at the time of birth. In the initial stage of development of brain, cerebrum and cerebellum gets developed. During the first year, weight of cerebellum gets triple, which plays an important role in bringing a kind of balance and postural control of the body. Body gets grow at the rapid pace in this period. Child gets to learn various kinds of activities, like walking and talking. To the outer environment, his circulatory and digestive systems get acclimatized, and during this period, all these systems start to function.

With the development, functions of the brain becomes more organised. Various kinds of voluntary motor behaviours take place. He becomes able to sit, creep and crawl and then after some time, he learns to walk without the help of anybody. With the time, an improvement comes in the various motor skills, which leads to a kind of cognitive development in the body of the child. With development of cognitive capacity, a child become more aware of himself. This kind of development of his cognitive capacity takes place as a result of his interaction with various people of the society. Social world of the infant is being dominated by his parents and other members of the family. After third month, muscles of the eye body gets stronger because of which they can move in a co-ordinated manner. By this time, their hearing ability also gets improved. It is at this stage that the process of socialization gets started in the child's life. Upto this time, they begin to turn their head, smile, and wave their arms in response to activity of some other person. They recognise the fact that they have been left alone by his parents because of which he starts crying. They begin to differentiate between the emotions of love and anger. After an age of one, they begin to respond to simple commands of yes or no and by the end of second year, they starts to take part in simple activities of adults. Thus, it can be said that this period in the life of a child is a period of self-assertion.

Childhood : Period in which the relative dependency of infant is over, is called the childhood. The time span of this period is very long, as it exist upto the period until when the child attains sexual maturity. Generally, this period differ with regard to the sex of the child. In boys, this age begins from two years and last upto fourteen years, however, in case of girls, this period ends upto they attain the age of thirteen.

Various kinds of physical and psychological changes take place within an individual's body. This period is being divided into two categories, namely, the early childhood and late childhood. From second year period known as early childhood begins and this lasts upto an age of sixth year. After this age period begins the period of late childhood, which extends upto the time when the child becomes sexually mature. During the whole period of childhood, a child growth at a uniform or considerable rate. Higher centres of brain of the child gets developed at a slower rate, however, during these years, it is being developed progressively.

Adolescence : This word has been extracted from the Latin word adolescence, which implies to grow into the stage of maturity. In reality, adolescence is a process and not a period. During this period, a child achieves the attitudes and beliefs which he need for participation in the society effectively.

In simple terms, the stage between childhood and adulthood is known as adolescence. This age begins from 13 to 19 years of age. This period consists of stress and strains of various kinds. First stage of adolescence is known as puberty, during which a child initiates his steps towards adulthood for the first time. It is during this period that primary sex characteristics of a child gets developed. In comparison to boys, girls enter this stage earlier. In case of boys this age is between 11 to 15 years, while in the girls, it is between the age of 10 to 14.

During the early adolescence age, a child is grown in a very disproportionate manner because of which this period is known as the age of awkwardness. Those adolescents are pre-occupied about their physical appearance who are adjusting to their growth spurt. The age in which girls and boys attain an increase is height is also different. In girls, this age begins from the age of nine while in the boys, it gets started from eleven, however, in all the children, changes in weight follow the same kind of pattern, which is being related to the height.

Adolescent spurt of growth is found in proportion to the magnitude for weight rather than for height, which is because of the tendency which is being found to accumulate large quantities of fat in sub-cutaneous tissues. There are various factors which give rise to this fact. Because of increase in weight, skeleton gets broader and massiveness of individual bones of the human beings get increased. This kind of increase in the stockiness of bones is more apparent in boys in comparison to girls. At this time, muscles of the body grows more rapidly. Various studies have proved that during this period, between the age of twelve to sixteen, strength of a child gets doubled, however, it reaches to the maximum level after utmost growth in height and weight. Continuous moderate improvements are being shown by motor abilities, however, this kind of improvement is more rapid in the periods of pre-pubescent and post-pubescent. During this period, physical and physiological abilities of a child gets developed to a lot of extent, which result in growth of mental abilities, with the help of which an individual can deal with various abstracted matters. During this period, mind of the child gets its own metamorphosis.

Abilities to concentrate properly and to keep the memories of various events also increases during this period. A child becomes more self-aware during this period of age. Various internal organs also gets developed. Size of the heart and blood vessels grow in size during puberty. Organics of various important systems of the body becomes more developed, which improves their ability considerably. All the changes help in improving the functioning of sex glands and the pituitary glands. Changes during this period affects the social life of a child also. They become emotionally more mature, and begin to participate in decision making processes. The impact of this period on all the children is not same. Some becomes tensed and feel stress, while some of the children get the opportunities to grow and develop their physical, intellectual and social abilities.

Adulthood : Adult life is the period for which infancy, childhood, and adolescence are considered to be the preparatory phases. When a child enters in this age group, he is considered to be prepared to face various kinds of challenges of life. This stage is considered to be the age of effective cognitive functioning. It is during period that a child has to decide or choose the proper profession in which he wants to enter.

It is during this period of life that a child gets confidence and ability to work independently. Various responsibilities are being laid upon him and he has to face various kinds of commitments. Process of aging takes place on a continuous basis, and when an individual attains the age of upto forty, a marked decline in seen in his mental and physical capacities.

Old Age : When an individual attains the age of sixty, he is considered to be in the old age. Generally people in these age group are known as senior citizens. During this period, in various ways, an individual capacities get deteriorated and declined. Various kinds of problems are being faced in doing some functions, however, by indulging continuously in some important kinds of exercises, one can cope with all these kinds of problems, however, to some extent.

Process of Growth and Development during the Period of Childhood

The span of life which begins with the cessations of infancy is known as childhood. This period begins from the age of two and extends upto a child gets into the stage of adolescence. At the end of this period, a child becomes maturer in all the respects. Thus, it is a long period of time, during which various kinds of changes take place within an individual. Into various categories this period can be divided, which are as follows :-

a. Early Childhood : At the conclusion of infancy, this period begins. In this period, growth of the body takes place at a slower rate. Process of growth does not get stopped entirely in this period, but pace of it gets reduced or somehow becomes static. Various kinds of changes are being shown in body proportion and the immatureness look starts disappearing. Manner in which the skeleton develops result in changes which occur in the body proportion. Change in body proportion is inevitable and most obvious change taking place in the body is of the lengthening process. Shoulders of the individual becomes broader and his hands and feet gets increased in size. Body of the individual becomes lengthy and it becomes thinner. When a child enters into this period, all the baby teeth of him gets developed. The total number of such teeth are 20 in number.

During this period of life, emotions are intense and temper tantrums occur at a frequent period. During the age from two to five years, perception of shape progresses at a rapid rate. It is at the age of three years that child learns to make various kind of judgements.

An individual has the capacity to learn various kinds of skills during this period. During this period, young child tends to learn the different kinds of skills as he has a very pliable body and he can adapt himself according to the needs and requirements. The kind of opportunities he gets determines the activities he will learn.

A child from poor family takes lesser time in learning skills in comparison to child from wealthier or richer families. If a child is being brought up in an over-protective environment, then his abilities to learn skills decreases considerably and vice versa. During this period, process of language growth take places at a considerable pace. Vocabulary of the child increases to a lot of extent and this helps him in expressing his emotions and feelings more easily.

b. Period of Later Childhood : This period begins when the child is around five or six years of age and it comes to an end when he attains the age of thirteen or fourteen. Sometimes, this period or age is also called the school age. In this period, one gets grow at a very leisurely rate. After the age of six, pace of physical growth comes to a decline and child loses his soft contours and top heavy stature. The growth rate of bones become slow and this tendency continues with the increase in the age.

During the early phase of this period, arms and legs grow at faster rate in comparison to the trunk of the child. The height of the child increases considerably. Body proportions of the child becomes quite same as an adult's, Child's limbs become lengthen, which brings various kinds of changes in his physical structure. Baby teeth are being over-thrown by the permanent teeth and various kinds of facial configuration take place in the child. Bones become longer as well as harder. Heart, and blood pressure of the child increases, while a decrease is found in his pulse rate. Hunger of the child gets increased during this age and children of both the ages become stronger.

Throughout this period, neural conduction rates and reaction speeds up. Child's reaction time decreases with increase in the age. Child becomes better co-ordinated and integrated and becomes capable of learning and executing more complex motor activities. This kind of co-ordination refined further during this period of time and it is being used in various activities.

Child become able to acquire adequate conception of himself as he gets a realistic conception of his environment. Size of child's conceptual world also increases. He can perceive efficiently and rapidly. They become more efficient in organising perceptual information in coherent ways. It becomes possible for an older child to process complex information.

Various kinds of new mental abilities got aroused in the age of six or seven. This period is considered to be very important for teaching the child new skills and knowledge. These kind of knowledge and skills will help him in his near future. He will become efficient in drawing various kinds of logical conclusions. His capacity to remember things increases.

A considerable growth is seen in the vocabulary and syntactic understanding of the language between the age of five and ten. Child becomes more perceptive in using the rules of language while communicating with someone. Till now, the main school from where child can learn manners and other social values remains his house. He considers his parents as the moral teachers. Thus, he is guided by his parents during this age group. Child's behaviour gets influenced by the parental behaviour and attitudes. Only that child can become confident who can have, beside his social interactions, a secure environment at home. In providing direction to the behavioural patterns to the child, home environment plays a much important role. These behavioural patterns, with the time take the shape of habits, and affect the personality of child to a lot of extent. Character of the child depends to a lot of extent on the kind of environment he gets at his house. On the child's personal and social adjustment, parental acceptance or rejection has very important influence. If child do not get support or love from his parents, he becomes emotionally insecure and unhappy, while those children who are being accepted by their parents feel emotionally secured and this provides them with the necessary courage and self-confidence. Thus, personality of a child is being affected to a lot of extent by the kind of learning situations he found at the home.

As said earlier that in the adolescent age, a child becomes self-dependent from the dependency he had earlier on his parents and other elders around him. In this period, a child becomes quite responsible and self-reliant. Thus, because of all these, child has to make various kinds of psychological adjustment through which he can adjust himself in the changed conditions, which are absent earlier.

If it is said that adolescent is the age in which a child do various kinds of experiments and adventures, it will not be entirely wrong. There is a tendency, which is being found in the adolescent that they like to behave contrary to accepted standards which are being set up by the adults. Some children becomes mature early and they set the goals they have to achieve, while some do not indulge themselves in any kind of planning, because of which they become maladjusted to the changed needs and conditions. At this stage, various kinds of problems are being faced out by the children, because of which this age is sometimes called the problem age. Only that child can successfully cope with these problems who will be given proper kind of responsibility at the proper time. Adults should provide the adolescents with adequate opportunity to make their judgements and solve the problems themselves.

Various kinds of new situations take place in the life of children during adolescent age and child who is over-protected and who is not prepared to face various problems arising during this period can become emotionally, socially and psychologically unbalanced. During this period of life, an individual tries to find himself as a person. If planned properly, one can very easily and comfortably enter into the state of adolescence.

Categorisation of Adolescent Age

This age period can be classified into three categories, namely, the pre-adolescence, early-adolescence and late-adolescence. All these periods have their own features and characteristics, which are discussed as follows:—

Period of Pre-Adolescence : During this period, childhood personality gets broken up and various kinds of changes take place in the personality of the child. All these changes lead the child towards period of adulthood.

In this age, a child has to cope with various kinds of problems which arises because of various changes taking place in his life. Generally, children in this age group are found to be restless and hyper-active. They seems to be rebellious in nature. They have to make various kinds of adjustments in order to adapt themselves according to the new or changed conditions and emotions. One's perception regarding the parents, peers and the self gets changed during this period of time. If children are not treated properly by the elders during this period, they can respond to them with irritation and distrust.

Children in this age group are emotionally very sensitive and sometimes become over-powered with their emotions. Until now, they do not learn the skills to get alongwith their adults. A kind of conflict is being found in between the children and the parents, and this makes them frustrated. He begins to argument with his own parents if they do not provide him the authority to take his own decisions. Children during this age group requires independence and they do not want others to interfere in their life. Pre-adolescent children want to enjoy full authority in all the matters. Sometimes, they feel guilt or shame because of their behaviour towards others, but it happens seldom. They have their own ideals and values and they misbehave or even ridicule the people who do not cherish their values. They like to come out of the jurisidication of house and desire to maintain friendly relationships with a large number of people. They like to participate in the activities in which children of his age group participate. They like the exposure to mass media of various kinds.

Period of Early Adolescence : During this period, various kinds of changes take place in a child, not exactly physical but in their feelings or psychologically. They provide more importance to their body, looks and stature. As known, various kinds of physical changes take place in a child during adolescent period, which leads a kind of self-rejection in them. In this age, chief criterion of social acceptability is considered to be the physical attractiveness. They find it interesting to know more about matters relating to sex. They feel anxious and curious if they do not get this kind of information. They begins to attract towards the people of other sex. They try to find out their self-identity. In achieving personal identity, becoming independent of parents and gaining acceptance of peers are important steps. Another important step in this process is to make a choice of and do various kinds of preparations for a career, which is being decided by the child.

Period of Late Adolescence : By this period of time, most of the children get entered into their career. They get the independence from their parents and other elders around them. They try to make their own perfect world in which they try to abolish all kinds of inequalities. Till the child gets entered into this phase of life, his outlook towards the people of other sex gets changed considerably. It is during this age that children become mentally mature. This period of age is also called the period of heightened social consciousness. During this period, adolescents provide special attention to the status and social acceptability. The desire to be popular in the society is dominating during this period of age. Only that adolescent can adapt himself in the changed condition who can appreciate the personality of others and can various kinds of changes in himself which can help him in maintain co-operative relationships with the others.

During this period, body image of the child gets changed, social roles which he is required to play also gets changed and sex role gets changed to a lot of extent, which create various kinds of problems in finding out the self-identity. As he gets certain independence from the parents, he tries to make his own values and beliefs. At various times, a controversy is found between the child and his parents. This results because of various transitions which take place during this period. He becomes mentally, psychologically and socially very mature which helps him in taking his own decisions and if he does not get such independence or authority from the parents, he becomes a rebel. He behaves or does things in the manner he likes and even does not consider what his parents or other elders say. Because of this, child feels inconsistent and confused within the world of adults, where he is not given the right to involve in decision makings.

Various kinds of problems are being faced by children in this age group. These problems are generally of the psychological nature. It is very necessary to solve these problems as soon as possible otherwise, they can take the shape of serious problems. Some of the problems which an adolescent face are as follows :—

a. Children in this age group wants complete independence. They do not like any kind of boundations from his family or parents. They want to take their own decisions independently. Generally, during this period of life, a lack of understanding is being found between a child and the parents. Parents do not recognise the changes which are taking place in the child and they try to impose on them their own wishes or decisions, but this irritates the child and he becomes a rebellion.

b. Various physical changes take place in a child during this age group and the problem arises because of the fact that these changes do not take place in a simultaneous manner, because of which, sometimes, children consider their physique as improper. This kind of feeling creates a lot of problems or depression among the adolescents as their find themselves deviated from the sex appropriate physique.

c. Various kinds of changes take place in the school environment of the adolescents. During these changed conditions, it becomes quite difficult for them to adjust themselves. Now each subject is being taught by different teachers and for this reason, children are required to adjust themselves according to the personality traits of all the teachers. At one time, they may be required to obey the orders of an authoritarian teacher and at the other time, they may be required to participate in the classroom planning. Today's world is a world of competition, and an adolescent should know the skill to make adjustments according to the failure and success. At this stage, various kinds of fears kept on brooding among the adolescents, such as fear of failure, fear of disapproval of teachers and fear of disapproval of peers.

d. During this period of age, a tendency takes place in a child according to which he wants to spend his life according to his desires. He does not want to obey the rules and norms set up by the society or the others on him. But, sometimes, the norms set up by the child do not seems appropriate to the new social life, which creates a lot of problem for him. In this kind of situation, he finds himself mis-adjusted in the society's values.

e. In our country, generally it is seen that a child is treated in different manner at home and in different in outside world. Sometimes he is provided with heavy responsibilities as he is very mature while sometimes he is over-protected as he is an innocent child. This kind of dual behaviour give birth to a kind of confusion in the mind the adolescent.

f. Adolescents try to find out their identity in this period of life. Some regard them efficient in facing various kinds of problems, while some consider them incomplete to do the same. They set up certain goals for their life and if they do not get them achieved, they feel distressed and stressed. A lot of psychological stress is being put on them because of the goals they have set out for the future.

Thus, various kinds of different problems are being faced out by the adolescents in this period of age. Only that child will become more able to solve the problems generally aroused during this period of time who are provided with proper care as well as freedom by the parents. Under guidance of self-disciplined adults, transition from childhood to adult status should be preceded in a gradual manner. Only this kind of development will be accepted by the society. If liberty is being provided to them suddenly, then they will become confused and can use their power in wrong manner. This kind of thing can make them socially maladjusted and emotionally unbalanced.

Physical Education and Problems of Adolescents

The children in adolescent period like to perform or take part in various kinds of physical activities. By taking part in the physical activities, they get various kinds of personal advantages, which help them in developing their personality to a considerable extent. An adolescent can engage himself in various physical activities through the field of physical education and sports.

To become a whole or complete man, one should have the quality of self-confidence and self-control. By becoming master in some physical skill, one can get self-confidence. All kinds of sports and games help in attaining some level of self-confidence in a child, however, different activities provide this quality in varying degrees. Activities offering a definite challenge to courage contribute in making self-knowledge to a considerable extent.

Man is considered to be a social animal, and it is necessary for acquiring emotional balance to fulfil his social needs or requirements. Two important social virtues are loyalty and un-selfishness. These two qualities can be developed in a child through the participation in team sports. This kind of games or sports should be given prominent place in the curriculum of the adolescents.

If any child is lacking in some specific quality, he can fulfil it by joining certain sports activity. For instance, if one lacks in keeping close co-operation with others, he should be included in some team sports, i.e., cricket, where will be required to play while maintaining a co-operation with other players of the teams.

By participating in the games and spots, a child can develop his total personality. He becomes physiologically as well as psychologically healthy, which helps him in solving various kinds of problems which can be of different nature.

If during this period, any child gets habitual to bad habits, he will remain to practice those habits throughout the life. These bad habits are required to be detected at proper time and it is also very necessary to correct them and an important means to correct these errors is by making the child participant of certain sports activity. Through various sports and games, bad habits of posture or function can be corrected.

Various kinds of opportunities are being provided to the children for acquisition of aesthetic satisfactions by participation in the physical activities. There are some sports events which are being organised in the natural surroundings which help the children in getting closer to the nature. Such kind of aesthetic contributions play an important role in the development of an adolescent's personality.

A large number of children are found who lack physical co-ordination. This kind of lack of co-ordination can be improved by the participation in physical activities and sports. Progressive course of training can be used on such kind of children, which help in correcting the fundamental weakness which is being found in them. This will influence the performance of the child on the other activities positively.

From the above discussion it is clear that physical education and sports play very important role in solving the problems which are generally faced by adolescents. Physical activities help them in becoming more maturer and also to cope with the difficulties generally faced by them properly.

Concept of Personality

Personality is a complex phenomena, which means

different to different persons. For a common man, it is nothing but the general physical appearance of an individual, while if seen from psychological point of view, it is the manner in which an individual sees the world and the things around him. It is this complex nature of the concept that various psychologists have done deep study relating to this concept and have defined it in various manners.

True Meaning of Personality

In the general concept of personality, it is nothing but an individual's manner of living. The way in which an individual spends his life, wears the dress and interact with other individuals is known as personality. But, this concept of personality is entirely different the psychological concept. According to the psychologists, personality is not only how an individual looks or wears dress, but it is very wider in nature. In reality, from the word persona, word personality has been derived, which is a Latin word. Word persona implies the mask, which was being worn in the ancient Greece by the actors with the purpose to hide their identity while they used to take part in the theatrical plays. To present the character, to whom actor was being portrayed that he used a mask. From their the concept of persona came into existence. Thus from the origin, it can be said that word personality implies effect one exerts on the other peoples around them.

Structure of human personality is very complex, which comprises of various emotions, habits, motives and thinking pattern of the individual. All the aspects of an individual are included in his personality. One's perception, imagination, attitude and habits are being reflected by the personality and all these are important constituents of an individual's personality.

Various biological and cultural heritages or behaviours affect an individual's personality. With some biological heritage, a child comes in this world and his personality is being moulded by the cultural environment in which he is brought up. Interaction of biological organism with the social environment affects the personality of an individual to a lot of extent. The manner in which an individual adjusts himself according to the external environment is what known as personality. Thus, the manner in which one responds to the outer environment is known as one's personality.

Every individual has an individual system which reflects his behaviour and the manner of thinking. Peculiar blend of characteristics that make a person unique are known as personality. Various features make-up one's personality. These features are external in nature that interact in different manners. Personality is the organisation of all the features found in a human being. The manner in which these features or traits are integrated in an individual is different as found in the other individual. Because of this reason it is said that personality of an individual is unique in nature.

Psychological make-up of an individual is revealed through the personality. In simple terms, it can be said that it is the quality of an individual's entire behaviour. Personality is a continuous process of learning under which an individual learns various modes of responses. All the factors which make up an individual are important constituents of his personality. It consists of one's psychological make-up, his ability to adjustment himself in the changed environment and the manner in which he behaves in different environments. It is not possible to define all the criterion or features which can help in making up a good and attractive personality, but self-acceptance, acceptance by other members of the society, and performance of work efficiently are some of the important criterion which can help one in developing an attractive and good personality.

One of the most interesting areas of psychology is personality. This topic has remained an important subject area for the researchers and various researchers have defined this concept differently. Some of the definitions provided by the psychologists are as follows:—

In the words of Dashiell "Personality is the whole picture of one's organised behaviour, which can be featured by his fellowmen in a consistent manner."

According to Munn "Personality is nothing but the integration of an individual's structures, manner in which he behaves, his interests, attitudes, abilities and capacities."

In the words of Gordon W. Allport "Within the individual, personality is the dynamic organisation of psycho-physical systems that determine the manner in which individual have adjusted himself to the environment."

In the words of Ulrich "Sum total of an individual's values and attitudes and all of his traits is known as the personality. The resultant of all these traits have a dynamic nature. In other words, personality is dynamic in nature.

According to J.B. Watson "Sum of all the activities which can be discovered by actual observations over a long period of time which can provide with reliable information is known as personality."

In the words of Carl Pearson "Personality is the effect of an individual' appearance and behaviour upon the persons coming in contact with him."

According to Buskist and Gerbing "Personality is a particular pattern of behaviour and thinking which prevail across time and situations that help in differentiating one individual from the other.

From the above definitions, one can grab out various features of one's personality, some of which are as follows:—

a. Product of Heredity and Environment : With various hereditary biological traits a child is born but by the socio-cultural environment in which he lives, his personality gets influenced. Through the interaction of heredity trait with environmental factors, personality of an individual gets affected to a lot of extent. Because of this it is said that an individual's personality is the product of hereditary and environmental factors.

b. Adaptable to Changing Conditions : Personality of an individual helps him in adapting himself to the environment or the conditions in which he is required to lead his life. With change in conditions, personality of an individual also gets changed. With this various kinds of changes or modifications take place in the behaviour and habits of the individual.

c. Components of Personality are Permanent in Nature : All the components which make up an individual's personality are more or less static or permanent in nature.

d. Everyone has Unique Personality : Personality

characteristics found in an individual are different as being found in other individual. These characteristics help in differentiating one individual from the other. No two individuals can have similar personalities and personality can be specific or unique to an individual.

e. Learning affects Personality : An individual's personality gets affected to a lot of extent by the his learning and the experience. The impact of learning on an individual can be evaluated from his personality.

f. Development of Personality is a Continuous Phenomena : Throughout the life of an individual, his personality keeps on developing. There can be no stage in an human being at which his personality can be said to have developed fully. It is because of this reason that it is said that personality of an individual has a dynamic nature and not a static one.

g. Various Constituents of Personality are Inter-Related to each other : Personality of an individual is made up by various components, but these components do not function in isolation, but they are inter-related and dependent on each other. It is the unified form of all the components that constitute the personality of an individual.

10

FOOD AND NUTRITION

Introduction

One of an important feature of found in all the living beings is that they experience hunger for satisfaction of which they have to take consuming some material by which they can get their stomach filled. Here it is important to note that mention has been made of all the living organisms as it is not only the human beings who sense such feeling of hunger, but all the animals and insects existing on the earth in any form. As human beings are considered to be superior creature of the god, thus, for satisfaction of their appetite, they first get such food items ready for consumption, while other animals and insects consume food items in their raw form. Today, various techniques have been devised by which human beings add taste to the food items. Not only this, for this purpose, they make use of various spices also, by which taste level of their food gets increased to considerable extent and their appetite level also gets increased. However, some people like to consume some vegetables in their raw form.

Human beings can sustain their life because they consume food items of different kinds. If human beings do not get food for a long period of time, then they can die. This is equally true for all the living organisms existing on the earth. It is because of this reason that food and role played by it has remained an important subject of study since a long period of time. It has been by the experts that most of human beings do not eat to sustain their physical survival, instead they eat food as their experience feeling of appetite, which in simple terms is the desire to eat. Human beings or all the living organisms consume food items when some inner signal tells them that it is time to eat. It is possible that a person can feel appetite even after consuming the food.

Varied kind of differences are found in the liking and disliking of people regarding food items. Not only this, different human beings take food in varying quantities. In reality, such habits or features are influenced to considerable extent by various factors. Feeling of appetite can get developed in human being when he is not hungry, which can take place as a result of sensory stimulation such as smelling, seeing and tasting delicious food items. Large number of people can be found who remain in a constant struggle to find the right balanced position in between eating to maintain body function and eating to satisfy their appetite. The factors which play important role in defining what a person is nutritionally are personal preferences, habit, availability of food items, emotional comfort, values, kind of body structure and nutritional values.

Thus from above discussion it can be said that there exist differences in the concepts of hunger and appetite. Hunger is the feeling which is associated with physiological needs of the human beings, while appetite is the desire to eat, which normally accompanies hunger and is psychological in nature.

Human beings consume various kinds of food items in order to satisfy their appetite. Although main function of food is to satisfy the appetite, but various other kinds of functions are also performed by it, some of which are as follows:—

a. It is only through the energy provided by food that human body can perform various kinds of mechanical functions.

b. Human body is composed of various muscles and cells. While performing physical works, some of the cells existing in body gets destroyed, for repair and development of new cells, energy is needed. Such energy for this purpose is provided through the food consumed by human beings.

c. Human body is a highly complex machine, in which various kinds of functions keep on taking place. Various kinds of chemical reactions take place in human body, by while body temperature gets increased. The energy which is required to keep body temperature under control is provided by the food items consumed by human beings.

Thus, apart from satisfying the appetite, food consumption performs various important kinds of functions, for which, human beings should consume proper kind of food in adequate quantity and at proper time. It is important to mention here that generally people believe that if they will consume food at short period of intervals, then energy level will get increased to considerable extent in their body, which is far from true. With such practice, extra energy will get stored in the form of fats under the skin of body, by which body will become over-weighted and person will get affected by the disease known as obesity, which in turn leads to various kinds of problems related to cardio-vascular system of the body.

Experts have provided some basis on which food

items consumed by human beings can be divided into various categories. The basis used for this purpose are : on basis of source, on basis of function and on basis of chemical nature. On basis of source of the food, food items can be divided into two categories, namely, vegetable foods and animal foods. In the category of vegetable foods, items such as rice, wheat and similar kinds are included which are generally sown in the farms, while in second category, those food items are included which are provided by nature, e.g., meat, egg and fish. Likewise, on the basis of functions performed by food items, they can be divided into three categories, namely, body builders, energy yielders and protectives. Those food items which perform the function of body building are included in the first category, in which items like meat, milk and fish are included, while items through which human body gets energy to varying degrees are included in the second category, which generally include the items like cereals and sugars, while food items which help in protecting human bodies from various diseases are included in the third category, in which items like vegetables and fruits are included.

After discussing these concepts at length, now it is reasonable to throw some light on the next concept under discussion, that is nutrition.

Concept of Nutrition

Science of food and it's relationship to health is known as the nutrition. In other words, it can be said that nutrition is the science that investigates the relationship existing in between the physiological function and the essential elements found in the food items consumed by living organisms. The constituents of food that sustain living organisms physiologically are called nutrients, and in this category proteins, carbohydrates, fats, vitamins, minerals and water are generally included. It is necessary for living organisms, and specially to human beings to take such food in which all the nutrients exist by which proper level of all of them can be maintained in the human body. In lack of any of the nutrient in the body, human beings can get attached by various diseases, for which it is necessary to make those provisions by which their body can get all the essential nutrients in proper quantity. Such kind of food which consist of all the essential nutrients in adequate quantity is called Balanced Food.

Unit of measure that indicates the amount of energy one obtains from a particular food is known as calorie. It is in the forms of proteins, fats and carbohydrates that calories are eaten by human beings. Other remaining nutrients are considered to be necessary for proper body function, but no calories to the diet is being added by them in any way. Situation of overweight gets developed as a result of excess calorie consumption. It is no so much the quantity of food human beings eat that is likely to cause weight problems and resultant diseases as it is the relative proportion of nutrients in their diets and lack of physical activity. It has been found from various studies that food which is generally consumed by majority of people in our nation contains high quantities of fat and carbohydrate and as people do not have enough time to get participated in the physical activities as a result of which their body weight gets increased to considerable extent, because of which they become pray of problem known as obesity, which lead to development of various other problems. Experts are of the view that most of the diet related diseases have resulted from the excess calories and increased consumption of fat by the human beings.

Essential Nutrients

As said earlier that it is very important to have some of the essential nutrients in desirable quantities for proper development of the body. As these nutrients are of such importance, thus, it is necessary to discuss them at length, mention of which are as follows :—

Proteins

This nutrient is the most abundance substance in the human body. They are considered to be complex nitrogenous compounds. In reality, proteins are major components of nearly all the cells present in human body. Experts consider proteins to be body builders as they play important role in developing and repairing bone, muscle skin and blood cells. Here it is important to mention that human body is made up of various muscles and cells, which gets damaged while performing different physical functions. For proper functioning of the body, it is necessary to have these damaged cells and muscles repaired, and this important function is performed by proteins found in the food, as a result of which they are considered to be of utmost importance. Not only these, proteins are also key elements of the antibodies which help the human body to be protected from various diseases. Chemical activities taking place in the human body gets controlled by proteins and they also control the hormones which play important role in regulating various functions performed by human body.

As known that various kinds of nutritious elements are obtained through food consumed by human beings, which is required by all the body parts. The function to transport all these nutritions to various parts of the body is also performed by the proteins. Proteins also play important role of supplying other sources of energy to cells situated in different parts of the body in situation when fats and carbohydrates are not available readily. Thus it gets proved by the discussion that adequate amounts of protein in the diet are vital to many body functions and ultimately to survival of human beings.

Proteins consumed by human beings are being broken into smaller molecules by the body parts, which are called amino acids. These parts are linked together like beads in a necklace, and there are total twenty in numbers, out of which three combinations are considered to be most essential for the body. Dietary proteins by which body gets all of the essential amino acids is termed as complete protein. Generally proteins obtained through animals products are considered to be complete in nature. Whenever human being consume food items in which some of the essential amino acids are found in less quantity that desired than whole amount of protein that can be synthesized from other amino acids gets reduced to considerable extent. Proteins that present in the digestible form are considered to be complete in nature.

Proteins obtained through plan sources are found to be incomplete in nature, as they generally lack one or two of the essential amino acids. Experts have divided plant sources of protein into three categories, namely, legumes, grains and nuts. In the first category, food items like beans and corn are included while in the second category falls various nuts. Likewise, various seeds are included in the third category. Certain vegetables also contribute valuable plant proteins. Human beings can get essential amino acids necessary to ensure adequate protein absorption through mixing two or more food items with each other. Incomplete plant proteins with complete low fat animal proteins can be combined by those people who are interested in obtaining all of their protein from plants. One can obtain high quality proteins through low fat cheese, skim milk and egg whites.

Although human beings should eat enough protein, but it should be ensured that you do not consume too much, as it can place added stress on the liver and kidneys. By it, calcium excretion in urine can also be increased, by which risks of bone fractures can get elevated. As cases of persons suffering from various diseases arising as a result of high amount of carbohydrates have come into notice, which has led to production of various food items which have low calories by which high levels of carbohydrates can be eradicated and people can be induced to consume food items rich in proteins. Although diets that deviate from a balanced nutritional approach are almost certainly flawed, most would not cause major health threats in otherwise healthy people when used for short periods of time. High protein diets should be avoided by those persons who suffer from kidney or liver problems.

If a person is fighting off a serious infection or is recovering from surgery or blood loss, then high amount of protein will be required by him. In such kind of situations, proteins that are lost to cellular repair need to be replaced, which can be done by proteins effectively. Protein deficiency continues to pose a threat to the global population, and large number of people in our nation also suffer from this same problem. Experts have recommended protein intake for the average man is only 63 grams, and the average woman need only 50 grams. But still number of people suffering from low level of proteins in their food is increasing with greater pace.

Vitamins

These are considered to be one of the most potent

and essential organic compounds for human body. These nutrients are required by human body in very small amount. No energy is being provided by this nutrient, but it helps in making proper utilisation of other nutrients found in the food. It is necessary to provide vitamins to the body through food as they cannot be synthesized by the body themselves. Vitamins help in maintaining nerves and skin every minute and every day. Human body requires blood cells without which various body parts will not be able to function properly. Vitamins help in making the development of blood cells in the body possible.

Human beings meet various kinds of accidents, as a result of which different kinds of wounds get developed on their body. In the absence of adequate amount of vitamin in the body, it will become quite difficult to heal the wounds. Vitamins found in the body can be destroyed by various factors, some of which are age, heat and various environmental conditions.

Categorization of Vitamins

Experts have classified vitamins obtained through various food items into two categories, namely, fat soluble and water soluble. Fat soluble vitamins get absorbed through intestinal tract with the help of fats, while water soluble vitamins get easily dissolved in water. Vitamins A, D, E, and K are grouped under the first category while Vitamin B and Vitamin C are placed under second category. Fat soluble vitamins are tend to be stored in the body and toxic accumulations in the liver may cause cirrhosis like symptoms which water soluble vitamins are generally excreted and cause few toxicity problems in the body.

Concept of vitamins cannot be understood properly without mentioning the sources through which various vitamins can be obtained and the important functions performed by them in length, mention of which are as follows :—

- Vitamin A : This vitamin is an unsaturated alcohol in reality. Carotene is the precursor of this kind of vitamin, which exists in three forms, namely, alpha, beta and gamma. This vitamin is considered to be very important for human body, as it performs various kinds of functions, some of which are as follows :—

i. It helps in production of retinal pigments in the body, with the help of which human beings become able to view things even in very dim light.

ii. It helps in maintaining the integrity of epithelial cells found in the human body.

iii. It saves human body from getting affected by various infections.

iv. It helps in getting the skeletal system of the body developed.

Importance of this kind of vitamin can be analysed from the fact that if found in deficient amount, then human body can get affected by various serious kinds of diseases some of which include Night Blindness, Bitot's Spots and Keratosis. It is possible to get this kind of vitamin from various food items, some of which are carrot, spinach, green vegetables and mangoes. It can be obtained through consumption of various diary products like milk, butter and cheese.

- Vitamin B Complex : Water soluble vitamins belonging to group of Vitamin B complex include the following :

i. Thaimine: It is also known as Vitamin B_1. One can obtain this kind of vitamin from food items like peas, beans, oatmeal, vegetables and fruits. A person having deficiency of this vitamin can get affected by the diseases known as Beriberi and Wernicke's Encephalopathy. An individual requires 2 mg of this kind of vitamin daily, which gets increased for the persons who take carbohydrate in more quantity.

ii. Riboflavine: It is also known as Vitamin B_2. One can obtain this kind of vitamin through milk, eggs, liver, kidney and green leafy vegetables. Importance of this kind of vitamin can be analysed by the fact that deficiency of this vitamin can lead to problem of Angular Stomatitis. Not only this, person having this vitamin in deficient quantity will be more susceptible to cataract. A healthy human being requires 2 to 3 mg. riboflavine in the food daily.

iii. Nicotinic Acid: Also known as Vitamin B_3. The main sources through which this kind of vitamin can be obtained include the meat, poultry fish and ground nut. A person having this vitamin in deficient amount can get affected by problem known as Pellagra. Generally it is found that problem of Pellagra gets developed more in the persons who consume maize or jowar in higher quantities. Person suffering from such disease should take a mixed diet which should consist of milk and meat while maize and jowar should be avoided by such person to maximum possible extent.

iv. Pyridoxine: It is also known as Vitamin B_6 is often found in the food items like milk, egg yolk, fish and vegetables. An adult requires two mg. per day of this vitamin and it's requirement gets increased for a pregnant woman, during which it rises upto 2.5 mg per day. Deficiency of this vitamin can lead to various problems in human beings, some of the important out of which are irritability, loss of body weight and shortage of red blood cells in the body. Adults having this vitamin

body organs against shock. An important role is being played by it in keeping the body temperature under control and in promoting healthy cell function. Through fats, taste of food items become better and it is through this constituent that food attains the quality of deliciousness. If there is absent of carbohydrate in the sufficient amount in the body, then concentrated form of energy can be provided by this nutrient.

Minerals

These are the inorganic and indestructible elements that provide help and assistance for various physiological processes taking place within the body. Human body consists of more than fifty chemical elements, which are being obtained through various food items. Around 1/20th part of body weight is made up by the minerals. It is not possible for body parts to get vitamins absorbed in the absence of minerals. Experts have divided minerals found in human body into various categories, two of which are Macrominerals and Trace Minerals. Macrominerals are those minerals which are required by human body in large amounts, for instance, sodium, calcium, phosphorus and potassium, while in the Trace minerals includes those elements which are required in trace amount by the body. Zinc, iron and copper are some of the examples of this kind of minerals. Although it cannot be denied in any way that minerals are necessary for proper body functions, however, they should be consumed within restricted quantities.

Sodium

This mineral is necessary for regulation of blood and body fluids. Functions of transmission of nerve impulses and heart activity are controlled by this mineral. This help in various metabolic functions taking place in the human body. It has been found that majority of people consume sodium in the quantity which is much more than the needed. Experts are of the view that an adult who does not sweat profusely needs very little amount of sodium, which has been set out to be 500 mg. per day.

One of the most common and important source of obtaining this form of mineral is table salt, however, table salt accounts to very little per cent of sodium intake, while the remainder comes from water and from highly processed food items which are infused with sodium and help in enhancing the flavour of food. Hundred milligrams of sodium per serving are found in the food items like pickles, salty snack foods and processed cheese. From various studies it has been found that there is a positive link between the excessive sodium intake and high blood pressure. In other words, it has been found that persons who take more salt in their diet generally face the problem of high blood pressure. To reduce risk for cardiovascular disorders, it is necessary to cut back on the sodium. It has also been prove by various studies that calcium loss in urine can take place as a result of high sodium intake, by which risk for debilitating fractures get increased with increase in the age.

Iron

It is considered to be one of the most important nutrient required by human body. Around three to four grams of iron is found to be present in body of an adult, out of which, a large proportion of which exists in hemoglobin present in the blood. There is around 3 to 3.4 mg of iron in each gram of hemoglobin. Iron deficiency is found to be one of the most common kind of nutrient deficiency, by which majority of people not only in our nation, but different parts of the world are being affected. This problem is more alarming in the developing countries like ours, majority of sufferers of this problem are children and women. When human body becomes unable to produce hemoglobin, then a disease called anemia gets developed in the body. In people affecting with iron deficiency anemia, a condition known as pica can also get developed which is an appetite for ice, clay and other non-food substances that do not contain iron and in fact may inhibit iron absorption to considerable extent.

In the person having deficiency of iron, various kinds of problems are faced. Generally it is found that body cells present in such person's body receive less oxygen as a result of which, carbon dioxide wastes are removed from body less efficiently. As a result of this condition, a lot of tiredness is felt by such person. Generally women are more likely to develop iron deficiency problems as they typically eat less food than men and their diets consist of less iron elements.

Significant role played by mineral in the form of iron can be analysed from the fact that it's deficiency can tax the immune system, causing it to function less effectively. Iron deficiency can also lead to immunity and decreased resistance to various infections. There appears to be a slight association between iron deficiency and cancer.

Calcium

This nutrient plays very important role in human body, some of the functions performed by it are as follows:—

a. It helps in building strong bones and teeth.

b. It helps in regulating the function of muscle contraction.

c. It provide assistance for various cardiac actions.

d. In the retina, light is being transformed into electrical impulses through this mineral.

e. It helps in keeping control over the heart beats.

f. It helps in keeping the fluid balance within the cells existing in human body.

Over half of the calcium intake usually comes from milk, which is one of the highest sources of dietary calcium. Other good sources of calcium are green and leafy vegetables. Cauliflower and many peas also offer good supplies of calcium to the body. Good amounts of calcium exists in various nuts, particularly almonds. Some fruits, such as citrus fruits have moderate amounts of this mineral.

One should not consume carbonated soft drinks in larger quantities as these consist of added phosphoric acid which can cause you to excrete extra calcium which may result in calcium being pulled out of your bones. Chances of development of kidney stones gets increased with existence of calcium quantities in much larger quantities than required.

Fluorine

This kind of mineral is considered to be one of the abundant element found in nature. This element in highly reactive in nature, as a result of which it occurs only in a combined form in form of fluoride. Major portion of fluoride in the body is found in the bones and teeth. Experts have recommended the intake of 0.5 to 0.8 mg per litre of fluorine in the water for a healthy adult. Various kinds of dental problems get arise as a result of deficiency of fluoride in the body, however, if taken in excess than required quantity, then it can lead to dental and skeletal fluorosis in the body.

The main sources by which fluorine can be obtained are drinking water, sea fish, cheese and tea. This mineral should be taken in the right or adequate amount as various kinds of important functions are being played by it. For instance, it helps normal mineralisation of bone and also helps in formation of dental enamel.

Iodine

This is considered to be one of the most important micro-nutrient. Generally it is present in the human body in quantity of 50 mg. Sea foods of various kinds are considered to be important source of iodine. In meat, cereals and vegetables also this mineral is found in moderate quantities. The best source of availability of this mineral is consumption of iodised table salt.

This mineral performs various kinds of important functions in the body. For instance, it helps in the synthesis of thyroid hormones in the body and it is also required for proper development of various body parts. It is very necessary to consume this mineral in adequate amount as it's deficiency can lead to various kinds of problems, one of an important and of serious nature of which is goiter. Not only this, this mineral should be consumed in higher quantities by a pregnant woman as it's deficiency can lead to abortion and mis-carriage.

Copper

This kind of mineral is required for the synthesis of hemoglobin present in the blood. It should be taken in adequate quantity as it's deficiency can lead to defective formation of elastic tissues and tissue matrix in the body. The main sources from which it can be obtained are common salt, tomatoes and green leafy vegetables.

Zinc

This kind of mineral is found in all tissues in form

of traces. It is one of an important constituents of several enzymes. The daily requirement of a human being is five to ten milligram. The sources through which it can be obtained include meat, fish and milk. It is very important to take this mineral in proper quantity as it's deficiency can lead to various kinds of sexual infantilism and skin disorders. Not only this, person having inadequate amount of zinc can suffer from problem of slow growth process as a result of which, he can become physically or mentally regarded.

Water

Human beings can survive for much longer without food than they can without water. Even in severe conditions, the average person can go for weeks without certain vitamins and minerals before experiencing serious deficiency symptoms. However, dehydration can cause serious problems within a matter of hours, after a few days without water, death is likely. Here it is important to mention that the condition in which water level gets lower than the adequate or required in the body, it is called dehydration.

Various studies show the fact that a health human being requires around six to eight glasses of water per day. Because of high concentrations of water in most of the food items human beings consumed, however, the actual number of glasses needed each day becomes somewhat less than this. On various factors individual need of water of human beings depend, some of which are age, body size and environmental temperature. Higher volume of fluid intake becomes necessary for persons suffering from certain specific diseases like diabetes. However, it should be born in mind that if clean water can prove be nectar for the human beings, dirty water can play role of poison for them. It is very necessary to take only clean drinking water, otherwise, various kinds of diseases will get arise in the body. Not only this, there are various infections which result as a result of drinking impure water. All the provisions should be made to keep the drinking water safe and clean. Firstly clean utensils should be used to store such kind of water and proper attention should be paid to the fact that no one puts his fingers in such water. Number of persons suffering from problems arising as a result of drinking dirty and unclean water are increased in our nation, the main reason of which is that no proper provision of safe and drinking water has been made in various parts of the nation inspite of various steps taken by government authorities in this direction. But still, significance of water as one of an important nutrient of the body cannot be ignored in any way. This should be understood by the politicians and service providers that without providing clean drinking water to the citizens, they even cannot hope to raise the level of their health in any way.

PART-II
ENVIRONMENT STUDY

1

ENVIRONMENT—FROM SOCIOLOGICAL POINT OF VIEW

Meaning of Social Issues

Activities of man right from birth to death on this earth are deeply related to social issues. He while living in society cannot detach himself from social issues of life. This is the reason that someone has rightly pointed out that society is the web of social relations and man is social animal. Social issues cover family, associations, institutions and communities. Perhaps family is the strongest agency of social issues. While being in society he has to undertake a number of socio-economic activities such as industry, agriculture, transport, construction of roads, and buildings etc., for surviving in the society.

These activities contribute much to environment degradation including water, soil and air etc. Socio-economic development is the call of the day because everyone desires to have a higher and better standard of living. The geographical land area with man is reducing day by day due to growing population. With the limited availability of land for cultivation purposes, the need for increasing the application of fertilizers, nitrogenous, phosphatic and potash are also necessary for appropriate pest control through pesticides is being made in order to ensure more and more growth of both food and fibre. These socio-economic activities hit environmental conditions. So the protection of the environment is an important issue of the day. There should be development without polluting the environment. Engineers in this respect have a major role to play. Many a time the question comes to our mind as to whether we want environment or development.

To this the straight reply is that, there should be development within the environment. One does not place these two things separate, i.e., development and clean environment. If one cannot breathe pure air, if he cannot drink clean water e.g., if you have come from west and live on mineral water because you do not dare touch water available here, there is something wrong somewhere, and if in the 20th century we have achieved the so called material benefits by the last decade is that we have polluted our land, air, water and food, then there must be something wrong in our achievements we have done for the last 90 years. So the real socio-economic development does not lie in producing and amazing material and non-material things but in having these along with a clean and pollution free environment.

Urban Residential and Commercial Energy Demand

As already explained, the amount of energy required for residential and commercial use varies greatly throughout the world. The economics of energy consumption describe that a country with high GNP use less per capita energy for residential and roughly national use less per capita energy for residential and commercial needs, than a less developed country like Africa and India. 30 percent energy used in North America and 90 percent used in India is for residential and commercial purposes. Reason is very simple. North Americans use air conditioning, refrigeration, water heating and space heating. So 75 percent energy is used in these gadgets. In India, almost all of the energy used in home is for cooking due to scarcity and high cost of fuel. About half of the energy demand in Africa is for cooking because they use an open fire instead of stoves. Using more efficient stoves instead of open fires could reduce these energy requirements by 50 percent. Similarity North America, and India could reduce energy consumption in many ways.

Urban- Industrial Energy Demand- Considerable variation is found in the amount of energy used for industrial processes. Facts speak that 60 percent of all the commercial energy was used in the former Soviet Union. About 30 percent of energy is used by USA for industries.

In the former Soviet Union large deposits of coal, oil and natural gas reserves were available. On account of this reason steel is processed from ore because energy is readily available. Spain and Italy lack large deposits of fossil fuel necessary for the extraction of oil and natural gas. So both Italy and Spain produce steel from scarp steel because it needs less energy. Producing 1 metric ton of steel from iron or in the former Soviet Union uses as much energy as producing a metric ton of steel from scrap in Spain or Italy.

Large capital investment is required to upgrade the process of industrial production, because updated and upgraded machinery and equipment reduce industrial energy consumption. Many countries of the world cannot afford to convert their existing processes due to financial and other constraints. Take the case of India, a nation with few coal deposits, still used the outdated open hearth furnace to produce steel. This process needs double the worldwide energy for producing a metric ton of steel on an average. India being a underdeveloped country if unable to change the process of modern methods has to continue to use energy expensive methods.

Transportation Energy Demand in urban areas. In India energy used in giga Joules per capita in transportation 2,103 in United States, 82 in Australia and 4 in Zimbabwe. These statistics with regard to energy demand in transportation clearly show that energy use for transportation is larger in developing and highly developed countries. Rail, water, private automobiles and mix bus service determine country's energy use for transportation. The places where public transport is efficient less private automobiles are used. This is so because automobiles require about four times more energy per passenger kilometer than bus or rail transport. But in developed countries, the situation is different. The government policy in these countries is different. Government in these countries keep the cost of energy low. Consequently, the automobile plays a dominant role, and public transport is primarily used only in metropolitan areas. Rail and bus transport are about twice as energy efficient as private automobiles. Air travel is relatively expensive in terms of energy.

Electrical Energy Demand in urban areas. Electrical energy consumption in different regions of the world varies widely. The amount of electricity used by all the less developed nations, with over 75 percent of the world's population, is only 66 percent of that used by the United States alone. North America uses electrical energy twenty-five times greater that average per capita use of this energy in less developed countries. The electricity used in industries by developed countries in comparison to underdeveloped countries is also much more.

Unsustainable to sustainable development

Unsustainable development or growth is one in which social issues of life do not progress in a healthy and ethical style. This style of living cover mismanagement of resources like large-scale deforestation, indiscriminate construction and expansion of settlement activities, discharging toxic wastes, pulling air water and what not.

As globalization in its current form increases, so too unsustainable development that it seems to prescribe. There is abudant evidence that the version of modernity demonstrated in current globalization trends neglects scientific evidence and tradition in equal measure. In contrast, the traditional approaches to natural resources management in many communities demonstrate sourced science than development does. Tradition in local resource management has survived over many generations of environmental degradation - which are evidently no longer future threats but very real current crises of - have resulted from approaches to modernity which, in throwing away such traditions aside, continue in denial about scientific evidence.

In many regions of the world, ecosystem stress can be seen due to human-intensive activities such as unsustainable resources extraction and exploitation via large corporations and international trading agreements that open these sources up for excessive extraction and consumerism.

Dropsy is a disease caused due to adulteration in mustard oil by greedy, dishonest elements of society with a motive to get rich at the expense of the lives of the general public in the society. Most of the adulterated mustard oil samples were found containing Argemone, and a few samples were found to be containing adulterants such as polybromide and even mobile oil.

This may be sustainable personal development of an industrialist but most unsustainable development for society as a whole.

All environmental issues involve consideration of ethics. For instance, sufficient food and fabric is available in the world to feed people. It is unethical to allow some people to starve and others consume more than what they need. Developed nations do not realize it. They have enough and still they need more. Their greed for more is ever increasing. They do not surrender before morals and ethics of life and share with others what they have. They must think less about conquering nature and more about learning to work with nature. Each person must realize his interdependence with the rest of the nature including his fellow human beings. To safeguard life on earth, people must learn to control and adjust the balances in nature that are altered by their activities.

One more reason is placed in this context. Members of the society very well realize this view. They view the world's energy situation as serious and have reduced their own consumption. But many do not believe and realize this problem. They continue to consume energy as long as it is available and do not accept any cut on the use of it. Other similar issues are the population problem and pollution. It is ethical to have more than two children when the world is facing problem of overpopulation? Similarly an industrialist may not probably look on the negative aspects of pollution compared to one who is outdoor. Some sixty American cities have been declared having unsatisfactory water supply due to toxicity of pollutants released by industries. Every year in the United States, 20 million tons of paper and 200 million tons of domestic garbage is junked. Keeping this in view the Massachusetts

Institute of Technology, USA reveals that there shall be disastrous collapse in the coming hundred years if both population growth and industrial growth are not brought to an immediate halt. So the first task is to educate economics harpers about the value of environmental ethics. Clean and unpolluted air away from the chimneys of industries, free from fumes and smoke has a great cleansing and purifying effect for sustainable growth. For this purpose, taking ethical stand is important regardless to those who disagree with it.

Emerson, a pioneer philosopher environmentalist in his first essay Nature published in 1836 objected fast economic development by way of invading nature. Another naturalist who held the beliefs similar to Emerson was Henry David Thoreau. According to Thoreu, "Truth in nature and wilderness over the deceits of urban civilization." He summarized his feelings about nature as But most men, it seems to me, do not care for nature and would sell their share in all her beauty, as long as they may live, for a stated sum-many for a glass of rum. He further concluded Thank God, men cannot as yet fly, and lay waste in the sky as well as the earth.

Urban Problems related to energy

Energy is a essential of a man where-ever he lives-urban or rural society. In urban areas the need of energy is increasing by leaps and bounds. Take the case of mega-urban dwelling places. Vehicles both petrol and engine driven are seen flowing like floods. According to one rough estimate nearly 40 lakh surface transport move on Delhi roads. These vehicles run with the basic input called oil which is one form of energy. What about other sources of energy-renewable and non-renewable being used by urban population. The world-wide demand for energy will be more than double by the year

2020.

Moreover, countries use energy in an uneven manner in the world. Some countries use more energy while many less. In developed countries the amount of energy used is much more compared to underdeveloped developing countries. Industrialized developed countries use energy for these purposes:)i) residential and commercial, (ii) industrial and (iii) transportation. In less-developed countries, most of the energy is used by individuals. Canada and United States use about twice as much energy as someone in France or Japan and over twenty-five times as much energy as a person in Africa. The consumption of energy in India is more than Africa because it is the second populous country in the world with population touching slightly more than 100 crores, according to the latest census.

In India, about 70% commercial energy is being generated through coalfired thermal plants. Coal consumption by thermal plants is nearly 130 million tonnes annually and is expected to rise to 272 million tonnes by 2002. There are about 40 thermal plants both big and small scattered all over the country. The Korba-Super Thermal Power Station is the largest. It has installed capacity of 2,100 MW. Power from the project goes into the western grid comprising the states of Madhya Pradesh, Maharashtra, Gujarat and Goa. However, Bihar, West Bengal, Delhi, Gujarat and Haryana are some of the main producers of thermal power in India.

Sustainable Development

Continuous and persistent rise in any system is known as sustainable growth. It means continuous rise in the GNP of the country resulting into the rising trend in per capita income of the country. The objective of sustainable development is to promote development which in turn reduces the disparities in life styles. Improve global consumption and maintaining a healthful local environmental and thereby contributing towards solving critical global environmental management problem:

1. Reduce disparity in life style.
2. Protecting soil from pollution.
3. Reduction in waste and prevention of pollution.
4. Integrated environmental systems management.
5. Efficient use of natural resources.

The 10th FYP envisages the provision of potable drinking water to every settlement in the country on a sustainable basis and the pursuit of all possible measures for the rapid expansion and improvement of sanitation facilities in rural and urban areas.

Water conservation, Waterland management and water-harvesting

Water conservation means saving water for future use. When water scarcity is felt storing water and avoiding wastage of water is equally important approach towards water conservation. Wetlands are found of course all over the country and are either natural or built by people. Over the years they have gradually depleted, leading to a number of problems such as flooding, water scarcity, and water logging. Keeping this problem in view, takes have been constructed in the catchment areas of cities that were not located near a river or a large lake. Rainwater or run-off would collect during the monsoons and be stored for the rest of the year in these tanks and lakes. The city would get its water supply from these.

In southern India, the towns were built around a temple, which always had a tank at the centre. Wells were located in the tank, which served as a link with the aquiferous. There were innumerable tanks dug by rules, most of which have been destroyed. In fact, in some areas tank building by the ruler was considered a noble deed.

In Karnataka, the Hoysalas built tanks all over the state. Some of these still exist. Festivals were organized around tanks; cleaning and de-silting the tanks were a part of the rituals. But over the years, human activity steadily destroyed these wetlands. In Bangalore, the city bus terminus has been built on the Dharmambudhi tank. A part of the Sampangi tank has given way to the Kanteerva stadium and the remaining to a housing colony. Another lake was filled up to house the city market.

The Cholas were well known for the construction of tanks in the state of Tamil Nadu. But today, despite heavy rains, Chennai reels under severe water crisis along with flooding. A number of housing colonies have been built on tanks and over the years the numbers are increasing. This is the case in most large cities in the country.

Energy problems of urbanized population

The details of energy demand clearly reflect that there is imbalance between demand and supply of energy. The demand of energy is more whereas supply is less. Demand is more because number of houses and vehicles are increasing day by day. Besides this, consumers of energy are abudant in number. We were 34-37 crores in 1951 but now we are more than 100 crores in India. Every one nearly is having electrical appliance. The energy consumption is therefore shooting up. On account these reasons urban people are feeling following energy demand problems.

1. Where you could walk, walk or at the most use a bicycle.

2. Eat grain based diets than carnivory.

3. Renewable energy damages are less in comparison to coal and oil. Use it frequently.

4. Create wind-break on the north side by house and plant deciduous trees on the south side.

5. Keep an eye on energy use habits. Turn-off lights, televisions, geysers, computers etc., when not in use.

6. Careful use of large electric or gas appliances such as stoves, refrigerators, washing machines and dryers.

7. To have sustainable life-styles, use of lesser voltage sources of light may be exercised to conserve energy so that even distribution of power is done.

8. Hydro-electricity is not sufficient and where there are no water flowing or perennial rivers, there were cannot depend upon hydro-electricity either.

9. Entropy is failure because eventual heat is not distributed within a closed system.

10. Transmission lines are not perfectly erected.

The Wetlands

Wetlands are areas lying along the banks of rivers and lakes and the coastal regions. They are life-supporting systems providing fish, forest products, water, flood control, erosion buffering, a plant gene pool, wildlife, recreation, and tourism areas. Though they are endowed with a rich biodiversity, yet of late they are being greatly exploited. Wetland come in many forms. Swamps are good example.

In most simple manner wetlands represented interface between land and water. Depth of wetland should be a maximum of 6 metres according to the Ramsar convention. For minimum depth there is no limitation, it can be 6 inches or no water at all in dry season. Wetland are important links between land and water. They are regarded as most important ecosystems on the earth, and called kidneys of the biosphere as they moderate flow of nutrients and silt from land to water by trapping them. About 6% of the land surface of earth is wetland. Many wetland species have become threatened and endangered because of their dependence on a particular type of wetland ecosystem, which has become seriously degraded or destroyed.

Functions of wetland

These high productive ecosystems have important benefits such as:

(i) maintenance of integrity of other ecosystem.

(ii) climate stabilization.

(iii) toxicant removal by doing water treatment.

(iv) salinity control.

(v) erosion control.

(vi) ground water recharge.

Types of wetlands

Wetlands can classified into three categories:

(i) Marshers, (ii) Swamps and (iii) Peatlands. Within each of these categories wetlands can vary widely, because wetlands depend on water resources, their boundaries can change. The characteristics that describe each category include vegetation, soil type, water supply and water chemistry.

Wetlands in India and Threats to Indian Wetlands

In India wetlands are distributed in different geographical regions. As per a survey conducted by ministry of environment and forests, the total wetland area of India is about 4.1 million hectares and the rest is occupied by man-made wetlands. Maximum number of natural wetlands are in Assam. Total no. natural wetlands in country is about 2,200. Main threats to Indian wetlands are:

(i) Use of poisons and explosives during hunting and fishing.

(ii) Grazing by domestic livestocks.

(iii) Degradation of waterlands, increased siltation of wetlands, deforestation and soil erosion.

(iv) Encroachments for road and other transportation facilities.

(v) Infestation with aquatic weeds uncontrolled growth of weeds and eutrophication.

(vi) Cutting of timber, trees and mangroves for fuelwood and domestic use.

(vii) Alteration of wetlands to other use categories such as for agriculture urban development, industrial sites, forestry operations etc.

(viii) Pollution from waterboats, domestic sewage, pesticides, fertilizers and effluents.

Environmental Ethics

Earth is the most beautiful object. It is unique among all the planets in our solar system. It is a pathway of sustainable development. We abuse land because we regard it as a commodity belonging to us. Once we see land as a community to which we belong, we may being to use it with love and respect. Environmental ethics teach us value of earth; interdependence; belongingness and ecological preservation-necessary for sustainable development. The treatment given to earth in the form of commodity is most unethical recognized by ethical environmentalists. This is so because many people see little value in an undeveloped river. They feel it is unreasonable to leave a river flowing in a natural state. This is the reason that many rivers throughout the world have been controlled to provide power, irrigation and navigation for the people at the expense of the natural world. Sarovar over Narmada and Rajasthan Canal Project are a few important river valley projects constructed by man for power generation, navigational, recreational and irrigational benefits. Power a most versatile form of energy is being used in the development of agriculture and industry.

To meet the ever increasing demand of electricity, public leaders are engaged in harnessing natural resources amongst which water is one. Not using such resources would be wasteful is a feeling quite common in their minds. A serious conflict is going on over the value of old-growth forests in the Pacific Northwest of the United States. Many economic interests are involved over this dispute. They want to use the forests for timber production. If not to make their use for the betterment of society, they feel. Those who support land as a community to which they belong to not agree with this attempt. They feel that all the living things that make up the forest have a definite value which we do not appreciate. Felling and removing the trees would destroy something that took much more time to develop and may never be replaced.

120 nations at a global meeting on CITES objected the trade sanctions against china and Taiwan when these two nations were found selling rhinoceros and tiger parts for medicinal purposes. The animals are killed to provide material for growing international market. Rhino horns and tiger bones are still used in traditional

Chinese medicines to treat fevers and joint as well as bone are available for sale in pharmaceutical shops as well as government run stores in China. This may be one important reason that fewer tigers and rhinos remain in the world. In view of this reality. CITES has proposed a cut on international trade in endanger species. Corporate leaders should support in leaving aside economic interests.

Though there may be many environmental attitudes yet for the sake of convenience three classifications are made and each one in labelled separately provided with suitable heading.

1. Conservation ethic - This is the ethic of environment. Conservation means maintenance and preservation of the environment to meet human needs for production while insuring that proper consideration is given to aesthetics and recreation. The conservation ethic is related to scientific preservation. Through it recognizes the desirability of decent living standard yet works toward a balance of resource use and resource availability. The reasonable use of Earth's natural resources such as water, soil, wild-life, forests and minerals is the major objective of conservation ethicists. The conservation ethic suggest a serious balance between total development and absolute preservation of resources.

An effective conservation programme results in continuous production of plants and animals and mineral resources which can create imbalance between availability and demand of such resources may not today but in future definitely. The goal and objective of conservation ethic is one people living together in one world indefinitely. Conservation is therefor very important in view of this fact. Environmental ethicist can better guide human beings over this issue and preach. As humanists and populists, they consider the goals of conservation to prevent waste and save resources for prudent constructive and efficient human use and absolute preservation of resources. Social ecologists suggest that the problem of human ignorance and greed can be solved by interacting with correct thinking people for the survival of planet. Canada's Green Plan developed in 1990 address current environmental problems. It contains comprehensive new programmes, policies and include: (i) Protecting and enhancing the quality of water resources and promoting wise and efficient use of water, (ii) Developing an environmentally healthy society, pollution problems did arise. Groundwater became contaminated with chloride from the drilling. Forest's most prized commodity solitude is lost. The case of the Pigeon River Forest is solitude versus oil. Agreed that a barrel of oil has direct economic value. But what value we can place on a day of solitude in nature is difficult to estimate. (iii) Cutting waste 50 percent by the year 2001. and (iv) Securing current and future generations a safe and healthy environment and a sound and prosperous economy.

The question arises what is enough, Many poor societies have little but do the rich societies agree to halt. The developed societies are over-ambitious. One thinker said The earth provides enough to satisfy every person's need, but not every person's greed. Contentment is great thing but bow many nations compromise over it. Growth and domination is the central sociocultural goal of most advance societies whereas economic growth and resource exploitation are attitudes shared by developing societies amongst which Indian society is one. We continue to consume natural resources with this feeling in mind that supply of resources will never end. This is reflected in our increasingly unstable relationship with the environment. Our desire for taking resources is growing day by day from the common lot regardless to future.

2. Preservation ethic - This ethic reserve special place for nature. Different preservationists have different reasons to preserve nature. Some have religious reasons while many shoe recreational aesthetic feelings towards preservation of nature. Those who have religious belief towards nature hold reverence for trees and respect the right of all creatures to live. To these preservationists social and economic costs are not so important. Preservationists opine that when a tree is hexed it may not show any visible feelings of suffering but that does not man that we can go to felling trees. Aesthenic or recreational preservationists believe that nature is beautiful and refreshing. It should be available cross-country skiing, picnics, hiking, camping and just for quietness and peace. Exploitation should be curbed. Glorious pursuits beyond sensible level of need must not be permitted. With these feelings, man can live more happily in the future because harmony between him and nature is created by way of eco-friendship.

The views of semireligious and recreational preservationists seems to be essentially scientific. These individual argue that human species depends on and has much to learn from nature. Natural resources such as trees and plants are the life and blood of human civilization. They have served human species in various ways from the days of yore. A large portion of the food, medicines and materials that man consuls is derived from some wild species of plants Catharanthus rosens is one such plant which originated in Madagascar when used in the form of herbal medicine, treated children suffering from Leukemia. Dr. Richard Evans rightly pointed out The drugs of future grow in primeval jungle. Man should know the immense value of nature by putting aside ignorance and shortsightedness. This ignorance has put about 25,000 flowering species on the verge of extinction. Preservation of nature alone can save human species. Preservationists comment and argue that rare and endangered species and ecosystems, as well as, more common one must be preserved because of practical utility. Remember natural diversity and wilderness is much more superior to humanized domesticity. If we care for Nature, it can be rich, bountiful and inhausibly sustainable.

3. Progressive ethic - It is also called development ethic. This ethic is governed and based on action. Progressive ethic reflect that human race is master of nature. Earth and its resources exist for the benefit and pleasure of man. Who denies than man should not make use of natural resources. It is called work of ethic which dictates that human should be busy creating continual change. The activities performed by him that are bigger, better and faster represent progress itself is good. This philosophy is encouraged by the idea that if it can be done, it should be done. Our actions and energies should be best harnessed in creative work. The dream of upward mobility is embodied in development ethic. The notion that bigger is better, definitely not new to us but is unpatriotic when one hit the environmental ethic. Preserve ethic and exercise growth is the answer.

Urban Wetlands

There are no rivers in the vicnity of Bhopal and the city depends entirely on lakes to meet the water needs of the city. Over the years, these lakes have become polluted due to the dumping of sewage into them. The government recently announced the Bhuj Wetland Project, a scheme to prevent the flow of liquid and solid waste into the lakes and also to desalt them. More than 2000 ha of land around the upper lakes, which feed water to the lower ones, is to come under plantation.

Once upon a time, these urban wetlands maintained a steady supply of water of the city, recharged the groundwater, cooled the city, and prevented flood as they have natural drainage system. Over the years, these very tanks and wetlands have been neglected, encroached upon either to accommodate more houses or to dump waste. This has caused large-scale water crisis and monsoon flooding and water logging, leading to misery and disease. These wetlands that have been protected for centuries are now being ravaged and destroyed in the name of development.

People in the urban areas learn to live in harmony with nature in their own habitat. The wetlands, the green belts, and the flora and fauna of these areas have to be preserved for urban areas to survive and remain healthy. Many people do not understand the value of wetlands, in support we give following cases.

1. Indore's water needs were met by a large numbers of wells and tanks located all around the city. But over the last few years, the tanks have gradually dried up, including the largest of them, the Yashwant Sagar Lake. Vegetable and fruit cultivation along the banks of the lake has caused pollution due to run-offs from the fields. This has caused eutrophication and contamination.

2. In Kolkata wetlands, both artificial and natural, have been a part of the city system. The main drainage for the city has been the Hooghly River; but the incline of the city is eastwards and this has led to the creation

of the East Kolkata Wetlands. The Salt Lake is one of the largest wetlands in the city and serves as a flood cushion for the city. Kolkata has no sewage treatment plant. The sewage is treated in the sewage-fed fisheries purify this water through a series of sedimentation tanks and use of the water for fish cultivation and agriculture.

Corporate Environmental Ethics

Corporation also called a corporate enterprise is a large business house managed by professional managers, designed to operate at a profit. Corporation have legal entities. Examples of corporate enterprises in India are D.C.M., Modi, Reliance and ABB. A corporate enterprise procure raw materials, manufacture and market the products so produced. These corporate enterprise when seen in the shape of industry appear dirty because all industries consume energy and resources. Some waste is inevitable when raw materials are processed. Some of the waste material may be simply useless. For instance, the food service industry use energy in the preparation of meals. Much of this energy is lost as waste heat. In addition smoke and toxic gases are released into the atmosphere. The cost of controlling waste can be very important in determining the company's profit.

Ethics are involved when a corporation do not maintain standard as prescribed of the product and waste disposal to maximize profit. Ethics appear when an industry cut corners in production quality and many times present adulterated items to the users. Reduction in cost in another issue before corporation. The cheaper it is to produce an item, the greater the possible profit. It reduces the cost of production by lowering the quality standards which is highly unethical. To an industry it is cheaper to dump wastes into a river than to instal wastewater treatment facility, and it is still cheaper to release wastes into the air than it is to trap them in filters. Pollution in this way released is considered immoral and unethical to many but to the corporations, it is just one of the factors that determines the profitability. This is true in chemical, oil and many other industries. If we question corporate leaders over this subject then the simple answer given is that stockholders expect a quick return on their investment. It is, therefore, observed that corporations often make decisions before short-term profitability rather than long-term benefit to society. It is not an unethical practice exercised by corporations.

The expansion of a corporation depends upon the amount of profit it realizers from a given investment venture. Higher profitability leads to higher expansion. Take the case of big corporation like Tata, Tata, Birla, Dalmia and IBM Corporation. Analyser predict more expansion of these organizations in future, because these corporations create increased demand fort their products through advertisement, publicity and other marketing strategies. The more they expand, the more power they attain and greatly influence decision makers who create conditions favourable to their expansion plans. So it becomes a never-ending spiral. Who stops their expansion provided these corporations do not show irresponsibility toward the environment. The corporate decision maker exercise minimum discount to the public interest, while maximum efforts are made to increase profitability. It is fair to enhance profitability by increasing social costs. One is amazed to notice that many political and legal institutions defend private property rights rather than social and environmental concerns.

To evaluate corporate environmental responsibility

Valdez Principles were coined as a result of the 1989 oil spill in Alaska. These principles were later adopted by the CERES organization. These are recognized as CERES Principles propagated by independent group of environmentalists and social investors. These principles are set of codes against which the working of business houses as well as corporations can be assessed and compared. The principles encompass making sustainable use of renewable resources by way of minimizing pollutants. Corporation are expected to make compliance with CERES principles for doing business. The need for developing such principles was felt due to deaths of ducks that occurred on account of oil spill in Alaska in 1989. There is no sanity to maintain higher industrial productivity at the cost of depriving a nation of breathable air and drinkable water, is clearly reflected by CERES principles. CERES principle as its core advocate environmental justice which means protecting health of human beings and the productivity of ecological systems upon which all human activities rest.

Societal Environmental Ethics

Societal environmental ethics concentrate on the development of environmentally literate society. Accomplishment of it is a difficult task because society is composed of a great variety people with different views and opinions. However, this variety can be distilled into a set of ideas and observed from the ethical point of view. Western developed societies accommodate unchecked growth and development because members of these societies accommodate unchecked growth and development because members of these societies feel and act that earth has unlimited reserves of natural resources and limitless ability to assimilate wastes.

Continual growth is the rationale of developed nations behind this thinking. Unfortunately the idea of continual growth has not always been carefully planned and implemented. This growth has resulted in the use of nonrenewable resources for comfortable homes and convenient transportation. Oil was discovered by man in a remote area of Michigan known as the Pigeon Reiver Forest in 1968. Its 37,600 hectares is considered to have all wilderness qualities because many animals inhabit this region. Oil wells were drilled in the area with a view to overpower energy crisis. Michigan would get several hundred million dollars of royalty against this venture. But what happened, much less oil was found beneath the forest than was originally predicted with all safeguards. This attitude of society towards environment is deeply rooted since time immemorial. The first settlers when arrived in North America considered nature an enemy. They viewed nature to be conquered and vanquished. Invading and exploiting wilderness were justified by religious beliefs by them. This attitude towards nature is still popular amongst them. Not developing a resource is considered almost a sin by many.

Pollution Abatement Eco-friendly

The chambers of Commerce and Industry Association have an important role in sharing the experiences of industrial units besides providing a form for exchange of ideas and technical knowledge in the implementation of pollution control schemes. A survey conducted by ASSIOCHAM revealed that one of the basic problems faced by the industry in implementing pollution control system is that proper monitoring devices are not available within the country. Based on the survey ASSOCHAM has submitted a list of monitoring devices which can be manufactured in India.

Various interactions between the industry and Government organised by ASSOCHAM have highlighted the following suggestions for effective management of pollution:

1. In setting standards, parallel supporting system and facilities for effective implementation to be given equal attention.

2. Creation of centralized data bank pooling all information on wastes particularly hazardous types.

3. Greater coordination between industrial units and multinational projects being set up in India with latest technology in this area.

4. One or more environment performance units can be set up to tackle the problems of pollution in the industrial sector enabling the other units to draw upon the expertise of these companies.

5. Many of the existing standards are unachievable for the existing units because of the type of technology in use, age of the unit, size of the plant, lack of economically viable pollution control technology, non-availability of testing equipment and non-identification of dumping sites for storage of wastes. In view of these considerations, there is need for evolving rational standards and different norms for new units and the old ones. Besides standards need not be the same as in developed countries.

6. The role of government enforcement agencies should not be restricted to only regulation but should also provide information education, guidance and counselling.

7. Removal of prejudices against recycled products through education campaigns and providing offtake guarantees by institutional buyers to promote waste

utilization for manufacturing useful products.

8. The proposed institute could also industry particularly in the small sector through constancy, training and providing technical assistance.

9. An autonomous industrial waste management institute as proposed by National Waste management Council should be set up to provide institutional support to the industry. The institute could also advise the Government on policy issues and evolve strategies for reducing waste and in managing it.

10. A national policy needs to be evolved on the management of hazardous and other wastes. It should aim at reducing the volume of waste, utilizing it for manufacturing recycled products to generate resources, treating and disposing the residual waste in an environmentally friendly manner.

Now standards for bottle water should be adopted. New BIS code says packaged water will have to be tested for 32 pesticides; individually, the quality of those pesticides cannot exceed 0.1 micro-milligram per litre and total pesticide residue should be less than 0.5 micro-milligram per litre. Licensed manufacturer shall have to obtain permission from Central Ground Water Authority, because most bottlers use laced with pesticide in most areas. Small companies will be wiped out because new plants could cost over Rs. 15 crores. Instead of burning the leaves, bury them in compost pits, by which it gets converted to natural manure, making it beneficial for the soil.

Economic aspects of environment

Many people hold the view that there is conflict between quality of the environment and economic growth. Working out environmental benefits quantitatively is a difficult task. Though economic growth depends upon environmental conditions yet it is difficult to work out cost benefit analysis between the two. Attempts have been made to estimate monetary losses and gains as a useful tool in the formulation of development objectives and in the execution of environmental policies.

Costs

A study revise that the effect of noise by London Airport on the value of property nearby and on the elimination of noise did not make people conscious about the monetary benefit represented. On the contrary the occupants of the expensive houses gave higher value to noise elimination while poor residents attached more value to being close to the place of work. The possible effects on the future generation whose voice is not heard make some of these views or estimates mor valuable.

Of all the various environmental factors which have economical consequences, the most well known and easy to identify and analyze is that of the industrial pollution and urban wastes. The economics of industrial pollution, which is basically in terms of effluents, wastes and residues, have been studied in many countries including Japan, Italy and United States. The economics have advocated that polluter must pay for the pollution. There are also other views that the industrial polluters pay charges which are directly proportional to the amounts of wastes or effluents discharged, as in the polluter pays principle used by Environment Protection Agency of the USA.

Scaled compensation in another economic method and aspect of environment. Though technically not possible, yet it has been introduced in Japan and Italy. The payment of compensation has been enforced by law courts under various environmental and civil laws. Under this, people are compensated if they are their property suffer from environmentally bad conditions.

One of the unresolved issues today is to what extent is the ecosystem and our environment going to remain stable under the stress of various development actions. Scientific research can throw some light on this issue in the future. Techno-economic analysis of the nature of developmental alternatives is also of crucial importance, to recognize the problem of harmonizing economic and environmental conflicts. Human settlements, industrial and agricultural activities lead to production of wastes of various kinds. The overall term generally used for these, are residues. If we use the term resume broadly then,

1. One part of the residues, again termed generally waste, can be completely foreign to nature and may represent a serious source of trouble for living organisms and the equilibrium of the ecological system into which these wastes are put. The polluting effect of a residue, in whatever category, has to be taken into consideration both the nature and the quantity of the waste discharged and the dimensions and capacity of the receiving system to absorb and transform it. Included in the concept of residues and wastes is also heat and this is termed as thermal pollution because a rise of temperature by even a few degrees in a lake or a river may change the ecological system and change the species composition drastically.

2. A part of residues which can be termed waste is biologically or geochemically degradable and at the end is converted into naturally occurring substances such a nitrogen, carbon dioxide, water, metal oxides and others. However, the process of natural degradation takes placed at the expense of the quality of the environmental

and, therefore, has an impact on human society. For instance, a human or animal excrement discharged in the water is degraded in lake or river but in that process takes up oxygen from the river or lake and decrease the capacity of these waters to receive further bio-degradable wastes. In fact, it may even jeopardize fresh water fauna through lack of dissolved oxygen.

3. A part of the natural resources is definitely subtracted from the reserves when they are used in buildings, roads and other semi permanent structure.

4. The amount of residues tends to be greater than or equal to the amount of natural resources subtracted from the reserves; because in the use of resources, in the manufacture of commodities or in the combustion, oxygen or water may be subtracted from the atmosphere or river and converted into products such as carbondioxide and water vapour which are also essential residues but which cycle quite easily in nature.

The number of pollutants are so many that it is often difficult to study the natural history of a single pollutant. There are also complicating possibilities of synergistic effects when two or m ore pollutants are present together. The economic effects in terms of costs of remedying or of prevention are difficult even to estimate. Nonetheless, there are costs or sacrifices involved in the process of absorption of residues even though they may not be toxic.

Handling of agricultural residues or wastes is comparatively easy, except for weedicides and pesticides, etc. The techno-economics of agricultural residues, however, provides exciting possibilities and challenges. The potential of utility of these residues can extend to the stage of complete recycling in an energy and ecologically efficient manner. Animal wastes or residues are also generally treated as part of agricultural wastes. However, the chemical composition of animal wastes can vary greatly depending on the nature of the waste and the manner in which these are collected and used. These wastes are a resource regular use by our people in a variety of ways but are often lost sight of. In fact, there is substantial resources value in animal residues which can be increased by suitable categorization and processing. When we use plant wastes as fuels it is necessary to make cases the gain may be significant. With the development of controlled microbial degradation, the potentiality of getting fuel as well as recovering a part of the nitrogen and phosphorus for recycling as fertilizers makes such economic calculations worthwhile under different assumptions and various models.

Similarly, on the negative side, for instance, the use of lead in petrol as an additive does not involve only an immediate hazard to man. Lead which settles on the roadside vegetations and soil can get into the cattle and indirectly into the human system. The economics of lead additive is not only the gain in improved combustion of petrol engines but the cumulative costs of lead in the vegetation of the neighborhood which has a substantial probability of getting into human and animal systems of inhalation of getting into human and animal systems of inhalation or through the food chain. The statement that the final destination of lead in soil or water does not give us any indication of the possibility of damage to human or animal health or the disturbance of biological equilibria in the process. Similar situations or comparable statements can arise about several other heavy metals. However for operational purposes, the pathways, alternatives, costs of amelioration have to be considered in the quantitative manner. Such studies are needed to evaluate technological and economic factors in the disposal and reuse of wastes.

One of the concepts often used to quantify some of the environment benefits is the concept of augmented gross national product. The AGNP is defined as the GNP plus the value of all other public golds and non-market services. If the industries on the banks of the Hooghly at Kolkata run efficiently to maximum production, then they are points on the production possibility frontier. Suppose we want a river-front park; it can reduce the production possibility by making less of river bank available for industrial use. However, efficiently run godowns or industries could give up some river front areas by reorientation and better use of land without losing access of the river.

Practical problems such as the choice of location of a new plant or the choice of a technology or a choice of an anti-pollution policy have financial effects as well as long-item economic and social effects. More accurate information is usually necessary on the entire cycle, energy needs and the types and amounts of various residues, to be able to quantify the increased benefits derived by taking environmental effects into consideration. The possible effects of residues on geographical, geochemical and biological conditions of the receiving bodies are necessary to determine such choices and to study comparative risks and costs over a longer time profile. Very often it may boil down to differing short and long term views. The estimated span of time during which a process or an industry will operate is used to calculate future residue bonds, due to explosion, or starting of new industries and possible changes of technology in existing industry.

Finally an important and developing concept is that

of considering residues are resources rather than wastes. For instance each market in Kolkata produces several forms of vegetable, animal and other residues. The management of urban solid wastes now being discussed by economists and technologists is utilization of organic wastes after separation of paper, metals, glass and plastics. Today these organic wastes are often used as landfills. However, they can be microbial degraded to obtain methane for fuel and the residues usually rich in nitrogen and phosphorus can be used as fertilizer. Sometimes some of the micronutrients are also present in such residues and improve fertilization of the soil. Human and animal excreta can also be similarly processed. Thus there are both economic and environmental gains in such approaches. However, changing costs ad improvements in technology will increase the attractiveness of the approach.

There are some problems with plastics, pesticides and other non-biodegradable mater when these are mixed with such wastes. Most of the plastics are not easily biodegradable and some plastics such as PVC cause problems by inhibiting microbial degradation. PVC an lead to the production of chlorine which is toxic, or hydrochloric acid on incineration. It is often recommended that the glass, paper, plastics and metals be separated from the rest of the residues as all these are amenable to reuses through appropriate processing. However, the degree of social organization necessary for such segregation and recycling has been difficult to achieve till now. This has made the problem at present unsolvable in our society. To some extent, however, glass, paper and metal is recycled because of small traders who buy waste paper, cans and glass from houses and sell to the reprocessing industries.

The problem of recycling also has to deal with the total energy and social costs in the process of segregation and recycling. In many countries, and this is particularly true of India, it appears that due to the rising costs of energy and extracting and processing minerals, recycling of some wastes of industrial processes and domestic use might become increasingly economic in the future.

Role of Science and Technology in Development

Interrelationship between Socio-economic and Scientific Factors : Scientific factors and socio-economic conditions are closely related to each other. As a cause, economic factors tries to know the level and type of technological needs, ability of society to procure them, resources availability for research and development and efforts and capacity to build scientific and technological institutions. There is no doubt that capital intensive technique ensure higher rate of production quantitatively and qualitatively but poor countries are not able to buy these due to a number of reasons. They lack scientific and technical manpower too. On account of this reason they do not have good science and technical colleges. They do not have sufficient resources for building industries and certainly nor for research and development. Similarly social conditions such as values, attitudes and motivations are necessary for promotion of science. Traditional societies are quite backward having no scientific temperament. In India political leaders, intellectuals and practicing scientists have often stressed the need to develop scientific temperament among the people which they find to be lacking due to various historical, ethnic and ethical forces active in society for centuries together.

It is, therefore agreed that science and technology

play a very crucial role in development of a country. The successive five year plans have stressed the need towards scientific and technological maturity. Per capita income and standard for living depend heavily on technology. Some significant contributions of science and technology towards development are stated below:

1. Development of innovation and discoveries.
2. Employment generation and removal of poverty.
3. Reduction and regional imbalance.
4. Development and growth of human resources including food, cloth, health, sanitation, hygiene, nutrition and water supply.
5. Conservation of resources.
6. Exploration and extraction of new natural resources.
7. Advancement and improvement in defence capabilities.
8. Increased productivity qualitatively and quantitatively in both agricultural and industrial sector.

Methods used by engineers for controlling environment and ecology

Two methods viz:

1. Cleaning gaseous effluents - Removal of gaseous pollutant emissions is important as complete source correction is not possible in existing units of production. It is cheap and economical too if pollution control equipments are installed for removing pollutants from the main gas stream. Such emission control equipment are classified into two categories. These are: Equipment for particulate control and Equipment for gases control. Particulate matter emitted in gaseous streams range in size from 100m down to 0.1m and even less. Following

types of equipment are used for removing particulate matter from gas streams.

(i) Elecostatic precipitators - It is process in which particles suspended, get separated in gas stream. These equipments are mostly used in powerplant, cement, paper mills and oil refineries etc.

(ii) Fabric filters - It is one of the efficient methods for removing particulate matter from industrial gases.

(iii) Cyclone operators - It uses centrifugal force generated by a spinning gas stream to separate the particulate matter from the carrier gas.

(iv) Gravitational settling chambers - It is a simple type of equipment used in gaseous stream with its entrained particles allowed to flow at a low velocity in the settling chamber. It provides sufficient time for particles to settle down.

2. Source Correction Method - The best way of controlling air pollution is preventing pollutants or minimizing the pollutants while planning the erection of an industry at the very stage of process and design. In an existing industrial units source correction is default. However some correction can always be applied in the industries which have already been installed by raw material changes, modification of process equipment and process changes. These are explained below:

(i) Process changes - Process changes involve modified or new techniques which lower atmospheric pollutant emission. For instance if we wash coal before pulverization then it can reduce fly ash emission.

(ii) Modification of process equipment - Emission of pollutants can be minimized by replacing process equipment. For instance unburned carbon monoxide and hydro-carbons can be made to burn fully by suitable modification in the carburation of automobile engines.

(iii) Raw material changes - It has been established that raw material is responsible for causing air pollution. Use pure and A grade raw material. It offers best solution as it reduces formation of undesirable impurities.

Role of Engineers in Environmental Protection

People are demanding as a fundamental right, not only clean air and pure water and food, but also decent housing, an unpolluted land, freedom from excessive noise, adequate recreation facilities, and housing in communities that provide comfort, privacy, and essential services. The engineers and planners must ensure at the planning stage itself that the projects are so designed as to pleasing and enhancing the well being of the community. Before any project is undertaken, a site is selected wherein following considerations are important:

1. In relation to occupational health-safety, toilet, shower and locker facilities, lunch room, clean air, safe water, accident and explosion hazards, pathogens and dust in work areas ventilation, general sanitation and compliance with the Occupational Safety and Health Act should be ensured.

2. Engineers should see that permits are obtained in compliance with the clean Air Act.

3. Solid waste disposal should be in compliance with Solid Waste Disposal Act and Resources Conservation and Recovery Act.

4. There should be perfect provision and arrangements with regard to waste water disposal from dumping platform, storage and charging areas, gas cooling, toilet, shower, dressing rooms, waste-water reuse and cross-connection control. All measures

adopted should be in compliance with Clean Water Act.

5. Planning of water supply should be done for drinking and sanitary purposes, for cooling water, for make up water, and cross connection control. Water resources, recreation and wildlife. There should be compliance with Safe Drinking Water Act.

6. Noise level should be controlled, hopper charging and truck delivery and leaving should be convenient.

7. Special care should be taken in matters of drainage and flooding. The site selected should be above the 100-year flood level before erection for the structure is started. Access to roads, well drained and above flood level, is equally important.

8. The site selected should be good from the geological point of view. It should have suitable foundation soils, and be safe from earthquakes. The use of limestone, dolomite or gypsum should be avoided.

Wild life Protection: Legislative Measures

Undomesticated animals living in their natural habitats such as forests, deserts and grasslands etc. refer to wildlife in layman's language. To an ecologists, the meaning of wild-life is somewhat different. An ecologist includes both fauna naturally occuring animals as well as flora plants in wild-life. Wild-life, endangered and super species are extincting from the lap of the nature.

Indian Board for Wildlife : It is the main advisory body to Govt. of India. At its first meeting, the Board made a recommendation for unified legislation for wildlife conservation in India. The wildlife Act was enacted in 1972 which has been adopted by all states. Biological diversity in an important and irreplaceable asset. We are adopting national legislation and international treaties to protect endangered species and biodiversity. Following steps have been taken in this direction:

1. The Biological Diversity Bill 2000, awaiting Parliamentary sanction and presidential approval, is a landmark legislation aimed at protecting India's bio-assets and ensuring equitable benefit-sharing by the users and the owners.

2. U.S., Endangered species Act of 1973 and COSEWIC 1976 provide powerful approaches to wildlife protection.

3. The endangered species Act and CITES represent a new attitude towards wildlife in which we protect organisms just because they are rared and endangered.

4. Worldlife protected area network comprise 84 national parks and 447 wildlife sanctuaries.

5. Recognition for Ecological conservation.

Consumerism and Waste-Products : Environmental protection Act

Consumerism is an activity performed by consumer in purchasing goods and services. Waste-products are residual left after consumption having no utility to consumer and thrown or put in waste pots also called litters as well as Garbage bin. The development of a nation can be measured in terms of per capita generation of garbage. The figure ranges from 0.5 kg. per head per-day in developing countries to 2.5 kg in advanced countries.

Waste Products are horrible because insects and rodents proliferate in garbage and transmit plague, typhoid, cholera, skin diseases and even malaria and filaria with the breeding of mosquitoes. Garbage dumps contribute to the seepage of toxic metals and other chemicals to ground-water and surface water. Waste products when kept uncycled add foul smells, unsighliness, additional dredging costs of water-ways, silting up of reservoirs, decrease in plant productivity, corrosion of structures and structural foundations and depreciation of land value.

Industries take the major blame for waste piles. A 1000 mega watt thermal power station piles up 3 meter deep ash on 20 hectares area in its life period of 40 years. Metal industries dump 50 percent of the ore volume they process or solid-waste. Consumer with snobbery for elegant packing of utility goods, foolish use of paper from elementary school to governmental correspondence practices, short lived consumers goods of use and throw-type and junk discarded due obsolescence add up to the municipal garbage. Construction debris and frequent demolition of structures to be replaced by more commercial profitable ones also add-up municipal solid wastes.

Individual and Global Environmental Ethics

Sanitation is the most sacred of all the activities performed by man. Aesthetic factors and ethics are the most important aspects in sanitation. Clean community with clean surroundings is a way of life. Physical health and development rest on man's physical environment. This is controlled by the water that man drinks, the food which he eats, the house in which he lives as well as disposal of wastes and other wastes matter in community. As human populations grow economic activities grow simultaneously leading to a number of environmental problems that threaten not only human health and the productivity of ecosystems, but in many cases habitability of the globe. Motor vehicles cause air pollution, petroleum refiners emit gaseous pollutants, fly-ash and hydro-carbons by thermal power stations, inorganic and organic pollutants presented by industries, chemical through agriculture discharges, phenyls, toxins and acids released by dying textiles, paper and pulpmills. Are they not creation of human activities. This show that each us is individually responsible for the quality, for better or worse. There are no two opinions over it that man and man alone is responsible for polluting the atmosphere. This show that each of us is individually responsible for the quality, for better or worse. There are no two opinions over it that man and man alone is responsible for polluting the atmosphere. This does not mean that he should stop performing everyday activities. What needed is real changes in individual behaviour. Environmental ethic can modify his attitudes and behaviour. Environmental ethics should not only be expressed itself in national laws but profoundly changing individuals the way they live their daily lives.

Americans think environmental problems can be solved through a quick technical changes. Raper Organization on environmental problems believe that cars, not drivers pollute environment, hence corporations should invent pollution free autos. This shows that many individuals want the environment cleaned up, but they do not want to make life-style changes to make that happen. Decisions and actions by individuals want the environment cleaned up, but they do not want to make lifestyle changes to make that happen. Decisions and actions by individuals when faced with ethical choices can collectively save the environment from further degradation.

Changes in individual behaviour are necessary but not enough. Increased awareness of global environmental change is important. This can be done by pooling our knowledge and coordinating our actions. Environment is a matter of global priority and action.

Whatever political differences between different nations have must be dropped/ After all, ecological degradation in any nation inevitably impinges on the quality of life in others. Studies reveal that much of the environmental crisis are rooted due to widening gap between rich and poor nations. Developed industrialized countries contain hardly 23 percent of the world's population and control 80 percent of the world's goods.

Environmentalists hold these countries responsible for pollution. Underdeveloped developing economies are hit by overpopulation, malnutrition, and disease. These nations struggle to catch up with developed nations. They make rapid efforts towards industrialization which poison their cities and attempts to increase agricultural production often result in feeling of trees which deplete the fertility soil. So the most important question of the future is put aside political differences and work together for global environmental course of action. The United Nations conference on Human Environment was a step towards this direction in 1972.

It is agreed the interactions between man and environment are not new. They are as old as human civilization. In past such interactions were less but now unprecedented increase in the rate, scale and complexity are observed. At one time pollution of any nature was a local problem but today it involves several countries. The discussions and debates over chemical and radioactive waste disposal are examples of international nature of pollution. The Gulf War which took place between Iraq and Kuwait in 1992 polluted the atmosphere. Pollution from the burning of about 3 million barrels of oil a day produced a pungent lmog. The polluted atmosphere created a very bad impact on human health. Reports reveal that babies suffered from lung problems; adults suffered from high blood pressure, physiological disorders, kidney failures and heart attacks. The burning wells produced huge amounts of smoke turned days into nights. The wind screens of the vehicles were found carrying black sports and in some cases turned grey and became untransparent. There were black rains in several parts of the world. The snow that fell in Kashmir during the post war period had black spots due to hydrocarbon pollutants. Should we not think less about conquering nature and more about learning to work with her.

2

ENVIRONMENT OF COMMERCE

The main function of commerce is to make the goods available to the consumers. Trade will not come into being unless goods are produced in excess of local needs. Thus, development of trade depends upon production of goods and services on a large-scale. The production of finished goods in the factories depends upon production of raw materials products. The primary products of raw materials have no utility or very limited utility in relation to man, for example cotton produced by the farmers to the textile mills. Moreover, cotton sold by the farmers needs to be transported to the textile mills. The finished goods produced by the factories need to be distributed to the different market places through different modes of transport. In the market areas goods are sold by the retailers to the consumers, which they purchase either from wholesalers middle men or directly from the producers. As wholesalers deal with the large-scale purchase and sale of commodities they are often required to use services of banks, warehouses, financial institutions, insurance and government offices. All these activities are necessary for the development of commerce.

Hence, these activities constitute environmental of commerce. Physical and man-made elements around man, constitute his environment. Similarly, the activities and services necessary for the smooth functioning of trade, constitute the environment of commerce. Variation in the development of these activities and services create commercial environment of their own king. Commercial environment of rural areas is different from that of urban areas.

The Service Sector Activities

The service sector activities can also be classified into two categories :

(i) Quaternary activities : These activities provide necessary infrastructure for the development and smooth functioning of all above mentioned activities.

(ii) Tetairy activities : These activities are concern with trade and aids to trade such as retailing, wholesaling, banking, insurance, transportation and communication and communication services etc.

Productive Sector Activities

The activities which are directly concerned with production of goods came under this category. These activities on the basis of the nature of products produced by them can be further classified into two activities, i.e., primary and secondary activities.

(i) Primary activities : These are the activities producing the products having raw or primary nature such as food gathering, hunting, fishing, grazing, farming, lumbering, mining etc. Through these activities man directly gets the raw materials or primary products from the nature.

(ii) Secondary activities : These activities are concerned which conversion of all kinds of primary products into a variety of useful of finished products.

Factors Influencing Environmental of Commerce

We have recognised the different forms and levels

in the trade organisations. The location and development of different trade organisations and the consequent development of commercial environment depends upon variety of factors such as physical and cultural factors. The nature of commercial environment in any region or in any country is greatly influenced by the physical factors such as availability of natural resources and their potentiality, level of development of agriculture mining, fisheries, forest and animal wealth etc. However, the role played by man-made factors in influencing the nature of environment of commerce is of vital importance.

Man-made or cultural factors such as size and quality of population, political and economic systems, government initiative and encouragement, play important role inn deciding the nature of environment of commerce. Let us study how these factors operate and affect the environment of commerce.

1. Man plays a unique role in the development of environment of commerce, being both producer and consumer of various goods. Man is the thicker, the planner, in inventor, the discover, the coordinator manager, the dreamer and above all the superior. He is an inexhaustible source of energy and skill on this planet. With all these tools he has created his own cultural world, a world of commerce and trade by bringing about revolutionary changes in the field of production, distribution and consumption of various goods of commodities.

2. Political Stability and Government Policy - They also influence development of commercial environment in a country as well as in the world. War between two countries Arab- Israel, Iran-Iraq not only affects the trade between such countries world trade in mineral oil was

adversely affected.

Government is powerful institution and plays a vital role in the development of commercial environment in a country. The Government, by its policy, is empowered to change the pattern of economic progress and trade through administrative process. It also controls credit it institutions, licensing import and export and trade process. It also controls credit institutions, licensing import and export and trade process. The form of government gives all kinds of freedom in trade and commerce and thus crates favourable environment for the development of commerce and trade. This is not so in case communist countries like China where trade activities are fully controlled by government.

3. Transportation and Communication Facilities - Development of trade and commerce is promoted by varied and efficient transport network. West European countries and eastern central pair of North America have become the leading commercial regions of the world, largely due to their dense network of roadways, railways, airways and even inland waterways. They also have the world's best communication systems. In contrast to this many African, South American and South Asian countries have remained commercially backward. They failed to create suitable commercial environment due to lack of these facilities.

4. Existence of Innumerable Differences in Human Needs, Wants and Desires - Human wants are ever increasing and never ending. These ever increasing wants of man provide scope to produce goods and services on a large scale. Consumer especially from urban areas in general and from western countries in particular have very high expectations. Technology has want more of many things than more of the same thing.

New varieties of products, superior in quality, free from pollution, more safe and comfortable, are to be produced and supplied to the affluent sections.

This calls for a massive investment in Research and Development. Japan is a fine example in the regard. Japan always takes care its customer's high expectations regarding design, sophistication, quality, delivery schedules and prices. Industry owners in japan swear by the dictum The Customer is God, who is always right. This attitude has enabled Japan to develop conducive commercial environment, making it one of the leading commercial nation in spite of lack of raw materials in the local areas.

5. Availability of Natural Resources and the Level of their Development - Development of trade and commerce, hence the development of commercial environment, depends upon production base of a country i.e., how much is the production of primary and secondary goods in country. Large-scale production of primary and secondary goods in a region of in a country depends upon its richness in commerce and trade, as they are rich in variety of natural resources such as cool energetic climate, fertile soils, basic minerals like coal and iron-ore, marine and animal resources. Moreover these countries being culturally well developed, have utilized their resources to their fullest capacity. In contrast to this, many African and South American countries have remained commercially backward due to unfavouable nature of their natural resources coupled with their cultural backwardness.

Consumer Space

From the above discussion it becomes clear that consumer space represents that section population space, which provides demand for certain goods.

Population space is a wider term. It includes all the people living in a particular region or country. All the people of a country or of a region do not purchase all the goods. They purchase goods as per their purchasing power, needs, liking, habits etc. In case of essential goods slide food grain, edible oil, cloth etc. the entire population space becomes the consumers space.

But this is not so, in case of luxury goods like, refrigerator, television etc. Thus, in case of higher order goods consumer space becomes more specialized and selective. It is because of this, while locating shops dealing in luxury goods, consumers space need to be taken into consideration. It will not be possible and profitable to open television and video shops in the villages or in tribal areas. Thus, while locations a shop or starting a business the study of consumer space becomes necessary.

We have studied that people in advanced countries enjoy higher standard of living. Their purchasing power as well as of consumption are very high and hence, provide demand for a variety of goods. Same is the with the people living urban areas. Hence, shops dealing in luxury goods are found well developed in these areas.

In U.S.A. level of consumption of people is so high that in spite of having large-scale production of milk and milk products, they import butter from Denmark, Netherlands and New Zealand. The temperate countries of southern hemisphere such as New Zealand, Argentina, South Africa and Australia export dairy products to the temperate countries. The people in tropical countries being economically backward cannot provide demand for costly dairy products. Thus, consumer space is very large in developed countries, though, their population space is comparatively smaller.

In contrast to this, in developing countries though population space is larger, consumer space is restricted. Similar condition are also observed in urban and rural areas. Therefore, while selling goods in the marked knowledge of consumers space is necessary. Nowadays consumer is considered as a king of God. His opinions, likes and dislikes, fashion guides etc. direct productions in the industries. If a consumer happens to dislike a particular product, its production, sour or later comes to an end. People in advanced countries as well as in urban areas have a variety in their demands and hence, to satisfy their demands careful study of consumers space is necessary. In fact, success of failure of any commercial organization largely depends upon its better understanding of consumers space.

Population Space

The word space refers to the geographical area. From the commercial point of view distribution of population across the geographical area is of utmost importance. It is because development of different commercial activities area depends upon the level of their demand. Demand for various goods and services depends upon density and distribution of population, i.e., how populations is concentrated and spread over in a particular area or a region. We have already studied, how population is found widely scattered in the rural areas but its is quiet compact in case of urban areas. Similarly, in villages number of people living is far less than those living in cities and towns. It is because of sparse and widely scattered population in rural areas that the organised markets and developed. Thus, a study of distributional and density of population is essentially useful for commerce. It helps us to know where demand for various goods is concentrated and hence, he location of the market. So, the study of he density and distribution of population is very important to understand the commercial environment. However, mere study of distribution, and density of population is not enough because demand for goods and services more precisely depends upon quality of population, i.e., purchasing power, standard off living, liking and disliking, fashions, customs, literacy ratio, male-female ratio, age and occupational structure.

All the above qualities determine the size of market. The size of market does not necessarily mean the number of customers. If that is the case China and India might have become the world's largest markets. Thus, it is the purchasing power of the people which determines the size of the market. For example, the population of U.S.A. Though far less than of India, has constituted one of the largest world. The higher level of consumption in such countries mainly attributes to their higher purchasing power.

In the world there are four major zones of high density. (i) Southern Asia, (ii) Eastern Asia, (iii) Western Europe and (iv) Eastern Central part of North America. In the first two regions, expect Japan, most of the countries are economically backward and hence, people in these countries have poor purchasing power. They cannot provide demand for various goods while in the other two productive capacities, there is always a demand for variety of goods. Thus, size of market does not necessarily depend on size of population but on quality of population.

Location and Development of Trade Organisations

Above, we have seen, how various factors influence, the environment of commerce in the world as a whole. Now we shall consider how different trade organisations get developed on a given geographical space. Also what factors influence their location and development in various areas leading to the development of their own commercial environment.

1. Normally wholesaling activities are found developed in cities and larger towns. It is because wholesalers deal with large scale purchase of different commodities, hence, require large size trading areas. In the cities and in the larger towns population being large in size to cater to the needs and wants of large number of customers, large numbers of retails shops get developed. They provide the necessary large trading areas to the wholesalers and hence wholesaling activities get developed in the urban and semi-urban areas. Moreover innovative urban transport and communication systems help the wholesalers to serve large number of retail customers not only from cities but even from neighbouring areas of cities and towns. Thus ultimately help them to earn large about of profit, thereby providing several facilities to retailers-their-customers-to earn their goodwill who give them business.

Within cities wholesaling activities show area specialization. They are found located close to central business district the most accessible part of a city and not the geometrical centre of the city. It is because, as wholesalers carry on business on a large scale, they are often required to use specialized services like the services to head offices of banks, insurance companies, industries as well as administrative offices etc. These services being meant for the customers, get located at the most accessible part of a city, i.e., C.B.D.

With the passage of time wholesaling activities developed closest to C.B.D. Show real specialization leading to organization of commercial business. We can identify different wholesaling zones in Mumbai such as Phule market for fruits, Kalbadevi road for cloths, Bhuleshwar etc. Here, they are benefited by their agglomeration. Hence, all these services and wholesaling activities form an integral part of the commercial environment which exists at such places in the cities.

Certain towns which are found centrally located with respect to the neighbouring villages producing a particular commodity on large scale as Pachora, Amalner, Dhuel towns in Maharashtra were known for their specification in wholesale trade of cotton. Khanna town in Punjab is known for wheat, Nagpur for oranges and Ratnagiri for mangoes. Thus, we observe areal affinities of certain trade commodities.

(ii) In a metropolitan city like Mumbai, as population is very large in size and having higher purchasing power, many departmental stores and shopping complexes have developed not only in the commercial centre of Mumbai. The areas in Mumbai which enjoy maximum accessibility have attracted location of super markets and consumers co-operative societies.

(iii) The shops dealing in same commodities are often found located at the places which are easily accessible to the large number of customers. Here, customers living on both the suburban railway lines, i.e., Central and Western, can easily come to make their purchases. Such location of retail shops dealing in same product on a particular road is beneficial for both retail shop owners as well as a change to compare quality and make their purchases form such areas. This provides large turnover of business to the retailers. Therefore, the get concentrated on a particular road. This leads to developed of commercial land use which is unique in nature.

Moreover, when customers come to such roads for making their purchases, they often combine purposes of their visits to such areas i.e., customers coming the Ranade read for purchasing clothes. They often purchase vegetables or shoes or ready-made garments and other goods for Dadar, which are very well available in their local areas. It is because of such multi purpose trips many shops dealing with vegetables, ready-made garments, plastic goods etc. have developed on the footpath of Ranade road and adjoining roads at Dadar.

(iv) Retail shops dealing with costly and non-frequently required commodities such as cloth, medicine, shoes, jewellery, radio, T.V. etc. are found located comparatively away form the residential areas. They are mostly found located on the main roads leading to a railway station or bus stand, if any. Once in a while customers don't mind travelling long distances while making purchases of such commodities.

Moreover the actual location of such shops also depends upon rent or cost of the land. The shops capable of paying higher rent or cost of the land are found to be located at the places having two shopping fronts or junctions.

(v) The retail shops dealing in cheap and those commodities required in daily life and found located nearest to the residential areas. This is because of consumer behaviour like customers not ready to travel longer distances for purchasing cheap and frequently required commodities. In fact, if the customers are forced to travel longer distance, to purchase such commodities, the cost of transport may exceed the cost of commodity itself.

Linkages between Producer and Market Environments

Commerce is unthinkable without linkages between producer and consumer. In fact, the linkages between producer and consumer form an integral part of the environment of commerce. These linkages may be in existence in a traditional form, as they where in the past in the form of barter system while transport of goods used to be carried out the help of man himself or animals. However, today these traditional linkages have been replaced by modern linkages such as cash or cheque payments instead or barter system and in case of transport of goods by means of containers, that too, through different modes of transport such as roadways, railways, waterways and airways. Thus, the linkages between the producer and consumer are of different types and vary from region forming their own environment of commerce. For example, in mountainous and desert areas, animals are still used as a beast of burden.

The linkages between producer and consumer are mainly with reference to transportation, payment, distribution agencies and price of commodities. These linkages along with their elements, play an important role in determining the nature of environment of commerce. For example, in advanced countries, banks, modes of transport, sales agencies and price guarantee system are well developed. In developing countries, these linkages are not well developed, especially in rural and tribal areas. This has affected the nature of commercial environment in these countries.

The various components of above-mentioned linkages also play an important role in the development of commerce. The linkages between producer and consumer are not only affected by man-made environment but sometime they also affected by natural calamities, such as heavy rainfall some mountainous areas and snowfall.

Internal Economies and External Economies

Internal economics are those economics which are open to an individual firm when its size expands. They emerge within the firm itself as its scale of production increases. Internal economies in the scale of its output cannot be realized unless the firm increases its output.

External economies are those economies which are shared by all the firms in an industry or in a group of industries when their size expands. They are available to all firms from outside, irrespective of their size and scale of production. They are the result of the growth and expansion of any particular industry of a group of industries as a whole. Thus, external economies are the functions of the size of the industry. They are not confined to one or two firms, but shared by the all the firms in an industry when its size expands. Thus, external economies can never be monopolized by any one in an industry.

3

GLOBAL TRADE

Environment of Commerce

The term trade refers to the exchange of commodities, services and know-how. Trade may be internal or domestic when goods or services are exchanged within the political and geographical boundaries of a nation or region; or it may be international or global when the exchange of goods or services is between two or more countries and across political boundaries. The latter is also known as intra-regional or foreign trade.

The economic progress of any country depends considerably on the development of trade relations with different countries. Different countries produce different types of minerals or crops. It is due to diverse geographical and economic conditions. Countries of the world have come closer due to effective development of transportation. There is no country in the world which is self-sufficient in the production of all foodstuffs and raw materials. Countries only specialize in different products under the particular conditions of physical and economic environment. Trade is the result of specialization which is a function of demand and supply.

Internal and External Trade

The Internal or domestic trade of any country is based on various factors, namely,

(i) Transportation.

(ii) Habits and size of population.

(iii) Differences in climate conditions.

(iv) Differences in the stage of Industrial Development.

(v) Uneven distribution of natural resources.

The fundamental basis of trade at any level is uneven distribution of natural resources. A large size country like India has developed internal distribution systems for coal, oil, iron ore, agricultural commodities and industrial goods. Certain agriculture products are produced in particular areas only, e.g., tea, jute, wheat, rice, sugar, etc. But they are consumed all over the country. There is a good deal of internal trade in these goods. Also we notice that there is an uneven development of industries are distributed all over the country. Sugar is produced more in Uttar Pradesh and Maharashtra. Other states are in deficit and therefore there is good deal of internal trade in sugar. Food habits of people in different parts of a country are different. Rice and coffee and more consumed in Southern India while wheat and tea are more consumed in the rest of India. If these commodities are not produced or are produced in deficit in area then naturally they are brought from the areas of surplus production. Thus the internal trade in these commodities is developed in India.

Size and type of population also helps to promote the internal trade. Larger the size of population of the area, larger the volume of internal trade. The types of the levels of economic standard of people also decide the volume as well as the kinds of commodities traded within the areas. The transport linkages play very important role to promote internal trade. Railways and roadways have been found to be more useful in internal trade of a country. They have not been adequately developed in India.

An external trade or a foreign trade of a country is influenced by following factors:

(i) Political relations.

(ii) A demand for a commodity or product.

(iii) Quality and cost in competitive world market.

(iv) Exportable surplus production of certain product.

The external trade of a country is a part of International trade. This king of trade is developed on account of uneven distribution and development of resources in the world, differences in the stages of industrial development, differences in the culture and skills of people, difference in climatic conditions, habits and tastes of people.

Besides above- mentioned reasons, the external trade is possible if their is an exportable surplus output of a particular commodity in a country and the commodity has a demand elsewhere. The trade develops from areas of surplus to areas of demand. The trade in particular commodity can last in this competitive world if better quality goods are sold at reasonable price. The surplus productions of better quality goods at reasonable price such as coffee by Columbia and Brazil; sugar by Cuba and Brazil; tea by India and Sri Lanka; synthetic fibre electronic goods, automobiles and ships by Japan, therefore, enter into world market on large scale. The demand for a commodity in foreign markets increases the trade of a country. The political relationship plays important role in external trade of a country. The strained political relationship between India and China could not allow to develop any trade during last four decades.

The positive balance of a foreign trade of a country helps to make the economic conditions sound.

Obviously negative balance of a foreign trade makes the economy weaker. The comparative territorial advantage is enjoyed in production of certain commodities by many countries in the world. It is possible for them to produce those commodities at least on cost production basis and in much exportable surplus output. Therefore some countries are specialised in the production and their export trade consists of these commodities, e.g., rubber and tin by Malaysia and Indonesia, tea by India and Sri Lanka, jute any India and Bangladesh, coffee by Brazil and Columbia, oil by the Middle East, sugar by Cuba and Brazil, paper and wood-pulp by Canada, etc.

World's Trading Pacts

The term trading pact or trade blocks refer to a group of two or more countries getting together for the purpose of promoting international trade. These trading blocs help to liberalize trade by lowering of abolishing tariffs. Economic integration initially helps to develop political integration. There are many advantages of forming trade blocks such as:

(i) The formation of a group for trade purpose has led to political unity. Apart from economic and commercial safety, political co-ordination and safety are two of the achievements of a trade bloc.

(ii) Free trade policy facilitates and encourages greater specialisation in particular field on production. A trading bloc may become specialised in agricultural or industrial goods. Sometimes it enjoys the territorial advantage because of its geographical location or geological structure.

(iii) Since trading restrictions are minimised, internal trade among the member countries and, therefore, each bloc is regarded as a single unit. Trading blocs and individual member countries, resulting in increased volume of trade.

(iv) Tariff concessions and abolition of trade restrictions help to promote trade among member countries. The volume of trade within the group has been growing very rapidly.

There are many trade blocs in the world. Some of the important ones are as under:

a. United Nations Conference on Trade and Development - It is the biggest pact ever entered into for trade and development at the international level. The organisations was set up to find out ways and means of expanding trade and upgrade the socio-economic status of people in the underdeveloped areas of the world. In 1964, when it was set up, UNCTAD has 120 members. Now there are more than 130 members. The problems of international trade and economic developing countries. After several conferences, it was decided to develop preferential arrangements of tariff in advanced countries to promote the export of several commodities to them by less developed countries. UNCTAD, therefore promotes the trade and development of all the developing nations of the world.

b. General Agreement of Tariffs and Trade - A pact was enter into in 1946 under the patronage of the U.N. to frame a charter for the International Trade Organisation in London. Seventeen countries including India were represented. The pact, however, was given shape at a meeting of 23 countries participating at Geneva in 1947. The GATT not has 86 members and its aim is to reduce tariffs and encourage world-wide trade links for mutual benefits. The headquarters of GATT is at Geneva in Switzerland.

c. South Asian Association for Regional Cooperation - It includes the countries of South-Asia such as India,

Bhutan, Pakistan, Nepal, Bangladesh, Maldives and Sri Lanka. One of these countries is being chosen as the chairman for a period of one year and every month an audio-visual film is shown on T.V. on the 1st day of every month. It is for promotion of cultural and commercial relationship among all the countries of the region.

d. Association of South-East Asian Nations - It is an association of South-East Asian nations, namely, the Philippines, Thailand, Malaysia, Indonesia and Singapore. Tariffs between these countries have been reduced, therefore, intra regional trade has increased. Simultaneously their external trade has increased very rapidly. Except Singapore, all the member countries are producers of agricultural products and industrial raw material. They supply these products to Japan, European countries, Australia and New Zealand. All of them import manufactured goods from Japan, Australia, Korea and European countries.

e. Latin American Free Trade Association - This organisation was formed in 1960 under the Treaty of Montevideo. All the South American Countries, excepts Surinam and Guineas, are members of this pact. Mexico is also a member. These is not much trade among the member countries because of the similarity of their products. It is not more than 10 percent of the total trade of Latin America within LAFTA. Most of the countries have trade links with the industrial nations in the northern hemisphere. LAFTA has either lowered' or abolished tariffs on agricultural products and assisted in the economic development of the sub-continent. A sub group of LAFTA from the Andean region Chile, Peru, Bolivia, Columbia and Ecuador has registered success in trade and economic integration and it is known as Andean group.

f. European Coal and Steel Community Bloc - A trading pact entered into by Belgium, Netherlands, Luxembourg, West Germany, France and Italy, to promote iron and steel industries in member countries by abolishing tariffs on iron and coal. The policy might help in developing monopoly in the production of iron and steel and the supply of steel in world markets. As a result of this pacts, there has been remarkable development in their iron and steel industry because of the exchange of material and technological know- how.

g. The Organisation of Petroleum Exporting Countries - The organisation cane into being in 1960. Thirteen major oil producing countries except, U.S.A. And the former Soviet Union, became its members - Saudi Arabia, Iran, Iraq, Nigeria, Gabon, Equator. Many of these countries have small-size populations, but are very rich in oil reserves and produce large quantities for exports. The organisation takes care of member countries and assists them in getting a better price for their oil by increasing or decreasing production, fixing the price for their oil by increasing or decreasing production, fixing the price of oil, and by giving advice on economic and technical matters. OPEC has shaken the economies of world's leading nations by increasing the price of oil in the world market.

h. Council of Mutual Economic Assistance - A trading partnership of former Soviet Union, Mongolia, Former East Germany, Poland, Czechoslovakia, Hungary, Rumania and Bulgaria, a group of communist countries, was establish in 1949. The former Soviet Union has greatly benefited by their partnership because she was the most advances country in manufacturing activities. She exported coal, oil, machinery, automobiles, mining equipment, agricultural machinery, transport equipment and chemicals to East European countries. She imported fruits, vegetables, textiles, etc.

(i) European Free Trade Association - This is an association of eight European countries: Iceland, Norway, Sweden, Finland, Switzerland, Austria, Protagon and the Faroe Islands. Iceland joined the pact in 1969, years after its formation. The United Kingdom and Denmark were founder members of the EFTA but left it to join the EEC.

In terms of the EFTA member countries agreement, tariffs on manufactured goods have been substantially reduced or abolished. This has promoted the industrial development of member nations and attracted foreign investors- especially American- for the development of industries in these countries. Its internal trade, however, did not develop substantially, may be because of the similarity of their products. The member countries of EFTA have strong trade links with the EEC and other countries.

j. The European Economic Community - This is an association of countries which has progressed very much in trade and general economic integration. It was formed in 1957 under the Treaty of Rome. There were only six members in the beginning- France, Germany, Italy, Belgium, Netherlands and Luxembourg. The trading conditions were changed in 1973. At that time, Britain, Denmark and Ireland joined the EEC. Norway became a member in 1981. Greece, Spain, Portugal and Turkey followed suit.

Though established in 1957, concessions in tariff and trading restrictions were not abolished immediately. But most restrictions on trade in industrial goods were abolished in 1967. However a common external tariff has now come into operation. The overproduction of agricultural and animal products because of the policy of interrogation of agriculture development by the EEC sometimes create problems. But the EEC has been successful in overcoming these problems. Therefore, it accounts for 33 percent of the world's trade and about 45 percent of the trade in manufactured goods. Five members countries are, of were, colonial powers, which helped in promoting the world-wide trade links of the EEC.

Basis of World Trade Patterns

(i) Political Influence on Trade - There has been a great political influence on world trade. Healthy political relationships between any two countries promote strong trade relationship. The political environments in different parts of the world have resulted into the regional trade carried through the trade blocks or trade organisations which enabled the member trade organisations which enabled the member countries to adopt Free Trade Policy or protected trade policy. Today we notice that the trades flows have emerged from the combination of Geographical, Economic, Social, Cultural and Political Environments at all levels.

(ii) Economic and sociocultural base - The countries with high economic and socio-cultural status are engaged in production of the goods of high production cost. Japan, France, U.K., U.S.A., with modern scientific and technological know how, sound economic base and high socio-cultural background produce exportable surplus sophisticate and fabricated goods as well as export scientific and technological know-how to rest of the world. Japan is specialised in electronic goods, automobile, chemical, shipbuilding, synthetic textiles etc. European countries and U.S.A. Are also specialised in automobiles, aircraft, chemical industrial plants and capital goods etc. A large surplus is produced in Asia, South America and Africa are the ready markets and very well linked by international trade routes. The high cost consumer goods produced by Japan, European countries and U.S.A., have good demand in the oil rich Middle East while other capital goods, fabricated countries. The multinational companies are also reaping heavy profit from developing countries- because of their dense population and high consuming capacities.

(iii) Geographical Base - The various commodities that enter into the world trade have geographical or natural bases. Among the food products, foodgrains and animal products, fish and fish products are produced in exportable surplus quantities for trade by some countries. Food grains were important commodities in the world trade till the second world war. The world's food production has outpaced population growth. During last decade the world's food production increased by 24 percent while its population grew by 20 percent. It is noticed only in Asia, Europe, South America and C.I.S. The food production increased because of increase in irrigation, mechanization, inputs of food grains and other products in developing countries are left for export because of large size populations. Rice producing nations of Asia are leading consumers of rice so, there is little trade in rice. Trade in wheat has also declined because developing countries have reacher a stage of self- sufficiency. Only developed countries, export wheat and maize to Japan, European countries and other deficit producers. Where is a major food item enters world trade. The U.S.A., Canada. C.I.S., France etc.

The industrial raw materials include agricultural products like cotton, jute, tobacco, minerals in the form of ores of semifinished products. Most of these industrial raw materials are produced in tropical countries and had a great demand after industrial revolution in the U.S.A. And Europe. The demand did decline after second world war. The new inventions by Americans and Europeans enabled them to produce substitutes. Moreover many tropical countries and developed countries has been declining. The industries in developed countries depend on others, especially, underdeveloped countries suffer for short supply of raw materials.

Broad Geographical Flow Patterns

Almost all countries are produces of primary goods which include minerals, agriculture products like food and industrial raw materials. The developing countries among tropical group have borrowed of hired or purchased scientific and technological know-how and started processing the natural resources they possess. Therefore either semiprocess or processed products are exported by them. Some of the developing countries like India export tools, machineries and engineering goods. She is one of he ten most industrialize nations in the world. However, most of the tropical countries export low value primary goods like agricultural commodities and minerals to temperate countries.

The temperate countries cannot produce certain agricultural products which need tropical climate as well as they do not possess industrially useful minerals. The import them but being industrially advance countries, iron and steel goods, transport equipment, machines and tools, chemicals, etc. The kind of flow of raw material and unfinished products from tropical countries to temperate countries and a flow of manufactured goods or finished products from temperate countries to tropical countries will continue till there is a gap in industrial development.

Northern Hemisphere and Southern Hemisphere

A flow pattern of trade between the countries of northern hemisphere and southern hemisphere is of a typical type. The countries of southern hemisphere are thinly populated and have poor industrial development. They are producers of agricultural commodities, animal products and minerals in exportable surplus quantities. Most of them were European colonies. They are all exporters of primary and unfinished goods to the countries of northern hemisphere. Foodgrains by Argentina, Australia; wool, meat, diary products by Australia, New Zealand and Argentina; Sugar, coffee by Brazil; coffee by Columbia; iron-ore, manganese, copper by Australia, Brazil South Africa; bauxite by Australia, Brazil; tin by Indonesia, Bolivia. The countries, e.g., Japan, European countries, U.S.A export machinery, industrial plants, chemicals, iron and steel goods, automobiles, aircraft, petroleum, petroproducts, textiles and variety of manufactured goods. Some of the countries, e.g., Brazil, Argentina, Australia are now developing modern industries to reduce the import of manufactured goods.

Trade Flow in the Last Two Decades

There has been a major change in pattern of trade flow between developed and developing countries during last two decades. There is a vast difference in the industrial development between these two groups in the world. The developed countries have achieved a very high stage of industrial growth. The developing countries in the world are generally termed as third world countries, mostly the tropical countries in Asia and almost all countries in Africa and South America.

They are industrially less developed. The export trade of developed countries consists of manufactured and fabricated goods the developing countries consists of agricultural commodities, industrial raw materials, including minerals, a relatively large share of their GNP. This trade has a lower economic and political countries of the world have dominated world trade, accounting for about 66 percent while developing countries contribute about 24 percent. Some of the developing countries have developed industries, therefore the trade pattern of those countries have changed during last 20 years i.e., India, China.

Euro-American and Asia Countries

The Ero-American countries are highly industrialized in the world. U.S.A. And Canada are rich in resources. U.K., France has colonies in Asian countries with a long time commercial ties. There is a flow of manufactured goods like chemicals, iron and steel goods, industrial plants, automobiles, petroleum and petroproducts, newspring, paper-pulp, variety of manufactured goods and scientific and technological know-how from Euro-American countries. On the other hand a flow of unfinished and semi-finished goods from Asian countries, except Japan is continued fro last more than two centuries. However, an import of finished goods by India and China has declined on account of progress in manufacturing after post-war period. Petroleum and petro-products from south West Asian countries are exported to Euro-American countries on large scale.

The Flow India to S.E. Asia, Africa and I.O. Islands

There has been good deal of trade between India and countries of S.E. Asia, Africa and Indian Ocean Islands. There have been separate agreements with these countries. Indo-Burma agreement, indo-ori Lanka

Trade Agreement the Indo-maldives Agreement. The major export by India to S.E. Asian countries and I.O. Islands includes of wheat, iron and steel goods, textiles, hosieries, transport equipments, electrical goods, machines and tools, etc. India imports from them rubber, copra, coconut oils, graphite, dry fish, palm oil, etc. India's trade with African countries is limited, but measures have been initiated to explore possibilities for increasing trade with these countries. Already joint agreement, bilaterial co-operation , joint ventures have been signed to establish trade link with them. There are offices of India trade agencies such as the Engineering Export Promotion Council at Abbidjan, the Trade Development Authority in Liberia, the Projects Equipment Corporation in Harare in Zimbabve and Ethiopia. There is ample scope for the export in manufactured goods to these countries and activation balance of trade with them.

Foreign Trade of India

Brief Review

In the pre-independence period, the pattern of India's foreign trade was traditional- the import of finished goods and the export of agricultural produce and industrial raw material. The bulk of her foreign trade was with Great Britain and Commonwealth countries. In view of the size of the country, and the size of her population, the volume of India's trade is very low. The reason are:

(i) The large size of the population, which used up some primary products, leaving a small surplus for export.

(ii) The near absence of roadways and railways connecting hinterland with ports to promote the export of unfinished products and the import of finished products.

(iii) Colonial period of about three hundred years, during which India was compelled to be a producer of low-priced primary goods for the colonisers.

(iv) ignorance, illiteracy and backwardness in scientific and technological know-how; hence, the absence of a scientific approach.

(v) The slow rate of development in agriculture and industry, resulting in low production.

In the post-independence period particularly from 1951 onward, there has been a remarkable image in the pattern of the foreign trade of India. She has now established trade links with practically every country in the world. She has now a fairly large volume of foreign trade and ranks sixth among the trading nations of the world. Her import of manufactured goods has been steadily declining; but her exports are on the increase. This change has come about because of improvement in manufacturing techniques and encouragement from the government. Her trade with U.K. has declined while that with U.S.A., Far Eastern countries, and the Middle East, in on the rise.

North/South

The pattern of trade flow between the countries of north hemisphere and south hemisphere more of less similar to that of developed and developing countries of the world, with few exceptions. The countries of south hemisphere are those in South America, half of Africa, Singapore, Indonesia, number of islands in South Pacific and Oceania. Except Singapore and Oceania all are economically and industrially backward countries. Their export trade consists of agricultural commodities, minerals and animal products. Similarly, their trading patterns in north hemisphere are mostly Japan, Russia, European countries, Canada, U.S.A., which export all kinds of manufactured and fabricated goods to them. The flow of animal products from the countries of southern hemisphere to the countries of northern hemisphere is remarkable.

South/South

There have been limited trade linkages among the countries of southern hemisphere. Most of them produce similar kinds of commodities. Many of them are thinly populated and maintain low standard of living, except Singapore, Australia and New Zealand. They have nothing special to exchange with each other. They are widely separated from each other by waterbodies, noon falls on he line of world trade route.

Pattern of India's Exports

In the pre-independence period, the exports of India consisted of primary products- generally agricultural products, such as tea, jute, cotton, species, tobacco and agro-based industrial goods like textiles, hides and skins and mineral ores. Some of these goods still enjoy prime importance in India's export trade trail development in the fifties, the pattern of India's foreign trade has changed. The number of commodities exported by her at the time of independence was only fifty. Now it is more than 3,000 and includes traditional goods like jute, tea, cotton, cotton goods, tobacco, hides and skins, lac, mica iron ores, magnese ores and spices, and many semi-processed and finished goods, engineering goods, transport equipment, etc. The sixties witnessed the development of industries which manufacture engineering goods, automobiles, other transport equipment, machines, tools, electorial goods and machinery, industrial plants for sugar, chemical industry, pharmaceutical industry, petrochemical industry, cement industries, paper industries, textile machinery and power plants. The exports have not yet wiped out our trade deficit. India is now among the first ten nations in the export of machines and tools. During the last twenty years there has been an enormous increase in the export of engineering goods, leather goods, chemical, jewelleries, readymade garments, handicraft goods, fish and fish products, sugar, and cashewnuts.

Until independence India's foreign trade balance was favourable. However after the independence, the trade balance has been unfavourable, except in 1972-73 and 1972-73.

Essential Features of India's Foreign Trade

The foreign of India is mostly seaborne, and takes place from major ports on the eastern and western coasts. There is very little trade by land routes because of the barrier of the Himalayan ranges. Moreover, the political relations with neighbouring countries are not very friendly.

The per capita share of India's foreign trade is much lower than that of other countries India has hardly one percent the world trade while the U.S.A. Has 16 percent, United Germany 10 percent, Japan 8 percent. Since independence, the foreign trade of India has been growing. The total value of her foreign trade in 1980-81 was Rs. 21, 413 crores and in 1989-90 was Rs. 63,093 crores.

Import Trade of India

In the pre-independence period, the import trade of India covered foodgrains, manufactured goods, machines, tools, electrical goods and transport equipments- foodgrain imports because of the large population and insufficient output, while that of other goods because of poor industrial development.

Greater emphasis was placed on improvement in agriculture by introducing land reforms and irrigation facilities, and popularizing the use of fertilizer and chemicals, high yielding varieties of seeds, mechanizations, and modern methods of farming. By the seventies India became self-sufficient in foodgrain. The imports of foodgrain declined. The process of industrialization has stated by that time. Initially, the machinery for the manufacture of agricultural equipment, machines and tools, transport equipment and industrial plants and their accessories were imported. Then, scientific and technological know-how to manufacture machines, tools and equipments. But industrial plants for heavy industries, such as the iron and steel industry, the petro-chemical industry, the automobile industry, were imported even in 1987-88. India has acquired knowledge in certain areas and will become self-sufficient soon. Industrial plants for the sugar industry, the cement industry, the paper industry, etc., are now made in India and installed by Indian technocrats.

The imports of petroleum and petro-products account abut 50 percent of India's import trade. The rise in the cost of these commodities in the international market has placed a heavy burden on India's economy. Therefore, she was forced to embark on oil exploration. Though she has not become self-sufficient, the pressure on the economy exerted by the import of oil has declined to some extent. In the eighties, 75 percent of her requirements of oil has been met from indigenous sources. But there has been an increasing demand by the increasing population. The imports of iron and steel, metals, certain chemicals, machinery and sometimes of essential commodities like foodgrains and edible oils still continue because of the increasing in the population.

New Trade Policy

The reversal of trends in exports growth during the last two years forced the Indian Government to announce the new export-import policy. The country-faced a serious economic crises with adverse balance of payment position and high inflationary pressure on the price level. There had been a steep decline in exchange reserves and there was not enough foreign exchange to earn import essential commodities and to pay off external debt. To bring the country out of such a difficult economic situation, the rupee was depreciated and it was followed up by major reforms in Trade Policy to boost exports.

In a world of growing interdependence and rapid technological advance, import substitution could no longer be followed at any cost. India has to become more modern, more efficient and more internationally competitive. Global developments like the oil crises of the early seventies and the early eighties forced India to adopt a pattern of development which would enable her to enter the export markets aggressively and earn foreign exchange needed to finance her essential imports. Last year, imports had gone up by 21-6 percent as against the growth in exports by 17-9 percent and the trade deficit reached a record level of Rs. 10,642.54 crores and hence, it was thought that unnecessary controls affecting the country's efforts in becoming globally competitive economy, should be removed. As a result of this the new export-import policy was announced by the Government in Parliament on 31st March 1992. The following are the highlights of the new export-import policy.

(i) The Ministry of Commerce has set up a High Level Committee on Trade Policy Reforms in order to progressively eliminate licensing and quantitative restrictions on capital goods and raw materials, components so that all these items can be placed under OGL.

(ii) Rationalization and simplification of the tariff structure has been undertaken in order to more towards international competitiveness.

(iii) EOU and EPZ schemes have been liberalised in order to attract foreign investment for tapping export markets.

(iv) The new policy aims at progressively reducing the extent of canalization. The Government has decontrolled 116 items, allowing their exports without any licensing formalities.

(v) The new trade policy includes measures to strengthen the development of export houses and Trading Houses in order to promote exports. The range of items permitted to be imported by Export Houses, Trading Houses and Star Trading Houses has been widened.

(vi) The procedure for import of capital goods has been simplified. New units and units undergoing substantial expansions will be automatically granted licences for import of capital goods. The negative list of imports is the smallest-ever. Consumer goods will continue to be under restraint.

(vii) The system of advance licences has been introduced to provide the exporters with duty free access to the inputs they need to produce competitively for world market.

(viii) The system of supplementary licences has been abolished.

(ix) The new trade policy makes major changes in the import licensing system by replacing a large part of administered licensing of imports by import entitlements linked to export earnings. The import replenishment system was enlarged and restructured and renamed as Eximcrips. Under this system all the export products of export services has seen enlarged. Eximcrips will be tradeable and can be used to import any item in the negative list of imports.

Indo-U.S.A. Trade -The large volume of India's trade is with U.S.A. In 1990-91 India's exports of the U.S.A. were 14-7 percent, while her imports in 1990-91 were of the order of 10-9 percent.

The major items of India's export to the U.S.A. are readymade garments, cashewnuts, diamonds, leather goods, jute goods, carpets, drugs, chemicals and allied products. She has started exporting many non-traditional items, including manufactured goods. Her major items of import from the U.S.A. are petro-products, chemicals, fertilizers, iron and steel, machinery, capital goods, spares, components and scientific and technological know-how. Her balance of trade with the U.S.A. is now been favourable.

Canada is another North American country offering a good market for the import of non-traditional Indian goods, The major items of her exports to Canada are textiles, engineering goods, chemicals, leather goods, tea, spices, jewellery, coffee, handicraft, etc. Traditional raw material is being increasingly replaced by finished goods. The imports to India from Canada consists of paper, newsprint, metals, etc.

Trade with South American Countries

India's foreign trade with Latin American and the Caribbean countries is hardly 6 percent of her total world trade. One of he reasons for this low volume in the distance, Nevertheless, India has forged trade links with Mexico, Venezuela, Columbia, Trinidad, Tobago, Cuba, Brazil, Argentina, Peru, Chile bad Guyana and the trade with them is increasing comparatively in the recent years. The major items of her exports to these countries are tea, jute goods, textile goods, machinery etc. India has no trade treaty with any individual country situation. There is a need for publicity for India's products and export capability inn the South American countries.

Trade with African Countries

India's trade with African countries is limited. But measures have been initiated to explore possibilities for increasing trade with these countries. Already, joint ventures, bilateral co-operation and agreements have been signed to establish trade links with them. There are offices of Indian trade agencies, such as the Engineering Export Promotion Council at Abiding, the Trade Development Authority in Liberia, the Project Equipment Corporation in Harare in Zimbabwe and Ethiopia. There is ample scope for the export of manufactured goods to these countries and for achieving a favourable balance of trade with them.

Trade with East-Asian - and Oceania

Among 27 countries in East Asia and Oceannia, only a few have trade-links with India- Japan, Korea, Australia, and New Zealand. Till 1978-79, the balance of trade with this region was favourable; thereafter it has become unfavourable mainly because of bulk imports of palm oil, woo, electronic goods, Natural Rubber, Zinc, Lead, Fertilizer, Coking coal etc.. Japan, of all the countries in trade with Japan recorded an all time high figures of Rs. 5547 crores manganese ore, mica, tobacco, leather goods, etc. Her imports from Japan cover silk, artificial silk, chemicals, electrical and electronic goods, machinery, iron and steel goods etc. There is ample scope for the export of Indian engineering goods and manufactured products of East Asian countries and Oceania.

Joint ventures and trade agreements with other countries have been functioning very efficiently and promoting India's foreign trade as well as increasing the country's participation in international trade.

4

FOREST RESOURCES

Natural Resources

Natural Resources means resources established by nature only. They are natural endowments in the form of land, water, vegetation and minerals. All natural materials with the passage of time become natural resources which provide base for economic development. By utilizing, natural resources, humans created their own world of living. They created houses, buildings, roads, railways, villages, towns, cities, machines industries and several other things. These are also very useful, and hence are called human made resources. Both natural and human-made resources are essential for living.

Resources have certain important characteristics as stated below:

(i) The help us to create goods and provide services.

(ii) The posses utility.

(iii) The are normally available in limited quantity.

(iv) Man has to exercise efforts in order to get utility from resources.

(v) Utility of resources change with the improvement in science and technology.

FOREST

Thirty percent of land area in the world is forest land. Trees are the most dominant living organisms in forests.

Forests function as huge biological filter systems that clean the environment by removing impurities from air and water. They restore oxygen in our atmosphere through photosynthesis, besides providing solvents, medicines, fuels and many other products that are important for our health and comfort. Briefly, forests play a vital role in regulating climate, controlling water run off, providing shelter and food for wild life. A part from it, forests have scenic, culture, and historic values that deserve to be protected. Forests have great biological and commercial values. These values of forests are discussed below:

Biological Values - A forest consists of an area where trees are the most dominant living organisms. The majority of forests are made up of different king of trees. Several layers of vegetation called strata are found in forest. These stratus are canopy, understory, shrubs, shrub layer, herb layer and forest floor. The tall broad leaf trees from the canopy are called ceiling. The areas beneath it is called understory. The lower strata of a forest having small woody plants is called shrubs. The shortest plants such as ferns, grassed and flowering plants are collectively called herb layer. The forest floor is composed of a layer of decaying plant materials.

Besides plants and trees that are found in the forests insects, birds, reptiles and fish are also included inn it. So all of the living organisms that found inn forest environments contribute to the value of forest. This is called biological value of a forest. Forests have some influence on the climate in the local area. They provide shade and cooler temperatures inside forest environment during summer months than in surrounding areas. Forest environments also contribute to comparatively warmer temperatures within the confines of the forest. Dense vegetation in the forest restrict the movement of air. This reduces the chill as well as limit evaporation of moisture from the forest floor. In contrast, large amounts of water are lost from plant leaves to the surroundings area. This results increased humidity in the air. This loss of water from leaf surface is called transpiration.

Trees are important to fish habitat in streams. They provide places for fish to hide and trees contribute to cool water temperatures by shading the water from direct sunlight. Trees protects streams from the heat of the sun that flow through forests. This is important to the survival of some kinds of fish such as trout that require cool water temperatures.

Forests provide food for many species of wild animals besides place of shelter. Animals and birds make their homes in forest environments. These predators use materials found in forests to provide dens and nesting places. Plant materials found in the forests is a big source of medicines that are of great use in our day to day life. Attempts are being made by botanists in the forests to identify unexplored herbs. So forests offer the potential for new medical cures. Research is being made continuously to find many new plant materials inn our forests that are valuable to a society.

Commercial Value of Forests

Forest products are important natural resource. A forest is renewable resources that replaces itself when conditions are favourable to new growth. Nearly 42% of the timber harvested in the United States is used for lumber. Lumber is an important forest products due to its widespread use in the construction of homes and commercial buildings. 20% of the wood harvests is still used for fuel in United States.

Wood is the most important energy source in many countries of the world. Energy is released form wood in the form of heat when commission of burning occurs. A recent development, in wood stoves is the use of wood pellets for fuel. Wood pellets are made from wood scraps, sawdust, shavings, and other waste materials. Charcoal and some kinds of coke are special fuels that are produced from wood for industrial and home uses. Biomass is defined as the weight of all the materials inn a tree that can be used as source of energy. Biomass production is measured as net weight of dry matter. Intensive culture of fast-growing trees has the capability of producing high tonnages of biomass when trees are planted in dense stands and harvested after twenty and thirty years of carefully managed growth.

Forests are the most important source of biomass. They constitute 42% of the total available biomass of the earth. Biomass includes vegetation and wastes that contain significant amounts of vegetable matter. Biomass is a modern wood product consisting of wood chips that are dried and burned as a source of e energy to generate electricity. Perhaps the best known use of the forest is the production of timber products.

Forests continue to hold appeal for people who enjoy outdoor environments, and many people use forests for recreation purposes. Some people enjoy the forest as a wild place where wild animals can be observed in their natural settings. Lakes and streams provide opportunities for fishing, boating and other water sports. Outdoor recreation has become a huge industry, and the citizens of many communities located in or near forest lands derive much of their income from sales of food or supplies related to recreational activities. The forest industry in north America has evolved from the harvest and sale of most timbers to more that $ 100 billion each year. Less developed countries, mainly in the tropics, produce more than half of industrial wood but use only 20 percent. Japan is by far the world's largest importer of wood, purchasing about 43 million cubic meters per year or 87 percent of net Asian imports, The average amount of wood used for cooking and heating in sixty-three less developed countries is about 1 person per year, roughly equal to the amount of wood that each American consumes as paper products alone. Many people in poor countries cook over the open fires that deliver only about one-tenth of the available heat to cooking pots. Jiko stove and clay pot used as an open fire. These stoves save forests, reduce air pollution, and save up to 20 percent of household income.

Types of Resources

Resources are classified in different ways namely as natural and human made, renewable and non-renewable, community and national resources. Natural resources are available with nature. Land, Water, Minerals and forests are some of the natural resources. They are of two types: biotic and abiotic: Land water and soil are abiotic whereas forests and animals are biotic resources.

Resources created by humans are called human made resources Engineering, technology, machines, buildings, paintings and social institutions are some of the human resources. Human resources are essential for development of natural resources.

As already stated, resources are further classified into renewable and non-renewable resources. Some resources have ability to renew themselves in a given period of time. Forests and wildlife are renewable resources. Similarity water, solar and tidal energy are renewable resources. Minerals are non-renewable resources. See below the classification Renewable and non-renewable resources:

Non-renewable Sources

Coal, Space of process heat, Natural Gas, Gasoline and fuel oil , Coal gasification, Oil shale, Nuclear.

Renewable Sources

Hydroglectic, Biomass methane, Wind, Solar electric. Attention mush be paid to the following important points with regard to natural resources.

(i) Resources Development - There are some resources, which cannot be used directly to satisfy human needs, One has to make an effort and develop it for human satisfaction. Land has to be cleared of unwanted materials and ploughed in order to grow crops. Water has to be e taken to fields to irrigate lands. Minerals have to be taken out from the earth and smelt before they are used for making machinery and implements. Resource development, thus, is a necessary exercise for its utilization.

(ii) Resources Planning - As the resources are limited and unevenly distributed over the country, their planning is essential. Resources planning is a technique or skill or proper utilization or resources. It comprises,

a. Planning for exploitation or resources.

b. Evaluation in terms of availability of resources.

c. Preparation of inventory of resources.

(iii) Conservation of Resources - Conservation means judicious and planned use of natural resources.

In other words conservation means preserving and maintenance of the environment to meet human needs for production while ensuring that proper consideration is also given to aesthentics and recreation. The reasonable use of the earth's natural resources- water, soil, wild life, materials is a major goal of conservation. Natural resources are a vital part of sustaining human life, and conservation measures are designed to control, manage and preserve them so that they can be used and appreciated to the maximum. The conservation of natural resources include (i) Mineral Conservation, (ii) Wild-life Conservation, (iii) Forest Conservation, (iv) Water Conservation.

Above described resources form a part of our environment. Proper utilization of these may sustain the environment. Inappropriate and reckless utilization and non-renewable resources, let us discuss forest resources which is renewable resources and contribute substantially to our economic development. They play a major role in enhancing the quality of environment. They perform various types of functions. They modify local climate, control soil erosion regulate stream flow, support a variety of industries, provided livelihood for many communities and offer opportunities for recreation. They reduce wind force and influence air temperature, The add to the forest floor large quantities of loaves, twigs and branches, which after decomposition, forms humus. They provide industrial wood, timber, fuel wood, fodder and several other minor products of great economic value. The national forest policy emphasizes the role of forests in maintaining the life support system. Detailed review of forest wealth is described below to know the value of this renewable source of environment, as well types of forest.

Types of Forest

Forest are classified in three types broadly for the

purpose of administration. They are:

(i) Reserved forest, (ii) Protected forests, (iii) Unclassed forest.

(i) Reserved forests are those which are permanently earmarked either to production of timber or other forest produce and in which right of grazing and cultivation is seldom allowed.

(ii) In protected forest, these rights are allowed subjects to a few minor restriction,

(iii) Unclassified forests consist largely of inaccessible forest of unoccupied wastes. Forests are also classified according to density. Namely: dense, open and mangrove forest.

Forest Management

The forest land constitute a massive renewable natural resources that should be available both for present and future generation of citizens. Forest management refers to the planning of sustainable harvests with particular attention paid to forest regeneration. The role of government in conservation and management of forest resources is to manage public forest lands to sustain the yields of forest products in a manner that is consistent with science validated Silviculture practices. Silviculture refers to growth of more and more trees. It is believed by the forest managements agencies in USA that forests are widely used and will always be available to the citizens who depend upon them Studies reveal and records speak that forests are shrinking rapidly. The man causes of diminishing forests are discussed below:

(i) Most countries replant less number of forest: to be converted uses. Due to divergent definitions of deforestation, rates of forest rates of forest destruction exist in many places. Some scientists and politicians while defining deforestation comment that it means a complete change from forest to agriculture and urban areas. Others define that if an area is logged and selective cutting of forests is exercised then natural growth will be rapid. Countries also have economic and political reasonable to hide or exaggerate the extent of their activities. Consequently, more than 20 million ha per year.

(ii) Incendiary fires account for over 1/4 of all of the forest in the World each year. This fire is stated deliberately by people and is called wilful setting fires. The practice accounts for nearly 40% of all forest fires in the region of United States. The objective of this fire is to control pests and to improve grazing for livestock.

Intense fires generate tremendous amounts of heat and by a fire of this type the combine and phloem tissue in the stem and branches and damaged restricting the flow of nutrients and water enforced. Wild fires often inflict serious damage to soils. This is because organic matter is destroyed, causing the soil structure to break-down.

(iii) Loss of control on a prescribed burn spread wild fire in the forest. A prescribed burn is a fire that is started in an established forest for the purpose of removing vegetation and fuel from the forests floor.

(iv) Human activities are equally responsible for most forest fires. A leading cause of these fires is failure to put out camp-fires, cigarettes, and matches before leaving or discarding them in forest.

(v) Volcano activity which is a rare cause of natural fires in the forest cannot be denied too. Volcanic explosion in 1980 demonstrated the intensity of this natural force. The trees within a radius of several miles of the Volcano were all blown down.

(vi) Fires, insects and diseases damage up to one quarter of the annual growth in temperate forests. The main causes of forest fires are lighting, human activities such as cigarettes, campfires, fireworks and so on. Fire types are determined largely by the kinds of fuels that are present. These fuels are of two types Surface fuels and ground fuels. Surface fuels are one located on the surface of the soil. They are dry leaves and plant materials. Ground fuels include combustible materials located beneath the surface. Duff is a ground fuel. A surface fire burns surface fuels consisting of the dry layer of twings, dead branches, grass and leaves that lie on the surface of the ground.

A ground fire burns ground fuels that are found on or beneath the surface of the ground. During dry periods, these fuels will burn, and a fire in a deposit of duff can smoulder for many weeks.

(vii) Another important reason for diminishing forests is huge profit earned by absentee landlord's and government agencies from plantations. Local people have least incentive to prevent fires or keep grazing animals out of newly planted areas. In some countries, such as Philippines and Israel, government reforestation projects have been targets and anti-government forces, with divesting environmental impacts.

Brazil as to the highest rate of deforestation in the World.

The coastal forests of Ecuador, Ghanna, Madagascar have almost destroyed their forests. Haiti waste once 80 percent forested and today all the forests are destroyed and the land lies barren and eroded. About 2/3 of the forest in Central America has been destroyed, mostly in the past few decades as land is converted to pasture or cropland. Unfortunately the soil is poorly suited to grain of farming. A variety of reasons lead to this deforestation. In Seacoast Rica, in addition to cattle ranching, banana plantations consume large areas of forest. In Brazil, invasion of immigrants from South are responsible for forest losses. Gold mining in Ecuador, Coca production in Columbia and Bolivia and logging of hardwoods for export in Malaysia are some of the causes of forest destruction.

The other major source of forest destruction is invasion by land-hungry people from other areas. The loggers are interests only in creaming i.e., the most valuable wood such as teak, mahogany, San sood, or ebony. Although only one or two trees per hectare might be taken, widespread usually results. Because the canopy of topical forests is strongly linked by vines and interlocking branches, felling one tree can easily bring down a dozen others.

Reforestation

It means re-plantation of forest than is harvested. Many outstanding examples of successful reforestation are recorded. China for instance, cut down most of its forests one thousand years ago and suffered centuries of erosion and terrible floods as a consequence. Recently in China massive reforestation campaign has been started. Korea has also followed the policy of reforestation. After losing nearly all its trees during the Civil War, 30 years ago, Korea has now about 70 percent forested again. Japan has increased forests to approximately 68 percent in spite of being biggest importer of wood.

Satellite Fire Surveillance

Forest fire management is based on the concept that it is neither necessary not cost-effective to suppress fire that has occurred. Plenty of evidence suggest that most fires that are allowed to burn will be extinguished naturally before they have burned a few acres of trees. To assess occurrence of fire lookout towers have been constructed in remote forest regions. A constant watch was maintained during the summer fire seasons to detect fires as they occurred. Some of these towers are used, although fires are usually detected more effectively using modern technologies such as remote sensing equipment an Satellite Surveillance. Cost effective analysis are very important in suppressing forest fire. When a valuable timber resource is located in the area where fire is burning, it may be cost effective to suppress the fire.

Agroforestry

Conservation and public service organizations are encouraging agroforestry plans. These groups encourage people to plant fast-growing multipurpose trees such leucaena. Leucaen is a legume, so it fixes nitrogen and improves the soil. Millions of seedlings have been planted in hundreds of self-help projects in Asia. Africa and Latin America. Its nutritious leaves are good livestock fodder. It can grow up to 3 meters per year and quickly provide shades. They protect watersheds, create windbreaks and also provide useful good and forest products.

Selective cutting in place of clear- cutting

Clear cutting is a harvesting stem in which every tree is given area regardless of size. This method enables large machines to fell, trim and skid logs rapidly, but wastes many trees. This system increase soil erosion, and eliminates habitat for many forest species. Most timber and plywood in the United States and Canada currently is harvested by clear cutting. Size and shape of clear cuts vary depending on topography and management policies. In a forests managed for these trees, or forestires, blue berries, deer, or grouse, this is a good method. Other harvest practices substitute clear cutting with strip cutting. Strip cutting entails harvesting all the trees in a narrow corridor. The leas disruptive method is selective cutting. Under this method only a small percentage of the mature trees are taken in each 10 year or 20 year rotation.

Debe-for-Nature Swap

Developed countries of the world can save tropical forest from diminishing. This cab be done by financing nature. Finance is a great need for developing countries to protect and conserve forests. One promising approach to over power this problem is debt-for-nature swaps. Banks, government and money-leading institutions now hold nearly 1 million dollar loans to developing countries. This debe is not collected. Bank sell bonds at a steep discount nearly 10 percent on a dollar. Forest conservation organization buy debt obligation at a discount as mentioned above and then offer to cancel debt provided. Debtor country agree to protect, to restore an area of biological importance. The first such swap was made in 1987. Agreements have been reached with Madagascar and Zambia to swap debts for nature.

Forest Protection from Extinction

This has been explained earlier that tropical forests around the world are being cut at an alarming rate. Often hundreds of trees are smashed down to a single teak tree. This is seriously realized by tropical countries and they are initiating steps to protect them. People on the grass roots level have started to protect and restore forests. Indonesia has announced plans to preserve 100,000 sq. kilometres. Brazil and Zaire plan for forest protection in the world. School children plant trees in a community deforestation project in Haiti.

5

WATER RESOURCES

It is believed that life first orginated in water before it invaded land. Water is in faxt a pre-condition of life. Agriculture and growing urbanization with its modern life-style has been demanding greater share of water day by day. The primary source of water on earth is precipitation that comes in the form of rain and snowfall. The average annual rainfall in India is estimated at 117 cm. in a year. Water is available as surface water. The Indus, the Ganga and Brahmaputra carry 60 percent of total surface water.

As already described water is essential for all forms of human life. The surface of the earth measures, 50,000 million hectares in area, 20% of this area is land and the rest 80% is all covered by water. A man on a average consumes about 2 liters of water everyday. More than 70% of human's body weight is made up of water. Water as a natural resource is limited and estimated 1,011 mmckms of water on earth, out of which 486 mckms or 97% is contained in the oceans , out mckms is buried underground of the remaining small quantity of water 1.100th of 1% estimated at 33,400 m, provides the water supply vital for life on this earth.

In Delhi alone 800 million gallons is needed everyday but the treated water supply is 600 mgd, the short fall of 200 mgd is met by drawing groundwater. The increased demand for water can be met, if following water use methods are adopted because water is precious environmental resource. It is scarce, save it.

Following are the common methods of saving or conserving water :-

(i) Use a map and bucket of water for washing the floor instead of a running hose. One bucket of water contain nearly 18 litres will do the same work as a 10 minutes use of hose pipe. It contains 400 litres of water. We can save 382 litres of water.

(ii) Use a mug of water while brushing your teeth instead running tap.

(iii) Repairing immediately the water supply pipelines to prevent wastage and pollution of water.

(iv) Preventing pollution of water bodies. Once it is rained it takes years for replenishment.

(v) Registering all water-extraction points like tubewells and borewells.

(vi) Stopping use of treated water for gardening, washing vehicles.

(vii) Rainwater harvesting a techniques to recharge of groundwater by capturing and storing rainwater by constructing structures, such as dug wells, [ercolation pits, check dams. Rainwater is stored in groundwater reservoirs by adopting artificial recharge techniques to meet the household needs through storage in tanks, with the objectives: to reduce run-off, to avoid flooding of needs, to increase groundwater storage, and to supplement domestic water requirement during summer and long dry spells.

(viii) Adopt water harvesting techniques to recharge ground water levels.

(ix) Collect rainwater and use it for gardening and recharging ground water.

(x) Make sure that water does not overflow from your

overhead tank.

Multipurpose River Valley Projects

To achieve self-reliance and improver the standard of living of its people after independence, a number of river valley projects were developed. Many of them are multi-purpose river vary projects. These projects are meant to tackle various problems in an integrated manner. They control flood, check soil erosion, provide water for irrigation and drinking purposes, generate electricity for industries, villages and cities, provide inland navigation, and several other facilities like recreation, preservation of wildlife and development of fisheries. A brief review of the major multipurpose projects is given below:

(i) Rajashthan Canal Project : Rajasthan Canal Project is one of the important river valley project in India. It is one of the world's largest single irrigation project providing irrigation waters to nearly 19-49 lakh hectares in the districts of Bikaner, Ganganagar and Jaisalmer in Rajasthan. It entails construction of canal measuring 523.93 cubic metres capacity taking off the Harike barrage and the distribution system. Rajasthan Canal Project has been divided into two parts viz. (a) Rajasthan Canal Projecty Feeder and (b) Rajasthan Canal. Rajasthan canal is being fed by the supply of water by Ravi and Beas rivers. Later, the flow supplies will be supplemented by stored waters from Beas dam and Pong dams. The entire length of Canal and the feeder will be lined to save water losses through seepage. The intensity of irrigation will now be increased from the present 78 to 110%.

(ii) Farokka Barrage Project : The Farakka Barrage Project constructed over Bhagirathi Hoogly river system is designed for the preservation and maintenance of the

Kolkata Port. The river Bhagirathi, the feeder cabal and the Navigation locks at Farakka Barrage from part of the Haldia Allahabad Inland waterway. The main components of the project are (a) Navigation works such as locks, lock channels, shelter bosins, navigation lights and other infrastructure. (b) A feeder canal of 11333 cumec carrying capacity and 38.38 km. long lacking off from head regulator on the right side of the Farakka Barrage. (c) A 2,240 metre long barrage across the Ganga with rail-cum-road bridge, necessary river training works and a head regulator on the right side. The barrage is designed to pass a flood discharge of 76,455 cumec. (d) A 213 metre long barrage across the river Bhagirathi and Jangir. The barrage is designed to pass a discharge of 1,700 cumec.

(iii) Bhakra Nangal Project : Bhakra Dam, 225.55 m high straight gravity structure, is a majestic monument across river Sutlej. Its construction water taken up just after independence, for the uplift and welfare of the people of Northern Region and it was completed in the year 1963. The lake created by the dam is 168.35 sq. kilometers in area gross storage of 9868 million cu. metre the water stored at Bakhra have tremendous potential of generation hydro-electric power. Nangal Dam, 13 km. Downstream of Bhakra Dam, diverts the water of river Sutlej into Nangal Hydel Channel for power generation and irrigation purposes. Nangal Hydel Channel is a lined channel 64.5 km. long off-taking from Nangal Dam. Two power houses have been constructed on Nangal Hydel Channel; the first is located at Ganfuwal and second is situated at Kotla. The total installed capacity of Bhakra Power House and Ganguwal/Kotal Power Houses is 1354 kW.

(iv) Sardar Sarovar Project - Investigations reveal that

the potential of water resources and power development in the Narmada basin was initiated sometimes in 1947. The project was opened by the Prime Minister of India, with the availability of more detailed modernized counter sheets, raising the height of the dam for optimum utilization was considered and series of negotiation took place at the political level as it was an inter-state protect. The matter was subsequently given to the Narmada water Disputes tribunal as no agreement could be arrived at.

The government of Gujarat established Sardar Sarovar Narmada Nigam Limited as a wholly owned Government Company under the provisions of the Companies Ace, 1956. This is perhaps the first state level autonomous Corporation constituted for implementation of such a large multi-purpose project. The protect is an inter-state multi-purpose project of four states viz., Madhya Pradesh, Maharashtra, Gujarat and Rajasthan. Some of its main features are us under :-

(a) The River Bed Power House will be located underground on the right bank and will accommodate six revisable Francis Type turbine units, each of 200 MW capacity. The Canal Head Port House, also on the right bank, will accommodate five units of conventional Kalpan Type each of 50 MW capacity.

(b) The length of distribution system network will be about 75,000 kms. The supply of water would be volumetric by rotation with automatic remote control so as economies the use of costly and scare water.

(c) A 460 km. long main canal will be construct which will reach upto Gujarat-Rajasthan Border. It will have the capacity of 1133 cumes the largest in the world and it will taper down to about 71 cumes at Gujarat-Rajasthan Border.

(d) Creation of concrete gravity dam of 128 M. from the river-bed and reservoir, with live storage of 5800 million cubic mtrs. enveloping about 214km of the Narmada Valley and surface area of about 3700 hectares.

Benefits on Implementation of the Sardar Srovar Narmada Project

It is envisaged that following benefits would accrue on implementation of the Sardar Sarovar Projects :-

(i) Since it is proposed to compress the construction schedule of the project from 17/22 years to 10/12 years, on account of its early completion then a saving of about 3,500 crores on account of cost escalation would result.

(ii) On completion, annual additional agricultural production would be Rs. 900 crores. Power generation would be Rs. 400 crores and water supply would be Rs. 100 crores aggregation to about Rs. 1400 crores every year working out to about Rs. 4 crores a day.

(iii) It would also create employment potential of 7 lakh workers daily during construction period and 6 lakh workers daily during the post-construction stage.

(iv) Since new industrial corridor will develop around narmada main canal, Ahmedabad-Delhi meter gauge Railway line and Eastern highway would be the extension of the present rail-road corridor to New Delhi giving further boost to trade and commerce between Gujarat and Northern States.

(v) It will be a permanent solution for drinking water supply problem of water hungry regions of Saurashtra and Kutch.

(vi) Water supply requirements of several industries will also be met from the project giving all round boost of the industrial progress of Gujarat.

(vii) 4720 villages and 131 urban centres in Gujarat

State would get a permanent solution as regards the drinking water supply needs.

(viii) Power generation capacity of 1,450 MW would be added.

(ix) It would generate 5000 million units of electricity.

(x) In Gujarat State 17.92 lakh ha. of land spread over 12 districts, 62 talukas and 3393 villages, about 75% of which is drought prone, would come under irrigation every year.

Present Status of the Project :-

You will observe from the Directors Report that progress achieved in construction of the dam and appurtenant works, hydro - power, Narmada Main Canal and Branches as also distributary system have already been highlighted in detail would, therefore, like to dwell upon the novel and unconventional methods adopted by the Corporation for expediting the implementation of the project, the importance of which is as under :-

(i) The task of testing soil samples for main canal work has been entrusted to the private laboratories after short-listing.

(ii) Work of survey and investigation as also preparation of plans and estimates for the work of distribution system have been entrusted to private consultants.

(iii) To expedite the land acquisition for the canal works, the land acquisition organisation has been expanded.

It is learned that the approval of the Planning Commission for the Project was received in October, 1988. It is also informed that some inter-state key problems were resolved. The Government of Rajasthan has also indicated the level at which the Narmada main canal should deliver water on Gujarat-Rajasthan border. Moreover the issue regarding provision of irrigation bypass Tunnel and sharing cost of Rock-fill dykes and inter-linking channels is also resolve. The Government of India has given clearance to construction of approach road from Gora to Dam site which was very vital for jet speed concreting to Dam.

In order to expedite implementation of the Project to meet with the construction schedule which has been compressed to 17/22 years to 10/12 years, the Corporation has expanded the organizational base at all levels. For simultaneous completion of canal along with main canal levels. For simultaneous completion of canal along with main canal three posts of engineer-in-Chiefs and two post of Chief Engineers have been created. At present works of Rs. 1032 crores are on hand. The projects is completed.

Energy

Energy is a very essential need of a man. Any body can do an amount of work only when the energy possessed by the body is released. The sources of energy in rural system could be broadly divided into two ; traditional and modern sources. The traditional sources would be fuels wood, fuelstick, crop residue and cattle dung. These are partly commercial, conventional and renewable. Electricity, kerosene and other commercialized expect biogas, wind and ocean energy. The source of energy would depend upon the type of energy required for the purpose it has to serve.

Residential and Commercial Energy Demand

The amount of energy required for residential and commercial use varies greatly throughout the world. The economics of energy consumption describe that a country with high GNP product roughly use less per capita energy for residential and commercial needs, than a less developed country like Africa and India. 30 percent energy used in North America and 90 percent used in India is for residential and commercial purposes. Reason is very simple. North Americans use air conditioning, refrigeration, water heating and space heating. So 75 percent energy is used in these gadgets. In India, almost all of the energy used in home is for cooking due to scarcity and high cost of fuel. About half of the energy demand in Africa is for cooking because they use an open fire instead of stoves. Using more efficient stoves instead of open fires could reduce these energy requirements by 50 percent. Summarily North America, and India could reduce energy consumption in many ways.

Industrials Energy Demand. Considerable variation is found in the amount of energy used for industrial processes. Facts speak than 60 percent of all the commercial energy was used in the former Soviet Union. About 30 percent of energy is used by USA for industries.

In the former Soviet Union large deposits of coal, oil and natural gas reserves were available. On account of this reason steel was processed from ore because energy was readily available. Spain and Italy lack large deposits of fossil fuel necessary for the extraction of oil and natural gas. So both Italy and Spain produce steel from serape steel because it needs less energy. Producing 1 metric ton of steel from iron or in the former Soviet Union uses as much energy as producing a metric ton of steel from scrap in Spain or Italy.

6

ENERGY RESOURCES

Energy is an important input for development. No country can develop and progress in material pursuits without energy. There are broadly two sources of energy - Non conventional and conventional. Non-conventional energy sources are also called renewable sources of energy. Non- conventional or renewable sources are non-exhaustible. They are physical resources like coal, oil deposits, natural gas, minerals, soil, materials etc.

The other resources of energy are conventional or non- renewable. They are mostly biological in nature and include forestry, agriculture, animals. Solar energy, wind energy, water energy and geothemal energy belongs to this category. They are available in an exhaustible form in nature.

To keep pace with the increased demand of energy in the world both renewable and non-renewable resources are required to be harnessed fully besides conserving energy, because energy conserved is energy produced. For energy sources both non-renewable and renewable sources. Both Nonrenewable and Renewable sources of energy are discussed below turn by turn in an elaborate manner.

Wind Power or Energy

Moving air is called wind. This wind has energy. It is natural source of kinetic energy. It can pick up things and send them flying; it can lift heaps of sand and pile them into big sand dunes; it can hit the huge trees and send them crashing. This shows that the wind has a lot of energy to smash and destroy. But the man is intelligent enough to make this wind energy to do useful work for him. The energy possessed by the wind is due to its high speed or motion.

The possession of energy in wind is called kinetic energy. This kinetic energy in wind is utilized for doing work. In the earlier days, the energy of wind was utilized to sail boats for transport purposes and in wind-mills to pump out water from earth. A sail boat and a wind-mill is a machine which works with the energy of blowing air or wind.

There is abundant energy in wind which can be tapped. The World Meteorological Organization has estimated that 20 million MW of wind power could be commercially tapped worldwide. The Windmill is a proven technology. Windmills have been used for more than 1000 years, mostly to pump water and grind grain. Windmills were brought to Europe by merchants and returning crusaders, In the United States, the old farm windmill was used for decades to pump water and generate electricity. It is still used for electricity in remote areas for rural electrification.

Denmark and California leads the world in where it lacks other energy sources. The largest current market for windmills ins in the United States. Because of the immense amount of energy that could be produced by tapping the winds, private companies are building machines to tap the winds, then selling electricity to power companies.

Historically speaking windmills played a crucial role in setting of the American West. They had abundant water in underground aquifers but little water on the surface. The strong, steady winds that blew across the prairies, provides the energy to pump water that allowed agriculture to move west across the prairies. By the level of the nineteenth century, nearly every farm of Mississippi ever had at least one windmill. Even today some 150,000 windmills still spin productively in the Great plains. Manufacturing, installation and repair of windmills was a major industry in America at that time.

The General Electric Co. Estimated that wind could provide 14 percent of U.S. Electric demand by the year 2000. One thousand MW of installed wind power could meet the energy needs of 400,000 households at present use levels and save 3-7 millions barrels of oil per year. The General Electronic research unit have also discovered more than 556,400 sq./kg of land in he United States alone that are suitable for wind generators.

Coal

Coal is a major non-conventional source of energy used throughout the world. It is India's number one energy source. It is used for domestic cooking and industrial heating to the production of electricity, in thermal power plants. Coal is most plentiful fossil fuel. Coal is largely carbon mixed with incombustible mineral matter of earth's crust. When coal is burnt, it produces carbon dioxide and flash which is a particulate pollutant. It is a fossilized plant material preserved by burial in sediments and altered by geological forces. Coal is non-renewable source of energy because it takes very long time to form fossil fuel. Studies reveal that about 6000 billion tonnes of coal lies under the earth and by now around 200 billion tonnes had been used. Coal is among the most important traditional source of energy in India. 60,000 million tonnes of coal is minerable and sufficient to meet country's coal demand for another 130 years. Maximum coal deposits are found in Bihar and West Bengal in India.

Coal comes in various grades : anthracite, bituminous, subbituminous, and lignite in descending order of energy content and hardness. Anthracite, almost pure carbon, is found in very small quantities. An average bituminous coal might have an energy content of 30 MJ/kg while lignite may have an energy content of 16 MJ/kg. As with oil some coal is left in place when it is mined.

Though coal is mainly composed of carbon yet, it contains hydrogen, oxygen and varying amounts of nitrogen, sulphur and other elements. Coal was formed by the decomposition of the remains of vegetation growing in swamps. It is one of the most important source of energy and an essential input in steel and carbo-chemical industries.

Coal reserves are spread over almost 100 countries around the world. It contributes over 25% of world primary energy consumption. Coal is a competitive primary source for generation of electric power, World's 40% and India's 50% electric power generation is from coal.

India is the third largest coal producing country in the world. Per man productivity of coal is highest approximately to 2-45 tonnes. It is attractive investment regime having closely monitoring mine effluents with prescribing time limits for disposal of applications for mineral concessions.

The coal belts in India are located mainly in Orissa, Bihar, U.P., M.P., A.P., Maharashtra and Bengal. Coal as a source of energy is used for different purposes. Coal deposits are not evenly distributed throughout the world.

Notice that the countries with the largest land area have the most coal North America has one-fourth or all proven reserves. Antarctica is thought to have large coal deposits. But it is difficult, expensive and ecologically damaging to mine in Antarctica. Coal mining is dirty and dangerous business.

Oil

Oil is an equally important source of energy. Its use has been encouraged as being more convenient and often less expensive than coal. Its use became popular when automobile became quite common in 1920. This facilitated, convenient and less expensive use of oil compared to coal, stimulated exploration of oil. Today geologists use a series of test to locate underground formations that may contain oil. The moment, oil potential area is identified, a test well is drilled to determine if oil is actually present. Easy-to-reach oil fields have already been tapped. Drilling is being done in less accessible sites where smaller amount of oil is available.

This is a very expensive process of oil extraction. Moreover oil deposits in land have become more difficult to locate. Geologists are therefore occupied in search of location oil from the search of geologists. The cost of building an offshore drilling platform is very high and may cost trillions of rupees. To reduce the cost of drilling many wells may be sunk from a single offshore platform. Once the drilling platform is secured to the Ocean floor a number of wells are sunk to obtain oil and gas. This technique finally reduce the cost of constructing platform on the ocean floor. By the year 1993, estimated oil was extracted to the order of 1000 billion barrels. Of this, more than three quarters are in OPEC countries and half lie in Saudi Arabia, Iraq, Kuwait and Iran.

Oil exploration in India dates back to 1866 when oil exploration began Upper Assam and adjoining areas. Oil exploration made headway only after independence, more particularly over the past two decades. Only after independence, more particularly with a modest level of indigenous crude critical to India's economy. Starting with a modest level of indigenous crude production of only about 0.25 million tonnes in 1950-51, the production of domestic crude oil reached the peak level of 33 million tonnes in 1990-91. The production of crude oil during 1997-98 was approximately 33.86 million tonnes. The major contribution to the crude oil production has come only after the discovery of the offshore ail fields. Mumbai is the most prestigious among them.

The world's oil production during the past five years has a declining trend. There are two reasons for this. First is Iraqi invasion of Kuwait and secondly decline in Russian oil production. In Russia, the world's biggest oil producer, output fell form 12.4 million barrels daily in 1989 to 11.2 million barrels daily in 1992.

Facts About Oil : Indian Scenario

(i) Petroleum bearing state in India are Rajasthan, Krishna, Calvary, Godavery basin, Andaman, Bengal and Himalayan foothills.

(ii) ONGC, since 19567 is engaged in oil exploration, production and refining is done is 15 refineries with the capacity of 60 MMT per annum. Scottish exploration firm Cairn Energy has struck an estimated 20 billion tonnes of oil and gas reserves in the Barner district Rajasthan.

(iii) In India, total consumption of oil production is used in road transport sector amounting to 40% and the balance in power generation, domestic and miscellaneous purposes.

(iv) Petrol from plastic : Nagpur- based scientist Dr. Alka Umesh Zadgasankar claims it is possible to derive petrol from plastic waste. And with all the plastic waste choking our rivers and adorning our garbage heaps, a fuel from plastic is probably just what our environmentalists ordered.

(v) By 2005 Indian oil demand is expects to reach 2.8 million bad representing a growth of 6-6.5 percent annually from 2001, and about to reach 3.6 million bed by 2010. Crude oil imports are expected to reach 70 percent of domestic consumption by 2005. India's dependence on imported oil not only continues to increase but also makes the country one of the world's largest consumer of oil.

(vi) Oil reserves in the whole world are estimated to around 1,000 billion barrels. Keeping reserves and annual production, oil shall last for about 45-50 years. India shall have oil only for another 15-20 years because reserves are just limited to 785 million tonnes. India is planning to increase production of oil from 32.24 MT to 50 MT very shortly.

(vii) Hydrocarbon is crude oil and is converted form the remains of marine organisms due to heat, pressure and catalytic action. Conversion took millions of years.

(viii) Oil or petroleum is a complex mixture of hydrocarbons. It averages about two atoms of hydrogen to each carbon atom.

Energy from Biomass/ Bio-Energy and Biogas

Energy is being produced from biomass. Biomass resources used for producing energy include fuel wood, wood chips, bark, branches, leaves, starchy roots new plant growth, residues and wastes, herbage, algae, agricultural and forest residues like bagasse, corn cobs, bark, saw dust, wood shavings, roots and animal dropping etc. Sewage, garbage and night soil also provide biogas. Biodegradable organic effluents from industries like sugar, slaughter house, meat packing plants and distilleries are equally important sources of bio-energy. Biomass is renewable source of energy. Energy from this source is determined advantageous over nuclear and fossil fuels because of its renewability and easy accessibility. All renewable sources of energy account for about 18 percent of total world energy use, and biomass makes up three-quarters of that renewable energy supply.

Sufficient energy have been collected and stored in photo-synthetic organisms. They have been storing energy for the last 2 billion years. Studies reveal that plants capture nearly 0.1 percent of all solar energy that reaches the earth's surface. Some energy collected by the plants is spent in metabolic activities, the rest is stored in biomass. The metabolic activities are pumping water and oils, mechanical movement, maintenance of cells and tissues, and reproduction. It is difficult to measure the magnitude of energy, but experts estimate useful biomass production is of fifteen to twenty times, the amount of energy from all commercial sources of energy.

Biogas

Biogas is a sustainable source of renewable energy. Maintenance operation and construction of biogas units are simple. It provides multiple benefits to users. Biogas is a gaseous mixture of methane, carbondioxide and certain traces of nitrogen and hydrogen sulphide. It is composed of 60% methane 40% carbon dioxide. New Delhi has developed technology of briqetting saw dust into smokeless fuel- a good source of energy which yields biogas and pyrogas. Depending upon the content of carbon dioxide, biogas has calorific value of more than 5,000 kcal. The calorific value of biogas cab be further enhanced provided content of carbon dioxide is reduced and biogas is passed through a limestone solution.

Burning Biomass

Since time immemorial world fires have been the main source of heating and cooking. Till 1850 wood supplied 90 percent of the fuel to so called developed countries. But now wood provides less percent energy due to these nations because they have invented new sources of energy due to scientific and technological advancement. But the condition of underdeveloped countries is entirely different. In these countries, wood and other biomass fuels provide up to 95 percent of all energy used.

In northern industrialized countries of the world wood burning as a source of energy is very popular because oil, gas and coal prices are high. In these countries the supply of wood is also enough. It is believed that wood burning may limit further expansion due to hazardous amounts of carbon monoxide and hydrocarbons due to inefficient and incomplete burning of wood. In hill areas wood burning as source of energy is not recommended because it can present a major source of air quality degradation and health risk. Wood burning in these areas produce polycyclic aromatic compounds worrisome to human health because these compounds are carcinogenic. The Environmental protection Agency recommend use of wood stoves nationwide to overpower this problem. Clean-burning woodstoves are available but they are highly expensive.

Fuelwood crisis in underdeveloped countries in general and India in particular shall be faced because other sources of energy in these countries are not harnessed. Increasing wood use lead to diminishing fuel wood resources and has many adverse environmental impacts. As sallen wood becomes scarce, people lop off branches and even fell trees. These activities have following results:

(i) Air pollution resulting from burning biomass cause acid rain. The pH scale is used to measure acidity. A pH of 7 is neutral; when the pH is less than 7, the liquid is acidic; when pH is greater than 7, the liquid is alkaline. Lakes with pH less than 5.4 have no reproducing fish.

(ii) Contribute to decertification land climate change.

(iii) Cause soil erosion making deserts.

(iv) Depletion in ground water supplies.

(v) Destruction of forests and decrease in wildlife habitat.

The match between aggregate demand fuel wood and its supply would be highly disturbed in future. Projections reveal that by 2025, worldwide demand for fuelwood will be 4400 million cubic meters, while supplies shall not cross the present levels. Situation in African countries like Sudan and Rwada would be worst because their demand of fuelwood is already ten times more than supply of fuel wood.

Sources of Biogas Production

(i) Some forms of biomass energy are well suited to developing countries especially biogas digesters which are widespread in China and India.

(ii) Biogas is chiefly produced from : Cattle dung, human excreta, straw, plant, leaves, algae, bagasse, paddy husk, water weeds, distillery sludge, wastes from tannery, food industries and paper mills.

(iii) The anaerobic digestion process constitute

complex series of reactions catalysed by a mixed group of bacteria, 90% of the combustible energy of the degradable organic matter is converted into methane and carbon dioxide. The manorial value of organic waste is not reduced. The slurry from biogas plant is enriched manure having high degree contents of nitrogen, phosphorus and potassium. So biogas plants help in obtaining both fuel and manure from waste.

(iv) It is naturally occurring biotechnological process and begins when anaerobic decomposition of organic matter takes place.

CNG and LPG

Natural gas is mostly made up of methane. The other 5% is made up of various gases along with small amounts of water of water vapour. These other gases include butane, propane, ethane and other trace gases. Methane is a hydrocarbon, meaning its molecules are made up of hydrogen and carbon atoms. It is simple, one carbon, molecular structure makes possible its nearly complete combustion.

Like oil, this common fuel comes from underground. However, natural gas, as the name implies, is a gas much like air, rather than a liquid like petroleum. It has been found to be one of he most eco-friendly fuels, and its popularity is growing.

Because of its clean burning nature and the fact that it is not made from petroleum, as gasoline are, may automakers around the world are developing vehicles to run on natural gas. Cars, vans, buses and small trucks generally use natural gas that has been compressed and stored in high-pressure cylinders.

Several vehicles are available today that operate on CNG. Some run on natural gas only and others can run on natural gas or gasoline called bio-fuel vehicles.

Most people call liquefied petroleum gas (LPG) propane. That is because LPG is mostly made up of propane. Actually, LPG is made of a mixture of propane and other similar types of hydrocarbon gases. Different batches of LPG have slightly different amounts of the different kinds of hydrocarbon molecules. These hydrocarbons are gases at room temperature, but turn to liquid when they are compressed. LPG is stored in special tanks that keep it usually about 200 pounds per square inch. Most LPG produced in the U.S. comes from natural. Gas well head processing. That is because natural gas has LPG gases and water vapour in it, which have to be removed before the natural gas can be sent away in pipelines. Most of the LPG produced in caligonia comes from petroleum refining.

LPG is also used in many homes in the country, where there are no natural gas pipelines. These homes use LPG for heating, cooking, hot water and other energy needs.

LPG fuelled engines can pollute less than gasoline and diesel engines. LPG usually costs less than gasoline for the same amount of energy. In some countries LPG is used much more for vehicle fuel. In the Netherlands over 10% of the motor fuel used is LPG.

Ethanol and Methanol

Alcohol have been popular alternative fuels for many years. In fact, Henry Ford's first car was fuelled with alcohol. Both ethanol and methanol are now used as transportation fuels and will likely to play an increasingly important role in the future.

Methanol can be made from various biomass resources like wood, as well as from coal. However, today nearly all methanol is made from natural gas, because it is cheaper. Methanol is also very poisonous and very harmful if swallowed. Methanol must not be confused with ethanol. As with gasoline, it is also wise to avoid skin contact with methanol, as it can pass through the skin.

Sunshine or Solar Energy : A Bonanza of Renewable Energy

Solar energy is an important, clean cheap and abundantly available renewable energy. The sun reduates heat and light and provide energy to society. It is a source of enormous energy. Its approximate age 4 or 109 years and is expected to radial energy for another 4 × 10 years. Energy from the sun inn the shape of radiations is called solar energy. So you will be astonished to learn that with just 0.1% of the 75,000 trillion kWH of energy from sun reaching the earth is enough to fulfil the need of planet earth.

The solar cookers were put to good use in after the Gujarat earthquake. Credit goes to one of the professors of the Indian Institute of Management, Ahmedabad for this achievement.

The solar cooker is a lifetime asset. If handled with care it can last 15 years or more. There is no moving part in it to go wrong. The only maintenance required is an occasional coat of black paint on the inside of the cooker and on the outer surfaces of the cooking pots.

The solar cooker can be used both in the rural and urban sector. In the rural sector it saves village woman from having to trudge for miles in search of scraps of firewood and spending her lifetime in smoke filled kitchens to the great detriment to their health and also saves the messy cleaning of smoke blackened pots and pans. In the urban sector, it saves energy on kerosene and LPG and makes cooking easy. The cost of petro-based fuels is going up all the time by the gradual withdrawal of the subsidies. The price of a cylinder of LPG has already reached Rs 260 after the recent budged, and even this forbidding price has a subsidy element of 20%. This subsidy might also go away inn the coming months and years.

But the cost of solar cooker which is around Rs. 1500 is all the cost you have to bear and there is no recurring fuel cost. Even so the poorer sections may have to be helped with a subsidy or a facility of payment in installments.

Solar cookers are not being subsidized by the Indian government they were until 1994 though some states like Gujarat have continued the subsidy after 1994. But commercial fuels like kerosene and LPG, which are imported at great cost and add to the pollution, are subsidized. Even other renewable energy systems are subsidized, e.g. improved chulhas, biogas systems, PV systems, etc.

There is another class of cookers called concentrating cookers or direct-focussing cookers, which are concave mirrors which reflect solar energy to a focal point where a cooking pot can be placed. They are available inn several models. These are the SK 14 cookers and the Scheffler cookers. These cannot cook more than one item at a time but they can take a pressure cooker. They are large, unwidely and have to be fixed at a place and tare prone to scratches on the reflecting surface.

India may be justifiably proud that the world's largest solar steam cooking system is operation in the Brahmakumari's ashram at Mt. Abu in India. Here the solar energy is concentrated by a battery of concentrators to convert water into superheated steam. The system can cook for 10,000 people. This is truly a fascinating achievement of human endeavour.

Another type of solar cooker is also now being made in India, the Sunstove, designed by Richard Warehan U.S.A. It has been popularized in South Africa. It is an insulated box whose sloping sides themselves are reflecting - thus doing away with the outside reflector - and has a plexiglass window. It has two large sized pots. It is being make in Kolkata, with assistance form Rotary International. Disabled children of a Ramakrishna mission organization assemble the cookers. It has good prospects since it dispenses with glass components, is very light to carry and also cheap - costing around Rs. 1000.

Many individuals and organizations are working in several developing countries promoting cardboard panel cookers such as the Cooking which is simply a sheet of cardboard coated with aluminium foil cut and folded in a particular way so that it will reflect sun rays on a pot kept at its centre in a plastic bag which functions as a greenhouse. The are a good beginning because the are cheap and the people are too poor to afford anything better. But by their very nature they are not durable; do feel that one being made in India are required. The Cook-Kits also make interesting projects for boys and girls in schools. The Renewable Energy Policy, which is under the consideration of the government makes no mention of solar cooking or solar drying.

Solar Space Heating of Buildings

Architectural design of building occupies important position for providing solar space heating. The building in which heat is to be provided through solar energy should have large-facing windows. More radical possibilities include provision of an entire wall of double-glazed windows.

An alternative technology of solar space heating exits where heat is to be exchanged through water tank. It is necessarily an extension of the technology employed in solar water heating except that energy has to be recovered from the tank through a heat exchange surface. In this system, air is used as the heat transfer medium. There is no need of an additional heat exchanger as was done in the case with water. However, between the two i.e. water and air, water systems offer better heat-exchanger performance. Solar water system has to disadvantages such as leakage and doubt of water freezing. For inclement heating system using electricity or any other heating system is needed to back-up.

Solar Water Heating

This system of water heating is usually used in hospitals, hotels, guest-houses and hostels. A solar collector are of 3-4 m2 having insulated tank of 200-400 litre volume can provide 200-400 litres of hot water nearly at 600 C per average sunny day. The climate should be favourable. If more hot water is required than solar collector are with proportionate increase in the size of insulated tank. Following systems are to be designed for solar water heating unit.

(1) The collector pipes and tubes are connected to a hot water storage tank. The collector absorbs solar radiations and transfer the heat of suns to the circulation water. This is done either by gravity or by a pump. Storage tank is usually located above the top of the collection so that natural convection is obtained. Water circulates from the collected to the storage tank and no pump is required.

(2) Metal tubes are used for water to remove the heat usually provided with a glass cover. Layer of insulation

is applied beneath the plate.

(3) The collector is typical having a blackened metal plate absorber containing metal tubes or pipes.

(4) A flat plate collector and an insulated storage tank.

Solar Refrigeration

Solar refrigeration and air-conditioning are nearly same thing. Solar refrigerator is used for preservation of food, biological and medical materials. A number of experiments have been conducted by USA. France and Sri Lanka on Solar-operated coolers using absorption cooling cycles Solar refrigeration is usually used at household level for food refrigerators or small scale ice manufacturing units. Though machines and units are quite simple in design yet too complicated to operate. On account of this limitation its use has been dropped by many people.

Solar Air-Conditioning

Solar air-conditioning cover three different types of SAC as mentioned below:

(a) Solar regenerated Desiccant cooling system.

(b) Absorption refrigerator systems.

(c) Solar powered refrigeration systems of Rankine cycle systems.

Out of these, 2nd one i.e. Absorption Refrigerator system seems to have best prospects. In a desiccant cooling cycle, ambient air is adiabatically cooled, dehumidified, cooled evaporatively and sensibly as well, and then detected to the living area. Air is evaporatively cool and heated at the regenerative stage because it cools the supply air stream, heated again by solar collectors, and humidified. Dessicant cooling system is best suited for regions with about heating and cooling loads and high humidity.

Solar Heating and Cooling

Drying the body or warming in the sun during winters were perhaps two earliest uses of energy from the sun. But with the advancement of science and technology a number of varied uses of energy have been introduced by man. Now solar energy provide : Heat, Electricity, Mechanical energy, and Chemical fuels.

Solar Desalination

The idea of capturing sun energy or solar energy was developed and given practical shape in 1892 in Chile where solar desalination plant operated nearly 30 years. Solar energy is used for desalinating well water has been shown in many countries like USA. USSR, Greece in moderate sized pilot plants. Though the idea is old yet adapted to modern materials now in a modified manner. The process is given below :

(a() Take a transparent air tight cover of slopping sheets of glass.

(ii) Place sheets of glass into a shallow blackened basin or pool containing brine. Brine is saline water. Place it is the sun.

(iii) Solar radiation passes through the cover is absorbed and converted into heat.

(iv) This process cause water to evaporate from the brine.

(v) The vapours so produced get condensed to form purified water on the underside of cooler glass cover.

(vi) It flows down the sloping roof. Thereafter it is collected in the troughs and from there into a water storage tank.

(vii) The excess brine not evaporated in run to waste.

Per litre cost of this water is cheaper compared to distilled water obtained by other electrical energy-based processes.

Solar Drying

It is the most ancient and traditional method used for utilizing direct solar energy. Agricultural items such as copra, grain, hay, fruits and vegetables as well as animal products. Like spray of milk and fish are dried up all over the world where direct solar energy is available. The technique used involve spreading of the material to be dried up in thin layer on the ground in such a manner that it is exposed to sun and wind.

Recently some innovation have been developed particularly to fruit drying. To dry agriculture products in the solar energy, a box is arranged insulated at the base, painted black on the inner side and covered with the glass. Ventilation holes are provided both at the vase and top of the sides of the box to facilitate the flow of air over the drying material. The material which is to be dried is placed on well designed perforated trays or racks inside the cabinet carefully. The adoption of this technique has resulted product quality.

Studies reveal that a large portion of the world's supply of dry fruit, crops and vegetables continues to be prepared by sun drying. It is the cheapest and simplest method where we have abudant sunshine and post harvest is featured by low relative humidity and minor rainfall.

Solar Furnaces

It provides extremely high temperature form the sun under very clean conditions. The temperature generated and provide from sun is nearly up 350000 C. The heat so generated by solar furnaces is used for melting refractory materials. To obtain high temperature in a solar furnace following arrangements are designed :

(i) Turnable mirrors should be arranged on a slopping surface.

(ii) Concentrate the solar radiations on a number of turnable mirrors called the liostats.

Solar furnaces are used to study the properties of ceramics at extremely high temperature and the manufacture of fused aluminium crucibles. Solar furnace accomplish heating process without any contamination, and the temperature can be controlled by changing the position of the material in focus. It is a specialized device with least impact on the fuel market as a whole. Scientists and environmentalists opine that solar furnace shall be used in the production of nitric acid and fertilizers from the air.

Solar Greenhouse

The greenhouse is a solar collector which utilize solar energy for the growth of plants. It is closed structure covered with transparent materials made of glass or plastic. The short-wave incoming solar radiations can pass through the greenhouse glazing but the long-wave thermal radiations emitted by the objects cannot escape through the glazed surface. On account of this reason, the solar radiations get trapped within the greenhouse. This process bring increase in temperature. The air inside the greenhouse gets enriched with carbon dioxide. Due to transpiration, the moisture loss is reduced. All these happenings assist the plant growth to sustain during night and colder months of the year.

Geothermal Energy

Geo means earth and thermal means heat. Thus geothermal energy is the heat energy from hot rocks present inside the earth. This heat can be used as a source of energy to produce electricity. It is one of the few sources of energy that do not come directly or indirectly from sun's energy heat. It is heat of earth and may be defined as naturally occuring thermal energy fount within rocks formations and the fluids held within those formations. According to geologists the earth's core is a molten mass of material having vast amounts of energy. In the molten core of the earth, temperature are as high as 440000 C. The heat from the molten core of the earth offers an unending source of energy. Though the quantity of energy or heat stored in the earth is in abundance yet energy cab be exploited only in few particular areas called hot spots. Volcanic eruptions, gears and bubbling mud holes are symptoms of such hot spots. We have in India these spots at Vashisht bath and Manikaran. Both these spots are located at Manali and the other around 150 km away from Bhunter Tattapani near Shimla also provide hot spot.

Sources of geothermal energy

So far, following sources are known to us:

(i) Hot dry rocks found near areas of volcanic activity and energy is provided from water free, impermeable rock at high temperature and at practical drilling depth.

(ii) Geopressured brines hot water traced at pressures above the normal hydrostatic gradient. Geopressured brine contain dissolved methane.

(iii) Hydrothermal fluids naturally occuring hot sprints or vents.

(iv) Molten mass magma with temperature 12000C of material with very high temperature.

(v) Natural stream, hot waters or dry rocks.

WAVE ENERGY

Ocean wave energy has gained attention during recent years. Periodic to-and-fro, up and down motion of water particles in the form of progressive waves provide ocean wave energy. The period of ocean waves is of the order of a few seconds. It is an important renewable source of energy possessing both potential and kinetic energy. The ocean waves originate in different parts of the ocean surface due to the surface winds. The height of the waves depend upon the velocity of wind, depth of the ocean and contour of the shareline etc. Waves have typical ranges. Average wave height is worked out be 0.2 m to 4 m i.e. Wave period denoted by varies between 4s to occur. The may reach heights of 10 meters and may topple ships and damage the ocean energy plants.

Ocean wave energy can easily be seen and felt on any seashore. The energy that waves expect as millions of tons of water are picked up and hurled against the land, over and over, day after day, can far exceed the energy budget for both insulation and wind power in localized areas. Before providing details of wave energy, let us have a clear understanding of the term wave. Wave is long body of water curling into arched form and breaking on shore. Wind blowing over water generate waves. Ocean waves are derived from of solar energy. Wind act as an agent in transferring energy of the sun on the surface of sea. Ocean waves can travel vast oceanic distances with negligible loss of energy. Wave energy generated anywhere within an ocean basin finally reach to same island.

Environmental scientists estimated that only 0.01% of the solar energy flux is finally expressed as wave power. While sunlight falls on the earth at a global rate of 1016 to 1017 W, wave energy is dissipated against the world's coastlines at a global rate of 1012 to 1013

W. Coalines total 3,36,000 km in length. Andhra Pradesh is having longest coastline in India's.

Motion of waves have both vertical and horizontal movement of water. Particles of water undergo nearly in a circular motion individually. Individual particles move up as the crest approaches, become forward at the crest, down as it recedes and backward in the trough. Waves generate energy in their continual motion as detailed in the preceding line of the text. The energy so generated is harnessed either by a water operated or air operated turbine.

Air operated turbine is preferred to generate electricity. The torque of an incident wave causes relative motion between an absorbed and reaction point in all the wave energy conversion processes. The relative motion between Absorber and Reaction point drives working fluid through a generator prime mover. The characteristic which distinguish one process from another are (i) mode of energy absorption (ii) type of absorption and (iii) type of reaction point. There are 5 types of wave motions that could be used alone or in combination to provide energy.

TIDAL AND WAVE ENERGY

Extraction and transformation of force from the movement of water is called tidal power. The tidal movement of water represents a great deal of energy. This is called kinetic energy. All the flowing water carry this energy with them. The situation is like this that a flowing water encounters a turbine, a part of the momentum of the flowing water is transferred on to the turbine. This process make the turbine to rotate. The rotation of the turbine is used to generate electricity. This is how energy is produced from tides. It is an inexhaustible and renewable source of energy, available to society. Ocean tides contain enormous amounts of energy that is being harnessed to do useful work, since time immemorial. For years, engineers have suggested that moving water could produce electricity and the principle is the same as that employed in a hydroelectric plant. It makes no difference whether the water is in the open ocean, in a estuary or in a river. The estimated tidal power potential in India is about 15000 MW. The promising sites for tidal power, plants are located in Gujarat State and West Bengal State. Non-conventional and Renewable Energy Department is engaged in surveying other sites in Orissa, Tamil Nadu, Kerala, Karnataka, Maharashtra and Andaman Nicobar etc. These sites have good prospects but require extremely high investments compared to conventional power plants of same rating.

Based on experience, scientists state that the tides occurring in the oceans are one source of energy. Occurrence of tides in the ocean results due to centrifugal action and appearing or tending to fly-off gravitational forces. These actions and forces are caused by the rotation of earth as well as changes in the relative position of the earth, moon and sun. The process in called law of tides. As the size of moon size of the moon is relatively small compared to sun yet it is small in mid-ocean, but becomes amplified near coasts. The amplification is governed by the shape of coastline. The tidal range is of a bay or esturary leads to resonance effects.

The rise of ocean water to the attraction of moon is called high tide whereas the fall of ocean water is called low tide. The tidal waves in the oceans build and recede twice a day. The enormous movement of water between the high tides and low tides provides a very large source of energy in the coastal area of the world.

SOURCES OF GEOTHERMAL ENERGY

So far, following sources are known to us :

(i) Hot dry rocks.

(ii) Geopressured brines hot water traced at pressures above the normal hydrostatic gradient. Geopressured brines contain dissolved methane.

(iii) Hydrothermal fluids naturally occuring hot springs or vents.

Having Motion

It is vertical motion developed by Godforsaken. It has a buoy pulls in sea water to pump through the hose next time. The wave energy conversion process is depicted below :

(i) Surging - It represents horizontal motion in the direction of water travel. As waves get over a concrete barrier the fill a reservour. The water in the reservoir flows out through a turbine. One such device producing 350 kW was installed in Norway.

(ii) Pitching Motion - It was designed by Sir Christopher Cockerel. Pitch is an angular motion about an axis parallel to wave crest. It is a device known as Salter's duck which consists of a series of wing like objects connected together and appears to absorb most of the energy in waves. The system was determined too expensive.

Ocean Thermal Energy

The water at the surface of an ocean gets heated by the heat of the sun and attains a higher temperature than the colder water at deeper levels in the ocean. So, there is always a temperature differences between the water at the surface of ocean and a deeper levels. At many places in the ocean, this difference in temperatures of water is upto 200 C. The energy available due to the difference in the temperature of water at the surface of the ocean and at deeper levels is called ocean thermal energy. The ocean thermal energy can be converted into usable form of energy like electricity.

7

MINERAL RESOURCES

Resources obtained by mining are known as mineral resources. Mineralogy is science of minerals. Economic mineralogy is the study of minerals that are heavily used in manufacturing and are, therefore, an important part of domestic and international commerce. In nature, mineral are normally found in solid, liquid and gaseous states. India is rich in mineral resources. It has fairly abundant resources of iron ore and mica, and adequate supplies of magnesium ore, titanium, bauxite and coal. In all, there are over 3000 mines in India. About 8,00,000 people are employed in the mining sector. It accounts for about 11% of the country's industrial output. Public policy in the United States has encouraged mining on public lands as a way of boosting the economy and utilizing mineral resources. So is being done in India. World industry depends on about eighty minerals, some of which exist in plentiful supplies.

Three-fourth of the eighty minerals are abundant enough to meet all out anticipated needs or have readily available substitutes. At least eighteen minerals, including tin, platinum, gold, silver and lead are short in supply.

Of these 80 minerals, between one-half and one-third are considered strategic resources. Strategic minerals are those that a country uses but cannot produce itself. Government consider these minerals capable for military strength if unstable global economics or politics were cut off supplies. For this reason wealthy industrial nations stock-pile strategic minerals in times when prices are low and the supply in available.

Types of minerals : Geologists classify minerals according to their chemical composition and crystalline structure. Generally the are classified into tow categories. Metallic and Non- Metallic. Metallic minerals are further classified into two parts - ferrous and non-ferrous. Ferrous contain iron. There are iron ore, managenese ore, chromite, pyrite, tungsten, nickel and cobalt. Non-ferrous metals are gold, silver, copper, lead, bauxite, tin and magnesium. Not- metallic minerals are limestone, nitrate, potash, alolomite, mica, gypsum, coal and petroleum.

Rocks and their types

The crust of earth has many types of rocks. The material that forms the curst of the earth is called rock. Natural minerals are the ingredients of the said material. These minerals have natural occurrence with definite chemical composition. So rocks are the aggregate material of various types including harder materials like granite and soft materials like clay and sand. Rocks are divided into three major groups, explained below one by one.

Environmental Hazards from Mineral Extraction

Both mining and extraction of minerals have environmental effects. The main environmental hazards encountered are stated below :

(i) Water leaking into mine shafts also dissolves metals and other toxic material. When this water is pumped out or allowed to seep into groundwater aquifers, pollution occurs.

(ii) Deeper ore beds are extracted by strip or open pit mining where overlying material is removed by large earth-moving equipment. The resulting pits can be many kilometers across and hundreds of meter deep. Even deeper deposits are reached by underground tunneling, an extremely dangerous process for mine workers. In one of the coal mines in Chasnella 350 workers died a decade ago, when water entered while mining.

(iii) Mining destroys stream beds and fills the water with suspended solids the smoother aquatic life.

(iv) Uncontrollable fires, producing noxious smoke and gases, sometimes ignite coal-bearing scrap heaps stored inside or outside the mine. Surface deposits called tailings can cause acidic or otherwise toxic run-off when rainwater percolates through piles of stored material. Tailings from uranium mines give rise to wind scattering or radio-active waste.

(v) In coal mines natural gas poses dangers of explosion.

(vi) Old tunnels occasionally collapse or subside.

(vii) One of the most notorious effects of earthquakes is the tsunami. The seismic sea swells can move at 1000 km/hr, or faster away from the centre of an earthquake.

(viii) Earthquakes and volcanic events are natural geological hazards that are result of movements of the earth, restless core and mantle.

(ix) Smelting and chemical extraction processes also create pollution problems.

(x) Surface mining results in removal of natural eco-systems, soil disruption, creation of trenches and open pits.

(xi) Fumes form smelters kill forest and spread pollution over large areas.

(xii) Mine drainage pollute thousands of kilometers

of streams and rivers.

Sedimentary Rocks

Sedimentary rocks are also called stratified rocks. These rocks are formed by the sediments or deposits laid down on the floor of the river beds, lakes or seas. Sedimentary rocks contain different types of dediments like sand, gravel, limestone, slate and chalk. History of geography reveals that chalk has interesting origin. The chalk is made up of skeletons of the tiny creatures that lived in ancient seas. When the creatures died, their skeleton fell to the bottom and over million of years layer of skeletons piled up which ultimately got squeezed into hard mass. So sedimentary rocks have enough contents of chalks. A distinguishing feature of sedimentary rocks is that they contain fossils. The fossils are greatly helpful inn estimating the age of the sedimentary rocks. Coal and limestone are the best examples of sedimentary rocks.

Igneous Rocks

These rocks are called the primary rocks because these were found first on the surface of the earth. These rocks are formed by cooling and solidification of the molten magma. Magma gets erupted by volcanoes. Basalt and granite are examples of igneous rocks.

Limestone

1. Country's production comes from Madhya Pradesh, Chhattisgarh, Andhra Pradesh, Rajasthan, Gujarat, Karnataka and Himachal.

2. Found in geological formations because of having sedimentary origin.

3. 75% used in cement industry and rest for smelting of iron.

4. Found associated with rocks composed ot calcium

carbonates.

Mica

1. Exported to U.K., U.S.A., Russia, and exported through Kolkata and Vishakhapatnam.

2. India produces 60% of the world's production of mica.

3. Occurs in Jharkhand, Bihar, Andhra Pradesh, and Rajasthan.

4. Used in electrical and electronic industries having quality to withstand high voltage.

5. It has insulating properties.

Bauxite

1. Occurs mainly in Jharkhand, Orissa, Gujarat, Maharashtra, Chhattisgarh, Madhya Pradesh and Tamil Nadu.

2. Widely distributed in India with vast reserves.

3. Used for manufacturing of aeroplanes and utensils.

4. Aluminium is obtained form bauxite.

Lead

1. Available at Andhra Pradesh, Rajasthan and Tamil Nadu.

2. Produced 25% of the requirement.

3. Imported from Australia, Canada and Myammar.

4. Used as constituted in alloy. Lead oxide is used in cable covers paints, glass, and rubber.

5. The ore of lead is called galena. It is soft and heavy metal./

Manganese Ore

1. Available in Karnataka, Orissa, Madhya Pradesh, Maharashtra where we have 97% mines of manganese.

2. Stands 2nd in the reserve of manganese ore in the world after Zimbabwe.

3. 1/5th exported. Only low grade manganese is exported to Japan. Which buys 2/3 of India's export.

4. 4/5 the of the production is consumed in the

country/

5. Also used to manufacture bleaching powder, insecticides, paints and batteries.

6. Used for making iron and steel, alloys etc.

Iron Ore

1. Available in Jharkhand, Chhattisgarh, Andhra Pradesh, Goa, Orissa, Karnataka, Tamil Nadu, Maharashtra and Rajasthan.

2. Iron ore is available inn 4 varieties : magnetite, Limonite, hematite and siderite.

3. Exported mainly to Japan through ports of Vishakhapatnam, Paradip, Marmagoa and Mangalore.

4. India's share is 20% of the world.

5. Used for manufacturing of machines and implements.

6. Backbone of modern civilization a metal of universal use.

8

SOIL RESOURCES

Soil is a thin covering over the land. It is marvelous substance a living resources of astonishing beauty. Soil is an organised and complex mixture of weathered mineral materials from rocks, living organisms, air, water and partially decomposed organic molecules. Soil is an essential component of the biosphere and must be natured and cultivated to bring to its highest potential. There are a least 20,000 different types of soils in the United States alone and many be hundreds of thousands throughout the world. Survival and growth of rural and urban population is governed by soil and its nature. In rural areas farmers are particularly concerned with soil because the nature of soil determines what kind of crops can be grown and what cultivation technique should be employed.

Urban dwellers are also concerned with the nature of soil because the health of soil determines quantity and quality of food they will eat. To understand the potential for feeding the world on a sustainable basis, we need to know the formation, composition as well as how soil is being lost and what can be done to protect and rebuild good agriculture soil.

Soil Profiles

A cross-sectional view of the horizons in a soil is called soil profiles. Classification of soil as per its thickness, colour, texture and composition determines soil profiles. The soil profile is a series of horizontal layers of different chemical composition, particle size, and amount of organic matter. Each recognizable layer is known as horizon. The different layers of soil differ physically, chemically and biologically. These layers are classified into different horizons. These horizons are three in order as per their profiles.

A - horizon : This is the top layer of soil. It contains most of the organic matter. The thickness of this layer of A-horizon may vary from less than a centimeter on steep mountain, slopes to over a meter in the rich grasslands. It is dark-coloured horizon with much organic matter mixed with mineral matter. The lower portion of the A-horizon often contain, few nutrients because water flowing through the soil from the top to deeper layers dissolves and transports nutrients to the B-horizon. This process is known as leaching.

B-horizon : This horizon is called sub-soil. It contains less organic material and few organisms. It has accumulated nutrients that were leached from higher levels i.e. A horizon. B- horizon is very valuable source of nutrients for plants. It also support root system of plants.

C- horizon : The area below sub-soil or B- horizon is known as the C-horizon. It contains weathered parent material. This parent material contains no organic materials but it does contribute to some of the soil's properties. The chemical composition of this soil helps to determine the pH of the soil. C- horizon soil also influence the soil's rate of water absorption and retention.

Factors contributing to soil development are extremely varied. Nearly fifteen thousand separate soil types have been classified in North America. In other countries of the world, there could be more types of soil. However many of the soils can be classifies into two broad categories isle. grassland soil and forest soil.

Grassland Soils : Soils formed in grasslands are known as chernozem soils and have deep A-horizon. The low amount of rainfall in grassland areas limits the amount of leaching from the A- horizon or topsoil. This lack of leaching also results in a thin layer of sub-soil.

Forest Soils : These soils develop in areas of more abudant rainfall. The rainfall results in a layer of topsoil that is usually not as thick as grassland soil. But the material leached from the topsoil forms a sub-soil which support substantial root growth.

Soil Properties

The properties of soil are explained below :

(i) Soil structure : Soil structure refers to the way various soil particles clump together. Sandy soils lack structure, whereas clay soil tend to stick together in large culpam. A good soil forms small clumps. Due to small clumps this soil crumble easily. The ability to crumble is called soil's friability. This characteristic of soil is determined by the soil structure and its moisture contents. Sandy soils are very friable. Clay soils do not have friability. A good soil will crumble because of has spaces to allow air and water to mix with the soil. The contents of air and water depend upon these spaces. In good soil, about 2/3 of the spaces contain air after the excess water has drained. The air in these spaces provides a source of oxygen necessary for plant cells. Water for the roots occupies the remaining soil space. The relationship between the amount of air and water is not fixed.

There are some typical inhabitants of soil stated below:

1. Bacteria : Bacteria and fungi are important in the

decay and recycling of materials. Their chemical activities change complex organic materials into nutrients that can be used by plants. These micro organism can convert the nitrogen content in the protein contained component of organic matter into ammonia or nitrate, nitrogen compound that can be utilized by plants.

Soil organisms usually stay close to the surface, the thin living layer can contain thousands of specials and billions of individual organisms per hectare. Algae live on the surface while bacteria and fungi flourish at the top, few centimeters of soil. A single gram of soil can contain hundreds of millions of these microscopic cells. Round worms, segmented worms, mites and tiny insects appear in thousands in that same gram soil.

2. Soil Texture : Soil contain rock particles. The size of rock particles within the soil determine soil texture. The largest size of rock particle in the soil is called gravel. Gravel consists of fragments larger that 2-0 millimeters in diameter. Particles between the size of 0-05 and 2-0 millimeters are classified and sand. 0.002 to 0.05 millimeters in diameter refer to silt particles. Smallest particles within soil are clay particles which are less than 0/002 millimeters in diameter.

There are many tiny spaces between large particles such as gravel and sand. The spaces between the two that is sand and gravel allow both air and water to flow through the soil. Water drains from this king of soil vary swiftly and often carry valuable nutrients to lower soil layers, where they are beyond the reach of plant roots. Clay particles being flat are conveniently packed together and form waterproof layers. Since water does not flow through clay very well, clay soils tend to moist and do not easily low minerals to flowing water. Soil consist of many sizes of particles. But an ideal soil is a loam.

Soil Composition and Formation

We know soil nutrients are depleted due to many farming techniques and exposure of soil to the erosive forces of wind and moving water. The lost nutrients of soil can be reestablished and renewed with careful husbandry. This soil becomes young by proper care and provide greater and greater productivity.

Building good soil is slow process. Good topsoil accumulates 10 tons per hectare per year under good circumstances and favourable environmental conditions. Under poor conditions, it takes thousands of years to build good soil. Topsoil is loosing its fertility much more faster than it is being replaced. Soil experts state that one third to one-half of the world's croplands are loosing topsoil faster than it is being renewed. In some parts of the world, erosion carries away about 2.5 cm of topsoil per year.

The formation of soil is a combination of physical and biological events. Soil building begins with the physical and biological events. Soil building begins with the physical fragmentation of the parent material. Parent material consists of ancient layers of rock as well as recent deposits from lava flow. It is the parent material and the climate that determine the kind of soil that shall be formed. Weathering bring about fragmentation of rocks. Large rocks get fractured the moment they are heated because rock does not expand evenly. Pieces of the rock flake off and are often reduced into tiny sizes by other processes. These processes are repeated freezing and thawing of water. Water that has seeped into cracks of rocks expands as it freezes. This process cause cracks in the rock to widen the crack in the rock fills with water.

As the water freezes and becomes ice, the pressure of the ice enlarges the cracks. The ice melts, and water again fills the rock. The water freezes again and widens the crack. Alternating freezing and thawing splits the rocks into smaller fragments.

Physical breakdown of rock also appear due to forces that cause rock particles to move and rub against each other. In many parts of the world, the parent material from which soil is formed consists of glacial deposits. Wind and moving water also cause small particles of fragmented rocks to collide. This process also assists in soil formation. The smoothness of rocks as well as pebbles seen on the shore line and river beds is evidence of this rubbing process.

Soil building process is also done through chemical weathering Small rock fragments when exposed to the atmosphere may be oxidized; that is, they combine with oxygen from the air and chemically change to different compounds. Other kind of rocks may combine with water molecules in a process known as hydrolysis. Hydrolyzed molecules are more readily soluble in water and can be easily removed by rain or moving water. Rain has slightly acid content which assist in dissolving rocks.

There are certain organisms which trap the modified parent material that contribute to the process of fragmentation. Lichens form an important community that trap small particles of fragmented rocks. These organisms chemically alters the underlying fragmented rocks. Other kinds of organisms such as plants and tiny animals become established and contribute increasing amounts of organic matter which are included with the fragments of rocks to form soil. Decaying organic matter called humus becomes mixed up with top layers of rock particles some nutrients needed by plants and also increase the acidity of Soil. Wheat and corn. Soils with the best texture for most crops are looms. If soil were 40% sand, 40% clay, it would be loam.

Burrowing animals like earthworm as well as roots of plants are equally important organisms that assist in the process of soil formation. One hectare of soil may support a population of five hundred thousand earthworms that can process as much as 9 metric tons of soil a year. Burrowing animals bring nutrients from the deeper layer of the soil up into the area where plant roots are more concentrated thereby improving the soil's fertility. Fungi and bacteria are important decomposers in improving the quality of soil. In certain countries of the world geologic forces like glacier, wind and water contribute enough to the parent material upon which soil composition depend. About 97% of all the parent material in the United States was transported to its present site by geologic forces.

Reasons and Mechanisms of Soil Erosion

A few mechanisms are involved in the process of soil erosion. These processes of soil erosion are recognized and called as sheet erosion, rill erosion, gully erosion and stream bank erosion. There could be other types of erosion too, but fact remains that wind and water are the main agents that move soil around. However, the type of erosion as mentioned in the preceding lines are explained below in a nutshell manner.

(i) Streambank Erosion : This erosion is caused by washing away the soil from the banks of established streams or rivers. Soil is washed as a result of removing trees and brush along stream-banks. Most soil erosion on agricultural land is sheet and rill erosion. Large amounts of soil is being transported by this mechanism without being noticed. A farm field can lose 20 metric tons of soil per hectare.

(ii) Gully Erosion : When rills enlarge to form bigger channels or ravines difficult to be removed by normal tillage operations, then this process is called gully erosion. Gully erosion is an advanced stage of rill erosion. Any concentration of surface runoff is a potential source of fulling. Unattended rills get deepened and widened every year and begin to attain the form of gullies. During every rain, the rain water rushes down these gullies, increasing their depth, width and length. Within a few year's the entire landscape may be filled with a network of gullies. Large areas of fertile lands thus get swallowed by the ever-increasing gullies and are rendered uncultivable.

(iii) Rill Erosion : The process is called rill erosion when little rivulets of running water gather and cut small channels running down in the soil. Rills develop when there is a concentration of fun off water which, if neglected, grow into large gullies.

(iv) Sheet Erosion : This erosion occurs when thin uniform layers are peeled of the land surface by water and wind. It is caused by rainfall and water run off. This type of erosion is extremely harmful to the land and usually show that the farmer is not conscious of its existence. It is common on land having gentle slope.

Causes and Reasons

Water and wind are important mover of soil. How water causes soil erosion has already been explained. In this section it is proposed to discuss how dust and wind, particularly dust bowls is responsible for replenishing soil. Wind erosion may not be as evident as water erosion, since it does not have gullies on the surface of the soil but erosion caused by water is quite evident. So the main causes of soil erosion as experienced from time to time by environmentalists and soil scientists in different countries of the world are discussed below :

(i) Agricultural Machinery : Farmland is being manages because agricultural machinery is becoming heavier, more powerful and more widely used, says a survey. The soil is the loser. It is increasingly compressed by tractors, combing harvesters and other machinery. The quality of farmland can decline markedly as a result. Inadequate nutrient supply used to be mainly to blame for low yields ; it is now often joined by damage caused by the soil being compacted. The survey, carried out for the Bavarian Environment Ministry by Rainer Horn, who is a Bayreuth University soil physicist, describes what happens when the soil is churned up by tractor types. Soil, he says, has a natural support, a structure consisting of expanded clay aggregate, clay, sand and humus. This substratum expands and contracts in the soil, forming a grid that supports the topsoil and ensuring sound soil structure. Healthy soil can withstand the pressure of tractor tyres and has sufficient bent to spring back into shape. Any compacting that occurs can at least be offset in part.

These stabilizing aggregates cannot withstand unlimited pressure. There is a limit to the stress a given variety of soil can withstand. If it is exceeded the aggregate is compacted, water is pressed out of the topsoil and soil is rutted for good. Deep ruts and churned-up soil are unmistakable danger sings. When this point is reached will depend mainly on the variety of soil and on its humidity. Heavy, clay soils are much more sensitive than sandy soil. The wetter soil is, the more readily it can be compacted. The reason for this could hardly be simpler. Soft and soggy aggregate is less firm than the hard, dry variety. The consequences for crop plants are serous. Soil ventilation deteriorates, leaving roots starved of oxygen and water less easily accessible. Cohesive forces in small-pore soil than they would in more loosely packed earth, which can lead to lower yields.

The growing threat of erosion is a further problem. Once the system of cracks and fissures in the soil has been destroyed, rainwater can no longer penetrate fast enough. It is drained off superficially and carries off topsoil with it. Compacting of soil is very difficult to reverse. Attempts to plough deeper and vermiculate it better have often failed, merely transferring the compaction to a lower stratum. Horn feels nature's self-recuperative capacity is the sole hope of recovery, nature in this case consist of a combination of the earthworm and ground frost.

Ice the freezes in the soil expands and can thus open up comacted earth. But even in fallow fields it can take years for the soil to be regenerative. So the aim must be, as far as possible, to prevent overexposure to stain in the first place. Horn has experimented with vehicles, drinking them over ground in which sensors that respond the pressure have been driven. He has found that soil is damaged less low-weight tractors crossing frequently than by juggernauts churning up the soil less often. A heavier vehicle weight, it was long felt, could be offset by a larger type surface area. But the Bayreuth readings disprove this assumption.

Type pressure spreads through the soil in what Horn describes as onion fashion. The narrow tyres of a light-weight tractor produce a correspondingly small onion. The jumbo tyres of a larger agricultural machine may generate the same pressure per square centimetre but the larger surface area makes the pressure onion expand. As a result the stain is sent deeper into the ground and the soil is impacted even further. So the only way to reduce the pressure is to fit larger tyres to smaller items of machinery.

(iii) Modern Agriculture : Organic decline in soil cause soil erosion due to the use of modern agriculture techniques. Two recent changes in farming techniques have helped to reduce the amount of organic matter in soil. First, farmers have ploughed up many old permanent pastures to plant crops. In other words, pastures growth is abandoned and in its place plant crop inn encouraged. Pasture crops maintain or even raise the amount of organic matter in soil, whereas arable cropping tends to reduce those levels. Secondly, inorganic fertilizers have largely replaced organic manure. Large applications of inorganic fertilizers can contribute organic matter to the soil by increasing the yields of crops.

However, where the land is continuously under arable crops, or where the residues of crops are removed or burnt rather than being ploughed back into the soil, the organic matter is lost more rapidly than it is replaced. Grass crops not only increase the amount of organic matter, but they also permanently cover the ground, affording greater protection to erosion by rain. Modern farming also famous large fields because they are quite suitable for modern machinery. But then large fields increase wind erosion, because hedges and shelterbelts slow the wind at ground level and decrease the distance of uninterrupted blow.

(iii) Dust Bowls : They are also called dust storms. These are worst human- caused environmental disaster ever experienced in United States, 10 billion tons topsoil was moved by these dust bowls in 1935. Thousands of people died of dust pneumonia while millions join the mass migration. A prolonged drought beginning in 1931 was the immediate cause of the dust storms had reached $ 25 per day. It seems incredible that something as basic as the very soil inn which we stand should be disappearing at such a rate that by the end of the century there will be 32 percent less person than at resent. And yet there it is. A fact that is a obvious as any to those who have seen the dust bowls of the American prairies. The spectre a now dust bowl and worldwide food shortages was evoked by US ecologists as dust clouds hundreds of miles wide swept by 60 mph winds from the drought-parched soil.

The demands made upon the Earth's agricultural are becoming greater, but the answer does not lie in the use of more and more chemical fertilizers. Neither does it lie in ploughing up more and more marginal land, or shortening cultivation cycles. And yet another stark fact on our list is that we have an increasing number of people to feed, and, just as important, a considerable and wealthy minority of them want to eat the type of foods that wasteful in the amount of energy needed to grow them. How do we reconcile this with the problem of erosion apparently caused by the practices that aim to alleviate hunger, and the rich world's greed?

Calculations suggest that by the turn of the century there will be third less topsoil throughout the world per person than at present. Almost half of American's farmland continues to lose soil faster than it is replaced : in the early 1980s, 1700 million tonnes of soil were lost each year. Where does all this eroded soil end up is note worthy point. Some of it is blown across land and out to sea. It shows up on satellite pictures or it is monitored by stations on islands that take air samples. Other quantities of eroded soil end up being washed out to sea or silting up dams and reservoirs considerable reducing their useful lives.

Soil erosion history

There is close relation between history of soil erosion and the history of agriculture. Expletive agriculture accompanied by the cutting of forests on the attachment of rivers began at the dawn of history. Soil erosion has been responsible for the fall of various ancient civilizations Mesopotamia, and land well developed in the time of the Babylonians, Assyrians and Persians in now virtually desert. In India, the Mohenjodaro and Harrappa civilization became extinct because of neglect of their lands. Rivers like the Saraswati have disappeared as their watersheds and river basins were exploited and mis-managed. A spectacular care of erosion in that of Punjab Shivaliks, a range of hills fringing the Himalayas. Along most rivers in India, soil erosion has led to the formation of a vest network of fissures and gullies interfering with the use of agriculture land. There is ravine land adjoining most of the Indian rivers, but Chambal is the worst offender in the respect, where several thousand hectares of land have been destroyed. Even in the great alluvial plains of India where the land is comparatively flat, the damage by gullying is considerable.

Soil Conservation Practices

Sustainable agricultural of regenerative farming depends upon careful husbandry of soil. The most productive layer of the soil is topsoil which is usually removed and lost by water or wind erosion. This has adverse effect upon agriculture output because agriculture is the area in which topsoil is most essential.

When the topsoil is lost, the soil's fertility decreases. To re-establish, this lost fertility fertilizers are used. This has the effect of raising the cost of the food we buy. Besides this, excessive movement of soil from farmland to streams have many undesirable effects as discussed below one by one.

(i) The soil carried by a river is eventually deposited somewhere and in many cases it should be removed to clear shipping channels.

(ii) A stream laden with sediment affects the fish populations. Fishing may be poor because of unwise farming practices hundreds of kilometres upstream.

(iii) Eroded and moved soil make streams dirty and muddy. So a dirty stream is less aesthetically pleasing than a clear stream.

In view of these reasons, proper soil conservation measures are required to be adopted to save the topsoil being eroded. These measures can be as detailed below:

(1) Windbreaks - In a relatively dry areas of the world soil erosion caused by wind is a serious problem. Wind erosion can be checked if the soil is protected from the wind. This can be done by planting generation over the surface of the soil. Soil is yet exposed to wind in spite of this practice. So the better way is to plant trees that protect bare soil from the full force of the wind. Windbreaks reduce the velocity of the wind, thereby decreasing the amount of soil that is carried away. In some cases, rows of trees are planted at right angles to the prevailing winds to reduce the force of the wind, while in other cases, kind of strip farming is practiced.

(2) Waterways - Though contour farming, strip farming and terracing are quite effective approaches directed towards soil conservation yet cannot provide wonderful results without the practice of waterways.

Waterways are depressions on sloping land where water collects and flows off the land. These areas are exposed to erosion when not properly maintained. If a waterway is maintained with permanent sod covering, the speed of the water is reduced, and soil erosion is decreased.

(3) Terracing - The terraces are very important for people who live in countries that have little flat land available. Terracing involves shaping the land to create level shelves of earth to hold water and soil. The edges of terraces are planted with soil-anchoring plant species. This agriculture practice though useful in controlling soil erosion yet quite expensive needing much energy and hand labour. Terrace farming use of land without serious erosion.

(4) Strip Farming - Strip farming consists of alternating strips of closely sown crops like hay, wheat or other small grains with strips of row crops like corn, soya beans and cotton. This method of preventing soil erosion is very effective where a slope is too steep or too long. Contour farming and strip farming together is used for raising crops when slope is too steep or too long.

(5) Contour Farming - This is the simplest method of preventing soil erosion. You know water runs downhill. The faster is runs, the more soil it carries off the fields. This is called run-off. Water run-off can be reduced by contour ploughing. This practice is useful on gentle slopes and produces a series of small ridges at right angles to the slope. This practice allow more water to be soaked into the soil. Contour farming reduces soil erosion by as much as 50 percent. Contour farming increases crop yields by conserving water. The soil conservation practice is useful on gentle slopes.

Soil Conservation Methods

Soil conservation problems vary with geographical

locations, soil types, land use watershed characteristics and climate. Major soil erosion problems and how these special problems can be solved with the application of remedial measures are discussed below.

Modern Farming

Modern farming favour soil conservation by checking soil erosion. This is a known fact that large fields enhance wind erosion, because hedges and shelterbelts slow the wind at ground level and decrease the distance of uninterrupted blow Hedges and ditches also play a similar role on sloping land that is prone to erosion by water. They break up the length of the slope, which slows the water running off and thus reduces its capacity to erode the soil.

Some sample measures can limit erosion without drastically altering current farming practices, farmers can grow grass of steep slopes, avoid cultivating up and down shallower slopes, and replace hedges and ditches on slopping grounds. These changes, however, will no stop the loss of organic matter in many soil is nor prevent damage from heavy machinery when the ground is wet.

Sea Erosion

Sea erosion is caused during rainy conservation by checking soil erosion. This is a known fact that large fields enhance wind erosion, because hedges and shelterbelts slow the wind at ground level and decrease the distance of uninterrupted blow Hedges and ditches also play a similar role on slopping land that is prone to erosion by water. They break up the length of the slope, which slows the water running off and thus reduces its capacity to erode the soil.

Some sample measures can limit erosion without drastically altering current farming practices, farmers can grow grass or steep slopes, avoid cultivating up and down shallower slopes, and replace hedges and ditches on slopping grounds. These changes, however, will not stop the loss of organic matter in many soils nor prevent damage from heavy machinery when the ground is wet.

Land slips and slides

This type erosion is usually seen in the hills of Himalayan region. Land slides caused to erosion block high ways and disturb the communication system. It destroys buildings constructed below as well as silt reservoirs, Land slips and slides are caused by the hydraulic pressure developed by the moisture penetrated in the soil to a saturation point during heavy rains.

The main causes of land-slides are under cutting of the base of the exiting slope, disintegration of soil through development of cracks and insufficient drainage in the sliding mass.

Remedial measure used are given below :

(i) Stabilization of small and big streams in the watershed in done by constructing a series of check dams.

(ii) Slipes are broken by contour planting to care the growth of vegetation.

(iii) Use logwood crib chen dams to cover the rills on landslide face.

Road side erosion

Some king of erosion take place along the roadsides and rail lines. This type of erosion is mostly found in the hills where the roads have been constructed by the cut and fill techniques and where the batters protected. On account of this reason, the situation gets aggravated when drainage in the area gets adversely affected.

The methods of checking roadside erosion are given below :

(i) In order to over power the adverse effects of meandering rivers on the railway lines guide bunds with pitched slops, are made.

(ii) Provide roadside drain for carrying the run off from the fill slopes.

(iii) To control the run-off from the cut-face catch water drains or gutters proper outlets should be constructed.

(iv) Turning, pitching and construction of retaining walls.

(v) Constructing interceptor drains about 3 to 5 meters away on the upstream side form the top of the cut face.

Stream bank erosion

Stream bank erosion takes place when the runoff flows over the side of the banks are devoid of vegetation due to overglazing. Velocity of the flow in the stream is considerable influences by the degree of erosion. Any obstruction to the stream flow forces the change in the stream course which cause stream bank erosion. When the stream or river gets loaded with sediments carried by the runoff the course of the stream gets shifted and in the process the stream banks get eroded. This is predominant in case of rivers and streams originating in Himalayas.

To prevent stream bank erosion, following measures are adopted :

(i) Afforestation and grassland improvement.

(ii) Soil conservation measures in the catchment areas.

(iii) Improving the capability of the channels to carry floods.

Torrents

They are popularly called as chaos in North and North-Eastern India. They carry large flows at high velocity and turbulence. The torrents cause destruction to life and property in valley reaches as a result of serious soil erosion hazard. In India, about 2.73 m. ha of land is affected by the menance of torrents.

This problem is showing upward trend. It is basically due to inherent geological and climatically features and further enhanced by human intervention, both on mountain slopes and foot hills. Torrents could be controlled to a large extent by adopting following remedial measures :

(i) Constructing spurs.

(ii) Constructing marginal bunds at a reasonable distance away from the edge of the banks.

(iii) Providing structures to control channel flow at permissible velocities.

(iv) Improving grasslands.

Four Classes of Land Suitable for cultivation

The US Soil conservation has established a system to classify land use possibility. The land is classified into eight classes and lists the characteristics and capabilities of each.

(i) Land class -I : It is suitable for cultivation. Its main characteristics are that it is excellent, flat and well-drained. It is capable for cropland. The conservation measures required for this class of land is nil.

(ii) Land class - II : This land is suitable for cultivation. It is good land with minor limitations such as slight slope, sandy soil with poor drainage. It is good for crop and pasture. This land is useful if strip cropping and contour farming is done because they are the two conservation measures.

(iii) Land class III - It is moderately good land with important limitations of soil slope or drainage, capable for cropland, pasture and watershed. It needs four conservation measures such as contour farming, strip cropping, terraces and water ways.

(iv) Land class IV - It is fair land with severe limitation of soil, slope, or drainage. This land is capable for pasture, orchards, urban, industry and limited cropland. Conservation measures are contour farming, strip cropping, terraces and waterways.

Four Classes of Land not suitable for cultivation

(i) Land class V - To be used for grain and forestry; limited by rockiness, shallow soil. Has capability for grazing, forestry, watershed, urban and industry. No special precautions of properly grazed or logged; must not be ploughed.

(ii) Land class VI - It has moderately steep slopes. This land is fit for grazing, forestry, watershed, urban and industry. Graining or logging may be done in a limited manner for conservation.

(iii) Land class VII - This class of land has severe limitations for grazing and forestry because of very steep slopes exposed to erosion. This land is capable for grazing, forestry, watershed, recreation wildlife, urban and industry. Careful management is required when used for grazing or logging from soil conservations point of view.

9

FOOD RESOURCES

Food means substance taken to the body to maintain life and growth. Food is necessary to supply energy to both living and non-living organisms. Food is essential to maintain vital functions and to rebuild tissues worn out in the day processes of living. Food intake is measured in calories. Food provide energy as already stated. The amount of energy each of us needs to remain strong and healthy depends on body weight, climate, state of health, stress level and basic metabolism. A small sedentary adult living in a warm climate a large, muscular person living in a vigorous outdoor life in a cold climate might need 6000 to 7000 calories per day to stay warm and active. FAO of UNO estimates that the average minimum daily caloric intake over the whole world is about 2500 calories per day.

Diet

Diet occupy important position and has a great effect on human health. There is a great correlation between cardiovascular disease and animal fat and salt in one's died. Highly processed foods, fat, smoke cured and high nitrate meats are prone to cancer. While grains, complex carbohydrates, fruits and vegetable often have beneficial health effects. Important dietary components are pectins; vitamins A, C and E ; substances extracted form vegetables such as cabbage, broccoli, cauliflower and brussels sprouts and selenium from plants have anticancer effects. Well-to-do people everywhere eat too much. This is often observed in developed countries. At least one-fourth of all Americans are considered overweight. Cutting back on the number of calories consumed reduces strain on bones including cardiovascular arrest, diabetes and may be cancer.

In some areas of the world, people have exceptionally long lives. They are Abkhasian of Soviet Geogia, Hunzans in the mountains of Pakistan and the Vilcabama villagers in Ecuador. Though some of these claim to be 120-140 years old yet, it is difficult to know the dates of their birth. Reasons of their high longevity are given below :

(i) Uncomplicated lifestyle as it reduces conflict and anxiety.

(ii) Enjoy clean air and pure water.

(iii) Diet is simple with low salt and fat: high fiber contents, little meat and lost of vegetables and fruits.

(iv) The whole family shares in decision making, recreation and religion.

(v) Do practical and physical work together for the common benefit of their community.

(vi) Low level of stress.

(vii) Uniform and predictable life in small villages.

(vii) Non-industrialized setting.

(viii) Active and vigorous life with low pressure.

(ix) Living at moderately high elevations with cool, sunny and dry climate.

Observe and experience the following national health recommendations and diet goals.

(i) Eat less radiative food.

(ii) Eat less red meat.

(iii) Eat more fish, poultry, beans and fruits.

(iv) Eat more whole grains, cereals, fruits and vegetables.

(v) Eat less sugar.

(vi) Eat less salt.

(vii) Eat less fat and cholesterol. Also Eat only calories enough to meet the need of body.

Highlights about food

1. Vitamins are organic molecules essential for life. Food sources of vitamins are fruits, milk and green vegetables.

2. Humans also require inorganic nutrients both for building cellular structures and for regulating many cellular reactions.

3. Lipids are an important source of energy. Most of us get adequate levels of lipids in out diet, but very poor people in some areas of the world exist on diet of starchy food.

4. Most people in the world derive the bulk of daily calorie intake upto 80% from carbohydrates, mainly starches.

5. In addition to calories, we need specific nutrients in our died such as proteins, vitamins and minerals. The average adult human needs 40 g of protein per-day.

6. Indians takes 2100 calories on an average while being in urban cities and 2400 calories in rural areas.

7. The average daily calorie intake in North-America and Europe is above 3500 calories, nearly 1/3 rd more than is needed for adequate nutrition. As least 20% of Americans are seriously overweight.

8. Grain supplies alone could provide everyone in the world with 2700 calories if that grain were equitably distributed.

9. People who receive less than 80 percent of their minimum daily calories requirements are considered seriously undernourished.

10. People who receive less than 90 percent of their minimum dietary intake one a long term basis are considered undernourished.

11. 60-90% of the food that consumers eat, digest and absorb is oxidized for energy, the remaining 10-40%, which is converted to body tissues is very important. This is the fraction that enables the body, to grow, as well as to maintain and repair itself.

Water food resources : By eating balanced diet, we can avoid malnutrition and the ill effects of obesity and cardiovascular diseased.

Food Security

In the past 50 years, the food grain production in the country increased substantially from 51 million tonnes in 1950-51 to 209 million tonnes in 1999-2000. During the same period the population if India increased from 361 million in 1951 to 1027 million inn 2001. Inspite of the constant rise of population, we have been able to build a food stock of 44.7 million tonnes in 2001. The country, on an average has enough in stock to meet the maximum food requirements of its citizens. But this situation is not likely to remains so easy in the years to come. The population of India by 2020 is likely to be around 1300 million. This would require a huge amount of food grain along with pulses, oilseeds, vegetables and fruits.

In spite of surplus food grain stock, it is also a fact that a vats number of people do not have enough money to feed themselves twice a day. Even inn 1999-2000, 26 percent of the population of India was below the poverty line. This ranged between 27 percent inn rural areas and 23.6 percent in urban areas of the country. Though the percentage of people below poverty line declined substantially form 36 percent in 1993-94 to 26 percent in 1999-2000, yet by no means a small number.

There has been a gradual shift from cultivation of food crops to cultivation of fruits, vegetables, oil-seeds and crops, which also act as industrial raw materials, This has led to the reduction in net sown area under cereals, millets and pulses. With the growing population puts a big question mark over the country's future food security. The food production has started to show a declining trend. In 2000-01, India produced only 199 million tonnes of food grain. The use of more and more land for construction of factories, warehouses and shelters has reduced the land under cultivation and new fertile land for farming is no longer available. The productivity of land has started showing a declining trend.

Fertilizers, pesticides and insecticide, which once showed dramatic results, are now being held responsible for degrading soils. Periodic scarcity of water has led to reduction in area under irrigation. Inefficient water management has led to reduction inn area under irrigation.

Under these situations, the key concern for agricultural scientists is to produce more food to satisfy the hunger of more than a billion people, through agricultural techniques which are environmentally sustainable. Biotechnology, as a supplementary tool, can be used for modifying different crops genetically to increase the yield per hectare. This will easily meet out our food, fodder and fibre requirements. Use of such technology has made the corps more resistance to insects, pests and diseases. This will greatly reduce the dependence on insecticides. Genetically modified crops require less water compared to other crops. This, ultimately, will reduce the cost of production and will help to improve the environment. Biotechnology is poised to give benefit to both rich and poor farmers equally, and is more environmentally safe and sustainable.

Hunger and Nutritional deficiency

The nutritional deficiency which means calories intake less than 1000 can effect individuals anywhere inn the world. Reason being that adequate diet is not available due to non-availability of wholesome food. Another reason is that people do not know how to choose right thing to eat. Food and water are our barest necessities to remain alive. One cannot easily imagine what would ti be without it. Let us a have a view about it.

(i) We usually think of hunger in terms of catastrophic famine and starvation, far more people in the world are affected by chronic food shortages in which they lack adequate nutrition on a long term basis. About 1 million people are thought to have died in Sub-Saharan Africa in the early 1980's as a result of drought related famine.

(ii) Similarly, the world was horrified by terrible photographs of starving children in Ethiopia and Sudan inn 1983 and 1984. More than 1 million people died in the Horn of Africa. Total food supplies dropped by 10 percent, the famine was severe.

(iii) The state of Maharashtra inn central India suffered a similar drought in 1971-73 that reduced crop yields by 50%.

(iv) Adverse weather, insect infestations and other

natural disasters cause crop failures and create food shortages. Problem arise because poor people can neither grow their own food nor find jobs to earn money to buy food they need. In 1974, a terrible famine struck Bangladesh and thousands died. The immediate cause was floods in June though August that interfered with rice planting, cultivating jobs on which many farmers depended. Fears about impending rice shortages triggered panic buying, hoarding by speculators and rapidly rising prices.

(v) Famines are characterized by mass migrations as starving people travel to refugee camps in search of food and medical care. Many die on the way or fall prey to robbers.

(vi) Starving people eat their seed again and slaughter their breeding stock to keep themselves and their breeding stock to keep themselves and their- families alive.

(v) Acute food shortage cause famines, characterized by large-scale loss of life.

(vi) Food shortages are the tragic scenes of mass starvation that come from countries like Ethiopia, Somalia, Sudan, or Mozambique.

Land and Major Crops

We have three crops seasons in India. They are Kharif, rabi and zaid, Khariff season starts with the onset of the monsoon and continuous till the beginning of winter. Cross such as rice, maize, millets, cotton, groundnut, moong urad etc., are grown in this season. Rabi season starts with the beginning of winter and continues till the beginning of Summer. Crops such as wheat, barley, gram and oilseeds are grown in this season. Zaid is short crop season of summer.

Watermelons and cucumbers are grown on the sandy tracts also the river channel. Rice, maize, vegetables and fruits and major crops.

Broadly, there are two types of crops. Kind and cash crops, Kind crops are : Rice, Wheat, Millets, Maize and cash crops are : Sugarcane, Rubber, Tobacco, Spices and Fruits.

Nutrition position In India

Although the country has been able to eliminate nutritional deficiency syndromes like pellagra, beriberi, scurry etc. yet chronic energy deficiency among adults, undernutrition among children and micronutrient deficiencies such as goiter, blindness due to vitamin-A deficiency and anemia are still prevalent across all section of the population. The country has adopted a multi-sectorial and multi- pronged strategy to combat these problems and to improve the nutritional status of the population.

One half of the children under the age of five years in India are moderately or severely malnourished, 30 percent of newborn children are significantly under weight and nearly 60 percent of women are anaemic. Under the Integrated Chile Development Scheme the Department of Women and Child Development implements the food supplementation programme for improving nutritional status of mothers and children. Ministry of Health and Family Welfare implements programmes for tackling major micronutrient deficiencies such as Vitamin A and Iodine deficiency etc.

To address the needs of undernourished infants and children below 3 years. 15 percent of the total Additional Central Assistance are earmarked for the nutrition component under the Pradhan Mantri Gramodaya

Yojana. ACA under the nutrition component of PMGY is an additionally for providing nutrition to children in 0-3 years. States are required to ensure that all below poverty line children by supplementing the States commitment for supplementary nutrition with adequate ACA under PMGY. During 2000-01 and 2001-02 the Department of Women and Child Development was the nodal Department for the implantation of the nutrition component of the programme. From 1st April 2002, the Planning Commission is directly implementing the scheme.

A National Nutrition Mission will soon be launched in selected nutritionally backward districts of the country to further carry forward the goals of National Nutrition Policy. The Planning Commission has allocated Rs. 103.33 crore for 2002-03, as Special Central Assistance to States to provide free foodgrains to undernourished adolescent girls and pregnant & lactating mothers in 51 identified districts. The first installment of Rs. 53.96 lakh has been released to all States for 2002-03.

Energy Conservation

Energy saved is energy produced is a common dictum. Energy conservation means saving of energy because we are short of energy in relation to its demand. Following tips may be adopted to conserve energy :

(i) Buy locally made, long lasting materials.

(ii) Eat locally grown food in season.

(iii) Use of recycled glass, metals, and paper : compost organic wastes.

(iv) Take shorter, cooler showers, install water saving faucets at shower heads.

(v) Stop faucet leaks, especially hot water.

(vi) Turn off light, television sets, and computers when not in use.

(vii) Insulate your house.

(viii) Joining a car pool or driving a smaller, or more energy efficient car.

(ix) Use of stairs instead of elevators if you are not sick.

(x) Use of public transportation, walk, or riding a bicycle.

Role of Individuals in Conservation of Resources and sustainable life style

The land which nature has endowed us is a common heritage. We have shared it with the past generations and will have to do so with the future generation. Human greed has increased so much so that we have almost stopped to think for the future. This is not a healthy trend. In an agricultural country like courts, we should not allow its depletion and degradation. Besides there are many natural resources such as energy, forests, water, soil and biodiversity. If every individual start thinking them as national wealth and a great use of generations to come then these precious resources can be conserved. We now take one by one how these should be conserved.

Home Energy Saving Through Energy Efficiency

Home energy efficiency means designing and building houses that incorporates methods and materials that have been proven to conserve energy. But most of us have to live in house and apartments that already exist. How can they practice home energy conservation. A few practices mentioned below can be adopted.

(i) Emphasize an greater use of non-conventional

sources of energy.

(ii) Switch off electricity whenever not required.

(iii) Use power saving devices.

(iv) Use more and more public transport system and less individual vehicles.

(v) Cogeneration which is as simultaneous production of both electricity and steam from the same plant is one of the fastest growing source of energy.

(v) For greater saving of energy, new houses can be built with extra thick super-insulated walls, air-to-air heat exchangers to warm incoming air, and even double-walled sections that create a house within a house.

(vi) Reducing air infiltration is usually the cheapest, quickest, and most effective way of saving energy because it is the large source of the oil.

(vii) Secondary recovery method may be used to recover a greater amount of the oil.

(viii) Municipal trash can be burned to produce heat and electricity. This will increase the additional supply of energy.

(ix) The easiest way to save energy is to keep an eye on energy-use habits.

(x) High- efficiency fluorescent lights emit the same amount of light but the quite less energy compared to conventional incandescent bulbs.

(xi) Some energy-efficient applications can save substantial amount of energy. Air conditioners and refrigerators with better condensers and heat exchangers use half to one fourth as much energy as older models. New improved furnaces can offer 96 percent efficiency, compared with conventional 70 percent efficiency in older models.

Conservation of water resources

In view of the limited water available, and that too, unevenly and polluted, there is need to adopt certain individual conservation measures because freshwater available on earth today is very limited. The amount of freshwater available on Earth today is no more than that was available 2,000 years ago when the Earth's population was less than 3% of its current size.

Rising demands of water in agriculture domestic consumption, and industry are forcing stiff competition over the distribution of scarce water resources, both amongst different regions and types of use. Water is likely to play the same role in world economy in the 21st century that oil played in the 20th century and will be the source of conflicts world over to pose a major threat to human security if proper preventive measures are not taken globally. Growing water scarcity has become very real.

Rainwater Harvesting

It is a technique of increasing the recharge of ground water by capturing and storing rainwater by constructing structures, such as dugwells, percolation pits, check dams, Rainwater is stored in groundwater reservoirs by adopting artificial recharge techniques to met the household needs through storage in tanks. The objectives of rainwater harvesting are :

(i) To supplement domestic water requirement during summer and long dry spells.

(ii) To improve the quality of groundwater.

(iii) To reduce groundwater pollution.

(iv) To augment the groundwater storage and raise the water table.

(v) To avoid flooding of roads.

(vi) To reduce run off.

(vii) To meet the increasing demand for water.

Watershed development

River basin is an area drained by a river and its tributaries. The watershed is the basin of a tributary. It may have a small stream or it may not have any such stream, but whenever it rains, the water flows through it finally to join some streams. The watershed, thus, is a physiographic unit and can be used conveniently for integrated development of small natural unit areas. The watershed development is holistic approach. It is includes programmes for soil and moisture conservation, water harvesting, afforestation, horticulture, pasture development and upgradation of community land resources. These plans take into consideration the land capability and the local needs of the people. It seeks participation of the local people. Several such programmes have been taken up recently by the central and state governments, with promising results.

Wildlife conservation

India has more than 89,000 species of animals, 1200 species of birds and 2500 species of fish. Besides, there are large varieties of amphibians, reptiles and mammals. Depletion of forests has endangered plant and wildlife. In order to preserve natural habitat and protect them from becoming extinct, the country has developed a network of 89 national parks, 490 sanctuaries and 13 biosphere reserves. The Biosphere reserve programme was launched by the UNESCO in 1971 to conserve representative samples of co-systems, to provide long term in-situ conservation of biodiversity and to promote appropriate and sustainable management of living resources.

In India first biosphere reserve-Nilgiri biosphere reserve came into existence in 1986. So far India have twelve biosphere reserves. Besides this a number of steps described below have been initiated to check wild life conservation.

During the year, ban on export of 29 species of plant, plant-portions and their derivatives obtained from wild, was continued. Export of six species of exotic birds was also continued subject to pre-shipment inspection and provision under CITES wherever required.

The Wild Life Amendment Bill, 2002 was passed by the Parliament during the Winter Session, 2002. The Bill proposes to enhance penalties for violation of the provisions of the Act. It also proposes to create two new categories of Protected Areas, viz., Conservation Reserve and Community Reserve.

A number of species reported as endangered were provided highest protection by including them in the Schedule I and part II of Schedule II of the Wild Life. The Standing Committee of the Indian Board of Wildlife met three times to discuss important aspects relating to wild life. The IBWL Apex Advisory Committee is headed by the Hon'ble Prime Minister. In order to monitor the implementation of the National Wild Life Action Plan, a Monitoring Committee has been set up.

There are 89 National Parks and 500 wildlife sanctuaries in the country covering an area of 1.56 lakhs square km. Financial assistance for development of National Parks and Sanctuaries was provided to 210 National Parks and Sencturies in 25 States including North-Eastern States and Union Territories in the country during the year.

Project Tiger was launch in 1973 on the recommendations of a special task force of Indian Board of wildlife to ensure maintenance of available tiger population in India and to preserve the areas such biological importance as a national heritage for the benefit and educational employment of people.

Conservation of forests

Conservation of forests is a national problem. It must be tackled with perfect coordination between forest department and other departments. People's participation in the conservation of forest is of vital importance. We must celebrate Van Mahotsava with great enthusiasm and zeal and plant trees in all such areas, which are unsuitable for cultivation of crops. We should also create public awareness about the importance of trees. All national day celebration programmes should follow a programme of tree plantation. Progress of forest conservation is detailed below :

(i) Forests Survey of India, Dehradun organized an International Training Workshop on Assessment of Trees Outside Forests from April 22, 2002. The Workshop was attended by 22 participants from 11 countries from South and South East Asia. Food and Agriculture Organisation of the United Nations sponsored the Workshop.

(ii) During the year the inventory data consisting of tree species and both collected from 51 districts, rural and urban areas of all 14 physiographic zones were used to estimate average number of trees per hectare in that zone.

(iii) Special studies for assessment of change in the forest cover of seven Biosphere Reserves, thirteen Tiger Reserves, twelve National Parks and fourteen Wildlife Sanctuaries have also been done.

(iv) Field manuals for forest inventory and TOF urban

have been finalized for data collection.

(v) Wood assessment of national forest cover 125 districts of Trees from 22 states and 15 districts of TOF urban from 13 states spread over 14 physiographic zones were surveyed and data was analyzed.

Assistance to Botanic Gardens

The Ministry has constituted an Expert Group to examine and recommend proposals received under the scheme on Assistance to Botanic Gardens to augment ex-situ conservation of rare endemic plants. One time financial assistance is provided under the scheme. The project for establishment of a National Botanic Garden at NOIDA - Delhi with an outlay of Rs. 3,777,85 lacks has been approved for implementation in the Tenth Five Year Plan.

Medical Plants

Medicinal plants have been identified as one of the thrust areas by the Ministry and different programmes encompassing activities in the area of medicinal plants were continued to carry out conservation of medicinal plants found in the forests and protected areas as well as cultivation of these plants in the degraded forest area.

Medicinal Plants Conservation Areas in the southern States of Kerala, Tamil Nadu and Karnataka and Medicinal Plants Conservation Network established for in-situ conservation earlier continued their activities during the year.

Animal Welfare

The Animal Welfare Division became a part of the Ministry of Environment and Forests in the month of July 2002. Earlier the Division was under Ministry of Statistics and Programme Implementation. The mandate of Animal Welfare Division is to prevent the infliction of unnecessary pain or suffering on animals. Under the Prevention of cruelty to Animals Act, 1960 a new set or rules namely, Animal Birth Control Rule, 2001 was notified on 24th December, 2002.

Under the scheme of Animal Birth Control and Immunication of Stray Dogs, during the year, an amount of Rs. 1.30 crore was released to 49 organisations in various states. The first National Seminar on The States of Animal Houses in India was organized in June, 2002. As an outcome of the Seminar, three sub-committees namely : Committee on Alternatives and Harmonistion with Global Guidelines on Alternatives, Committee on Norms of Rehabilitation of Animals used in experimentation.

An Institute is being set up at Ballabhgarh, District, Faridabad, Haryana for providing various Graduate and post Graduate sources on animal welfare. The Institute would also offer incentive specialized Diplomas inn specific streams.

Equitable use of Resources for Sustainable development

Resources both renewable and non-renewable are scarce in supply to match the demand besides being unevenly distributed. Some countries are using more resources and may have little to use. This is because there is drastic change in life-style. Life style changes may involve such things as switching to a more fuel-efficient car, recycling paper, cans and bottles. Similarly underdeveloped developing countries are adopting new life-styles in an unsustainable manner. Studies reveal that developed countries are more rapidly changing their life style. For instance USA has more aeroplanes compared to many Asian countries.

Poor nations produce only small amounts of

greenhouse gases compared to development nations. Reason being that rich countries continue to lead energy consumptive material life styles. Europe and Japan are responsible for about 2/3 of all potential global warming with them. Mismanagement of natural resources, large- scale deforestation, unplanned discharge of residues wastes, handling of toxic chemicals, indiscriminate construction and expansion of settlement activities pose threat to the environment because equitable use of resources is being hit hard by both rich and poor countries. This attempt has shaked sustainable life-styles. See ozone layer is as wide as the united states and as high Mount-Everest and opens over Antarctica every year. Ozone depletion has been occuring since 1960's but water not grown larger.

Dallas nay have 162 days per year that hot that 100 as it does not. Ecological disruptions could be severe. There shall be a rise in sea level due to global warming. A few oceangraphers are of the opinion that thermal expansion alone could raise the sea level by one meter or more in the next century. Global warming might cause increase in violent storms such as Hurricane.

May scientists state that global change in environment has already started. They point to the fact that four of the five warmest years on record were in the late 1980s and early 1990s. A new approach to gauge earth's climate has found that the atmosphere would witness more warming during 21st century. It is said that the global warming would be faster than what has been anticipated till now.

The approach, developed as the Handley Centre for Climate Prediction and Research inn Bracknell in UK and published in Nature, said average global temperature could be 5.5 degree Celsius higher by 2100, which is around 1.5 degree Celsius higher than a forecast accepted worldwide.

Contrary to earlier estimates which are based on limited factors only, the new approach says that the warming of earth's atmosphere would depend on a host of other factors like volcanoes, fluctuations in the sun's activity and changing levels of greenhouse gases and ozone. It also allows oceans to affect the land and vice versa.

James Baker, former administrator of the US National Oceanic and Atmospheric Administration while being in India some time back, commented that the world will see a definite impact of global warming within the next 10 years. Increase in global warming will make society more vulnerable to climate change. Policy- makers all over the world will either have to learn to do with lesser greenhouse gases or learn to live climate change. More scientists are convinced that we are seeing human influence on the climate what we are worried about is the enhanced Greenhouse Effect, With carbon dioxide levels in the atmosphere growing. Barker admitted that Developed countries have no right to tell developing countries to slow down their economic growth.

Developed countries need to find solutions and help developing countries leap frog over polluting technologies in their quest for raising standards of living. Indeed, we are all involved whether we recognized it or, not in degrading environment. Simply by out existence on the planet; everything we do- the car we drive, the product we use, the wastes we throw-away, virtually every choice we make and action we take-has certain environmental impact and certain consequences for the future. Therefore, it is not a matter of having an effect ; but of what and how great that effect will be. It is a matter of each of us asking ourselves.

Life Cycle Assessment

Life Cycle Assessment is a decision cum management too which provides information on the environmental effects of various products and processes so as to arrive at necessary corrective measures to make the entire process efficient with optimal utilization of resources and minimal wastes generation. LCA studies have been initiated in various sectors namely : Steel, Pulp and Thermal Power. The study in the Steel Sector was completed earlier and the report is under preparation. The study relating to the Thermal Power Sector has been completed during the year while the study in the Pulp and Paper Sector is progressing as per schedule.

Development of Natural Dyes from Forest Wastes

A three years duration project has been sponsored to Forest Research Institute, Dehradun for development of natural dyes from forest waste.

Bio-remediation of Raladevi Lake in Thane, Maharashtra

A project relating to cleaning of Raladevi Lake in Thane District in Maharashtra using bio-remediation technique has been sponsored to Thane Municipal Corporation.

Environmental Statement

Environmental audit is a management tool and provides a structure and comprehensive mechanism for ensuring that the activities and products of an enterprise do no cause unacceptable effects on the environment. Submission of the Environmental Statement by polluting units seeking consent either under the Water Act, 1981 or both and the Authorization under the Hazardous

Wastes and Handling Rules, 1989 has been made mandatory through a Gazette Notification of April , 1993 under the Environment protection Act, 1986.

The Environmental Statement enables the units to undertake a comprehensive look at their industrial operations and facilities, understanding of material flows and focus on areas where waste reduction and consequently saving in-put cost if possible. The primary benefit of environmental audit is that it ensures cost effective compliance of laws, standards, regulations, company policies etc.

During the year, action has been initiated to evolve model environmental statements in various sectors for facilitating comparison in use of raw material, water conservation, energy consumption etc. A project has been sponsored to Central Pollution Control Board for evolving model environmental statement in the eight sectors viz. Sugar, Thermal Power Projects, Cement, Paper and Pulp, Pesticides, Bulk Drugs, Tanneries and Textiles Activities.

Recycling of Marble Slurry in Udaipur, Rajasthan

A two years duration project has been sponsored for the manufactures of bricks and tiles from marble slurry in Udaipur, Rajasthan with the aim of utilizing wastes arising out of marble cutting and processing for the purpose of improving the local environment.

Field Demonstration and Development of Bamboo Based Composites/Panels

The ongoing project on field demonstration and development of bamboo based composites/ panels was continued during the year. Under this project, commercial production of horizontal and vertical laminates have been made using Bambusa bamboo

Species. Construction of demonstration house will be taken up during the current year.

Development of Market Based Instruments for Regional Environmental Management in the Kawas-Hazira Region in Gujarat

The ongoing project on Development of Market Based Instruments for Kawas-Hazira Region of Gujarat has been completed. The study report has observed that the taxes and incentives based on efficiency improvements align the pollution control agencies better with the polluters that the Command and Control regime. Such an instrument also facilitates prescribing incentives for achieving the triple bottom line, viz economic-efficiency, environment-responsibility, and social-relevance entitling the Corporate to Clean Development Mechanism and other cleaner-production benefits. The recommendations of the study have been discussed in a workshop with all concerned.

Industrial Ecology Opportunities in Ankleshwar and Nandesari Industrial Estates, Gujarat

A study was undertaken to develop and implement Industrial Ecology Opportunities in Ankleshwar and Nandesari Industrial Estates of Gujarat. The study has examined technologies used by industries in this region and suggested possible approach to achieve eco-efficiency within the industrial estates to reuse and recycle wastes and affluents generated from different industrial units. The recommendations of the study have been discussed in a workshop with all stakeholders including State Government Agencies for their implementation and an Action Plan is being drawn-up by them.

Environmental Statistics and Mapping

For sound Environmental Management, reliable information base and the mapping of areas needing special attention for pollution prevention and control are a prerequisite. As a step in the direction, projects and pilot studies have been initiated various research institutions and organizations. Under this program, following studies have been initiated and are in various stages of completion :

GIS base Hydrological Modeling for Water Quality and Quality inn Cauvery River Basin by IIT, Delhi. Geochemical baseline Mapping for Environmental Management by National Geophysical Research Institute, Hyderabad.

Waste Minimization/Cleaner Production

Waste minimization is one of the strategies adopted for minimizing the industrial pollution. The objective of the scheme is to assist the small and medium scale industry inn adoption of cleaner production practices. A project has been sponsored to National Productivity Council on Waste Minimizations in Small Scale Industries for establishment and running of waste minimization circles in clusters of small scale industries, capacity building in area of cleaner production, establishment of demonstration units in selected industrial sectors etc.

So far 115 waste minimization circles have been established through out the country and a large number of Organizations and Institutions have been trained in waste minimization activities. The project was executed till November, 2002 under the World Band project on Industrial Pollution Prevention as Phase - I and Phase - II is now being continued with Ministry's internal funds. Implementation of this project has helped in identification of more than 200 options for resources and energy conservation in various small scale industries.

Industrial Pollution Abatement through preventive strategies

This scheme is an amalgamation of the three on-going schemes viz. Environmental Audit, Adoption of Clean Technologies in Small Scale Industries and Environmental Statistics and Mapping, which have been continuing since eighth Five Year Plan. Due to encouraging results and benefits to various small scale units, these schemes are being continued during the 10th Five year Plan also.

Goals toward Sustainable life-styles and development

(i) Take a leadership role in the development and implementation of global sustainable development policies.

(ii) Move towards stabilization of population.

(iii) Create full opportunities for citizens, business and communities to participate in and influence the natural resources, environmental and economic decision that effect them.

(iv) Encourage people to work together to create healthy communities where natural and historic resources are preserved, education is life long, transportation and health care are assessable, and all citizens have opportunities to improve the quality of their lives.

(v) Use, conserve, protect and restore natural resources in ways that help ensure long-term social, economic, and environmental benefits for ourselves and future generations.

(vi) Sustain a healthy economy that grows, sufficiently to create meaningful jobs, reduce poverty and provide the opportunity of high quality of life.

(vii) Ensure that every person enjoys the benefit of clean-air, clean-water and healthy environment at home, at work, and at play.

10

ENVIRONMENT AND HEALTH CONCEPTS

Introduction

Today various kinds of changes have taken place in different spheres of life. With such kinds of changes, dramatic kind of change has taken place in the outlook and thinking pattern of common men. Earlier he was only concerned with finding out the means by which he can live a comfortable life, but now he tries to find out those means by which he live a comfortable and healthy life. People have now become health conscious. One of the main reason of this happening can be the fact that a paramount increase in the number of people suffering from various diseases has been noticed in the recent past. Not only this, as the literary level is increasing in the nation, various kinds of information relating to healthful living is being made available to them, because of which they have understood the value and importance of living a healthy life.

Now even a commonman knows the importance of health. Thus, if you are also concerned about your health, then you are not alone as at this time, majority of people are also concerned with their health. This can be considered as one of the main reasons that why number of private organisations and clubs making arrangements of various physical activities have increased in today's time. People belonging to higher strata of society do not get indulged in such organisations, but people belonging to middle classes or strata of society have also now become highly health conscious. Now everyone knows what to eat, when to eat and how much to eat. Before taking or consuming any food article, everyone give consideration to the nutrients value it possess and also the effects which the food item will mark on the health.

Although number of people becoming health conscious or making use of health services has increased to considerable extent, but still number of people suffering from problem of obesity and various other diseases arising out of this problem has increased to considerable extent, because of which maintaining health and leading a healthful life has now become a challenge for us. Various people will pose and ask the question that why is being healthy so challenge for so many of us. What can we do to overcome these challenges, make better decisions about our behaviour. There are no easy answers, because health is influenced by various factors, out of which some that we can control, some that we cannot. But the good news is that many people have found the skills and motivation to look objectively at where they are, plan carefully, and make decisions that improve their life and health.

As health has become so important concept in today's life, because of which it has attracted the attention of various researchers and experts. It is on the basis of best available research that health decisions should be based. All the decisions taken on such bases should be consistent with who you are, your values and beliefs, and who you want to become. Although health is not always totally within your control, some behaviour choices that affect health are certainly under control. The choices one makes can enhance his health, as well as reduce future health threatening risks. For those risk factors that are beyond one's control, one can learn to react, adapt, respond in appropriate manner and use a reasoned, rather than purely emotional, rationale method for taking the decisions. Quality and length of the life can be improved with the help of making informed and rational kinds of decisions. Not only this, such decisions also effect the persons around you in a positive manner.

As is clear from the preceding chapters that although term health is used by almost all the people of world, but there are very few out of them who understand properly what it really means. For some, health simply means the antithesis of sickness. To others, it means being in good physical shape and having an ability to resist illness. Still others use term such as wellness or well being to include a wide array of factors that seem to lead to positive health status. The main reason of existence of such kind of differences lies in the fact increasingly enlightened way of viewing health has taken shape over time. In addition, as collective understanding of the concept of illness has improved, so has human being's ability to understand the many nuances of health. In reality, one's progress to current understanding about health has evolved over centuries, and a long way has to be covered even till now in order to achieve a truly comprehensive view of this complex subject. Much discussion on the topic of various concepts relating to health had been discussed in the preceding chapters, because of which, they will not be discussed at length in this chapter. This chapter is designed to provide fundamental knowledge about various health topics, so that you can utilise personal and community resources for creating your own health profile, and to challenge you to think more carefully prior to making any kinds of decisions that affect your health status.

Evolution of Health Concept

Prior to 1800s, a person who was not sick was being regarded as not only lucky, but also healthy. When deadly epidemics such as plague, influenza etc., killed millions of people, survivors were believed to be of hearty, healthy stock, and they congratulated themselves on their good fortune. Poor health was not often associated with poor hygiene and unsanitary conditions, and certain stigmas were attached to households that harboured any of these illnesses. It was not until the late 1800s did researchers discover that victims of these epidemics were not simply unhealthy or dirty, rather they were victims of environmental factors which made them sick and over which they often had little or no control. Public health officials moved swiftly to address these problems, and as a result, the term Health became synonymous with good hygiene. Various schools began of offer courses in health and hygiene. It was into the 1900s that investigation into the environment as the primary cause of disease continued to take place, which was as a result of outbreak of tuberculosis and influenza surged i many regions of the world. People who made it through the first few years of life without succumbing to an infectious disease usually were able to survive to old age. Continued improvements in sanitation brought dramatic changes in life expectancy, and the development of vaccines and antibiotics added even more years to the average life of common men.

It was in around 1940s that progressive thinkers in public health began to note that there was more to health than hygiene or disease. They took into notice the definition provided by World Health Organisation in one of the conferences held on international level, in which he defined the term Health as the state of complete physical, mental and social well being. Scientists took a long time in accepting the fact that health included much more than physical, social or mental elements of life. Other elements, such as environmental, spiritual, emotional and intellectual aspects, helped to define whether a person was truly capable of optimal functioning. In addition, the new voices and views suggested that it is not just length of life or the number of disease free years that matters, but rather achieving your potential for a happy, healthy and productive life also.

Today, there is treatment of various diseases, which were once considered to be incurable in nature. As a result of such developments, mortality rate has lower down to greater extent. Morbidity rates also indicate that people less frequently contract the common infectious diseases that devastated previous generations, but still it cannot be said that these facts are indications of healthful living people. If one view the conditions in which major portion of population in our nation live, then all these factors, who are regarded as indicators of health, will be banished by the expert. Although number of persons getting dead as a result of various diseases has decreased and most childhood diseases are preventable or curable and massive public health efforts are aimed at reducing the spread of infectious diseases, but still longer life and less frequent diseases are not proof that people are indeed healthy and leading a healthful life.

In accordance with some experts, Health is a quality of life, involving social, emotional, mental, spiritual and biological fitness on the part of the individual, which results from adaptations to the environment. The concept of adaptability, or the ability to successfully cope with ups and downs of the life, became a key element of overall health definition. Eventually, the term wellness became popular which implied that there were levels of health in each category. In order to achieve a high level wellness, a person moved progressively higher on a continuum of positive health indicators. Those who failed to achieve these levels might move to the illness side of the continuum. Today, health are wellness are often used interchangeably to mean the dynamic, ever changing process of trying to achieve one's potential in each of several interrelated dimensions. Physical Health, Social Health, Mental Health, Emotional Health, Spiritual Health are some of the important dimensions of the concept of health. They are not discussed here at length as mention of these has been done separately in the preceding chapters.

Various scientists and experts have put forward the features which generally exist in healthy persons, mention of which are as follows :—

- A healthy person possess a realistic sense of self, including personal capabilities and limitations.

- Such a person possess the willingness to understand imperfections in himself and also in the persons living around him. Not only this, he possess the ability to analyse all the situations.

- Such a person possess the ability to laugh, to cry and to genuinely feel emotion without getting lost in emotional upsets.

- Such a person possess a sense of satisfaction with life and from whatever functions he perform. Not only this, he possess the ability to appreciate stages of life experiences.

- A healthy person has feeling of self-respect as well as respect for others.

- Such a person possess a zest for living a comfortable and successful life, which is being coupled with a curiosity about what each new encounter and each new day will bring.

- Such a person knows how to keep everything in life under control and in balanced position.

- Such a person likes to accept the challenges imposed by the life on him and never tries to escape from harsh realities of the life.

There are number of people who are of the view that wellness can best be achieved by adopting a holistic approach, which emphasises the integration of and balance among mind, body and spirit. Achieving wellness implies attaining the optimum level of wellness for a give person's unique set of limitations and strengths. A physically disabled person may function at his or her optimum level of performance, can enjoy satisfying interpersonal relationships, can maintain emotional, spiritual and intellectual health and have a strong interest in environmental concerns. On the other hand, persons who spend hours lifting weights to perfect the size and shape of each muscle, but pay little attention to nutrition may look healthy, but they may not maintain a good balance on all areas of health. Although generally we consider physical attractiveness and other external trappings in measuring the overall health of a person, appearance and physical performance are actually only two signs of wellness, indicating little about the other dimensions of health in any way.

Promoting Health

The term health promotion or promoting health describes the educational, organisational, procedural, environmental, social and financial supports that help individuals and groups reduce negative health behaviours and promote positive changes in the behaviours. Health promotion programs identify the healthy people who are engaging in risk behaviours, or behaviours that increase susceptibility to negative health outcomes, and motivate them to change their actions or behavioural patterns.

Effective health promotion programs provide information about risk behaviours and possible consequences of various harmful kinds of behaviours. Such programs also encourage those with sound health habits to maintain them. By attempting to modify behaviours, increase skills, change attitude, increase knowledge, influence values and improve health decision making, health promotion goes well beyond the simple information campaign. By basing programs and services in communities, organisations, schools and other places where people spend their time, health promotion increases the likelihood of long term success on the road to health and wellness.

Whether we use the term health or wellness, we are talking about a person's overall response to the challenges of living. The ability to recognise that each of us is an imperfect being, attempting to adapt in an imperfect world, signals individual well being. We must also remember to be tolerant of others. Rather than be warriors against pleasure in our zeal to change the health behaviours of others, we need to be supportive, understanding and non-judgemental. Health basing, i.e., intolerance or negative feelings, words or actions aimed at people who fail to meet expectations of health, may indicate our own deficiencies in the psychological, social and spiritual dimensions of the health continuum.

Preventing the Diseases

Most health promotion initiatives include the term disease prevention. Historically, the health literature describes three types of prevention, namely, primary, secondary and tertiary. In a general sense, prevention implies taking positive actions now to avoid becoming sick later. Getting immunized against diseases as polio and chickenpox constitute primary prevention, which are in reality actions designed to reduce risk and avoid health problems prior to they begin. Secondary prevention involves recognising health risks or early problems and taking action to stop or to bring them to an end on the behaviour it leads to actual illness. The third kind is tertiary prevention, which involves treatment and rehabilitation after the person is already sick, which is generally offered by medical specialists.

Number of deaths taking place as a result of wrong habits of consuming harmful substances is increasing in recent times in our nation, which implies that primary and secondary prevention offer our best hope for reducing such incidences. Time has come when we need to move from a mind set of tertiary prevention to focus on earlier intervention designed to remove barriers and help individuals succeeded in their behaviour change strategies.

Health Behaviours

Individual behaviour is a major determinant of good health, but heredity, access to health care and environmental factors can also influence health status. When these factors are considered together and form the basis of a person's lifestyle choices, the net effect on health can be great. Most experts believe that several key behaviours will help people live longer, some of which are as follows :—

i. Getting a good night's sleep, which should be minimum of seven hours.

ii. Maintaining health eating habits, by which human being can attain all essential nutrients by which he can develop at proper pace and manner.

iii. Participating in physical recreational activities, for which membership in the club or organisation established for this purpose can be taken.

iv. Avoid substances having injurious and harmful effects on the health.

v. Limiting intake of alcohol and to practice safer sex by making use of various intraceptives.

vi. Forming and maintaining meaningful and healthful relationships with family and friends.

vii. Controlling the real and imaginary stressors in life.

viii. Participating in atleast one fun activity every day.

ix. Enjoying the environment in which you live and also respect the others around you.

x. Understand the health care system and to use it wisely.

xi. Be as kind to yourself as to others.

Although it is much more easy to list things that one should do, and it is not very easy to bring changes in the behavioural pattern. All of us, irrespective of the fact that where we are on the health continuum, have to start from somewhere. All people have faced personal and external challenges to their attempts to change health behaviours. Some have not done so well, some have been extremely successful, and some have made only small changes that add up to significant improvements in how they feel and how they live. But still, it is very necessary to adopt some of the healthy habits in life, for which behaviour should be modified in a positive and encouraging manner.

How to Prepare for Changing Behaviour

The possibilities of successfully changing negative behaviour improve when you make gradual changes that give you time to unlearn negative patterns and to substitute positive ones. In order to understand the process of behaviour change, it is first important to identify behaviour patterns and attempt to understand the reasons for them. There are various factors which affect or influence behaviour change to considerable extent. Experts have divided these factors into three categories, namely, Enable Factors, Predisposing Factors and Reinforcing Factors.

Enabling Factors

All the factors which make a behaviour change decision more convenient or difficult are included in this category. Enabling factors include one's physical, emotional and mental capabilities, one's skills and one's access to resources. Positive enablers encourage a person to carry through on his intentions, while negative enablers work against one's intentions to change. One must possess the ability to identify the positive and negative enabling factors and to devise alternative pans when the negative factors outweigh and the positive factors are part of planning for behaviour change.

Predisposing Factors

One's life experiences, knowledge, cultural and ethnic heritage and current beliefs and values are all included in the category of Predisposing Factors. These factors influence behaviour and behavioural changes to considerable extent. Age, sex, race, income, family background and educational qualifications are some of the important factors which can play major role in predisposing a human being.

Reinforcing Factors

Presence or absence of support, encouragement or discouragement from significant people in your life are all some of the important reinforcing factors. The manner in which one reward or punish oneself also plays an important role. Accepting small failures and concentrating on the success can foster further achievements. Telling yourself that you are worth the extra time and efforts and giving yourself a pat on the back for small accomplishments are often overlooked factors in positive behaviour change.

It is very necessary to mention that want and an urge to change is a prerequisite of the changing process, but there is much more to the process that motivation. Motivation must be combined with common sense, commitment, and a realistic understanding of how best to move to healthy lifestyle. Readiness is the state of being that precedes behaviour change. People who are ready to change possess the knowledge, attitudes, skills and internal and external resources that make change a likely reality. To be ready for change, a person must take certain basic steps and make adjustments in thinking pattern.

Generally it is assumed that when rational people realise what they are doing carries a risk, they will act to reduce that risk, but this is not necessarily true. There are number of health professionals who even smoke and consume high fat diets. They surely know better, but their knowing is disconnected from their doing. There are two strong influences on behaviour which are found to play effective role by the experts. These two influences are beliefs and attitudes. A belief is an appraisal of the relationship existing in between some object, action or idea and some attribute of that object, action or idea. On the other hand, an attitude is a relatively stable set of beliefs, feelings and behavioural tendencies in relation to something or someone. Various studies have depict the relationship between beliefs and health habits, which show that although beliefs can subtly influence behaviour, they may not actually cause people to behave differently.

From a study, it has been concluded that several

factors must support a belief before change is likely, which include the perceived seriousness of the health problem, perceived susceptibility to the health problem and cues to action. Three other factors are linked to perceive risk for health problems, which include demographic variables involving qualities like age, gender, and race; socio-psychological variables, involving features like personality traits and social pressure and structural variables involving knowledge about or prior contact with the various health problems.

A person's attitudes reflect his emotional responses to situations and follow from his beliefs. According to an expert's views, our behaviours result from our intentions to perform actions. An intention is a product of our attitude toward an action and our beliefs about what others may want us to do. A behavioural intention, then, is a written or stated commitment to perform an action. The more consistent and powerful your attitudes about an action and the more you will be influenced by others to take that action, the greater will be your stated intention to do so. The more you verbalise your commitment to change, the more likely you are to get success.

There are various people who are highly influenced by the approval or disapproval of close friends, loved ones and the social and cultural groups to which they belong. Such influences can support healthy behaviour or they can interfere with even the best intentions. From the time of birth, a child's parents give him strong cues about which actions are socially acceptable and which are not. Brushing the teeth, bathing, wearing clothes and chewing food with your mouth closed are all behaviours that a child learns from the family members. A person's family culture influences his food choices, religious beliefs, political beliefs and all other values and actions. If person gets deviated from his family's norms, then any member of the family will probably let him know fairly quickly. Good family units share a dedication to the healthful development of all family members, unconditional trust and a commitment to work out difficulties in the life. When the loving family unit does not exist, when it does not provide for basic human needs, or when dysfunctional, irresponsible individuals try to build a family under the influence of drugs or alcohol, it becomes difficult for a child to learn positive health behaviours in such environment. Healthy behaviours get their origin in healthy homes, unhealthy homes breed unhealthy habits. Healthy families provide the foundation for a clear and necessary understanding of what is right and what is wrong, what is positive and what is negative. Without this fundamental grounding, many young people have great difficulties in adopting healthy behaviours.

A child's world remains limited to the house or to the family members but when he gets entered into the stage of adolescent, then his world boundaries get extended. He comes into direct contact with other members of the society. Thus the conditions and atmosphere in which he now stays got distinguished from the environment prevailing in his family or at house. In such kind of situation, he has to maintain healthy and co-operative kinds of relationships with the other members. Mostly at this stage, he encounters the persons with varying interests and views. It has been found that more a person values the opinions of other people, the more likely he will be to change a behaviour that offends them. If a person cannot care less what others think about him, he probably brush off their negative reactions or suggested change. Often people say that they do not care about the others, but in reality, most of us care too much about what even the insignificant people in our lives think. In simpler terms, it can be said that lower your self esteem and self efficacy, the higher the chances that others will influence your actions. Sometimes, the influence of others can be a powerful social support for positive behaviour changes. At other times, we are influenced in some wrong practices because we do not want to be left out or criticised. Learning to understand the subtle and not so subtle ways in which other people influence our actions is an important step toward changing behavioural pattern.

Important Techniques for Changing Behaviour

After analysing all the factors that influence what you do, you must decide which behaviour change technique will work best for you. There are some specific kinds of techniques or strategies which help in bringing various kinds of changes in the behavioural pattern of human beings, mention of some of which are as follows:—

i. Visualisation : Mental practice and rehearsal can help in changing unhealthy behaviours into healthy ones. Athletes and others use a technique known as Imagined Rehearsal to reach their goals. By visualising their planned action ahead of time, they are better prepared when they put themselves to the test. For instance, if someone has to appear in an interview then he will make all efforts by which he can improve his manner of communication. For this purpose, he will make rehearsal the manner in which he will reply the questions of concerned person, in which he can take the help of his friend also. Thus, through this technique, he will be able to reply the answers imposed in the interview more effectively and efficiently.

ii. Shaping : There are some behaviours to which it is impossible to change immediately. To reach your goal, you may need to take a number of individual steps, each designed to change one small piece of the larger behaviour. This process is known as Shaping. For instance, suppose that you have not exercised for a while. Now you decide that you want to get into shape, and your goal is to walk three to four miles every day. You realise that you have face a near death experience if you tried to walk even just a few blocks in your current condition. So you decide to start slowly and build up to your desired fitness every other day at a slow and relaxed pace. After some time, you will walk for the same amount of time, but will speed up your pace and cover slightly more ground. After some more time, you will speed up even and will try to go even further. In this way, you will continue taking such steps until you reach your goal. There can be difference in the desired behaviour change, but all shaping involves certain specific kinds of items, mention of which are as follows :—

- Beginning with slow pace and trying not to cause undue stress during the early stages of the program.

- Keeping the steps small and achievable.

- Being flexible and ready to bring any kind of change in the plan if original plan proves to be uncomfortable in any way.

- Refusing to skip steps or to move to the next step until the previous step has been mastered.

It must be kept in mind that as behaviours do not develop overnight, so it is not possible to change them also overnight.

iii. Reinforcement : A reward given with the purpose to increase the likelihood that a behaviour change will occur is known as a Positive Reinforcement. Each of us is motivated by different reinforcers. Experts have classified most positive reinforcers into certain specific categories, which are : manipulative, activity, possessional and social. While making choice of reinforcers, determine the fact that what would motivate you to act in a particular way. Various researches have shown that people can be motivated to change their behaviours if they set themselves up on a token economy system, whereby they earn points that can be exchanged for meaningful rewards, such as financial incentives.

It is quite a difficult task to determine which incentive will be most effective. Your reinforcers may initially come from others, but as you see positive changes in yourself, you will begin to reward and reinforce yourself. Always keep in mind that reinforcers should immediately follow a behaviour, but beware of overkill.

iv. Controlling the Situation : Sometimes, the right setting or the right group of people will positively influence your behaviours. Many situations and occasions trigger certain actions. Usually attempts are made to influence a behaviour by making use of situations and occasions to control it, which is generally known as Situational Inducement. You should know the art of carefully considering which setting will help and which will hurt your effort to change, and by making a firm decision to seek the first and avoid the second, you will improve your chances for chance.

v. Modelling : This is considered to be one of the most effective techniques for bringing positive kinds of changes in the behavioural patterns. This involves learning behaviours through careful observation of other people. Generally people becomes motivated to participate in various health care organisations when they find that someone they know have also joined such any organisation. Thus, this technique can play an effective role in bringing positive kind of changes in the healthful behaviours of people.

Steps for Changing Behaviour

As said earlier that changing behaviour is not a simple process in any way and it comprises of certain steps which should be taken carefully, mention of which are as follows :—

a. Self Assessment : An important fact regarding behaviours, thoughts and feelings is that they always occur in a context of the situation. Experts have divided various situations into certain categories, which are the events that come before and after. Antecedents are the setting events for a behaviour, they cue or stimulate a person to act in certain ways. Antecedents can be physical events, thoughts, emotions, or the actions of other people. Results of behaviour, which are called consequences, affect whether a person will repeat that action or not. Physical events, thoughts, emotions or the actions of other people are included in the category known as consequences. One of an important method of changing behaviour is learning to recognise the antecedents of a behaviour and acting to modify them.

b. Analysing Personal Behaviour : Successful behaviour change requires determining what you want to change. Determining the specific behaviour you would like to change in contrast to the general problem will allow you to set clear and realistic goals.

c. Decision Making : After proper analysation, function of decision making should be performed. Now it is a time to make a decision that will lead to positive health outcomes. It is not easy to make choice among various available alternatives. Just saying no is usually easier and said than done, however, if you are trying to fit in, be liked, or satisfy other emotional needs, decision making will become even more difficult. That is why anticipating what might occur in a given setting and thinking through all possible safe alternatives is important as you implement behaviour change. It should be remember that things typically do not just happen. By staying alert to potential problems, being aware of your alternatives, maintaining a good sense of your own values, and sticking to your beliefs under pressure, you can gain control over many situations in your life.

d. Set Achievable Goals : It is not an easy task to bring any kind of change in the behavioural pattern in any way, but sometimes we make it even harder by setting unrealistic and unachievable goals. Before setting goals, one should analyse the fact that what kind of changes he wants to bring in himself, and which change is the greatest priority at this time in his life. He should also analyse the fact that why he regards one change more important than the other and what will going to be positive outcomes of potential change.

It is only through taking all the above mentioned steps that positive kinds of changes can be brought in the healthy behaviours. People can learn to know how to develop positive and healthy kinds of behaviour only by bringing positive kinds of changes in their outlook, for which they require proper motivation and encouragement. Although health educator is the best person to perform this function properly, but family members and other people around the person can also help in performing this function to considerable and maximum possible extent. They should keep a check on the habits of person in order to ensure that he does get indulged in any kind of harmful behaviour. Not only this, they should pin point the kind of deformities or problems arising in his physical health, as it will encourage the person to make use of some health program or to get participate in some physical activities carried out in organisation or club situated near to his house or place of work.

11

TRANSPORT SYSTEM AND ENVIRONMENT

Essential Elements of Transport

The four elements of transport are (i) the way, (ii) the unit of carriage, (iii) the motive power unit, and the terminal.

(i) The way. Natural ways are cheap and free, and have no maintenance costs unless we try to improve them artificially. The sea, the air, the rivers, and footpaths are all natural ways. Being natural they are subject to the whims of nature, and this often requires, that they be improved artificially. Rivers are subject to controls to prevent flooding in wet periods and insufficient flow in dry periods.

They are dredged to maintain a channel and locks are built to improve navigation in the upper reaches, Bridlepaths are made up and turned into roads. Highways and motorways, canals, railways, tramways tunnels, and monorails are similarly constructed. Clearly these are not 'free' like may be borne socially rather than privately. If the costs are borne by the ratepayer and taxpayer we may have what is an apparently free way built the owner usually has sole use of it. This owner then charges for its use by other persons, to recoup the capital costs.

(ii) The unit of carriage. Whatever we call it, some vehicle or craft must be used in transport. The efficiency of the mode of transport depends to some extent on the flexibility and adaptability of the unit of carriage used. Road vehicles are adaptable than railways rolling stock because they are not entirely tied to the way : aircraft and ships are even less tightly bound by the way on which they travel.

Even a pipeline can be considered as unit of carriage. It is not very adaptable in its behaviour: we cannot expect it to carry gas until noon, milk from noon till 3 p.m., and petrol from 3 p.m. to midnight. In choosing our method of transport the adaptability of the unit of carriage will be a major consideration.

(iii) The motive power unit. Every vehicle must be driven and the choice of a propulsion unit depends upon the strength of the vehicle, the speed required, the available fuel, and other factors. Today the steam engine, the first great prime mover, has been largely replaced by the petrol engine, the jet engine, the diesel engine and the electric motor.

(iv) The terminal. Nearly every journey involves junctions where we can transfer from one form of transport to another. A port is usually regarded as a terminal for ships, but in fact it is also a terminal for trains, roads, pipelines, and aircraft.

In planning efficient transport systems, commercial firms and transport authorities must view the interchange of facilities as being part of a unified whole. Congestion in terminals in the past has spelt the death of transport system, as it did when the congestion on the canals led to the growth of railways.

The Position of Transport in the Pattern of Commerce

If specialized production is how advanced societies create the utilities they need to satisfy their 'wants,' some way must be devised to bring to the market-place the surpluses created by each specialist. The function of transport is to more goods and passengers geographically.

It is part of tertiary production, satisfying 'wants' by making goods available and by giving service to those who need, for family, business, or recreational reasons, to travel in their day-to-day affairs.

It also enables a fuller use to be made of the division of labour, because transport increases the size of a market and therefore permits a higher degree of specialization to employed. An improved transport system makes possible an increase in the scale of production so that the wealth of the whole nation increases.

Road Transport

Road transport has great advantages over inland raid and waterways, now that petrol, diesel, and jet engines have furnished a variety of cheap motive powers. The chief advantages are as follow:-

(i) Road vehicles are extremely flexible, and computerized route-charts can now be prepared which give the most economic route.

(ii) Specialized vehicles of great variety have been produced by the road-vehicle manufacturers. They include specialized vehicles for containers, packaged timber and other loads.

(iii) Intermediate terminal handling is laminated by door-to-door delivery. The operators' terminal is under his personal direction and control, designed to do what he requires. Delivery is made direct to the consignee's premises, and if these premises are not equipped to handle the goods being delivered this can often be overcome by appliances actually on the vehicle.

(iv) Although slower than rail fright when in actual transit, the slow speed is more than made up by the elimination of transhipment, the directness of the journey and the personal control of the entire movement. Two-way radios even enable drivers to report their exact positions so they can be called to assist other drivers to report their exact positions so they can be called to assist other drivers to pick up new loads.

(v) The 'way' is at present still great, if one ignores vehicle taxation. Proposals that electronic devices should be fitted to vehicles to charge them for use of busy roads have not yet ben implemented.

(vi) Low capital requirements are a feature of the industry, which permits a new entrant to start with a single vehicle. True, he has to face a licensing problem with certain kinds of vehicle, but many new operators do secure licences especially since the industry is continually expanding.

Solving the Inland Transport Problem—Integrated or Co–ordinated Services?

Since the Transport Act of 1947 first se up a nationalized system, inland transport in Britain has been bedevilled by politics. For many years we were in the position of operating a system which had now become law, but was about to be modified by the next

Government.

The discussion revolved around whether we should have an integrated transport system or a number of co-ordinated services each of which was a separate organization. An integrated system of transport would be operated by a central authority with the power to say who should operate certain services.

It would clearly be an enormous organization, and experience has already shown that a system of this size suffers from the diseconomies of large-scale operation.

On the other hand, it does provide an overall body to control the opposing faction in transport systems, much of it socially provided, are wisely spent. An integrated service will be governed by the basic precept that what is needed is a cheap, efficient transport system which provides consumers with goods and services at the minimum personal and social cost.

Three White Papers issued in late 1967 outlined the Labour Government's proposal, which were put into effect by the 1968 Transport Act. This Act proved to be a very effective Act and for several years the turmoil in transport subsided with a reasonable amount of agreement on all sides. The reasons seem to have been:

(i) Passenger transport—The solution here has been to set up local Passenger services by bus and rail. A national bus company has been get up to take over the bus services previously run by the Transport Holding Company, and with power to acquire voluntarily other under takings.

(ii) Road Policy—The close control of road haulage, which had been a feature of transport policy since the

1930s, was drastically reduced. Directly the Bill became law all vehicles less than 30 cwt. were freed from licence requirements. This meant almost a million tons of capacity became available to carry small loads.

Road transport is particularly suitable for small loads over short distances. The control of larger vehicles, which previously had to e licensed individually, was changed to a system of operators' Licences. This meant that a firm which could rove that it had properly qualified drivers, mechanics, etc., and an adequate financial structure could obtain a licence as a vehicle operator.

It was then free to buy as many vehicles as it liked to operate, and a strongly competitive situation developed, with larger firms able to develop a full service to customers without objections from small operators.

(iii) Railway Policy—The railways were thus forced to face quite severe competition from an increasingly efficient road haulage industry, but were compensated to some extent by being set free from the accumulated debts that had developed over the years since nationalization. Fuller use of railway workshops and vehicle-maintenance departments was made by permitting these organizations to compete with private companies in the sale, manufacturer and repair of a wide range of goods.

The official view her is that is ridiculous to have these expensive assets which have been provided at public expense, under-utilized. Since 1975 the Government has provided large sums to assist the transfer of goods from road to rail to subsidize uneconomic but socially desirable lines.

There has also been in the last few years an agreeable

amount of railway enterprise shown in chasing new sources of revenue, with special terms for pensioners, family travel, etc.

As the United Kingdom transport system enters the 1980s the 44 tonne lorry has been sanctioned, the motorway system is almost complete, and some residual cuts in the rail network are being proposed.

Road Transport—A Growth Industry

There are 200,000 miles of roadway in Great Britain, of which about 9,000 miles are trunk roads, 80,000 miles are classified roads, nearly 1,800 miles are motorways and the rest are minor roads.

In 1980 the railways carried 18,000 million tonne-kilometres—in other words, more than four times as much. 70 percent of rail traffic was coal, coke, iron and steel. The 30 percent of general cargo represents only about 7 percent of the general cargo being carried by road haulage. This gives some idea of the importance of road haulage in recent years.

Use of Containers in Transport

Container services were started as early as 1928 by the four British main-line railway companies, but they have now become firmly established in road, rail, and sea transport. A wide range of off-the-peg containers is now available in a variety of materials, and, while standardization of size is important, containers suitable to the personal needs of most private users can be obtained.

The basic advantages of containers are low freight charges and door-to-door security. Where individual parcels, cartons, or crates are sent by a carrier the work involved in loading and unloading many small items makes for expensive use of labour. If a shipper or distributor is moving large enough consignments go fill a container he can load it himself, either by stacking goods on one another or by making use of the shelving and portioning systems devised by the designers.

The container is then sealed, and moved as one unit with the advanced lifting equipment available. It is impossible to tell what is in it, which is a deterrent to thieves, and without lifting tackle it is impossible to spirit the whole consignment away. Freight charges, insurance, and losses due to minor pilfering are reduced. Container design is important, and handling presents problems. If sea-going containers are to be piled six high, which is no uncommon, the containers must be strong enough to take the weight.

This usually requires a steel framework, but steel is corrosive. Stainless steel is better, but is more costly, and stainless-steel framework with aluminium panels is a useful compromise. Bottom-lift handling devices reduce the need for strength in the container. Top-lift handling devices rely on the container itself to support the weight and place considerable strains upon it. It appears that current container rates are working out about 25-30 percent cheaper than ordinary freight charges, and therefore considerable advantages are offered to commercial firms. In 1979, 32 million container units were moved through ports around the world.

Motorways, Bridges and Tunnels

Road transport growth has slowed down since 1973, when increased fuel charges caused firms to improve economic use of road haulage fleets, but an expanding road network is crucial to progress.

The motorway is the answer to some of the problems giving fast journeys between towns. A start on the motorway network in Britain was made in 1958, and considerable progress has been achieved already in linking the main areas of the country. By 198 Britain had about 1,800 miles of motorway, compared with Germany's 4,200 miles, Italy's 3,500 miles and France's 2,600 miles.

The dilemma of transport is revived by these modern highways, for while the cost is borne socially the benefits in cheaper running costs and faster journeys are enjoyed by the individual families and firms who use the motorway. Tolls have been suggested as a way of reducing the social costs of these projects, but vehicle taxation is still the favourite method of paying for motorways.

The effect of motorways on the location of industry and the availability of labour is considerable. Country towns which once had an unemployment problem, and where emigration to the cities has been the solution for two centuries, suddenly find that land values are soaring as access to the motorway makes the town a desirable site for industry of every sort. Workers begin to travel in from farther afield to take employment.

Bridges and tunnels are essential if motorways are to take direct routes across river estuaries, and some splendid work has been done since the War in bridging the Firth of Forth and the Bristol Channel. The drawings of the Seven Bridge, and its position in the motorway network to South Wales illustrate the grandeur and utility of such engineering feats. The Darford-Purfleet tunnel is a similar link across the Thames estuary.

It has recently been duplicated, so that now two one-way tunnels are available. It is being paid for, like the bridges mentioned above, by tolls charged to users. By giving direct access to Kent and Essex from the other side of the river it is promoting the prosperity of both counties.

Rail Transport

For a century the railways were supreme in inland carriage, both for goods and passengers. Today there is hardly a country in the world where the railways do not lose money. In Britain the railways were nationalized in 1974, and a complete overhaul of the railways system has replaced steam power with electric or diesel-electric rolling stock. High degrees of efficiency have been achieved on particular trunk routes, yet the overall system is still losing money.

Advantages and Disadvantages of Rail Transport

(i) Railway transport is dominated by the 'terminal' problem, for heavy capital costs preclude running a line to every customer's door. Goods must therefore be loaded and unloaded at terminals to complete their journey by road vehicles.

Even though sophisticated handling equipment is now available to load and unload trains, delay seems inevitable and demarcation disputes between group of workers are common.

(ii) Rail transport is impersonal, so that pilfering, delay, and negligent behaviour are difficult to locate and remedy. The consignors and owners of goods are powerless themselves to expedite the handling of goods. One Wiltshire firm sending daily supplies of packages perishable foodstuffs to South Coast towns found it could not get its packing cases back in less than an average of three weeks.

This may not have been any fault of the railway, the may have lain with the retailers, but the impersonal nature of the service operated against the supplier and forced him to invest in much larger numbers of containers than would have ben necessary otherwise.

(iii) Traffic density presents a problem to railways, which operate ideally when the train is full. Highly concentrated traffic is the best. Even very dense traffic at very high speeds can be sagely operated with modern equipment. The Inter-City trains run by British Rail commonly reach speeds of 100 miles per hour.

(iv) Rail traffic is fast when actually moving, for it has a private way which is kept clear. It follows that if goods are to go a long way, rail transport is probably best. The economic limit seems to be about 200 miles. Below that limit the disadvantages of rail traffic make road transport more economic.

(v) It is economical in the use of labour, one driver and guard can take 60 carriages or trucks. Compares with road, transport, where long-distance lorries carrying with the train.

(vi) Because of the nature of the way, a breakdown, strike, or go-slow movement holds up all traffic behind so that its effects are cumulative, building up an enormous backlog of goods which may include perishables, live-stock, etc.

Freightliners—The Railway Container Service

In March, 1963 the Beeching Report 'The-Re-shaping of' British Railways' proposed that freight thinner trains be introduced. They were to use road and rail transport for door-to-door delivery of 'containerized' goods, the change-over from road to rail being effected by completely mechanical means at special rail terminals.

By 1970 the scheme had developed to the point where a national freight grid had been established between 29 freightliner terminals in main industrial and commercial centres. Four of these are in London, at King's Cross, York Way, Stratford, and Willesden.

Others are a Glasgow, Manchester, Liverpool, Aberdeen, Birmingham, Cardiff, Edinburgh, Hull, Leeds, Newcastle, Sheffield, Stocketon, Belfast, Dublin, Felixstówn, Harwich, Nottingham, Southampton, Swansea and Tillbury. All these terminals passed into the control of the National Freight corporate under the 1968 Transport Act in an attempt to integrate road and rail transport more effectively.

The experiment was not really successful, and control of the Freightliner system reverted to British Rail in 1978. Despite fierce competition from a thriving road haulage industry the Freightliner system has certainly kept a useful amount of traffic off the highways, and at times of industrial disputes in the road haulage industry it has proved invaluable.

Beeching Report on the Railways

Continuing heavy losses on the railway network led the Government to appoint one of Britain's leading businessmen, Dr. Beeching, to head a full scale inquiry into the railway organization. His report made drastic suggestions for ending the deficit. They included the following:-

(i) Reducing the rail network itself from 17,000 miles to 8,000 miles, eliminating in the process many rural passenger services, suburban services, stopping passenger trains, and country stations.

(ii) Uneconomic freight trains were to be replaced by liner trains running at regular times with a limited number of stopping points. By having fewer but larger depots increased efficiency could be obtained, but at some loss of convenience to the customer.

(iii) Concentrating on the profitable, long-distance, dense traffic routes, chiefly London-North, London-Midlands, London-West-South Wales, and Glasgow-Manchester-Bristol lines. Nearly all the these were carrying 1,000 tons per day in each direction; some were carrying almost 2,000 tons.

In fact, for political reasons, the full Beeching scheme was never introduced and Dr. Beeching himself left the railways system at 11,000 miles, and the Transport Act of 1968 has implemented a modified scheme. The effect of the Beeching Report has still been very great.

Air Transport

The transport of goods and passengers by air is the greater transport achievement of the post-war era. The great advantage transport is its speed, and for this reason it is particularly suitable for the transport of passengers. Shipping lines that once were prosperous, with full bookings on the New York, South Africa, and Australia runs, have had to turn to cruises and the emigrant trade to earn a living.

However, air transport is expensive, since aeroplanes are sophisticated technical products. Design, operation, and maintenance are all costly, and the actual pay load is small. Even the giant air-buses now in service carry only a few hundred passengers.

The se of aircraft as freighters has been slower to develop because the advantages of air freighting have been less obvious. Only when Air Canada began to publish its market research on air-freight costs did the work wake up to the fact that air freighting was a practicable and economically advantageous method of transport for many industrial and commercial enterprises.

Previously it has been thought that it was advantageous only for perishable commodities or small packets of high value, or for freight directly related to passengers. Even so, the cheapest place for cargo is on the passenger aircraft.

The Economic Viability of Air Freighting

The essential point concerning the transport of goods by air is that the actual cost of the air-freight ticket is less importance than the overall cost of moving the goods from their present position to their destination. The overall cost includes may other expenses besides the actual carriage charge, some of these are listed below.

(i) Factory Condition can be preserved. In many trades goods are finished at the factory and sent to the consumer in first-class condition: dresses and suit are pressed; motor bikes are tuned; bicycles are assembled for delivery.

The need to pack and ship goods destroys this sort of activity, which has to be done at the destination, with high costs of establishing depots, employing and training skilled labour, etc. With air freight, special racks installed in the aircraft rises are high, but the duration of the journey is so short that for any given transit the risks are much smaller than by surface vehicle.

(ii) The saving of time may prevent losses by idle factories or overstocked warehouses. One case on which Air Canada reported concerned a leading German hosiery-making firm which ordered 230 machines from Pennsylvania. The air-freight charge was Rs. 2400 per unit, six times more then the cost of dispatch by sea.

The machines were installed ten days ahead of schedule as a result, and turned out 207,999 pairs of hose in the ten days. This was more than enough to yield a handsome profit on the venture. Another firm flew in its raw materials and components from suppliers daily, so that there was no need to warehouse or stockpile these goods.

Its saving in warehouse space alone permitted an extension of plant layout to achieve economies of large scale, which more than off-set the high cost of air freight.

(iii) The cost of packing. Packaging can be very expensive for a sea voyage, where inclement weather may damage the goods salt air may taint produce, humidity may rust metals, etc. With air freighting most packaging is quite unnecessary. Modern aircraft fly above the clouds nowhere near the sea, and apart from possible effects of cold, the goods in transit are unlikely to come into contact with 'weather.'

(iv) Insurance costs are lower by air. Aircraft risks are high, but the duration of the journey is so short that for any given transit the risks are much smaller than by surface vehicle.

(v) Where goods are fashionable, they sell best on the crest of the wave. One manufacturer of wallpaper filled a charter aircraft with rolls showing a popular recording groups and followed them around America selling at fancy prices.

These are some of the aspects which, when taken into account, make air freighting an extremely useful solution to man's transport problems.

Sea Transport

Since the massive development of the air transport industry the passenger trade for long-distance sea voyages has almost disappeared, and the types of vessel in sue have changed. The chief ones are:-

(i) Container Ships—These are a ships which carry cargo in containers, rather than in conventional holds. The cellular construction permits containers to be loaded into the holds. The cellular construction permits containers to be loaded into the holds quickly, the actual 'stuffing' of the containers to be loaded into the holds quickly, the actual 'stuffing' of the containers having been done on shore.

The containers may be stacked up to seven high, and an entire ship can be turned round in twelve hours.

(ii) Bulk Carriers—A ship built for a particular type of cargo, e.g. iron ore, is often called a bulk carrier. The emphasis these days is on larger and larger bulk carriers, because the cost per ton of cargo is reduced.

(iii) Oil Tankers—In the last forty years the tanker had become the commonest ship on the high seas, and a wide variety of them is available. The largest are the V.I.C.C's which operate from the oil-producing countries of the Middle East, Nigeria, Venezuela, etc., to the refineries of Europe, North America and Japan.

(iv) L.N.G—Carriers are special refrigerated tankers for liquefied natural gas, while L.P.G. carriers carry liquefied petroleum gas. Clean product carriers, often quite tiny, carry refined products from oil refineries, chemical works etc. Bulk transport of liquid products is cheap and convenient. In former times oil, for example, was moved in barrels, which had to be lifted on and off the ship by cranes.

(v) Roll-on roll-off Ferries—There are great advantages in sending goods by road on long-haul journeys. The roll-on roll-off ship enables lorries and cars to drive onto the ship to cross from one land mass to another. Even the transport of cars from continent to continent is economical by this method.

(vi) Passenger Liners—As explained, the huge passenger liner has largely disappeared from the seas except as a cruises liner for holidays at sea. There are passenger cargo liners which are chiefly concerned with cargo to and from the major ports of the hull is taken up with the holds of the vessel.

(vii) Lash Ships—'Lash' stands for 'lighter aboard ship.' These huge ships carry barges from fiver mouth to river mouth, collecting loaded barges at the mouth of the Mississippi and releasing them to journey from Rotterdam up the Rhine to Germany, or up the Thames to inland wharves. Bacat stands for 'Barge-aboard-catamaran,' a similar type of vessel to a lash ship.

(viii) Tramps are pure cargo ships which travel anywhere in the world to earn a living. Like a tramp they have no steady home. A typical journey might be as follow:-

(a) Form Australia with wheat to China.

(b) Japan to West Africa with manufactured goods and electrical engineering equipment.

(c) Cargo of motor vehicles and engineering parts for South Africa.

(d) Across to India for a cargo of cotton goods for Australia.

(e) From China to Japan with iron ore.

(f) Home to the United Kingdom with cocoa and palm oil.

Terminals for Ships

Passengers and cargo have to have access to ships. The terminal is the port, where ships can be serviced, provided with all their requirements before the voyage, and take on passengers and cargo.

The Importance of Shipping

Britain is an island inhabited by over 50 million people. We could not possibly grow sufficient food to feed our vast population ourselves and we have insufficient supplies of most raw materials. We therefore need to import food and raw materials of every kind. In order to pay for these we must export all sort of finished goods and services. These quantities of goods can be moved only by sea, for air transport is too expensive for heavy goods. Shipping is our most important link with foreign parts, and on it depends the prosperity of our people.

Reference is often made to liner Conferences. The conference system is a way of protecting the liner trade from unfair competition from tramp shipping at times when there is excess capacity in the tramp market. If liners are to provide regular services calling at scheduled ports and leaving at stated times irrespective of the cargo position, they must be assured of reasonable freight rages. Tramp freight rates fluctuate with supply and demand, but liner freight rates are held steady. At times when tramp rates are high the liners carry at their steady rates.

When tramp rates are low there is a temptation for liner customers to transfer their cargoes to the cheaper tramps. If this happens the liners will suffer losses and may be driven out of business. To encourage regular support from traders, the conference system offers rebates which can be enjoyed only if the trader can prove that his goods have on every occasion in the previous trading period travelled by the conference liners.

This conference 'tie' permits a trader to ship his goods by any line that is a member of the Shipping Conference. These liners charger similar freights, but it is unfair to regard them as price-fixing 'rings' since they have in no way a monopoly of shipping, which is international in character and highly competitive.

The International Chamber of Commerce, which represents the liners' customers, itself approves the conference system because of the security and reliability of service that the liner owners give to businessmen.

Requirements of a Good Port

(i) A clear channel—This may mean dredging, or blasting rocks out of the may, or marking the deep water with buoys and lights. It will certainly be necessary to avoid blocking the channel with sunken ships. Pilots who know the way into the harbour are given sole charger of vessels entering and leaving.

(ii) Government offices for customers control, emigrating, immigration, licensing, quarantine centres, police and security establishments, public health and sanitation.

(iii) Deep water—This may be permanent deep water or, if it is tidal water, the water in the dock must be kept in by lock gates when the tide goes out. Southampton is a port with a natural advantage; it gets four tides a day.

(iv) Shelter—This may be in a natural bay or harbour, or it may be provided by the banks of a river. If these are not available groynes must be built.

(v) Supplies of coal oil, water, food, and electricity for ships calling at the pot. When a ship arrives it will need to re-fuel and replenish its stores of water and food. While its engines are not working it may need to use the shore supply of electricity.

(vi) Wharves, Cranes, floating cranes, and brags are needed to help unload the ship, and turn it round quickly. A vessel is wasted in port—its function is to sail the seas. A labour force of coders and stevedores is needed to carry out the work of loading and unloading.

(vii) Commercial Premises—warehouse, bonded warehouses, refrigerator stores, grain elevators, forwarding depots for packaging exports, insurance offices.

(viii) Dry docks, repair yards, workshops, disinfestation equipment and maintenance centres.

The Chief Ports of the British Isles

The map above shows the ports of the British Isles, and the shipping lanes which terminate in them. The importance of any port depends to some extent on its position and the industries and population it caters for.

1. London—London, under its Port of London Authority, is still wrestling with the problems of adapting to Britain's changed position in the world, and the technological changes in shipping since containerization began in the sixties. Once the busiest port in the world, its up-river docks are now inaccessible to the supertakers and bulk carriers; its passengers trade is dead except for a tiny cruise trade and the economics of the container trade favour a major stopping place in Europe for most Rhine for bare traffic and its absence of serious tidal problems, is a major competitor. P.L.A. plans to build a major deep-water port at Maplin near Shoeburyenees have been frustrated by official policies, but are not quite dead. It is a major container port. Far enough down river to accommodate large ships, it has been chosen as Britain major container terminal.

The facilities when have come into use are some of the most advanced in the world. Six Paceco-Vickers container cranes straddle carriers and other handling equipment provides rapid turnaround for container ships.

The British container consortium O.C.L. uses Tilbury for its Australia service. There are roll-on-roll baths, a common-user berth and also two prepackaged timber berths for the handling of wood products, manned by a permanent crew of skilled dockers who have set up new handling records with their side-loader fork-lift trucks. Just outside the container port in the main river a new grain terminal has been completed which can turn round large bulk carriers in two days. Land has been developed by the creation of modern mills and grain-processing plants and plans are in hand for four deep-draught riverside berths.

2. South-East Ports and Trade with the E.E.C— Two fifths of all U.K. exports and imports now go to, or come from, the South-East ports, While London dominates the South-East, its port is less well placed, partly because of the tidal nature of the River Thames, but also because of excess costs imposed by a traditional dock labour force.

Other ports have been able to expand more easily, with less sophisticated labour, shorter sea routes and absences of tidal problems. Southampton Dover, Harwich and Felixstown have picked up the profitable short-sea container trade at London's expense. They have all expanded threefold in the decade.

Milford Haven is Britain's second largest port in terms of tonnage handled, but nearly all its cargo is petroleum products.

Immingham, across the Humber Estuary from Hull, is now the third largest port, also handling mainly bulk cargoes.

Southampton, the next most important port of the

British Isles, has a residue of passenger trade with cruise ships taking a larger share of this business in recent years. It has become an important container port too, adding this type of packaged cargo to its traditional high-speed cargoes of refrigerated meat, fruit and vegetables.

Liverpool has declined in influence as U.K. trade has become increasingly Europe-orientated. Its rise to power began with the cotton and tobacco trade about 250 years ago, but its growth has been hampered recently by the decline in foreign and non-European trade.

Hull, the convenient port for the industrial cities of the West Ridding, is another important British port. Its fish trade has declined, but it imports wool from Australia, wheat, and a wide variety of general cargo.

Glasgow grew to importance when the New World was opened up in the sixteenth century, handling in particular the tobacco trade. Later, the fortunate discovery in the Glasgow area of coal and iron ore led to the growth of heavy industries and a large export trade.

Designated as Britain's first M.I.D.A., the Clyde Port Authority has deep water suitable for large bulk carriers, but is on the wrong side of the U.K. remote from Europe. The For the part Authority, which includes Leith and Grangemouth, is the port authority for East Scotland. It handles cargoes from Scandinavia, the Baltic and the Low Countries.

Bristol, a port that once gave its name to the British sailor's idea of efficiency—'ship-shape and Bristol fashion'—has declined because it is too shallow for modern shipping. Instead the port of Avonmouth was built nearer to the sea by the Bristol authorities, and a recent addition has been a now dock, the Royal Portbury

Dock.

Other ports. Several small ports have demonstrated since the Second World War that the smaller terminal has much to offer the carrier. Outstanding among the small ports are Flisxstowe, which developed a container berth before the bigger ports had realized the revolution that was to come over shipping. Middlesbrough now handles 16 million tonnes per year and the Midway Ports, in Kent, 11 million tonnes.

Advantages and Disadvantages of Sea Transport

(i) The 'way' is free, and gives access to most parts of the world.

(ii) Small power is needed to drive a vessel, so that large vessels are practicable and economies can be achieved.

(iii) Transport by sea is relatively slow, so that passengers are easily lost to airlines when speed is important.

(iv) The possibility of determination of cargo is great because sea water is corrosive and also liable to affect the quality and flavour of cargoes.

(v) Because weight is not important, ships can be massive enough to be strong.

(vi) Buoyancy of the effective weight zero. Hence sea transport is very suitable for heavy goods.

(vii) Pilfering of cargoes is not uncommon, though 'containerization' is doing much to reduce this.

(viii) Ports are expensive and delays not uncommon.

Other Transportation Systems

Hovercraft. Hovercraft operate on a cushion of air which is pumped under the vehicle and kept in by a skirt of heavy material. They are particularly effective over water, where they enable much higher speeds to be achieved than by the conventional ship. There is no water resistance worth speaking of, and a cross-channel ferry is now operating from a base at Pegwell Bay near Dover, carrying vehicles and passengers at about 80 knots.

The hovercraft is particularly advantageous in estuaries where its ability to ignore sandbanks and shallow water means it can operate by more direct routes. The use of longer skirts, possibly up to 12 feet deep will improve the ability of these craft to negotiate the larger waves. A second use for hover skirts has been found in moving heavy loads over bridges which are not strong enough to carry the load. By fitting a temporary skirt to lorries carrying heavy loads of this type the weight which is usually borne by the axle assembled, and enabling the load to cross without damage to the bridge.

Pipe lines are increasing in importance for the transportation of natural gas and oil field from the ports to inland depots. While the capital cost is great, the savings on motor-vehicle costs for comparable movements by road, quite apart from the social costs of congested highways, make this form of transport both economical and socially desirable. Pipelines cannot however compete with tanker costs, especially giant tankers on long hauls.

12

PROBLEM OF ENVIRONMENT POLLUTION

Environment

On the earth, various kinds of living creatures lead their life. Various kinds of things surround them. Whatever surrounds these creatures is collectively known as environment. In other words, all the external things or situations in which human beings are forced to live is known as their environment. This kind of environment is known as external environment. There is another kind of environment also, which is known as internal environment which rests inside the body and mind of the individual. Between these two kinds of environment, a balance is always kept by body however because of various factors or reasons, this balanced state can be disturbed. Out of various factors which can bring a kind of imbalance between external and inner environment is environment pollution.

By living in a polluted environment, an individual can get affected by various kinds of diseases. Whenever any foreign substance enters in the environment, it gets polluted and affects the life of human beings or other living creatures in different ways. Because of this foreign substance, its various constituents, namely, the air, water etc. also gets adversely affected and they also get polluted. In this chapter, we will discuss about various kinds of pollutions which is being found in the constituents of environment, the reason of such pollution and the consequences of their polluted states.

Water Pollution

An important constituent of environment is water and when water gets polluted in an way, it is known as water pollution. Whenever any foreign substance, which can be organic, inorganic, biological or some physical substance, enters in the water, the quality of the water gets deteriorated and this kind of water does not remain fit to use. Polluted water is not unfit for human beings, but also for the other living creatures. The qualities of polluted water get changed. For various purposes, water is being used by human beings in different functions, namely, for quenching the thirst, cooking food, agricultural purposes and washing clothes and utensils.

Polluted water consists of various kinds of impurities and when this kind of water is being used by human being in any of the functions, person or involved persons gets affected to some extent. By using polluted water, various kinds of intestinal infections can take place in human beings, because of which it is always better to avoid using this kind of water.

There are various reasons which led to pollution of water. It is because of various activities perform by human beings that water gets polluted. Two important factors are urbanisation and industrialisation. Today, we see that various people have migrated in big cities from the small villages because of which cities have been over-crowded. Various factors have been established for different purposes because of which water gets polluted.

The main activities which led to the pollution of water are as follows :—

i. Industrial Wastage : Various kinds of products are being prepared in the factories, in the production of which various waste products emerge. These waste are highly chemical products consisting of complex synthetic organs. Water gets polluted when the waste products originating in the factories get mixed with it.

Almost in all the factories, provision is made that waste products are being thrown in the water river and when these products get assimilated in water, various kinds of impurities in different forms enter the water and make it imperfect to use. When these chemicals are absorbed by the sand or the earth, the quality of underground water gets deteriorated. In big industrial cities, this kind of problem is increasing day by day. The substance from manure factories, the waste material from the mills preparing the chemicals render water impure. By living in impurer water, health of the living creatures living beneath the water also gets affected.

ii. Sewage : An important source of pollution in urban cities is sewage, which consist of decomposable organic matter and pathogenic agents. In developing countries, people are migrating in a large number to the big cities, because of which sewage is being produced in large quantity, but disposal of these products cannot take place accordingly. When the impure liquid get merged in the water, or they are being stored in any open space, after some time, mosquitoes breed over them and various kinds of bacterise and impurities enter into the water, which makes the water impure. With this, oxygen contents in the water get depleted.

iii. Physical Polluteness : Thermal pollution and radio-active substances are the main constituents of physical polluteness. Therma pollution takes place because of hot water. It is due to this hot water that the temperature of aquatic environment get increased. With this, aquatic animals and plants get affected adversely. When radio-active ash falls into the water, it gets polluted, which result from processing of uranium or research laboratories where isotopes are being used. On coastal areas of lakes, seas and oceans, oil gets spill. Oceanic water also gets polluted. Marine pollution results by the mineral oil which is being discharged from ships. By all these ways, water of ocean or sea gets polluted, which affects the fish or living creatures leading their life under the water. When these fishes are being eaten by human beings, their health also get affected adversely.

iv. Agricultural Activities : Today our country is developing or progressing in all the fields and this kind of development can be seen in the agricultural sector also. Today, primitive means of agriculture are not used, but various kinds of advanced equipments or methods are being used. To protect fields from insects, various kinds of chemicals are being used. If these chemicals or fertilizers are being used in greater quantity, they affect the quality of land adversely. When these fertilizers get dissolved into water, they remove the hydrogen present in water, which affect the life of various living creatures leading their life under water. When this kind of polluted water is being taken by human beings, their health gets deteriorated and they get affected by various diseases.

Thus we see that there are various causes which lead

to the water pollution. The main reason which emerge from the above discussion seems to be increasing population and the increasing migration from villages to towns.

Today, water pollution has become one of a big hazard to the health of the people. Various kinds of diseases emerged out by using polluted water. All the living creatures become affected by polluted water directly as well as indirectly.

Various measures or steps have been taken by the government to clean the water of various rivers and in making this kind of polluted water clean, large amount of money is being spent every year. Thus, water pollution leads to economic loss to the human beings indirectly.

Water pollution is the consequences of use of various modern industrial technologies and increased population. Now the problem which is being faced is to determine the optimum level which can permit economic and social development of the people, without affecting health in any way. For controlling or putting the stoppage on the water pollution, various measures are being used by the government, some of which are as follows :—

a. Population Control : As mentioned earlier that one of an important cause or reason of water pollution is increase in the population. Various programmes or policies have been designed by the government of India to control growth rate. Because of the tremendous population, people do not get the opportunity to get educated and in case of illiteracy, it becomes very difficult to convince them that they are responsible for water pollution. For this purpose, government should educate the people as well as try to control the population of the country.

b. Making waste water Clean : Industries and tremendous increase in the urban population are considered to be the two main causes of water pollution. Industrial waste is known as effluent, while the urban liquid waste is being called sewage.

Sewage is being produced by domestic as well as from the industrial area. This kind of product is being produced from various human activities. Sewage consists of pathogenic germs, and is very harmful and hazardous for the health. Sewage should nøt be thrown into water body without being treated properly. By their treatment, we mean extracting impurities from them. When sewages are being treated properly, the chances of spreading the communicable diseases from them gets reduced. Collection, treatment and re-use are the main steps which are being included in the treatment process of sewage. All the pathogenic agents preset in the sewage are being destroyed through the various treatment processes. From treatment processes, sewage becomes suitable for re-use.

Another measure which is being used by government of India is use of various methods in relation to industrial waste water treatment. For this, three steps are being identified, under which, various kinds of pollutants are being recognized. Pollutants are considered to be of three different kinds, namely, the floating pollutants, suspended pollutants and dissolved pollutants. Oil, grease and fat are the main kinds of floating pollutants. These kind of pollutants generally affect the growth of the plants. Suspended pollutants can be either organic or inorganic in nature. Acids, alkalis, heavy metals and insecticides are known as the dissolved pollutants, which can affect the aquatic life adversely.

Dissolved air, floating, chemical treatment, biological treatment are main methods with the help of which industrial waste water is being treated. If water is being treated properly, it can be re-used in various functions which can also solve up the problem of water shortage in big cities.

iii. Legislation : Water of ocean, rivers, canals get polluted in various ways because of which problem of polluted water has become a globalised one. To protect the water from being getting polluted, some important steps have been taken by the government. In 1974, parliament passed the water act, the reason of which was increase in quantity of polluted water. For controlling pollution, this act is provided with constitution wide powers. It is through this legislation that it was being set out that no industry is permitted to establish without furnishing the certificate by the owner in regard to re-treatment of waste water of the industry.

Method to Purifying Surface Water

As mentioned earlier that water is one of an important constituent of human body and water of canals, rivers and lakes is mostly used for drinking, but water in these sources do not remain clean or purified. Before consuming this kind of water, it is necessary to make them fit to drink. There exists various kinds of impurities in this water which make them unfit for the people to drink. With the help of some special kind of processes, water can be purified, some of the methods being used for this purpose are as follows :—

a. Decantation : In this process, impure water is being

pumped and collected in a decanting basin when soil and other waste products get settled down after some period of time.

b. Filtration : From settling basin, water is being transferred from filter, which consists of sand in some quantity. With this process, almost maximum impurities lying in the water gets destroyed. It is necessary to clean the filter regularly.

iii. Chlorination : After bringing the water out of filter, the next step is to mix chlorine in it. With this method, bacterias present in the water can be removed.

Air Pollution

Air cannot remain pure for a long period of time. For all the living creatures, air is the important and one of the closest component of environment. Oxygen for respiration is being provided by the air. It is through the air present in the atmosphere that the various kinds of sounds and smells are being transmitted from one place to another. When the various hazardous elements get mixed in the air, air becomes polluted. When foreign matter in the air get concentrated in a large quantity, air is called to have been polluted. Throughout the world, the problem of air pollution is becoming more serious.

Various experts have devoted their time in analysing the problem of air pollution, and it has been found by them that there exist some specific causes or sources which can pollute the air, some of which are as follows:—

i. Combustion Sources : By combustion of various fuels, various harmful smoke gets mixed in the environment which also make the air dirty. In the combustion sources, dust from domestic as well as from industrial sector are being included.

ii. Industrial Processes : Various kinds of processes are being performed in the industries and these processes result in various polluted gases and dust. When these gases merged with the air, they make air polluted.

iii. Motor Vehicles : Today, our life has become mechanized and for moving from one place to another, we make use of various kinds of motor vehicles. These vehicles are run through motors and they produce smoke which is very impure. Upto a normal limit, this kind of smoke emerges from the engines, but when there is any defect or problem in the engine, the amount of dust increases, which makes air polluted.

Although through the world, problem of air pollution has taken a serious face, but people of under-developed countries have to face them utmost. In such countries, processes of industrialisation and urbanisation are done without any kind of planning. Various air pollutants have been chosen and all these are considered as indicators of air pollution. Sulphur dioxide, carbon-oxide, and nitrogen are some of the important pollutants. Firstly, it is measured that in what quantity these substances are present in the air and if they exist in excess to the permissible limit, the air is considered to be polluted.

Consequences of Air Pollution

By living or breathing in the polluted air, health of the living creates get affected to a lot of extent. By air pollution, respiratory system gets affected to considerable limit. Chronic bronchitis is the disease which generally affects the people who breath in polluted air for longer period of time.

In the polluted air, plants and animals do not get grow to their maximum capacities. Plants grow improperly and the leaves of these plants get burnt or destroyed within short period of time. By inhaling in polluted air, animals suffer from various respiratory diseases.

Air pollution is effecting ozone layer adversely, because of which percentage of ultra-violet rays on the earth has increased, because of which plants and animals are being affected in various ways. By pollution, property and material are also affected considerably. Pollutants of the air pollution are so strong that they can corrode various metals, stones and marbles. Rubber can be cracked by the ozone depletion.

Social and economic aspects of an individual get also affected by the air pollution. Visibility of the people have affected adversely because of increase in the air pollution.

Important Ways to Control Air Pollution

For the prevention of air pollution, various steps have been taken by various international societies, and one such society is World Health Organization, which have done an enormous step in 1968 by publishing a document entitled Research into Environment Pollution, recommending certain measures with the help of which air pollution can be controlled, which are as follows :—

a. Replacement : In this measure, those products or processes which can result in air pollution are being replaced by other products and processes which do not create any kind of pollution. It is according to this concept that government of Delhi has introduced the concept of CNG instead of diesel buses.

b. Containment : Provision of various enclosures, ventilation and air cleaning are introduced in this process, the main object of which is to stop the release of toxic substance into the air. Various engineering methods can be used for this process.

c. Legislation : For controlling the problem of air pollution, various legislations have been adopted by various countries of the world. It is according to this process that government of India has passed Nuisance Act in our country.

iv. Dilution : By planting more and more plants, pollutants are being controlled under this method. An attempt in this regard is to establish green belts between industrial and residential areas. This means or mechanism proves to be fail when the amount of pollutants increase in the air.

Concept of Ozone Layer

The air in which we breath is composed of various gases, two of these main gases are nitrogen and oxygen. In addition to these, carbon dioxide, hydrogen and ozone are some of the important constituents of the air. It is believed by some people that the refreshing air we breathe in at the sea-side is known as ozone, however, the truth is that ozone is a poisonous kind of oxygen. Very little ozone is being found at the ground level. Around 24 km above the earth, there exist a very thin layer of this gas. Ultraviolet rays emitted by the sun are being blocked out by this ozone layer. Ultraviolet rays are very harmful for the living creatures thus, this layer prevents this rays to reach on the earth.

Because of the increasing pollution, this invaluable layer is destroying day by day. Ozone layer is getting depleted with the increase in air pollution. It has been found by the experts that there exists a large hole on the north pole of the layer. For saving the ozone layer from deterioration, it is becoming very necessary to control the air pollution with any means.

With the depletion of the ozone layer, all the living creatures will be affected adversely. All the human beings then have the small sized eyes. They will have long nose and small height.

Noise Pollution

Another problem related to the polluted environment is noise pollution. Generally, this kind of pollution is found in big cities or in the over-crowded places. Unwanted sound is known as noise. When the wrong sound is being produced in the wrong place and at the wrong time, it is called the noise. The condition in which excessive sound is being forced into the atmosphere without any use or necessity, it is called the noise pollution.

Fundamental Causes of Noise Pollution

There are various sources which can give rise to the noise in one way or the other. All the sounds emerging from household and industrial areas are included in it. Importance characteristic of noise, which differentiate it from the normal sounds are as follows :—

a. Noise has a high level of loudness. It is on the amptitude of the sound waves produced from the source that the intensity of the sound depends. The measurement unit of noise is decibel. Human ear can hear one decibel, which is the small amptitude.

b. Noise has high frequency, which is being denoted by Hertz.

To measure noise level frequency, duration and other environmental factors which are being used in industrial places, various kinds of instruments are being used.

Consequences of Noise Pollution

Unwanted noise affects the health of human beings adversely. An individual can be affected by noise pollution in various means. Simple effects of noise pollution are annoyance, irritation and disturbing sleep. If someone remains constantly in an environment in which noise has very high level, various kinds of serious diseases or effects can be found in him. Hearing power of such individual can be impaired and after a long period of time, he can become deaf. Various kinds of psychological and physiological changes can result in human beings because of noise pollution. Researchers has found a direct relationship between the levels of noise pollution and heart diseases. Efficiency to perform various functions can be affected by noise pollution. Behaviour and habits also get changed after some time living in an environment affected by noise pollution.

Controlling the Noise Pollution

While adopting remedial measures, some aspects should be provided the consideration, which includes the source of noise, medium of noise and the object being affected by noise.

To control the noise pollution, people should be made aware of the reason and consequences of noise pollution, for which various kinds of means or mediums should be used. Steps should be taken to put a kind of control on the source of the noise. Factories, in which noise machines are being used should locate at far distance from the residential areas. The limit should be imposed on the level to which loudspeakers can be used and time duration should also be defined by the government. If any vehicle is producing greater sound, the user can be asked to send the vehicle for service, or a penalty can be imposed on him. Horns of the vehicles should not be very loud.